BATTLE FOR THE ISLAND KINGDOM

OSPREY
PUBLISHING

For my patient wife, Teri,
so that she is remembered too.

DON HOLLWAY

BATTLE
FOR THE
ISLAND
KINGDOM

ENGLAND'S
DESTINY
1000–1066

OSPREY PUBLISHING
Bloomsbury Publishing Plc
Kemp House, Chawley Park, Cumnor Hill, Oxford OX2 9PH, UK
29 Earlsfort Terrace, Dublin 2, Ireland
1385 Broadway, 5th Floor, New York, NY 10018, USA
E-mail: info@ospreypublishing.com
www.ospreypublishing.com

OSPREY is a trademark of Osprey Publishing Ltd

First published in Great Britain in 2023

A catalog record for this book is available from the British Library.

ISBN: HB 978 1 4728 5893 1; PB 978 1 4728 5892 4; eBook 978 1 4728 5891 7;
ePDF 978 1 4728 5894 8; XML 978 1 4728 5895 5; Audio 978 1 4728 5896 2

23 24 25 26 27 10 9 8 7 6 5 4 3 2 1

Image captions and credit lines are given in full in the List of Illustrations (pp. 7–8).
Map in plate section by The Map Studio, previous published in CAM 13: *Hastings 1066:
The Fall of Saxon England* (Osprey Publishing, 2000)

Index by Alan Rutter

Typeset by Deanta Global Publishing Services, Chennai, India
Printed and bound in Great Britain by CPI (Group) UK Ltd, Croydon CRO 4YY

MIX
Paper | Supporting
responsible forestry
FSC® C171272

Osprey Publishing supports the Woodland Trust, the UK's leading woodland
conservation charity.

To find out more about our authors and books visit www.ospreypublishing.com.
Here you will find extracts, author interviews, details of forthcoming events and the
option to sign up for our newsletter.

CONTENTS

PART TWO. THE ANGLO-SAXONS: AD 1042–1065

PART THREE. THE NORMANS: AD 1066

LIST OF ILLUSTRATIONS

The vast majority of 11th-century Anglo-Saxons lived in humble thatch-roofed shacks no bigger or better than these recreations at West Stow village in Suffolk, England. (Midnightblueowl, Wikimedia Commons, CC BY-SA 3.0, https://creativecommons.org/licenses/by-sa/3.0/)

In 1013, with Viking Svein Forkbeard on the verge of conquering the Island Kingdom, the English king Aethelred sent his wife Emma of Normandy and their children to safety with her Norman kin. Illustration by Matthew Paris, 13th century. (Reproduced by kind permission of the Syndics of Cambridge University Library, MS Ee.3.59, f. 4r)

In 1016 Forkbeard's son Cnut and Aethelred's son Edmund Ironside agreed to rule England as co-kings, as shown in this romanticized 19th-century depiction. (Photo by: GHI Vintage/Universal History Archive/Universal Images Group via Getty Images)

In this illustration from the *Encomium Emmae Reginae* ("Elegy of Queen Emma"), the anonymous author presents her with her copy of the book, as her sons Harthacnut and Edward the Confessor look on. (© British Library Board. All Rights Reserved / Bridgeman Images)

Under the gaze of Christ, saints and angels, King Cnut and his queen "Aelfgyfu" donate a golden cross for the altar of the New Minster at Winchester. Aelfgifu was Queen Emma's regnal name, but also the name of Cnut's first, handfast wife. (The British Library, Stowe MS 944, f. 6, https://www.bl.uk/manuscripts/Viewer.aspx?ref=stowe_ms_944_fs001r)

In this 13th-century illustration by Matthew Paris, King Harold Harefoot orders the blinding of his rival Alfred Aetheling, while his housecarls bully the English. (Reproduced by kind permission of the Syndics of Cambridge University Library, MS Ee.3.59, f. 6r)

"Where Harold made an oath to Duke William." Whether by trickery or coercion, William claimed Harold swore fealty to him on holy relics. Scene from the Bayeux Tapestry, 11th century. (Photo by: Photo12/Universal Images Group via Getty Images)

Anglo-Saxon England was twice the size of Normany, even including its dependencies. To invade required William to leave his duchy defenseless against the Continental enemies surrounding it. (The Map Studio)

The Norman invasion fleet first sailed at night, following a lantern at the masthead of Duke William's flagship *Mora*. However, the Normans were not skilled sailors and did not complete the crossing until the next day. (Artwork by Steve Noon © Osprey Publishing)

Legend has it that at Stamford Bridge one Viking warrior single-handedly held the entire English army at bay, killing 40 of them with an axe before he was himself slain. (Artwork by Peter Dennis © Osprey Publishing)

The height of the Battle for the Island Kingdom. At Hastings, Norman knights charge the Anglo-Saxon shield wall. On the Bayeux Tapestry both Duke William and his half-brother Bishop Odo are shown wielding a *baculus*, a wooden club symbolic of religious or royal authority but also used to beat a man to death inside his mail armor. (Painting by Tom Lovell)

The famous "arrow in King Harold's eye" on the Bayeux Tapestry is thought to have originally been a spear upraised by an Anglo-Saxon housecarl, shortened and fletched by a later embroiderer to better depict the legend. Judging by more contemporary descriptions of the battle, the king is more likely the axeman struck down at right. (Pictorial Press Ltd / Alamy Stock Photo)

After the battle King Harold's body was said to be so mutilated that his handfast widow Edith Swanneshals ("Swan Neck" or "Gentle Swan") was brought to search the battlefield for it, identifying it by marks known only to her, as shown in this romanticized Victorian-era illustration. (traveler1116/Getty Images)

Senlac Hill. On October 14, 1066, the Normans and their Continental allies made repeated charges from this position, up the slope toward the Anglo-Saxon line across the crest. King Harold Godwinson is generally thought to have made his stand where Battle Abbey was built. (Ealdgyth, Wikimedia Commons, CC BY-SA 3.0, https://creativecommons.org/licenses/by-sa/3.0/)

AUTHOR'S NOTE

In the year 1724 historian, archivist and royal secretary Monsieur Antoine Lancelot presented a series of sketches to Paris's *Académie des Inscriptions et Belles-lettres*, in charge of royal inscriptions and mottoes on monuments and medals. The academy's task entailed the study of ancient medals, relics and rarities, and therefore archeology and history in general. Lancelot had recently acquired his drawings from the estate of the late Nicolas-Jean Foucault, a state councillor, intendant and scholar of Normandy. Their depiction of mounted knights, kings crowned and a bloody hilltop battle was, in his opinion, copied from some tomb carving, wall fresco, stained glass window or tapestry. The original source was unknown.

The drawings swiftly came to the attention of Dom Bernard de Montfaucon, a monk of the Benedictine Congregation of Saint Maur, renowned for their literary and historical scholarship. A former captain of grenadiers who had served two campaigns in the Franco–Dutch War of 1673, since taking the cloth Montfaucon had become France's premier archaeologist. Today he is still considered a founder of the science, who invented the term "paleography" for the study of historic writing systems and the deciphering and dating of historical manuscripts by studying their script. His *Palaeographia Graeca*, dating Greek manuscripts according to their lettering and abbreviations, was a work of such expertise that it would still be the leading source on the subject 200 years later. None of this was to the neglect of his religious studies, either; in 1719 he had been appointed as confessor to nine-year-old King Louis XV.

Montfaucon had doubtless heard rumors and legends of some tapestry dating from the Norman era, but like most Frenchmen of the day thought nothing more of it. Yet the clues had been there all along....

Around the year 1100 the French chronicler and prelate Baudri of Bourgueil composed a poem for Countess Adele of Normandy, daughter of William the Conqueror, in which he wrote of a silken tapestry embroidered in gold and silver, depicting the Norman conquest of England. As described, Countess Adele's tapestry (which perhaps never existed) could not be Foucault's, but had plainly inspired Baudri's poem.

Then again, in AD 1476, an inventory of the possessions of Bayeux Cathedral listed "a very long and narrow hanging of linen, embroidered with images and inscriptions, representing the conquest of England, which is stretched around the nave of the church during the day and during the octave of the Feast of Relics [July 1]."

In 1562 the monks of Bayeux, forewarned of the imminent arrival of a troop of Huguenots (French Protestants in that country's Wars of Religion), had hidden the tapestry away – wisely, as the Huguenots sacked the cathedral, destroying its stalls, organs, icons and relics. Perhaps the tapestry was thought long lost as well. Over 160 years later, Montfaucon wrote:

> It took a long time to discover the place where this artwork was found. Not doubting that M. Foucault, who had been Intendant in Normandy, had taken this masterpiece from Caen or Bayeux, I turned to our colleagues in that country. From the letters that they sent me, I believe that it is a length of tapestry that is kept in the Cathedral of Bayeux, and that is exhibited on certain days of the year. This cloth taking the length of the Church, it is to be believed that what we have here is only a small part of the story.

No French historian worth the title could be unfamiliar with that story: the conquest of England by Duke William of Normandy. By Montfaucon's time the tale had been told by any number of chroniclers, historians and writers, on both sides of the Channel. In addition to their duke, there was a plethora of Williams among them: William of Malmesbury, William of Jumièges, William of Poitiers; few people used surnames in those days. In retelling the story for a modern audience, let us differentiate them like English aristocracy, by their place names only, by the abbeys in which they wrote: Malmesbury, Jumièges, Poitiers. And for consistency, our other sources as well:

Worcester, Gaimar, Huntingdon, Wendover, Rievaulx. (I'll introduce them at length where each comes into the story, but for easy reference, see the complete list in the back of this book.) Many of these writers were anonymous, and some so far back in time that they did not even write in Latin, but in archaic forms of their own languages, which has made trouble for historians and authors ever since.

The tongue in which Anglo-Saxons framed their thoughts, Old English, *Aenglisc*, was very different from modern English, more resembling modern German. The meaning of a sentence depended less on word order than on inflections denoting case and gender. For readers who might like a slightly deeper dive into the mechanics of Anglo-Saxonish – and why this story is written as it is – we might (briefly, I promise) dig right down to the letters used. Initially, the literate Anglo-Saxons wrote with the old runic alphabet, *futhorc,*[*] suitable for short inscriptions on weapons, runestones, magic incantations and the like. Long passages were not written down but, in the tradition of most illiterate societies, passed on orally. When it became necessary to compile the annals of their history as a people, Anglo-Saxon scribes employed the *Læden stæfrof*, the version of the Latin alphabet used to write Old English. Before the Norman Conquest, with J, K, Q, V and Z unused, it consisted of just 24 letters. Two – *ash* (Æ, lowercase æ) and *eth* (Ð, lowercase ð) – were derived from existing Latin letters, and two others – *wynn* (Ƿ, lowercase ƿ) and *thorn* (Þ, lowercase þ) – were from the runic system. Since none of these letters appear in the modern English alphabet, I have followed convention in substituting *ae* or *e*, *d*, *w* and *th* respectively, so that a modern English audience may read, for example, King Aethelred rather than Æþelræd. In a few instances, though, I have chosen to keep the original letters for sheer effect. (My book, my rules.)

As in *The Last Viking*, I have used a similar approach for Old Norse names in this book, and have dropped the nominative case endings (for example, *Haraldr* becomes Harald, and *Sveinn* becomes Svein). In addition, bearing in mind that certain spellings will be more

---

[*]The Anglo-Saxon *futhorc* differed from the Germanic Elder Futhark in having 26 runic characters instead of 24. The Elder Futhark rune ᚨ, called *ansuz* (transliterated as the letter *a*), became three: ᚫ, *æsc* (*æ*); ᚪ, *ac* (*a*); and ᚩ, *ōs* (*o*).

familiar to readers, I have gone with Anglicized versions of names such as Eric Hakonsson (*Eirikr Hakonarson*).

Also, in Old English the letter C originally represented the hard C sound, for which Old Norse uses the letter K, which is how Danish Prince Knut became English King Cnut. (It was later Norman and French authors, writing in Latin and unsure how to phonemicize "Cn," who spelled out his name as "Canute.") Since this is a book about England, I have gone with his English name throughout.

I have also updated translations, whether from the original Old English, Latin, French, archaic or even Victorian English (which never uses five words when ten will do) to more modern speech patterns, not striving for a word-for-word match but, to the best of my ability, preserving the original writers' intent as I see it. Any transcription errors are therefore mine.

I suppose I should address any objections to the use of BC/AD dating (Before Christ/*Anno Domini*, In the Year of the Lord), rather than the "religiously neutral" BCE/CE (Before Current Era/Current Era). Since both systems use Christ's admittedly arbitrary birthdate as a dividing line, and both refer to the same numerical years before and after, it seems to me rather contrived to require non-religious terms for dates still framed in terms of religion. The Venerable Bede for one, although writing in Latin, used BC and AD in his 8th-century treatise, *De Temporum Ratione*, "The Reckoning of Time." The Anglo-Saxons measured their years in terms of BC and AD; therefore, so shall we.*

More recently, and sadly, as I write it appears the term "Anglo-Saxon" itself is deemed by some to be offensive and a term of pride among so-called "white supremacists." The argument seems to be that the medieval English did not refer to themselves as Anglo-Saxon – in Old English, *Angelcynn* – and that the term only came into vogue during the period of imperial British colonialism and expansion, and of American slavery and racial division. I am lucky enough to have

---

*As shall be seen, exact dating for events in our story will prove problematic, since January 1 was not universally accepted among Anglo-Saxons as the start of a new year. Some annalists set it at the preceding Christmas or winter solstice, others with the spring equinox in March or even the fall equinox in September. According to Bede, the Anglo-Saxon calendar, following the cycle of the moon, was further complicated by the occasional addition of a thirteenth month in midsummer, to stay in step with the seasons. For much of the Middle Ages in most of Western Europe, including England and Scotland, New Year's Day was March 25. Scotland did not convert to modern dating until January 1 of the year 1600, and England not until 1752.

gained audiences on both sides of the Atlantic, and the term "Anglo-Saxon" has traditionally had a less toxic connotation in the United Kingdom than that being assigned to it in the United States. However, since this is a book in part about the historic Anglo-Saxons, let me just say this.

I suspect none of us will ever really know what the great majority of the Anglo-Saxons called themselves, because it was hardly ever written down in their language. I would concede that most of them did not think of themselves as *Angelcynn*, or even English, but as Mercian, Northumbrian, Kentish, West Saxon, *et cetera*. Those kingdoms originally spoke separate, unique dialects of Old English, mutually comprehensible but clearly identifying the speaker as "different," the way international speakers of English can recognize each other today – evidence of how insular those peoples were. By far the vast majority of Anglo-Saxons, illiterate and tied to their own little plots of land, thought of themselves as nothing more than members of their village, viewing anyone from beyond a radius of a few miles as an outsider. That disunity is one of the reasons why they were overrun by the Danes, who were from a country smaller and more tightly knit than most of those in England at the time, and who further altered the speech of their eastern and northern parts of England with their Old East Norse.

All that said, what matters is not what the medieval English called themselves, but what others called them. It was medieval chroniclers on the Continent who first referred to *Angli Saxones*, *Angulsaxones*, *Angolsaxones* or *Anglosaxones*, to distinguish them from the continental Saxons who didn't make the Channel crossing. Pre-Conquest English kings adopted Latin terms in manuscripts, charters (land deeds), legal documents and, importantly, their title, even in their very coronation rites: *rex Anglorum [et] Saxonum*, *rex Angulsaxonum* and *rex Anglo Saxonum*, King of the Anglo-Saxons. The very first inscriptions in the late M. Foucault's sketches were of a seated king, REX, and a horse-borne warrior, HAROLD DUX ANGLORUM.

Montfaucon recognized those figures on sight. Later he recalled:

To draw it I sent to Bayeux M. Antoine Benoît, one of the most skillful draftsmen of that time, with orders to reduce the images to a certain size, but not to change anything in the historical style of the artwork. Even flavor of the coarsest and most vulgar kind must not be changed, the preservation of crudity being, in my opinion, an important part of historiography. We learn here many customs of that time, of arms, of war, of the navy, and of many other subjects. The history represented in the artwork and in the inscriptions of the tapestry is in perfect conformity with the best historians of its era, and teaches us many things that they passed over in silence.

In that same manner, let us now uncover that which is also too often passed over in silence: the six and a half decades leading up to those first panels on the Bayeux Tapestry, and the eighteen or so months leading to its bloody conclusion.

Don Hollway
December 2022

DRAMATIS PERSONAE

THE VIKINGS

Cnut Sveinsson, the Great: Son of Svein Forkbeard, King of England 1016–1035, King of Denmark 1018–1035, King of Norway 1028–1035

Eilif Thorgilsson: Brother of Ulf, *jarl* under King Cnut

Eric Hakonsson: Jarl of Norway 1000–1012, Earl of Northumbria 1017–1020s, father of Hakon Ericsson

Hakon Ericsson: Son of Eric Hakonsson, Jarl of Norway 1012–1015 and 1028–1029

Harald II Sigurdsson, the Hard Ruler: Half-brother of Olaf, uncle of Magnus, King of Norway 1045–1066

Harald II Sveinsson: Son of Svein Forkbeard, King of Denmark 1014–1018

Harold I, Harefoot: Son of Cnut, King of England 1035–1040

Harthacnut: Son of Cnut, King of England 1035–1042

Heming Haraldsson: Jomsviking, brother of Thorkell the Tall

Magnus Olafsson, the Good: Son of Olaf, King of Norway 1035–1047

Olaf I Haraldsson, the Stout: Father of Magnus I, King of Norway 1015–1028

Stigand: Chaplain and advisor to Cnut, Harefoot, Harthacnut, and Emma of Normandy, Archbishop of Canterbury 1052–1070

Svein Haraldsson, Forkbeard: Father of Cnut the Great, King of Denmark, 986–1014, King of Norway 986–995 and 1000–1014, King of England 1013–1014

Thorkell Haraldsson, the Tall: Leader of the Jomsvikings

Ulf Thorgilsson: Jarl of Skane, later *jarl* and regent of Denmark

THE ANGLO-SAXONS

Aelfgar Leofricsson: Earl of Mercia 1057–1062

Aelfgifu of Northampton / Alfifa: Daughter of Aelfhelm of York, wife of King Cnut, mother of Svein Cnutsson and Harald Harefoot

Aelfhelm of York: Ealdorman of Northumbria, father of Aelfgifu of Northampton

Aelfric of Hampshire: Ealdorman of Hampshire, turncoat

Aethelred II, the Ill-Advised: King of England 978–1013 and 1014–1016

Aethelstan Aetheling: Eldest son of Aethelred II

Alfred Aetheling: Eighth son of Aethelred II

Eadric Streona: Ealdorman of Mercia, turncoat

Ealdgyth: Widow of *thegn* Sigeferth or Morcar, later wife of Edmund, Queen of England 1016

Ealdred: Bishop of Worcester, Archbishop of York, diplomat

Edith of Mercia: Daughter of Aelfgar, Earl of Mercia, widow of Gruffydd ap Llywelyn, wife of Harold Godwinson and Queen of England 1066

Edith of Wessex: Daughter of Earl Godwin and Gytha Thorgilsdottir, wife of Edward I, Queen Consort of England 1045–1066

Edith Swanneshals, the Fair: Common-law wife of Harold Godwinson, 1045–1066

Edmund Aetheling, Ironside: Third son of Aethelred II, King of England 1016

Edward I, the Confessor: Seventh son of Aethelred II, King of England 1042–1066

Edwin Aelfgarsson: Second son of Earl Aelfgar, Earl of Mercia 1062–1071

Godwin Wulfnothson: Son of Wulfnoth Cild, Earl of Wessex and Kent 1020–1053, father of Sweyn, Harold, Tostig, Edith *et al.*

Gytha Thorgilsdottir: Sister of Jarl Ulf Thorgilsson, wife of Earl Godwin. Also known as Gytha Thorkelsdottir

Hakon Sweynson: Son of Sweyn Godwinson, hostage

Harold II Godwinson: Son of Godwin, Earl of Wessex, King of England

Leofric: Son of Leofwine, Earl of Mercia, husband of Godiva, father of Aelfgar

Leofwine: Under Aethelred, ealdorman of the Hwicce; under Cnut, Earl of Mercia

Morcar Aelfgarsson: Youngest son of Earl Aelfgar, Earl of Northumbria 1065–1066

Northman: Son of Ealdorman Leofwine, brother of Leofric, follower of Eadric Streona

Sweyn Godwinson: Eldest son of Godwin, English earl, outlaw, exile

Tostig Godwinson: Third son of Godwin, Earl of Northumbria 1055–1065, exile, usurper

Uhtred the Bold: Ealdorman of Northumbria 1006–1016

Ulfcytel Snilling: Ealdorman of East Anglia 1004–1016

Waltheof Siwardsson: Son of Earl Siward, Earl of Northamptonshire and Huntingdonshire 1065–1072, Earl of Northumbria 1072–1076

Wulfhild: Daughter of King Aethelred, widow of Ulfcytel Snilling, widow of Thorkell the Tall

Wulfnoth Cild: Ealdorman of Sussex to 1014, father of Godwin

THE NORMANS

Emma of Normandy: Queen consort of England 1002–1013, 1014–1016, 1017–1035, Queen consort of Denmark 1018–1035, Queen consort of Norway 1028–1035

Fulbert of Falaise: Father of Herleva, grandfather of William I

Gilbert of Brionne: Count of Eu and Brionne, 1015–1040

Guy of Burgundy: Cousin of Duke William, rebel

Herleva of Falaise: Consort of Duke Robert I, mother of William I

Mauger: Son of Duke Richard II, Archbishop of Rouen 1037–1054

Néel I de Saint-Sauveur: Vicomte of the Cotentin to 1040

Néel II de Saint-Sauveur: Son of Néel I, Vicomte of the Cotentin 1040–1047

Osbern fitzArfast, the Steward, the Peacemaker: Steward of Duke Robert I 1027–1035, Steward of William I 1035–1040

Ralf de Gacé: Lord of Gacé, son of Archbishop Robert II, cousin of Duke Robert I, first cousin once-removed and regent of Duke William I

Ralf of Mantes, the Timid: Nephew of Edward I, Earl of Hereford 1051–1057

Richard II, the Good: Father of Richard III and Robert I, brother of Emma, Duke of Normandy 996–1026

Richard III: Son of Richard II, Duke of Normandy 1026–1028

Robert I, the Magnificent _or_ the Devil: Son of Duke Richard II, father of Duke William I, Duke of Normandy 1028–1035

Robert II: Son of Duke Richard I, brother of Duke Richard II, uncle of Duke Robert I, uncle of Mauger and William of Arques, great-uncle of Duke William I, Archbishop of Rouen 989–1037

Robert fitzWimarc: Landholder and castle-builder in Essex, died _c._ 1075

Robert of Jumièges: Archbishop of Canterbury 1051–1052

Roger de Beaumont, the Bearded: Seigneur of Beaumont, father of Roger, advisor to Duke Willam I

Roger de Montgomery: Seigneur of Montgomery, vicomte of the Hiémois, rebel, exile

Roger de Montgomery, the Great: Son of Roger, Earl of Shrewsbury, Earl of Arundel

Roger I of Tosny, the Moor Eater: Seigneur of Tosny, rebel

Walter of Falaise: Brother of Herleva, protector of William I

William I, the Bastard, the Conqueror: Son of Robert I, Duke of Normandy 1035–1087, King of England 1066–1087

William de Montgomery: Son of Roger de Montgomery, brother of Roger the Great, murderer

William fitzOsbern: Son of Osbern, seneschal of Duke William I 1040–1066

William of Arques: Son of Duke Richard II, brother of Duke Robert I, Count of Arques 1037–1054, rebel

William of Bellême: Father of William Talvas, Lord of Bellême 1005–1028

William Talvas: Son of William of Bellême, Lord of Bellême c. 1028–c. 1060

OTHER

Alan III: Duke of Brittany 1008–1040, cousin of Duke Robert I, guardian of young Duke William

Baldwin IV: Father of Baldwin V, Count of Flanders 988–1035

Baldwin V: Father of Matilda, half-brother of Judith, Count of Flanders 1035–1067

Conan II: Son of Alan III, Duke of Brittany 1040–1066

Enguerrand II: Brother-in-law of William I to c. 1049, Count of Ponthieu 1052–1053

Eustace II: Count of Boulogne 1049–1087

Geoffrey II Martel, "the Hammer": Count of Anjou 1040–1060

Gruffydd ap Llywelyn: King of Wales 1055–1063

Henry I: King of France 1027–1035

Henry III: Holy Roman Emperor 1046–1056

Judith of Flanders: Daughter of Baldwin IV, half-sister of Baldwin V, wife of Tostig Godwinson, Countess of Northumbria 1055–1065

Matilda of Flanders: Wife of William I, Duchess of Normandy 1052–1087, Queen of England 1066–1087

INTRODUCTION

A New Millennium

*We, too, should translate those books which are of highest
importance for most men to understand...until they learn how to
read English writing. Let men afterwards also teach Latin to willing
students, whom they desire to educate to a higher state.*

Alfred the Great

Today the Cathedral Church of the Holy Trinity in Winchester, England is one of the largest cathedrals in Europe.* Every year several hundred thousand visitors marvel at its architecture, a pastiche of styles from across the centuries of its construction: the Norman-style transepts, seventy-five feet high; the Early English-style retrochoir, built over a century later to house a shrine for Saint Swithun; and its late-Gothic nave, with spectacular vaults over eighty feet across, soaring almost as high. The church was built over the course of nearly 500 years, using hand tools to carve marble, honey-colored Bath stone, and limestone from as far away as the Isle of Wight and Normandy. Visitors wandering the outer grounds, craning their necks upward to admire the 150-foot Norman-era bell tower, might completely miss the odd brickwork paths beneath their feet: right angles and semicircles, leading nowhere.

Those outlines were there when Winchester was *Wintanceaster*, the capital of Wessex (to the extent there was one) and, for much of the

---

*It has also inspired two pieces of modern popular music: "Winchester Cathedral" by the New Vaudeville Band, 1966 (which reached No. 1 in the USA and Canada, and No. 4 in the UK) and "Cathedral" by Crosby, Stills & Nash, 1977.

19

island's subsequent history, of Anglo-Saxon England. They trace the foundations of the town's Old Minster, the church that stood on the site for over 400 years prior to the construction of the modern cathedral, and probably for a good 200 years before St. Swithun himself was born. More modest than its replacement, the Old Minster nevertheless had been one of the largest, most impressive and most important buildings in England. In those days churches were not only the center of civic life but seats of learning, home to the very few people who were literate: monks, priests and clergy. Sons of nobility, and some daughters, too, were sent to monastic schools to learn Latin and, as shall be seen, written English (Old English). Churches became repositories of knowledge, where books of the day were laboriously copied by hand in monastic *scriptoria* and stored in their libraries, *bibliothecae*.

A thousand years ago, in the *scriptorium* of Wintanceaster's Old Minster, an anonymous scribe sat bent over a writing table, carefully replicating, word by word, a medieval folio, itself perhaps a hundred years old. Every step of the process required meticulous labor. Lamb-, kid- or calfskin vellums had to be soaked in urine to remove flesh and hair, then washed, scraped, stretched and dried before being cut into sheets and scored with parallel scratches to mark lines and margins. Black ink was manufactured from crushed oak galls, scarlet from red mercury and egg white, and green from malachite, all using gum arabic from African acacia trees as a stiffener and applied with quill pens. Wing feathers from geese or swans (the curvature of left-wing feathers being preferred by right-handed scribes) constantly needed their quills sharpened, up to sixty times a day. Each scribe kept a small knife ready in his off hand for that purpose, and to scrape away errors in transcription before the ink set on the skin. The work was slow, tedious and exacting.

As a result of all this intensive labor, books were incredibly valuable. Our medieval scribe at millennium's end would not be working on mundane texts. Among many others, of course, he – or they, as, to judge by the handwriting, over the centuries up to fifteen monks carried on the work at Winchester alone – was updating a year-by-year recounting of people and events, the greatest annal in early English history. It had no known title in its day. The first printed edition, in 1692, was arbitrarily titled the *Chronicon Saxonicum*. Since 1861 it's been known as the *Anglo-Saxon Chronicle*.

Its writing had probably first been undertaken right there in Winchester, by the vision and at the command of King Alfred the Great (r. 871–899). Knowing that his capital was constantly at risk from a sack by Vikings, most of whom considered books as little more than handy fire starters, he had seen to it that copies of the original were sent for safekeeping to monasteries across England – Abingdon Abbey, Worcester Cathedral, Peterborough Abbey and others, probably including a number whose copies have been lost. (Today at least seven editions and a number of fragments survive, though not all date to the beginning of the millennium, being transcribed later. The copy from Winchester is thought to be third-hand, a copy of a copy of the original.) Each site updated its edition independently, sometimes taking second-hand news, rumor and hearsay as fact. This naturally led to some divergences, discrepancies and errors, and only by comparing and contrasting the various accounts can something of a consensus be made. Taken as a whole, however, the *Chronicle* offers the first post-Roman European history written by a people in their own language.[*]

Its earliest entries far predate its actual inception, going as far back as 60 BC, the date of the Roman invasion of England, and a genealogy in the Winchester chronicle claims the descent, and therefore the legitimacy, of West Saxon kings all the way down from Adam. For events prior to Alfred's reign the annalists could draw – as might we – on earlier historians and their monastic forebears.[†]

Even after the fall of Rome, many of these historians continued to write in Latin, in which even Anglo-Saxon clergymen were educated, and as would their counterparts on the Continent, the anonymous authors of, say, the *Encomium Emmae Reginae* and *Vita Aedwardi Regis*. Alfred, however, recognizing that few of his subjects spoke the Roman tongue, and that most were illiterate and would never read the annals themselves, decreed that an Anglo-Saxon chronicle should be written in Anglo-Saxon English, for an Anglo-Saxon audience. With its reliance on alliteration (both vowels and consonants), Old English was meant to be heard, not read. But Anglo-Saxons might listen to their history read to them by a cleric educated in Latin, who

---

[*]Since these multiple versions and fragments of the *Chronicle* for the most part paraphrase each other, I will not be noting which version I'm quoting unless that quote differs greatly from others.
[†]After a thousand years, we have access to sources unknown or unavailable to the old scribes. Again, see the complete list in the back of this book.

in turn might not be able to read the old Scandinavian runic alphabet, the *futhorc*. So the scribes used Roman lettering to approximate Old English word sounds.

The difference is telling, and important. In medieval society the church's mastery of the written word gave it control of narrative, of recorded history – in effect, of the truth. The writers of the *Encomium* and the *Vita* wrote on behalf of aristocratic sponsors, to present their version of events for posterity, and the annalists of the *Chronicle* likewise, on behalf of the king in the name of the English people. By recording Old English words in the Latin script popular across the rest of Europe, Alfred was striving to preserve his people's heritage for foreign readers as well, to prove them worthy of inclusion among the great peoples of history.

For hundreds of years that worthiness had been in dispute. Most of England, except for Wessex and Mercia, had long been under Danish domination, in effect part of Scandinavia. The Anglo-Saxons considered Viking depredations as God's divine punishment, perhaps for the crime of allowing their own culture to decline so far from the greatness gifted them by Rome. The annalists, ticking off the years on their pages, could attest that, more than a century after Alfred's death, Anglo-Saxon versus Viking was still an ongoing struggle.

It had always been the Island Kingdom's curse to be just visible enough to observers across the water, to tempt the boldest to try conquering it.

Before the Romans it had been the Celts, crossing the Channel from Gaul. It was a Celtic tribe, the Belgae, who had settled the site of three Iron Age forts and called it *Wenta* or *Venta*, "town." The Romans, when they in turn conquered the Belgae and fortified the place, named it *Venta Castrum*, "town castle." The Romans themselves had been, if not the most enduring, by far the most advanced and successful of these waves of invaders. Over more than 350 years they had cultivated a high level of art, culture and engineering among the natives, enforcing a kind of *Pax Britannia*. By the end of their tenure, though, when their own empire was falling apart at home, the island's eastern coast was already plagued with Germanic raiders: Jutes, Angles, Saxons. In the power vacuum left by Rome's departure, these had come to stay, either assimilating the native Celts or driving them into Cornwall, Wales and Scotland. (It was the Germanics who had named the ex-Roman town Wintanceaster.) For four and a half centuries these Angles and Saxons mingled, interbred, founded kingdoms, and ultimately fell to fighting among themselves. First the King of Kent took dominance, then the lords of Northumbria and Mercia, then Wessex. They had proven unable to unite to form a common front when a savage new breed of raiders, Scandinavians whom they called the *Denes*, "the Danes," arrived to prey on them as they had once preyed on the Celts. Their mindset in those hard-pressed years is likely best captured in the *Codex Exoniensis*, the "Exeter Book," a collection of Anglo-Saxon poetry dating from the late 10th century, though probably composed much earlier. The poems are full of lament and woe, mourning lost loved ones and dead lords. Looking back, the 12th-century Cistercian abbot Aelred of Rievaulx described those times simply: "Fear, death, desolation, and mourning reign everywhere."

Only Wessex and Mercia held out against the Danish onslaught, and those only by the virtue of Alfred's guile and force of will. He saw all Anglo-Saxons as one people, the *Angelcynn*, the "English race." Together they withstood the Viking pressure and began to push back. In 878, at the Battle of Edington, Alfred defeated the Viking king Guthrum, had him baptized under the *Aenglisc* name Aethelstan, and named him King of East Anglia.

The peace was uneasy. In 885 Guthrum resorted to calling the Viking chieftain Hrolf away from his siege of Paris to help put down an uprising among his subjects. According to the Picardish historian of the Normans, Dudo of Saint-Quentin, Hrolf dropped his siege and came to England, pledging Guthrum he would remind the Anglo-Saxons of the Vikings of old:

> I will crush whomever you please, I will destroy whomever you choose. I will level their cities and I will set fire to their houses and villages, I will tread them underfoot and scatter them, I will make them your slaves and kill them, I will take their wives and children captive and I will devour their herds.

Hrolf made good on his promise. After Guthrum was restored to power, he was so grateful (according to Dudo) that he offered the

Viking half his kingdom to stay in England. Hrolf nobly declined, choosing instead to return to Francia. Though he never did conquer Paris (if he had, it might have changed European history as much as a later invasion of England by his descendants), the Franks ceded Neustria, the western, coastal part of their kingdom, to him. Over successive generations, as shall be seen, that land and its people – part French, part Viking – would acquire a new name, the same way Hrolf would be remembered as their father, Rollo.

Meanwhile in England, for seventy years Anglo-Saxons and Vikings maintained an uneasy, troubled equilibrium, but when the last Norse ruler of York, Eric Bloodaxe, died in 954, in battle or murdered, the Danish tide finally washed back out to sea. What had been *Britannia* under the Romans; *Britene, Brytene* or *Britenlond* among the Germanics; and the Danelaw, Mercia and Wessex to Alfred's *Anglecynn*, was now united as one: the *Angelcynnes lond, Aenglelande, Engla-land.*

The northern Anglo-Saxons, though, having lived so long under Viking rule, were half-Viking themselves, clinging to Scandinavian ways. In the 980s the Danes returned, and though they did not manage to reestablish their ancestral Danelaw on English soil, they soaked it in blood. For the entire reign of English King Aethelred II (at thirty-seven years, the longest of any Anglo-Saxon king), Vikings were the bane of his existence. Not for nothing would he become infamous as Aethelred *Unraed*, "the Unready."* He had tried fighting, but at Maldon in 991 the Norwegian reiver Olaf Tryggvason dealt his army a decisive defeat. Aethelred then tried to buy them off, but payments of *gafol*, later to be known as *Danegeld*, the "Danish tax" or "Danish tribute," only encouraged more raiding.† In 994 Tryggvason allied with the Danes under King Svein Haraldsson, called *Tjuguskegg*, "Forkbeard." They returned to besiege *Lundenburh*, "Fort London," built within the walled confines of Roman Londinium, already the largest city in England and Aethelred's capital. Both Tryggvason and Forkbeard were Christians, but apparently only Olaf had a Christian

---

*As is now well known, *Unraed* is more accurately translated as "the Ill-Advised," a pun on Aethelred's name, which means "Nobly Advised." He was not widely called *Unraed* until at least 150 years after his death, and it is doubtful anyone called him that during his lifetime.

†In Aethelred's defense, payment of tribute to Vikings was a tradition going back to the days of Alfred the Great and even among the Franks across the Channel, most of whom had little more luck than Aethelred did in battle against the Vikings.

conscience. Aethelred and Winchester's bishop Aelfheah prevailed upon him (with the added encouragement of 16,000 pounds of gold and silver) to agree to raid England no more.* Olaf had gone home, become king, and forcibly converted Norway to his faith. In England, for the time being, it had seemed the Viking menace was over.

But now Olaf was dead, outnumbered, surrounded and slain at the naval Battle of Svolder in the western Baltic, by his erstwhile ally Forkbeard. Nor was Forkbeard – so cruel that he had driven his own father Harald Bluetooth to death in exile – satisfied to be king of Denmark and Norway. He had turned avaricious eyes toward England, which in those days was seen as the most southerly, warmest part of Scandinavia. Vikings raided right up the Thames, laid waste almost all of Kent, and threatened London, while the *Chronicle* lamented Aethelred's feckless response:

> The king and his councilmen decided to move against them with both the army and navy, but every time the ships were ready there was a delay, which was very annoying for the eager sailors aboard. Again and again the more urgent anything was, the longer it took to begin it. Meanwhile they were allowing their enemies' strength to increase, and whenever they retreated from the sea the enemy moved closer. When all was said and done these naval and army plans were an utter failure, succeeding only in alarming the people, wasting money, and encouraging the enemy.

Aethelred did, however, manage to take out his frustration on any neighbors who supported the Vikings. He marched his army north to ravage *Strath-Clota*, "valley of the river of (the Celtic goddess) Clota," in Alba, modern Strathclyde in Scotland. His fleet raided the Isle of Man in the Irish Sea. And the English chroniclers, in charting the Vikings' depredations, took note to add one more hostile neighbor to their list: "The enemy fleet had sailed off to Richard's realm."

---

*It's nearly impossible to make a straight conversion of an Anglo-Saxon pound – a unit of finance as opposed to weight – to modern currency. In those times one pound equaled 240 silver pence, at very roughly a gram each, so in terms of weight the 994 payment might have come to some 8,400 pounds of silver, four and a quarter tons. (I leave it to the reader to look up current silver melt values.) Back then, however, silver pence had much greater purchasing power, perhaps as much as ten to thirty modern pounds sterling *apiece*. (According to contemporary accounts, a slave girl could be expected to live all winter on three pence.) One Anglo-Saxon pound might be worth £2,400 to £7,200 in today's money, bringing the 994 payment from £38,400,000 to £115,200,000.

This realm, just across the English Channel (which the Anglo-Saxons called the *Sud-see*, "South Sea") was the dukedom of Richard II of *Normaundie*, modern Normandy. Unlike the Danes in the Danelaw, however, and more like the Angles and Saxons in England, rather than remain a Scandinavian colony the descendants of Rollo had interbred and assimilated with the local Franks and Celts, becoming vassals of Francia. They stopped being Norsemen and became Normans. Yet they were hardly less warlike than their forebears, and maintained better connections with Scandinavia than with England. Relations between Aethelred and the previous count, Richard I, called *Sans-Peur*, "the Fearless," had soured to the point that in AD 991 Pope John XV intervened, sending a legate to bring them to an agreement. By the Peace of Rouen, both agreed not to aid each other's enemies. In 996, however, both Richard and John died, and as Richard II – the first Norman to be styled as Duke – was still in his minority, his Danish mother and Norman uncle ruled as regents. For them to allow Forkbeard and his Vikings to cross the South Sea, shelter safely in their harbors, and sell their ill-gotten English booty was a violation of the peace.

Now it was 1001, the dawn of the new millennium. To the poor beleaguered English it seemed nothing had changed. As the *Chronicle* records, "In England this year there were constant raids by the pirate army, who harried and burnt almost everywhere."

The Danes came raiding into Hampshire, practically to the doorstep of the Old Minster at Winchester. They sailed up the River Exe and laid siege to *Escanceaster* ("Fortress on the Exe," modern Exeter), but the town was more than the typical Anglo-Saxon *burh*, a village defended by earthworks and stockade. Like London, it had been founded and fortified by the Romans as a military post, with stone walls the Vikings were unable to overcome. They vented their frustration on the surrounding villages, and defeated the armies of Devon and Somerset in the field.

But if Aethelred could not stop Vikings from preying on England, he could at least see to it they found neither shelter nor markets in Normandy.

Our story begins the way it will end: with invaders from the sea.

PART ONE

THE VIKINGS

AD 1001–1043

Night-shadow darkens, sending from the north fierce hailstorms
to punish warriors.
Everything is hardship in the earthly realm.
The fates' creation changes the world under the heavens.
Here wealth is fleeting, friendship is fleeting, man himself is fleeting,
kinship is fleeting.
All the underpinning of the earth will become as nothing.

From "The Wanderer"
Anglo-Saxon, late 9th/early 10th century

I

NORMANDY INVASION

1001

How Aethelred, King of England, who married Emma, sister of the Duke, sent an army to conquer Normandy, and how Néel of Cotentin defeated and utterly destroyed this army.

Jumièges

The sight would have been terrifyingly familiar to anyone living along the Channel coast in the centuries leading up to the turn of the millennium...that is, anyone lucky enough to have survived it the first time: longships, high-prowed, low in the water, closing in from the horizon with astonishing speed, oars sweeping across a high tide and hulls scraping to a halt on the silty shore. Men in chain-mail hauberks and leather byrnies, bearing shields and naked blades, leaping over the gunwales into knee-deep surf to wade onto foreign soil. And soon, the screams of victims and the glower of flames rising from thatched roofs.

Except these invaders weren't Vikings. By their leaders' elaborate full-face helmets, their single-edged, clipped-point swords, and their banners – Roman-style windsocks in the form of golden wyverns, the two-legged winged dragons symbolic of Wessex – they would have shown themselves to be Anglo-Saxons, sent by their king Aethelred to punish the Norman duke Richard II for his flirtation with Vikings. The 11th-century monk William, of the Benedictine abbey at Jumièges in

Normandy, was born right around the time of this raid, and devoted a chapter of his *Gesta Normannorum Ducum* ("Deeds of the Dukes of the Normans") to it. According to him, Aethelred had ordered the raiders to lay waste Richard's land with iron and fire: "He further commanded them to capture Duke Richard, bind his hands behind his back, and deliver him into the royal presence alive."

They had landed on the banks of the Saire River, which winds halfway across the Cotentin Peninsula to its outlet on the east coast. In their shallow-draft longships, the Vikings had routinely exploited river routes to penetrate deeply and unexpectedly into enemy territory. The Saire, however, today at least, is more of a winding creek, barely three or four yards across – deep enough to bear longships, but not wide enough to accommodate the sweep of their oars – and the Anglo-Saxons, as shall be seen, did not have the seagoing Vikings' aversion to long overland marches. They beached on the tidal flats at the river mouth and waded across the rich offshore oyster beds which are still farmed to this day. The 12th-century Norman writer Master Wace probably used Jumièges as a source for his *Roman de Rou*, a history of the Norman people. He confirmed, "Disembarking, each tried to outrace the others, and quickly made their way to the beach. They took plunder and food, captured sheep and cattle and razed and burned houses. Women wept and peasants fled."

The English would find, however, that times had changed in Normandy. The kings of Francia relied on their Norman vassals to repel seaborne invaders, and the Normans took their royal duty seriously.

It should be noted that historians regard accounts of this episode with various-sized grains of salt. Wace and Jumièges were Norman writers after all, writing to please their Norman patrons. No mention of the raid is made in English accounts, including any version of the *Chronicle*, which does mention Aethelred's expeditions to Strathclyde and Man in 1000. Neither Wace nor Jumièges bother with exact dates, and those historians who take the story of the Anglo-Saxon invasion of Normandy at face value date it anywhere from the 990s to 1003 or 1004. Most seem to settle around the turn of the millennium, but as the *Chronicle* notes, that year the English army and navy were in the north. In medieval times, men had to be home for the harvest. There was a narrow season for military campaigns, and it is doubtful Aethelred would have conducted two such wide-flung offensives in the same summer. More likely the English warred on their northern neighbors in 1000, and against the Normans in 1001. The Viking incursions in Devon and Somerset that year were much closer and more important to English scribes, to whom the Normandy landing may have been of little consequence. Since Aethelred, who led the northern invasions, evidently took no part in this one – presumably his hands were full with Forkbeard's Vikings – it may even have been an unsanctioned raid by English pirates, simply played up for maximum political effect by the Normans.

But England and France would be at war, on and off, for the next 800 years. If the Norman writers are to be believed, it was England that struck first.

At the other, eastern end of Normandy's flattened U-curve, across the Bay of the Seine from Cotentin, rises what the French call the *Côte d'Albâtre*, "the Alabaster Coast," for its Dover-like chalk cliffs, a hundred meters high. Where the River Valmont cuts through them to the sea lies the village of Fécamp, today a modest fishing resort but a thousand years ago the seat of the dukes of Normandy. In the 990s, Richard I, the Fearless, Count of Rouen, raised an abbey on the hilltop overlooking the town, on the site of an old Merovingian nunnery destroyed by Vikings 150 years earlier, and the beginnings of a castle as well. (This was probably no more than a wood palisade, as the Normans were then only beginning to dabble in building stone castlework.) Around the turn of the millennium Duke Richard ordered the initial expansion of the keep, with a square wooden tower, in 1001 likely still under construction. Probably the growing family simply needed the extra room. Richard was only about twenty-one, but already married with two baby sons. His four brothers, three sisters and their Danish mother Gunnor were also crowded into his hall, but there was a prospect of some moving out soon. The eldest sister, Emma, was of marriageable age.

Her birthdate is uncertain. In 1001 she could have been in her late teens, or not yet even a teen, but as shall be seen, she was probably near the higher end of the range. There are no images of her at this time, but she is said to have been "very esteemed and honored," and "a very beautiful daughter, a well-behaved maiden." Her brothers and sisters would go on to become variously counts, dukes, duchesses and an archbishop, but Emma would outshine them all.

That, however, was all in the future. Right now, if the English had their way, it was possible the entire House of Normandy would be rendered abruptly and prematurely extinct.

If the English really wished to capture Duke Richard, as Jumièges asserts, it made little sense for them to land at the far end of the dukedom. To reach Fécamp from Cotentin would have required them to march practically around the whole curve of Normandy. There were probably a few of Forkbeard's ships tied up at the town docks as well, possibly even something of a Danish fleet. A direct assault would mean fighting both Normans and their Viking allies. Medieval lords, however, often roamed at large over their realms and lived off their underlings' largess, and the English may have hoped to intercept the young duke at the other end of his duchy, far from the safety of his fortress. If so, they were mistaken. The Val de Saire was the fiefdom of Néel I of Saint-Sauveur, the *vicomte* (viscount, vice-count) of Cotentin, Richard's vassal on the peninsula. Normally his job entailed nothing more than enforcing ducal law and collecting taxes, but an Anglo-Saxon invasion brought out his Viking blood. *Every* Norman's Viking blood. "He summoned liegemen and servants, knights and farmhands, townsmen, peasants and footsoldiers," wrote Wace. "Even the old women came running with spears, cudgels and clubs, their skirts and sleeves rolled up, ready to fight."

This is probably his patriotic way of making the most of what was in fact a very typical medieval army – a small core of well-equipped, skilled fighting men that medieval Scandinavian scribes would call a *hird*, backed by a larger militia of poorly armed, ill-trained farmers and villagers that the English called a *fyrd*, all accompanied by various women and children, camp followers. Yet the lords of Normandy had a few surprises in store for the English.

In the Val de Saire, Aethelred's raiders were having their way with the locals. "From forest and field alike they seized and carried off loot, chased and hunted prey," wrote Wace. "They beat and killed peasants and thought they could conquer the entire region."

The Anglo-Saxons warred in the manner of Vikings, surprising and overwhelming hapless country folk before any effective defense could be organized, preferring to avoid pitched battle. Yet by lingering too long in the Cotentin, they invited it. The Normans knew their home ground and could choose the point of attack. Somewhere along this venture, evidently on the march, the invaders were surprised by the oncoming rumble of hoofbeats. "Suddenly the men of the Cotentin were there," wrote Wace, "and did not waste time making threats, but savagely attacked. Then you would have heard blows and shouting."

The scribes are vague on the details, but we know enough of Anglo-Saxon and Norman tactics to surmise how went the Battle of Val de Saire. For their part, the English fought like Vikings: on foot. Having to control a horse in battle was, to them, a needless distraction. "The Battle of Maldon," an Old English poetic account of Anglo-Saxons fighting Olaf Tryggvason's Norwegians just ten years earlier, tells how the English leader Byrhtnoth ordered his men to release their horses and chase them off prior to the fighting. The 12th-century English monk and chronicler Orderic Vitalis recalled, "The English scorn warhorses and, trusting in their ability, stand fast afoot."

The Normans, on the other hand, fought the way the Franks did, since the days of the Carolingian Empire centuries past: on horseback. The continentals had become well versed in cavalry tactics in Roman days, with a refresher course taught to them by the Huns in the 5th century. Emperor Charlemagne's armies had needed to cover ground in the course of his conquests, did so in the saddle, and eventually didn't even dismount to fight. They developed a cavalry tradition, and passed it on to their Norman vassals.

At Val de Saire, the Anglo-Saxons would have mounted their typical defense: a wall of shields, bristling with spears, two-handed axes adopted from their age-old Danish enemies, and their distinctive single-edged swords.* For their part the Normans would have attacked in their usual fashion: an all-out cavalry charge, with the aim of preventing the shield wall from ever forming or, failing that, of getting around and behind it. A shield wall could only face one way. Once broken or outflanked, it was defeated. Norman horsemen could ride down fleeing Anglo-Saxon footsoldiers, leaving the vengeful townspeople to finish off the wounded. "There was a great tumult and the battle was severe," recorded Wace. "They killed and slaughtered everyone, as long as any Englishman still stood."

The crews guarding the beached fleet were alerted to the disaster by the return of a single survivor. He had evidently sat down for a breather on the march and fallen behind before the Normans attacked. The sight of the massacre gave him a second wind, enough to run for his life. Wace has him telling the shocked sailors, "Flee, flee flee! If you hesitate you are all dead. If you are found here, you will be slaughtered like sheep.... Not one would live to be ransomed. Those you await are already dead."

Only enough English remained to man six ships, which they hastily slid off the tidal flats and sailed for home. When they arrived back at the English court, King Aethelred naturally inquired after the capture of Duke Richard. Jumièges has them admitting, "Most Serene King, we never saw the duke."

"You have lost all your men except us," Wace continued. "You sent them to the slaughter and will not see them again.... There was a battle, a truly awful one, and misfortune fell upon us."

For Aethelred this was just the latest in a series of disasters. First Forkbeard demanding protection money and stepping up his predations regardless, and now this defeat of an English army at the hands of a petty duke and a people who weren't even Viking anymore. His mother, the dowager queen Aelfthryth, passed away

---

*The Saxons' iconic weapon, the *seax* or *sax*, from which they took their name, had evolved from a short dagger in the 5th century to a full-fledged short-sword by the 9th, yet always defined by its tapered, clipped point. The 10th-century Seax of Beagnoth, recovered from the Thames in 1857, has a blade almost two feet long, inscribed in silver and brass with the Anglo-Saxon *futhorc* and the owner or swordsmith's name, Beagnoth. It was probably a prestige weapon not meant for battle, but is similar in design to three other period blades found in southern England. The narrow point may have evolved from that of a utility knife into a stabbing weapon capable of penetrating and bursting links of chain mail.

around this time. On top of that, his consort, Aelfgifu of York, had also just died. Some say she had been the daughter of an ealdorman, the king's representative in Northumbria, others that she was of low birth, but in any case they had been together the better part of twenty years. She had given him six sons and three daughters, and may have died attempting to bear another.

"He was filled with grief and sorrow for his commanders and his men. He regretted his foolishness and left Normandy in peace," declared Wace. "What cheered Duke Richard caused the king great sadness."

In this first contest between Normans and Anglo-Saxons, the latter had come out second best. Unknown to the players, of course, the contest was to continue for over sixty years. For now, in his quest to make himself appear worthy of his Viking-conquering ancestors, the hapless king of the English would feel compelled to bully more helpless victims, even closer to home.

II

FOREIGNERS

1002

*While Normandy prospered in the happiness I have recorded,
Aethelred, king of the English, defiled the kingdom which had
long flourished under the power of most glorious rulers, and
committed a treason so appalling that even pagans judged this
execrable crime horrible.*

Jumièges

In Normandy, Duke Richard was in a predicament. His duchy had
been gifted to his great-grandfather Rollo by the King of France as
a buffer state against Viking invasions. The dukes had solved that
problem by making the Scandinavians partners in trade, but perhaps
the only thing they had traded was one set of invaders for another.
The defeat of Aethelred's raiders was no guarantee the Anglo-
Saxons would not come again, and in greater strength. Normandy
was on only intermittently good terms with its neighbors in France
and Brittany, and Richard's own vassals might rise against him if
he showed weakness. He had made peace with Forkbeard. Now he
needed to make it with Aethelred.

The death of the English queen, Aelfgifu of York, created an
opportunity.

Richard's sister Emma would have been raised knowing it would
be her duty to wed some foreign noble or another, as a bargaining
chip in diplomacy and as a more-or-less hostage against any break

in the peace. If she was to be married off, best to be married off to a king, and to a king of England at that. Norman women were more or less the property of their fathers or husbands, but Anglo-Saxon women could own land, slaves and other property in their own name, sell it or give it away without a man's consent, defend themselves in court, and even have their marriages annulled. Aethelred, then around thirty-five, was probably twenty-odd years older than Emma, but hardly an old man. To be the wife of a king, a mother of kings? Emma's own mother and sisters must have looked on her with envy.

Norman envoys found Aethelred amenable to such a match. According to Geoffrey Gaimar, an Anglo-Norman chronicler writing about twelve decades later, "These men advised that he should immediately cross the sea, ask for Emma, Richard's sister, and bring her back. With the Normans as his friends, he could easily intimidate his enemies. Duke Richard would back him."

What middle-aged widower, in those rough-hewn days, would refuse a beautiful girl in his bed, obliged to give him children? Eventually, of course, there would be a question of inheritance. Aethelred's eldest son by the late Aelfgifu, the *aetheling* (prince) Aethelstan, was about Emma's age, a warrior who would likely press his claim to the throne as rightful heir to the king. That was in the future. For now, there were myriad other details to be worked out.

In Scandinavian terms there was the *brydceap*, the "bride-price" the groom gave her family to compensate them for the loss of such an asset; the *brydgifu*, the "bride-gift" or dowry that her family provided her as security in the event she was widowed or divorced; even the *morgengifu*, the "morning gift" or dower to be presented by the groom to his new wife as the price of her virtue. These were not small matters. Among his wedding gifts, Aethelred gave Emma properties in Winchester, Northamptonshire, Devonshire, Suffolk and Oxfordshire, not to mention the entire city of Exeter.

Such negotiations took time, especially since Aethelred's rule was not absolute or even hereditary in the manner of feudal, continental rulers. Anglo-Saxon kings did little without the approval of the *witan*, the "wise men" of the advisory council. (The Vikings would have called the meeting a *thing*.) It was they who confirmed new monarchs, theirs the choice of making a Norman girl an English queen. Evidently they were not opposed, but it was not until Lenten season of 1002 that Emma and her bridal party, including her personal retainers and men-at-arms, made the Channel crossing.

The first meeting of the new royal couple must have been quite the experience for all concerned – a match not only of politics, but matrimony, akin to a president of the United States not just meeting, but marrying, the Queen of England, or more accurately of some non-English-speaking country. Unless they were mutually educated in Latin, Aethelred and Emma might even have needed an interpreter, since Old English and Old Norman were not the same and not yet widely spoken outside their native lands. According to Wace, "The Normans claim the English bark, because they cannot understand their speech."

Decades later the monks John and Florence, in the cathedral at Worcester on the River Severn, had never met Aethelred, but knew church elders who probably had. They described him as "a youth of good manners, handsome appearance, and fine personality." That, however, was Aethelred as a young man. He was no longer young, and was beaten down by years of near-constant defeat and submission at the hands of the Vikings. Whatever Emma thought of him was not written down, for in those patriarchal times it was immaterial. Of her Gaimar would write, "A more beautiful woman there could not be," but he wrote that over a century later, without ever knowing anyone who had ever met her. Whether Aethelred was happy with his new bride (and to judge by his future behavior, he was at best ambivalent) was equally immaterial. This slip of a girl – half-Danish, half-Norman, all Viking – was the future of England.

Her new country, and subjects, must have presented something of a culture shock to a Norman noblewoman. "The English in those days," wrote the 12th-century English chronicler William of Malmesbury, "wore short tunics reaching to the mid-knee. They had their hair cut short and their beards shaved. Their arms were laden with golden bracelets and their skin decorated with tattoos."

From the crumbling Roman ruins on the coast, Watling Street – *Wæcelinga Stræt*, the "street of the people of Waecla," today's A2 or Great Dover Road – led through hamlets of what Malmesbury disparaged as "mean and despicable houses," little thatch-roofed, wattle-and-daub shacks very unlike the "noble and splendid mansions" of the Normans and French, peopled with dirty peasants muttering in their strange guttural tongue as she passed. But then, whether a French *paisant* or English *ceorl* (churl, lowest of the low, little better than a slave), a commoner was a commoner on both sides of the Channel. As queen, Emma would not have to associate with her husband's subjects any more than she had her brother's.

The 400-year-old cathedral at *Cantwaraburh*, modern Canterbury, "the city of the men of Kent," had already been rebuilt at least once, along the lines of a Roman basilica (in fact, on the site of an old Roman-era church). It was even then one of the largest in Europe, as befit the *cathedra* (Latin, "seat") of the church in England. No descriptions of royal wedding ceremonies survive from this period, but in its cavernous interior, echoing with the hymns of the choir, repeating her vows in Old English from rehearsed memory, Emma was married to King Aethelred. Her name in Old English being Imme or Imma, she was given the regnal name Aelfgifu, the same as her husband's dead wife, but more likely in remembrance of his sainted late grandmother. Meaning "elf-gift," it was a common Anglo-Saxon girl's name; Aethelred also had a daughter named Aelfgifu.

In his chronicle of the royal family, the 13th-century monk and artist Matthew of Paris enthused, "They were beautiful as sapphire and glittering gold, or the lily and the rose in bloom." But the *Chronicle*, a copy of which was maintained at Canterbury, reveals the somewhat cooler attitude of Emma's new subjects toward her: merely that "the Lady [*Hlæfdige*, meaning queen], Richard's daughter, came to this country."

And there is no record of what Aethelstan Aetheling and his brothers, Ecgberht and Edmund (who were about Emma's age), thought of the match. They surely attended the wedding ceremony, but for them Lady Emma was nothing but a threat.

Thus was peace made between England and Normandy. Yet there were still the Danes to contend with. That year Aethelred had already paid them 24,000 pounds of silver. These payments had been going on now for ten years, with no sign of abating. After so many years of conquest, many of the invaders had simply settled on English soil as unassimilated immigrants, as Wace recorded: "In England the Danes lived alongside the English, married English women and raised many sons and daughters. They had lived there so long that they had greatly increased their number and power. The English thoroughly hated them, but could not rid themselves of them, for they did not dare meet them in battle."

Their foreign ways were anathema to right-thinking Anglo-Saxons, or at least the Anglo-Saxon aristocracy. Malmesbury was half-Norman on his father's side, and had a low view of his Saxon mother's people:

> The clergy, content with the slightest degree of learning, could barely mumble their way through sacraments, and anyone with a knowledge of grammar was beheld with awe and amazement. The monks ignored their order's rules, wearing fine vestments and enjoying every kind of food. The nobility, giving in to luxury and debauchery, did not go to church in the morning like good Christians, but simply, carelessly heard prayers and services from a hurried priest in their chambers, along with their wives' flattery. The defenseless commoners became prey to the powerful, who made fortunes by either seizing their goods, or by selling them bodily in foreign lands, although it is characteristic of this people, to prefer revelling, rather than accumulating wealth.

"Drinking at parties was common practice, at which they passed entire nights as well as days," he added. "They were accustomed to eat until they became glutted, and to drink until they were sick."

On the other hand, John of Wallingford, a 13th-century Benedictine monk at the Abbey of St. Albans, famously declared the Danes did not have to kidnap Anglo-Saxon ladies to steal them away. They simply practiced good manners, kept their hair combed, bathed weekly, changed clothes regularly, and smooth-talked English wives and daughters into their beds, the cads.

Ethnic hate was rife among the Anglo-Saxon populace, especially as whipped up by Wulfstan, the firebrand Bishop of London. England could absolve itself of the sins for which God had punished it with Vikings, he promised, by driving them out in turn. And Wulfstan sat among the *witan*, where he would have recommended such a course to the king. Aethelred was informed there was a plot afoot among the

Danes settled in the country. According to the *Chronicle*, "The king was advised that they wished to kill him, and all his councilmen with him, and then seize the kingdom."

Once a Viking, always a Viking. If the English could not eliminate the Danish threat on the battlefield, or by bribery, then they would accomplish it by guile.

Never in his long reign was Aethelred, the Ill-Advised, so ill advised.

In January 2008 laborers on a construction site at St. John's College in Oxford had to halt work upon striking archaeological gold. Among the finds uncovered by specialists called to the site were a Stone Age earthwork enclosure, pottery, the remains of food, and a mass grave: human skeletons dumped together so haphazardly that a month was required to excavate them all, and two years to count them – between thirty-four and thirty-eight; even the experts could not piece enough together to be sure. Bone analysis indicated they were Scandinavians, all males. All had suffered appalling cut and puncture wounds. Many had skull fractures. Some of the bones were charred. Radiocarbon analysis narrowed the date of burial to between AD 960 and 1020.

In June 2009 another mass grave was uncovered, this time at Ridgeway Hill, down in Dorset: over fifty dismembered skeletons, dumped in an abandoned Roman-era quarry. Again, all males, in their teens to mid-twenties, their wounds not indicative of death by battle, but by execution – decapitation. Their skulls were all piled together off to one side, but only fifty-one of them, three heads having been retained, presumably as trophies or souvenirs. As before, the date of death was estimated at AD 970 to 1025.

Though nothing is certain, historians have linked these atrocities to a specific day in English history: November 13, 1002, the feast day of St. Brice of Tours, a 5th-century Frankish bishop reviled for his youthful decadence but later venerated for his humility. The date was not random but carefully chosen. St. Brice's Day is two days after the feast day of St. Martin. Traditionally Martinmas marked the start of the slaughtering season, when all the country folk brought their fattened cattle, sheep, poultry and other livestock into town for butchering and marketing – along with all their axes, cleavers and knives.

After consultation with his *witan*, Aethelred chose St. Brice's Day to put his plan into action. Jumièges scoffed, "The king, driven by a blind hatred and without accusing them of any offense, ordered the peaceful Danes of his kingdom to be massacred."

Aethelred himself admitted as much a couple years later, in a royal document: "I sent out a decree as advised by my lords and magnates, ordering that all the Danes living in this island, sprouting like weeds amongst the crops, were to be slain by a most deserved extermination, and so this decree was to be put into effect even unto death."

"The plans and the treachery were so well hidden," wrote Wace, "that they were all slain at one and the same time, wherever they were found."

In England the event is remembered as the St. Brice's Day Massacre. Across the North Sea it is called the *Danemordet*, the "Danish murder." Today the practice, like more recent activities in Armenia, Germany, the Balkans, Rwanda and more, would be called by other terms.

Genocide. Ethnic cleansing. Extermination.

"With great knives and axes they slit their throats," attested Wace. In Dorset, it is thought the prisoners were stripped naked and beheaded from the front, so they could stare their deaths in the face. In Oxford it was mob violence. The Danes sought refuge in St. Frideswide's, the minster church named after the town foundress. The townspeople locked them inside and set it afire, incinerating them. The 13th-century English chronicler Roger of Wendover reported, "The decree was mercilessly carried out in London town, to the point that a number of Danes who sought refuge in a church were all butchered in front of the very altars."

Nobody knows to what extent the sentence was carried out. Wace wrote, "They slew and murdered so many that no one could count the dead and left many unburied."

In the old Danelaw, the greater part of the population would have had Danish blood. Maybe the victims were only Scandinavian mercenaries in English service – the mass graves in Oxford and Dorset hold only men – but according to the chroniclers, women and children were not spared. Wace went into horrific, possibly overwrought detail:

They dragged babies out of their cradles and smashed their heads against the doorposts, knocking their brains out. Some they disemboweled. The women and maidens they buried in the earth up to their breasts. Then they loosed their mastiffs, their dogs and hounds, who tore out their brains and ripped off their breasts. They left no Dane alive, man, woman or child.

Legend has it that one woman was specifically targeted: Gunhilde Haraldsdottir, wife of Pallig Tokesson. A Dane who had entered English service, Pallig had been named by Aethelred as Ealdorman of Devonshire and become rich, but soon reverted to his Viking ways and joined the plundering of AD 1001. Gunhilde was a Christian and had pledged herself to peace, but now the whole family, taken prisoner, was to pay the price for her husband's treachery.

According to Malmesbury, one Eadric Aethelricsson (more of him later) acted as the king's enforcer: "In his cursed fury, Eadric ordered her, even though knowing that her death would bring great evil on the entire kingdom, to be beheaded with the other Danes."

Gunhilde's husband Pallig was executed in front of her, and likewise their son, speared through four times, before Gunhilde faced the sword. Wendover recalled her bravery: "She confidently predicted in her last moments that her death would cause great damage to England."

"She suffered her end with courage," attested Jumièges, "and she neither paled at the prospect, nor, when dead and her blood stopped, did she lose her beauty."

Gunhilde Haraldsdottir was singled out for mention in the chronicles not just because she was the wife of a Danish ealdorman. She was the daughter of Harald Bluetooth, once King of Denmark.

And the sister of Svein Forkbeard.

III

WOE TO KING AETHELRED

1003–1009

While on the day of this massacre the streets of London were
littered with dead due to the brutality of the murderous English,
some young men got away clean, took over a ship, and by rowing
down the river Thames made their escape to the open sea. Crossing
the vast expanse of water, they finally arrived at their destination
and, disembarking in a port of Denmark, set out to tell King Svein
of the bloody calamity of the Danes.

Jumièges

Today Roskilde, Denmark, at the southern end of the fjord named
for it, about twenty-five minutes from the capital of Copenhagen, is
famous for its annual rock festival – the largest in Scandinavia – and
its 12th-century cathedral, built of brick, which set an architectural
trend through medieval Europe and is the traditional burial place of
Danish royalty. A thousand years ago, however, Roskilde (Hrothgar's
spring, after its semi-mythical 6th-century founder) was the capital of
both Denmark and Norway. On the high ground above the harbor,
on the site of the modern cathedral, stood a wooden stave church
raised by King Harald Bluetooth some sixty years before, and beside
it his royal palace, also of wood and probably (as no trace of either
remains) more of a large mead hall. The crew of a ship from London,
emerging from the narrow fjord onto the expansive inner harbor,

would have been both relieved and anxious to see the banners of King Svein Forkbeard flying atop the snowy hill. Relieved, because these Danes had launched in haste from London – according to Jumièges, escaped, just ahead of Aethelred's executioners – and after a hazardous midwinter crossing of the North Sea, had finally reached the safety of their own people.

But anxious, too, because it is dangerous to bear bad tidings to a heartless king.

Svein's hall would have been a scene of relative warmth, peace and comfort. In medieval times winter – at least, until the food stores began running low – was a time of plenty, of reaping what had been sown, of living off the fat of the land. And Viking sea rovers lived off the fat of many people's lands. The *Knytlinga Saga*, the chronicle of Forkbeard's family, declares, "King Svein was a noble warrior and a strong king. He raided far and wide, both to the East Way [*Austrvegr*, meaning Sweden and the Baltic] and further south in Saxony [modern Germany]." And Wace agreed: "He was a powerful king with many warriors, many allies, much land and property, a man of great ability."

Svein's *huscarls* – housecarls, household troops, his personal cadre – were likely seated around the great central fire, quaffing ale and mead from drinking horns and earthenware tankards, but in moderation. Not for these men was the drunken debauchery of Vikings past, who risked life and limb for matters as trifling as the favors of lowborn women and the roll of dice. Svein was a war king and did not stand for such frivolity. These men of Roskilde were the culmination of an age – the sons of generations of warriors, the highest evolution of the Viking fighting man. Relentlessly disciplined, drilled and trained by their king, they were all dedicated to their task, which was to make him the greatest of all Viking overlords.

Said by some to be the son of a Wendish, Slavic princess – but by others, including his father Bluetooth, the illegitimate whelp of a nameless serving girl – Forkbeard had wrested the crown from his father's hands to become the greatest Viking king in a generation, lord of two lands and scourge of a third, and was yet only about forty years of age. If he had his way, his sons Harald and Cnut, though still only boys, would be the foundation of a new Scandinavian dynasty.* Svein's treasure chests were full of English silver, grudgingly but willingly paid by King Aethelred, and his benches were full of chieftains loyal to him and to that silver. Whenever he ran low on either, he could always make another run across the North Sea to gain more. The city of Exeter had successfully defied him the previous year, but that was a matter of little consequence, especially since he had gone on to defeat two English armies outside its walls. Exeter would still be there whenever he chose to come back for it.

Imagine, for a moment, the entry of these wet, shivering, exhausted survivors, the impatient questions of the king and their hesitant answers – the news of alliance between England and Normandy, and finally the shocked silence upon news of the St. Brice's Day massacre. Many of the Danes in that hall, like Svein himself, had kin in England who had learned to live as the English, as subjects of that king, and many had kin there no more. True, like Forkbeard's brother-in-law Pallig, they might change allegiances if a better offer came along, but in those days that was only to be expected. Men followed their lords, lords followed kings, and kings – good kings – were supposed be above such treatment of their subjects. But this – *this* – was an unwarranted betrayal by a king of his own people, so unimaginable that even the Vikings were left aghast. "Svein was filled with sorrow," conceded Wace. "He would never be happy, he said, until he humbled the English who had murdered his Danes."

Yet not even a king of Denmark and Norway could act without the support of his men. According to Jumièges, "The king, broken-hearted with grief, summoned all his chieftains to him, explained the situation, and demanded to know what they wished to do about it."

There could be only one answer. Medieval Scandinavia's proto-democratic assemblies – Viking *things*, Anglo-Saxon *witans* – were

---

*The name "Harald," in English "Harold," is a common Scandinavian name, derived from the Old Norse *herr*, "army" and *vald*, "leader." On the other hand, "Cnut" – in Danish, *Knut* – "knot," was an uncommon Viking name and might owe more to the Middle High German *knuz*, "daring" or "bold." Cnut's mother was likely Polish, and he was said to have been raised as a foster child on the Pomeranian coast. Over centuries prior to this time, the Old High German spoken there underwent a consonant shift in which *t* became *z*, but West Germanic, Scandinavian languages were less affected by the shift, and Old English not at all, so the old-style spelling represented a different meaning.

the most egalitarian governments in Europe. Yet the basis of Viking law – of Viking justice – was still the blood oath, an eye for an eye. Wrong done to one was wrong done to all, and everyone knew where the king stood. Jumièges wrote: "The Danes, moved by sorrow and mourning their kith and kin, agreed to campaign together as one and avenge the blood of their people."

Bullying English peasants out of their food, women and silver was merely business.

This would be vengeance.

Back across the North Sea in England, around the new year the royal court vacated London. Not in expectation of Viking attack, but in anticipation of an equally momentous event. The date is uncertain but was at least nine months after the marriage of Emma and Aethelred in 1002. The young queen was preparing to deliver her first child.

The king had chosen to spare her the noise and stress of the city for the quiet of the countryside. Anglo-Saxon kings often hunted northwest of the city in Oxfordshire, in what had once been Mercia, and the crown reserved several estates in the area for that purpose. One of these manors was known in Old English as *Githslepe*, "a slippery place by the river Giht," today Islip, on the River Ray. Aethelred's hall is long gone but is thought to have stood just to the northeast of today's parish church.

Aethelred was no stranger to fatherhood. By most counts this was the tenth or eleventh time he had gone through it, but that was no guarantee of success. Medieval men bet their lives in battle, but women wagered theirs in childbirth, at arguably poorer odds. Modern studies suggest that in those days one in ten pregnancies, and perhaps as many as one in five, were fatal to the mother. Anglo-Saxon graveyards are full of women who never survived their childbearing years, as well as babies just months old or stillborn. Aethelred's late wife Aelfgifu, mother of all his children so far, is thought to have died trying to beat the odds. Her sons, the *aethelings* Aethelstan, Egbert and Edmund, might well have been hoping their father's new wife would fail to deliver as well. The fate of realms rode not only on the deaths, but also on the births of kings. At the moment the only thing standing between the eldest, Aethelstan, and the English throne was their father. That would all change if Emma bore a prince.

It was said the queen, young as she was, had already taken all this into consideration and – according to later biographers, perhaps to justify events – prevailed upon her husband to give any prince born of her precedence: "When the royal wife of King Aethelred was pregnant, all the men of land swore an oath that if the fruit of her labour was a son, they would serve him as their lord and king and he would rule over the whole English race."

Emma and her ladies, in her hour of seclusion, would have withdrawn even further from the menfolk for her lying-in. (This was a noblewoman's luxury; a common wench might have to work right up to the onset of contractions.) Anglo-Saxon childbirth is poorly documented, women's business: private, intimate, presided over (again, in cases of highborn women) by the mother's attendants. There is no specific record of Emma's delivery, but that both mother and child survived counts as success. She bore Aethelred a son.

King and queen took the little prince to the abbey on the Isle of Ely, the "Island of Eels" in the fens of eastern Cambridgeshire, to be blessed on the high altar there. They christened him *Eadpeard*, Edward. It was a proud old Anglo-Saxon name meaning "wealth protector," the name of, among others, King Aethelred's elder, martyred half-brother, his predecessor as king.

That other Edward's death – murdered, many said, on the orders of his stepmother, Aelfthryth, to put her son Aethelred on the throne – had resolved a succession crisis that had seen England plunged into chaos and nearly civil war. This Edward's birth would set off another struggle for the crown of England, to last decades and involve three realms, in which he and his mother would be two of the main players.

It is uncertain, but probable, that Emma toured at least southern England early in her reign, as an introduction to her new subjects. She would certainly have wished to visit the city gifted to her as part of her dower: Exeter.

With a population of about 2,000 (probably a fifth of that, it must be said, when the town had been the headquarters of the Roman

Second Legion), Exeter was the last Anglo-Saxon outpost on the frontier with Celtic Cornwall, yet one of the largest towns in Wessex. As one of the southernmost ports in England, it had a thriving trade in wool, tin and leather with France, Spain and even the Mediterranean. It was sited on a stony ridge above the river, but surrounded with verdant pastures and floodplain meadows for cattle and sheep. With its own market, mint, and over twenty churches and chapels, Exeter was a prime, ongoing source of tax revenue for its owner. And it was effectively under new management.

Emma was duty-bound to accompany her husband the king on his travels around the realm and could not remain in the city to rule. To oversee her interests, she designated as her *gerefa* (her reeve or magistrate) one of her escorts who had crossed the Channel with her from Normandy. He is known to history only as "Hugh," the Anglicized version of the Old French "Hugo," more specifically the Norman "Hue." He would undoubtedly have been of warrior stock, and besides the queen's authority, furnished with a small retinue of staff to enforce his will – Emma's will – as necessary. If the Vikings returned, he would have to depend on the locals to supply fighting men, but mostly he could rely again on Exeter's city wall.

That wall was of Roman brick, already a thousand years old but strengthened by Alfred after he drove the Vikings from the city in 877, and again by Aethelstan in 928 after he drove out the Britons. (About three-quarters of the wall survives today, a 2,000-year-old layer cake of Roman, Saxon, Norman and later stonework.) Almost one and a half miles around, it was this wall that had kept the city safe from the Viking attack in 1001.

But Exeter was an unplucked fruit, and now belonged to Queen Emma, the representative in England of the treacherous Normans. That made it an irresistible target for Forkbeard.

In the summer of 1003, a Danish fleet hove into the river mouth to beach on the wide mud flats. The Vikings had no catapults or siege towers with which to overcome the defenses, nor any intention of trying. They laid siege to Exeter, according to some sources for two months, during which Aethelred apparently did nothing to help. In August, with starvation stalking the streets, Hugh the Reeve had a decision to make. He was Norman, perhaps, like his queen, of Danish blood himself, and might have had kin outside the walls and more sympathy for them than for the English in his charge. The *Anglo-Saxon Chronicle* demonizes him forever as that "French churl," for making the decision to open the gates.

Going all the way back to Roman days, by the rules of war cities which surrendered were to be spared a sack. By his treachery against the Danes, however, Aethelred had done away with the rule book. Svein and the Vikings had been suffering their grief and fury for the better part of a year. Now they unleashed it on the people of Exeter. The *Chronicle* admits, "The army utterly razed the *burh*, and seized much booty there without anyone fighting back."

They looted, murdered, raped and enslaved at will, emptying the mint of silver and gold, burning everything that would burn, pulling down the churches and even some of the city walls to render Exeter less defensible in the future. For his treachery, it is said, Hugh the Reeve kept his life, but was led away in chains.

And when Exeter was a smoldering ash heap, Svein and his warriors took a look around to decide what part of England to level next. For Forkbeard intended to make it his life's work to torment King Aethelred and his new Norman queen.

It was poor Aethelred's misfortune to find himself on the wrong side of two saints, when it was nobody but priests and clerics who wrote all the historical accounts of his reign. They started with the story of his christening by Archbishop Dunstan, later St. Dunstan, in Canterbury Cathedral in 966. As befits a young princeling, it was attended by his father King Edgar the Peaceful, his mother Queen Aelfthryth, his elder half-brother Edward, and all the nobles and bishops of the land. In front of them all the infant Aethelred, when dipped in the baptismal font, defecated in the holy water. Dunstan did not take it well, declaring, "By God and the Mother of God, this will be a sorry fellow."

Beyond taking offense at Aethelred practically from birth, Dunstan was appalled at the assassination of his elder half-brother, King Edward the Martyr, and had a hand in forming his cult. Aethelred was only ten or twelve at the time and could hardly be held responsible for his brother's death. It was said that upon hearing the news he wept, infuriating his mother Aelfthryth. She, having no switch at hand, beat him with a candle (instead of a thin taper candle, think of a pillar candle, thick as a club, and of beeswax, which doesn't bend), so badly that for the rest of his life the king was said to suffer a fear of candles and candlelight. Yet he, and she, profited by the murder, and if anyone was ever punished for the crime, Aethelred was. Malmesbury recorded that at Aethelred's coronation Dunstan practically cursed him: "The sin of your forsaken mother, and of her accomplices in her foul plot, shall not be washed clean except by the blood of the poor subjects, and such evils shall come upon the English nation as they have never suffered since they came to England."

Not long afterward Dunstan retired – or was retired – but he wasn't finished with Aethelred. In 986, when friction arose between the king and Aelfstan, Bishop of Rochester – probably a property dispute; land-grabs among the clergy and aristocracy were endemic during his reign – Aethelred actually called up his *fyrd* and marched on the city, only calling off a siege when Aelfstan bought him off with a hundred pounds, cash. Astonished by such a blatant protection racket, Dunstan scolded the king: "Since you prefer silver to the Lord, money to the Apostles, and greed to me, the evils which God has ordained will shortly befall you, but not while I live, for this too has God said."

Dunstan died in 988 (and was canonized, with a cult of his own, who faithfully documented his poor opinion of Aethelred), but his curse soon bore itself out. Not long afterward, Forkbeard and Olaf Tryggvason had begun stepping up their bloody raids on England.

And now Forkbeard was back.

Having destroyed Exeter, Forkbeard and his men next drove deeper into the heart of Wessex. Their dragon ships sailed some eighty miles eastward along the coast to Twynham (modern Christchurch), but there's no record the Vikings attacked it. It was then the most important harbor town in England and one of King Alfred's fortified *burhs*, protected on three sides by water, with an earthen wall fronted with stone and topped with a wooden palisade and, unlike Exeter, no traitors within to open its gates. Forkbeard bypassed it.

Twynham's harbor was fed by two rivers, the Stour and the Avon. (The town's name in Old English, *Tweoxneam*, derives from *betweoxn*, between, and *eam*, rivers.) This Avon was not Shakespeare's Avon, and is sometimes called the Salisbury Avon or the Hampshire Avon to distinguish it from other Avons in Bristol, Devon and Warwickshire. It wound up into Wiltshire, a land of chalk hills, prehistoric stone circles and, more to Forkbeard's interest, the market towns of Wilton and Salisbury. This was no longer Emma's territory, and was entirely too close to Winchester for Aethelred's liking. He ordered the *fyrds* of Wiltshire and Hampshire to be levied, under the command of the ealdorman Aelfric of Hampshire. This Aelfric had betrayed the king once already, not long after the Battle of Maldon, warning the Danes of an impending attack, for which Aethelred had ordered his son blinded. Ten years had passed, and Aelfric was no more inclined to follow such a king. "Ealdorman Aelfric should have led the advance, but went back to his old tricks," declares the *Chronicle*. "As soon as the armies were in sight of each other, he feigned illness and began to retch, claiming he was sick, and so betrayed those whom he should have led."

Salisbury, then called Sarum, was the site of a hill fort dating back to the Iron Age, but without an army to support them the citizenry abandoned it, and Wilton too. Svein ordered both towns burned. Probably the only thing that saved Winchester from similar destruction was the time of year. Weighed down with treasure, and with their thirst for vengeance temporarily slaked, the Vikings returned to their ships, put to sea and went back home for the winter.

Not all of Aethelred's nobles were as craven as Aelfric, particularly when fighting for their own homes. Malmesbury declared, "Ulfcytel, ealdorman of East Anglia, was the only man who offered any resistance to the invaders." When the Danes returned the next year, this time attacking East Anglia, they surprised the locals, who were unable to draw up their levy in time to save Norwich. Svein added it to his growing list of burned cities. At the bidding of his own council, Ulfcytel (Wolf Kettle or Wolf Helmet) first tried to bargain with the Danes, but they violated the peace and burned Thetford too.

Rather than attack them directly, Ulfcytel sent men to destroy their dragon ships at their anchorage, but when they failed as well, no choice remained to the East Anglians. They met Forkbeard at Wretham Heath, north of Thetford, and fought the Vikings to a bloody draw. Casualties were heavy on both sides, including many of the East Anglian chieftains. The surviving Danes were able to reach their ships, barely, and according to the *Chronicle* admitted they had never met with harder swordplay than that dealt by the East Anglians. They gave Ulfcytel the nickname *Snilling*, meaning Valiant or Bold, or possibly just Good Talker, and had not heard the last of him. He wedded Aethelred's daughter Wulfhild (or Wulfgyth, the two names having the same meaning, Wolf Battle). With this marriage Ulfcytel made himself one of the most powerful earls of England.

The year 1005 saw the Island Kingdom given a respite from Viking attacks, but only because of a greater scourge. Malmesbury recorded, "At this time, so King Aethelred's misery might be complete, a famine ravaged all England, and those whom war had spared died of want."

English weather was unpredictable and harvests subject to failure. No grain meant no bread, a catastrophe when, for commoners, meat was a rare luxury and bread or vegetable stew was the staple food. The famine of 1005 was so severe that even the Danes, unable to live off the land in England, packed up and went home.

The next year, however, they made up for lost time. The 12th-century English historian Henry of Huntingdon recorded, "the daring Svein reappeared off Sandwic [modern Sandwich on the Kentish coast] with a large fleet, along with his three usual servants – fire, slaughter, and pillage – and all England trembled, like a reed-bed shaken by the west wind."

The combined armies of Wessex and Mercia could do nothing against the Danes. They were becoming so comfortable in England that, come autumn, they overwintered in the Isle of Wight and launched a midseason campaign in the south, up to fifty miles inland. Hampshire, Berkshire, Reading, Wallingford and Cholsey all fell. The Vikings defeated an English army at Kennet before heading back to sea, in their boldness marching past within sight of the walls of Winchester. The *Chronicle* admits, "So great was the terror of the enemy, that no one could come up with a plan to drive them from the land, or to hold the land against them, for they had left their terrible mark on each shire in Wessex with flames and destruction."

Aethelred, however, wasn't at home in Winchester. He had long since fled across the Thames to safety. His utter uselessness against the raiders was apparent to everyone, not least the ruler himself. As Malmesbury put it, "The king, ever inclined to sleeping, did nothing but dither and delay, and if ever he came to his senses long enough to rise up on one elbow, he quickly lapsed back into his original despondency, either from depression, sloth, or ill fortune. His brother's ghost, demanding awful vengeance, tormented him too."

In his shame Aethelred shamed Queen Emma as well, and in public. Malmesbury confided, "He was so disloyal towards his wife, that he rarely shared their bed, and demeaned the royal dignity by his relations with whores. She too, a woman aware of her noble blood, became offended by her husband, as he loved neither by her innocent modesty nor her fecundity."[*] In a royal charter of 1004 which Emma, as part of her royal duties, had signed as a witness, her position at court was given as *thoro consecrata regio*, "dedicated to the royal bed."

It's hard to make that sound flattering to a modern ear, but the phrase had a different connotation in those days, more of an honorific. And Emma had made that bed – or, more precisely, King Aethelred and her brother Duke Richard had made it for her – and as a wife, even a royal one, she was compelled to lie in it. She was not the first Englishwoman to find herself in such a bind. For all their relative freedom compared to Norman women, Anglo-Saxon wives, even queens, were not so free of their male relations that they could act with impunity. Emma, barely an adult herself, was as much a subject of her king as his lowliest commoner. Her power base, the city of Exeter, lay in ruins. By now she doubtless knew Old English well

---

[*] Malmesbury was unrelenting in his scorn for his mother's people. "They had an abhorrent custom," he wrote, "by which they sold their female servants, after they had slaked their lust and made them pregnant, into either public prostitution, or foreign slavery."

enough to appreciate the sentiment of one of the earliest Anglo-Saxon poems, "The Wife's Lament," as found in the *Exeter Book*:

> My lord had ordered me to make my home here, though in this land I had few dear friends, and so I mourned. And then I found that my ordained one was ill-starred, and filled with sadness, hiding what he felt, with murder in his heart. Smiling at each other, we often vowed that nothing but death could part us. All that is in the past. It is as if we never loved. And near or far, I must suffer my dearest husband's hate.

To her credit, if her task was dedication to the royal bed, Emma took the job seriously. By this time she had borne Aethelred two more royal children, the princess Godgifu and another *aetheling*, Alfred.* Yet even the status of her eldest, Edward, was in question. Prince Aethelstan, in order of precedence, had signed that same charter directly underneath Emma, where he was titled *regalium primogenitus filiorum*, "firstborn of the royal sons" – technically true, of course, but it would seem to imply the prince was reneging on any vow that Edward would precede him to the throne.†

Edward was only three or so. He could hardly have understood his father's antipathy toward his mother, and was likely ignorant of it. Like most aristocratic children in those days, he was not raised by his parents. Noblewomen's duties included birthing children, but they had more important things to do than nurture them – in Emma's case, manage the royal household and her own personal estates and properties, as well as court gossip and politics. By this time Edward may have already been shipped off to be raised by the monks of the abbey of Ely in the fens of Cambridgeshire. A royal charter of 1004 awarded them twenty hides of land, at roughly

---

*Huntingdon and Malmesbury, both writing about a century later, inexplicably list Alfred rather than Edward as Emma's eldest son. Both first appear by name in the *Chronicle* in 1013, but Edward's name appears on royal charters in 1005, within a few years of his birth, whereas Alfred does not attest a royal charter until 1013. The *Encomium Emma Reginae*, their mother's approved account of events, plainly states Edward was the eldest. He was probably born around 1003, Godgifu circa 1004, and Alfred 1005.

†Viewing the line of succession with cold-hearted math, in 1005 everyone else's position in the royal pecking order moved up one notch due to the death, apparently of natural causes, of the king's second-eldest son, eighteen-year-old Ecgberht Aetheling.

120 acres each, but in monetary terms each enough to produce a pound of income per annum, probably in compensation. That Edward resided at Ely is confirmed by the *Liber Eliensis,* the annals composed there: "According to the church elders who witnessed it and took part in it it, he was raised there in the monastery for a long time with the other boys, and like them learned the psalms and hymns of the Lord."

To be raised by the church and destined for a life in the priesthood was not an uncommon fate for younger sons of nobility, and Edward was far down the line behind his older half-brothers. In many ways, though, he could be glad to be so far removed from his father's court. Aethelred may have been powerless to stop the Vikings, but he could still persecute his own subjects.

Vikings in the south were not the only threat to England. To the north, the realm of Alba (modern Scotland) had a new king, Malcolm II, anxious to prove himself in war. In 1005 he had attained the throne by killing his predecessor on the battlefield, and seeing Aethelred preoccupied with Danes, he immediately sought to demonstrate his power against the Celtic Scots' ancestral enemy, the English.

Malcolm's target was Durham, the holy city founded in the late 990s to keep safe the remains of Cuthbert, patron saint of Anglo-Saxon Northumbria, from coastal Viking raids. On a wooded hilltop above a horseshoe bend in the River Wear, a little stone church had been raised. It was of special interest to one Uhtred of Bamburgh, on the Northumbrian coast, who helped the monks clear the site of trees, and probably to build the wooden stockade which blocked the peninsula off from the surrounding country. Uhtred had married the bishop's daughter and for his efforts received several church estates.

When Malcolm laid siege to Durham in AD 1006, the local ealdormen, Uhtred's father Waltheof of Bamburgh and Aelfhelm of Northumbria, declined to come to Durham's rescue. (Waltheof was too old, and Aelfhelm, whose seat was in the old Viking capital of York, may have been more inclined to support Malcolm against a common enemy, Aethelred.) It was Uhtred who raised an army of

Northumbrians and Yorkshiremen, led the relief of the siege and defeated Malcolm on the field. Tradition has it that local women were paid one cow each to cleanse the heads of Scottish dead, for mounting on spikes on the town stockade.

In thanks for handling the northern incursion, King Aethelred named Uhtred, to be called "the Bold," as Ealdorman of Bamburgh over his father. For Aelfhelm he reserved more special treatment, which would affect the future of England. The 12th-century courtier Walter Map, a Welsh-born official in the court of Henry II, like everyone else held a low opinion of the *Unraed*, in part for his choice of henchmen: "He preferred his men to have hearts like his own, and he empowered them for all the degrees of brutality."

Eadric Aethelricsson – the same royal enforcer who had beheaded Forkbeard's sister Gunhilde in the St. Brice's Day Massacre – is remembered as Eadric Streona, literally "the Aquisitor" or "Acquisitive" but in more vernacular English as "the Greedy." There are few Englishmen in history, and certainly none from this era, more universally reviled than he. Virtually every chronicler of the times waxes near lyrical in their hatred of him.

"He was a truly a man of low birth," wrote the monks of Worcester a few decades later, "but his smooth talking brought him wealth and high rank and, gifted with a sly and persuasive tongue, he rose above all his contemporaries in malice and treachery, as well as in pride and brutality."

Malmesbury was similarly scathing, calling Eadric "a scheming villain who had risen to his station not by nobility, but by lies and audacity."

Eadric invited Aelfhelm to a feast at Shrewsbury in western England. In the course of the multi-day event, the two went out hunting. At an appointed spot a local thug named Godwin Port-Hund (Town Dog), in Eadric's pay, leaped from hiding and stabbed Aelfhelm to death. Furthermore, the ealdorman's sons, Wulfheag and Ulfgeat, were dragged before the king and, on his orders, blinded. Only Aelfhelm's daughter Aelfgifu was spared, being about sixteen and perhaps beneath royal notice, relatively powerless compared to her brothers. She would not be powerless forever, though, and she would neither forget nor forgive what had been done to her family.

Such treachery, though, worked for Eadric, who had a singular talent for ingratiating himself with powerful men. Like Ulfcytel Snilling, he even went on to marry another of Aethelred's daughters, Eadgyth (Edith), and the next year Aethelred named him Ealdorman of Mercia.

It is a sad reflection on any king, to surround himself with such men, and associate himself with such deeds, and yet show himself so pathetic in the face of his enemies. In 1009, in deliberation with his ministers, Aethelred decided to pay off the Danes yet again, this time to the amount of 30,000 pounds. It bought him some time. The annals record no Viking raids in 1008, but in full expectation they would eventually return, the king determined again to meet them at sea, and ordered the construction of another fleet to be assembled at Sandwich on the Kentish coast. Here, however, Aethelred's duplicity, and that of his men, would be the undoing of all that expense and effort.

While the navy was being assembled, one of Eadric Streona's brothers, Brihtric – "a slippery, ambitious and prideful man" according to Worcester – accused their nephew Wulfnoth, called Cild (the Bold Wolf's Child), himself a minor lord of Sussex, of some kind of treason. Ahead of his own arrest, Wulfnoth and his men – and, given Aethelred's penchant for blinding the sons of royal enemies, presumably taking along his son Godwin, then just eight or nine – escaped with twenty ships. Whether or not they had been guilty of Brihtric's accusation, they promptly made good on it now, turning pirate and plundering along the English coast. With eighty ships Brihtric set out in pursuit, but a storm shipwrecked his little fleet, whereupon Wulfnoth attacked and burned what was left.

With his own men battling each other and a hundred ships lost without ever having seen the enemy, Aethelred gave up on the idea of fighting Vikings at sea and took the remainder of his fleet up the Thames to London. So, as Worcester put it, "in this way the hard work of the entire kingdom was thrown away."

It was all too typical of Aethelred's reign. Malmesbury bemoaned: "Who can say how often he levied his army, how often he ordered the building of ships, how frequently he summoned commanders from all regions? And yet nothing was ever accomplished."

But King Aethelred was setting more of an example than his contemporaries knew. His queen Emma, little Prince Edward, young Aelfgifu of Northampton, and even Wulfnoth's son Godwin, were all learning a hard lesson from their king: how not to rule. They would be the next generation of Anglo-Saxon leaders. And England would need them.

For there was an entirely new threat facing the Island Kingdom.

IV

THE JOMSVIKINGS

1009–1012

When this naval expedition was thus concluded, then soon after
Lammas came the powerful army of the enemy, Thorkell's army...
they looted and burned, as is their way.

Anglo-Saxon Chronicle

Portus Ritupis, modern Richborough on the Kentish coast where
the English Channel narrows into the Strait of Dover, was the initial
landing point for the Romans in AD 43, and probably where the
last of them stepped off the island over 350 years later. It's thought
that in the dark times after the Roman departure the place was a
religious center, with a wooden church, a nearby amphitheater used
as a graveyard, and a pier extending out from the shore. Today the
harbor has silted full and lies two and a half miles inland from the
coast, but in 1009 it was still the most convenient spot for a landing
from across the Channel.

The men tying up to the medieval dock and wading ashore from
their beached ships would have found the place defenseless. They
swiftly took over the streets of nearby Sandwich, still recovering
from the Danish invasion of 1006. These were not the same Danes
as then. There were Danes among them, yes, but Norwegians as well,
and Swedes and even Wends (Poles, Slavs). Pleading with them for
Christian mercy was pointless, since few of them spoke any English,

and none of them was Christian. They were the most feared of all Scandinavian warriors: the Jomsvikings.

Feared, yes, but in Scandinavia the Jomsvikings were so admired that an entire saga was written about them. They adhered to a strict code of honor. No women were allowed inside their fortress at Jomsborg (thought to have been located near the town of Wolin, Poland, in an estuary connecting the Oder River with the Baltic Sea). Any male warrior between the ages of eighteen and fifty could join them, proving himself by defeating a Jomsviking in a duel. The Jomsvikings were one of the first European military orders, before there was anything like the Knights Templar, Knights Hospitaller or the Teutonic Knights. They were all steadfast pagans, but would sell their swords as mercenaries to the highest bidder – even a nominal Christian like Forkbeard.

They would be useful to him, for the days of the Great Heathen Army and Danelaw, when the Danes had put down roots in England, were in the past. That England had been a disjointed clutch of kingdoms, fighting each other as much as the Danes. Now it was unified, even if under an ineffective king. Forkbeard didn't have the manpower to push the entire island around forever, let alone to recolonize England while simultaneously holding Denmark and Norway.

According to some of the sagas, the Jomsvikings' leader, Thorkell *inn Havi* – Thorkell the High or Thorkell the Tall – was Forkbeard's uncle and served as foster father to Svein's son Cnut. This was common practice among Vikings, who called such parents *fostra*, foster mother, or father, *fostri*. It's just as likely, though, that Forkbeard had left the boy in Jomsborg more as a hostage for peace with the Jomsvikings. He needed a spare army more than he needed a son.

The Jomsvikings wasted little time on the coast, but drove straight inland. The *Chronicle* relates, "Soon they turned their march to Canterbury, which they would quickly have stormed, if they had not rather desired peace."

They did not desire peace. They desired payment. The citizens of Canterbury quickly gave it to them, to the amount of 3,000 pounds. The invaders then either marched or sailed to the old Viking haunts on the Isle of Wight, from which they drove once more through the south lands, Sussex, Hampshire, Berkshire. Aethelred called out his levies, and even managed to head the raiders off from their ships, but Eadric Streona talked him out of risking battle. It was getting late in the year. These Jomsvikings were not like the Danes of years past, who had come to England to stay. These would soon go home for the winter.

He was wrong. Thorkell and the Jomsvikings did not go home. They were not farmers. They had no fields to reap back in Jomsborg. More than any other Vikings of the age, the Jomsvikings lived by plunder. They sailed back up the Thames to beach their dragon ships at present-day Greenwich, where Watling Street's proximity to the river permitted quick movement by land or water, and settled in for the winter on the hill above the U-bend in the river, from which to threaten London.

By this time the city was the largest and most heavily defended in England. Besides the old Roman wall and defensive ditch, a separate fortification protected the south end of the bridge over the Thames, crucial to troop movements over the river (and probably rebuilt around this time). When Aethelred mustered his army there, the Vikings simply went where the army wasn't, scouring the surrounding countryside. They burned Oxford and Northampton. A *burh* in the old Mercian days, Northampton had been fortified with a stockade and earthen rampart when it was part of the Danelaw, but it was no London to stand firm against a Viking onslaught.

Some of its citizens may even have welcomed them.

In any military occupation there is a certain segment of the captive population who readily cooperate with the enemy, if only to save their own lives, and often to prosper under the new regime. The Jomsvikings had proven themselves the dominant warriors in England at the time, who might easily have been seen as more capable providers – better men – than forlorn, defeated Englishmen. Not all female captives went with them unwillingly. Viking raiders even had a term for such women: *frillur*. In the early years of Viking expansion, a *frilla* meant little more than a sex slave, but as time went on and the Vikings became (relatively) more civilized, it became more like the Latin *concubina*, a second wife.

An English woman, particularly one of good breeding and noble birth, might have something more than sex to offer an ambitious Viking, especially if she still harbored a grudge against the House of Wessex.

In 1010 Aelfgifu of Northampton was about twenty years of age and still unmarried, likely due to the stain of treason on her family name. No image or even description of her survives, but to judge by her later career she had a certain appeal to men, and a willingness to use it.

Thorkell numbered among his men a young warrior, Olaf, son of King Harald Grenski, a petty monarch of Norway. Just fourteen years old, the young prince was already a veteran of several battles in Denmark and Sweden.* According to the saga later written about him, it was Olaf's own mother who sent him out on his first raid, at age twelve, to learn the ways of war under the tutelage of more veteran warriors: "When Olaf thus acquired a ship and men, the crew titled him king, for it was the custom that those leaders of men who were of royal parentage, on going out upon a Viking raid, received the title of king immediately even if they had no land or kingdom."

Olaf and his men had met Thorkell and his men in Denmark and partnered with them in several raiding ventures, including this invasion of England. Despite his young age, or perhaps because of it, Aelfgifu may well have sought Olaf out. His saga describes him, now in his mid-teens, as "not tall, but of average height, although very thick, and strong. [As an adult he would be called Olaf the Stout.] He had light brown hair and a broad face which was white and red. He had notably fine eyes, beautiful and piercing."

An older woman exploiting the infatuation of a young admirer is a tale old as time. Though a connection between Aelfgifu and Olaf was thought common knowledge for centuries, it should be noted that the story ultimately derives from one passing mention, by the

---

*For most of history child soldiers have been a common feature of war. In medieval times life was short, and boys and girls alike grew up fast. The 10th-century Norwegian king Eric "Bloodaxe" Haraldsson began his military career at age twelve. Eric Hakonsson, Svein's son-in-law and Jarl (Earl) of Norway, reportedly killed his first man at the age of thirteen or so.

12th–13th-century Danish historian Saxo Grammaticus, who referred to her as "Olaf's *frille*."* Some historians now surmise that Saxo, writing 200 years after the fact, got her mixed up with one Alfhild, Olaf's concubine later in life.

Perhaps. Yet an affair between Aelfgifu of Northampton and Olaf Haraldsson goes a long way to explaining future events.

The next summer it was East Anglia's turn. This was still the land of Ulfcytel Snilling, who had given the Danes such a bitter victory back in 1004, and now he had the armies of both East Anglia and Cambridgeshire at his command. The Jomsvikings were not in the least intimidated. On May 5 they met him at Ringmere Heath, on much the same ground as before, in one of the biggest battles of Aethelred's reign, though the king, as now might be expected of him, took no part – a wise move, for shield wall to shield wall, the Jomsvikings were nearly invincible. English *seax* swords and two-handed Dane axes rose and fell, shields splintered, helmets split and caved. The East Anglians broke and ran before the Viking assault, and then the men of Cambridge too, having lost a number of high-ranking warriors, including the king's son-in-law Aethelstan.

For the next three months Thorkell and his men ravaged the countryside. Malmesbury attested, "Out of thirty-two counties of England, they overran sixteen." In desperation the king offered once again to buy them off with silver and provisions. They accepted, and went right back to looting. By September there was hardly any place in southeast England they had not ravaged, except Canterbury and London. Thorkell, Olaf and their men set about rectifying that.

This time there was no talk of payment or peace. According to Worcester, the Vikings cut a trench around the old Roman wall of Canterbury and laid siege to it. The English were unable to break out, and in almost three weeks Aethelred sent no one to their rescue.

---

*He also referred to her, depending on the translation, as Alwina or Alwine, but that is easily forgiven, as what your name was in those days depended on who was calling you by it. The Norwegians would later call her Alfifa, and recall that the Anglo-Saxons renamed Emma of Normandy Aelfgifu.

The delay infuriated the Vikings. At this point, the city archbishop was Aelfheah, the former Bishop of Winchester who had helped make peace between the king and Norwegian Olaf Tryggvason back in 994. He was unable to make any peace with Thorkell. Or, he never got the chance. One of his archdeacons, Aelmar – a man whose life, according to the chroniclers, Aelfheah had once saved – through treachery, or fright, or in hopes of mercy for the city or at least for himself, opened one of its seven gates to the Jomsvikings.

The lesson of Exeter had not been learned. A city which surrendered could expect to escape a sack…except from Vikings.

They burned a quarter of Canterbury, including the cathedral where Aethelred and Emma had been wed. The entire adult population, holy orders included, underwent a kind of inverse decimation – reportedly nine out of every ten slain, to the amount of 800 people. Worcester described the scene in lurid terms:

> Some townsmen died by the sword, others in the flames. Many were tossed headlong from the walls, some were hung by their private parts till they died. Matrons were dragged by their hair through the city streets, and then thrown into the fire to burn. Babies torn from their mothers' breasts were impaled on spearpoints or crushed to bits under wagon wheels.

The treacherous archdeacon Aelmar escaped the sack of Canterbury with his life, and Archbishop Aelfheah as well, though that was slim comfort. Worcester noted, "When the citizens had been slaughtered, and the city pillaged and razed to the ground, Archbishop Aelfheah was brought out in irons and dragged along, badly wounded, to the ships, where he was imprisoned and underwent great sufferings for seven months."

That was seven months, however, for an archbishop to proselytize to the heathen. Some were more than usually receptive to his preachings, for seemingly like God's punishment a painful, fatal bowel disease ran through their camp, according to Worcester killing some 2,000 men, ten and twenty at a time.

This sounds like dysentery or cholera, carried by the Thames from London downstream to the Viking camp. In those days when hygiene was unknown, streets were filthy and streaming with sewage, and everything from garbage and manure to dead animals was tossed into the nearest ditch or river – the same water people drank – no one was immune. (Aethelred's fourth-born son, Eadred Aetheling, presumably in London, also died of unknown cause about this time.) Random death was so common in England that the Anglo-Saxons had a word for it, *aelfscot*, "elf shot," struck down by an invisible, otherworldly arrow. If Thor and Odin were helpless against such a plague, even a Jomsviking might have considered commending himself into the hands of another deity.

Meanwhile, in London, King Aethelred assembled the *witan*, including the treacherous ealdorman Eadric Streona, to yet again try to come up with some solution to the Viking problem. Since no one wanted to fight Jomsvikings, it was finally decided to – what else? – pay them to go away. This time, 48,000 pounds of silver. The bribe was to be paid around Easter.

By then many of the Jomsvikings were literally sick of Aelfheah and his god. They convened a *thing* meeting and offered to ransom him for 3,000 pounds, but he declined, conceding they could do as they wished with his body, but his soul belonged to God. With no further use for him, and according to Worcester drunk on wine (which, if they had drunk more regularly, might have spared them their stomach bugs), they were through with this bothersome priest.

What happened next was so heinous that word of it reached as far as Saxony, where Thietmar, Prince-Bishop of Merseburg, heard it from an eyewitness and wrote it down. Seeing his men's mood turn murderous, Thorkell tried to intervene: "Stop, I beg you! I will give you gold and silver – with the exception of my ship, everything I own or can get. Only do not harm this man who is the chosen of the Lord."

"Such sweet words could not appease the unleashed rage of his companions, more unbending than iron or stone," wrote Thietmar. "Indeed, their wrath could only be slaked by the innocent blood."

Worcester continued, "Presently they set in, knocked him [Aelfheah] to the ground with the backs of their battle-axes, and pelted him with stones, bones, and ox-skulls."

Finally a Viking named Thrum, whose conversion to Christianity Aelfheah had achieved just the day before, returned the favor. He put the archbishop out of his misery, splitting his skull with an axe.

Even in death, however, Aelfheah managed to awe the heathen. According to Wendover, "Where he died, a dry log, spattered with his blood, overnight sprouted again, and grew shoots and leaves. The sight of this miracle so terrified the pagans, that, eagerly kissing the holy man's body, they allowed it to be taken to London, where it was given an honorable burial."

Utterly disgusted by his men's brutality – or their stupidity in killing a cash cow – Thorkell had Aelfheah's body delivered to London, where it was received with reverence. (Some sixty years later Aelfheah was canonized as a saint, his symbol being an axe.) Almost certainly, secret missives were sent along with the procession to Aethelred and the *witan* from Thorkell, who must have had much to think about. A Viking chieftain whose men felt free to disobey him could never sleep easy again.

After the 48,000 pounds of tribute was delivered, the Viking fleet broke up. The dragon ships went their separate ways. Some went home to Scandinavia and Jomsborg. According to Malmesbury, however, fifteen ships – and according to the *Chronicle*, forty-five – remained in English waters. Aelfheah's proselytizing had been more effective than he knew. He had driven a wedge into the ranks of the Jomsvikings. Perhaps having an attack of Christian conscience, as Olaf Trygvasson had almost twenty years earlier, Thorkell and the men still loyal to him – apparently including young Olaf Haraldsson (who might equally have chosen to remain behind for Aelfgifu of Northampton) – had decided to enlist in the service of King Aethelred of England, and swear to defend his land against all invaders.

Even Svein Forkbeard.

V

HNEFATAFL

1012–1014

If any one wishes to know this game fully, before all the lessons of this discipline it is necessary for him to have these seven in mind, namely, dukes and counts, defenders and attackers, city and state, and nine degrees twice.

From *Alea Evangelii* (*Game of the Gospels*)
Irish, mid-12th century

A millennium ago the board game that would eventually evolve into modern chess had only just begun to spread out of the East into the Mediterranean and southern Europe, and had not yet reached Scandinavia.* Vikings and Anglo-Saxons played their own kind of chess, called *hnefatafl*. Its rules have long since been lost and there were variations, but we do know that *hnefatafl* was played on a square board, with all pieces except one, the king, identical (though differently marked or colored for the two sides), and all moving like a rook in chess: any number of squares in a straight line, but not diagonally. Pieces were captured by being surrounded on two or, depending on the rules, three sides. Unlike chess, the two opponents did not start at opposite ends of the board. The defender's

---

*The famous "Viking" chess pieces discovered on the Isle of Lewis in the Outer Hebrides of Scotland date from AD 1150–1200.

pieces surrounded their king at the center, with his goal to escape to the edge of the board. The attacker, with more pieces but no king, started from all four edges, with the goal of capturing the king before he escaped.

Capturing a surrounded king. Whether influenced by medieval Scandinavian battle tactics, or influencing tactics itself, the game of *hnefatafl* was to have symbolic effect on ensuing decades.

In his capital at Roskilde in Denmark, Forkbeard must have received the news of Thorkell's betrayal with less shock than the news of the St. Brice's Day massacre ten years earlier. The Jomsvikings' loyalty to him had not exactly been rock solid in the past, and that Thorkell might not be completely trustworthy would have come as no surprise. It did, however, change the strategic situation entirely. In the past, to raid England had meant Forkbeard's Danes and Norwegians against Aethelred and his weak-willed, divided, vacillating Anglo-Saxons. Now everything he had gained in England was lost, and to regain it would require fighting another Viking army.

His men, at least, were undaunted. According to the *Encomium* – the author of which was biased, but who learned of events not long afterward – they told their king, "Our lord should not suffer such a loss, but lead his willing army. We will defeat that traitorous Thorkell and his men and his English allies."

Still Svein was hesitant. The risks were higher, but so were the stakes. He had been raiding England for ten years, never aspiring to take it and keep it. If he was to risk all, it could only be to gain all. Not only his empire, but his legacy. His eldest son, Harald, could be left in Denmark as regent while his father was away, but what of the second son? His birthdate being unknown, Cnut was now anywhere from about ten – unlikely – to his early twenties, about the same age as Forkbeard when he ousted his own father, Bluetooth, and took over his kingdom. If he wasn't already, Cnut would soon be desirous of his own realm. Forkbeard had to provide one, or risk forfeiting his own. According to the Encomiast, Emma's biographer (who may have heard the story from Cnut himself), Forkbeard summoned the boy to ask his opinion of the venture. "Questioned by his father, and fearing to appear weak if he opposed it, he not only approved of invasion, but that it should be done without delay."

With both father and son talking each other into it, and their nobles and warriors all for it, another invasion of England was inevitable. According to Malmesbury, "Svein was naturally brutal, and did not require much persuading."

But Malmesbury also throws another wrinkle into events. He claimed Thorkell sent word to Svein, encouraging him to return to England. King Aethelred, he said, concerned himself more with wine and women than war. His subjects hated him and his nobles, who spent their time quarreling with each other. Faced with an invasion, they would flee or capitulate.

If Malmesbury's claim is true, then while in Aethelred's service Thorkell either secretly switched sides yet again, or had signed up for England with Forkbeard's blessing. Either way, the prospect of the Danes facing Jomsvikings in combat had just been drastically diminished, and the total conquest of England looked much more promising.

In July of 1013, Forkbeard's army mustered to his fleet. The Encomiast waxes positively poetic in describing the longships' upraised prows, adorned with gold dragons, lions, bulls, dolphins and centaurs, their hulls brightly painted, gilded and silvered, birdlike wind vanes spinning at the mast tops. Oars threshing the water, sails billowing in the summer breeze, the fleet rounded Jutland and moved down the coast of Saxony to France. Before his conquest of England, Forkbeard wished to mend fences with Duke Richard of Normandy, who received him at Fécamp. They pledged to maintain the peace between them, and that the Danes could sell their goods (meaning loot) in Norman markets and see their wounded cared for by Norman physicians. This sounds remarkably similar to the state of affairs between Danes and Normans that provoked the Anglo-Saxon invasion of Normandy in 1002. Forkbeard was simply resetting the entire relationship of Danes, Normans and Anglo-Saxons back by a decade, to when it was much more favorable to him.

That done, the Danes landed at Sandwich on the Kentish coast, just as Thorkell's Jomsvikings had two years earlier. Initial resistance by the local *fyrd* soon melted away. Sandwich had been repeatedly sacked by Vikings in recent years and picked clean. Canterbury, the next stop inland, could not have been much better.

The Danes did not immediately march for London, though, or sail up the Thames to make a landing there. Forkbeard may have had misgivings about Thorkell and his men. Given the Jomsvikings' treacherous history with Denmark, it was entirely possible they really had switched sides and joined the English, and Thorkell had sent his invitation only to lure Forkbeard into a trap. If so, the Danish king did not wish to meet them head-on, but commenced to playing *hnefatafl*. Let Aethelred believe he had strengthened his army with Jomsvikings. Forkbeard would strengthen his with English.

The Viking fleet moved north, around the curves of East Anglia, Norfolk and Lincolnshire into the Humber, the tidal estuary that cuts from the North Sea into the heartland of northern England. Only a few generations past, this had been the Danelaw. The English had reclaimed it but done little to keep it English. Aethelred had sent no aid to Uhtred the Bold to repel the Scots those few years before, and he had brutally punished Aelfhelm of York for doing the same. The Northumbrians had no love for the House of Wessex.

The Humber is fed by two rivers, the Trent from the south and the Ouse from the north. Here Svein divided his force. Heming Haraldsson – brother of Thorkell the Tall – took sixty ships up the Ouse to Slessvik, about fifteen miles from York. Svein took the rest up the Trent. Twenty-five miles upriver, and fifty-five miles inland from the sea – in fact, at the furthest reach of the tidal bore which causes the river to flow upstream with the tide – the Vikings reached *Gegnesburh*, modern Gainsborough, Lincolnshire. In centuries past this had been part of the Anglo-Saxon kingdom of Lindsey, then the capital of Mercia, and then a Viking stronghold in the Danish days. Forkbeard intended it to be the latter again. It was not even required of him to conquer the northerners. After thirty-five years of Aethelred's rule, they knew better than to think any help was coming from him. They had a choice of watching their towns and houses burn before they themselves were slain, or acknowledging their new overlords.

Uhtred the Bold, Ealdorman of Northumbria, was the first to kneel. Routing Scots was one thing, but getting in the way of Danes was another. The *Chronicle* admits, "Uhtred soon submitted, and all the Northumbrians, and the people of Lindsey, and afterwards those of the Five Boroughs [of the old Danelaw: Derby, Leicester,

Lincoln, Nottingham and Stamford], and soon the entire army north of Watling Street, and each shire gave hostages."

It was a stroke of strategic genius. For years Forkbeard had demonstrated that he was a mightier king, a greater warrior than Aethelred, but he had largely confined his predations to the south. The north – the Danish blood of England – he had left relatively untouched. And when he came demanding the northerners' help, they gave it. The business of hostage-taking was mere insurance. Svein Forkbeard, King of Norway and Denmark, was effectively King of Northern England.

He requisitioned supplies and horses for his army and, leaving his son Cnut in charge of the fleet and hostages, undertook his invasion of the south. This was no mere raid, but a campaign of terror and scorched earth. Worcester recounted, "Crossing Watling Street, he commanded his warriors to destroy the fields, raze the villages, plunder the churches, kill every male captive without mercy, slake their lusts on the women and, in short, cause all the suffering they could."

About a hundred miles south of Gainsborough, Northampton would still have been recovering from the Jomsviking sack of three years earlier – good reason why it, and the rest of the surrounding lands, quickly capitulated to Forkbeard.

Some citizens, if we are to believe Saxo Grammaticus, capitulated more easily than others.

Now in her early twenties, Aelfgifu of Northampton would have become used to a life of hardship and bleak outlook. Daughter of a murdered earl, sister to his blinded sons, her family name stained with treason, she had (perhaps) served as *frilla* to the Jomsviking boy-raider Olaf Haraldsson. If so, it had done her no good. By this time Olaf was probably in the south, at the side of Thorkell the Tall, serving her family nemesis King Aethelred. Manless in a patriarchal age, getting no younger, Aelfgifu was fast running out of options in life.

Yet Forkbeard evidently saw more in her than a mere Anglo-Saxon wench to be used and tossed aside. The unmarried daughter of an ealdorman – in Danish terms, a *jarl*, an earl – was a rarity, a treasure, and in Danish eyes treason against Aethelred was no treason at all.

If Aelfgifu intended to set her hooks in the king, she was too late. Forkbeard already had more than enough wives and children. He had moved beyond all that and was playing the game at the next level: securing his legacy. His goal in England was to acquire a realm for his son, and part of that was finding him a queen. Aelfgifu of Northampton, Anglo-Saxon and living proof of everything wrong with the Anglo-Saxon king, was an ideal match for Cnut.

In his new hall in Gainsborough Castle – probably a Scandinavian-style wooden fort about two miles north of the modern town, where the local manor hall now stands – Cnut must have been surprised to have a wife delivered to him. He seems to have quickly gotten over the shock. Her dalliance with Olaf Haraldsson, if there ever had been one, was left unspoken and best forgotten. For her part, Aelfgifu could be thankful to gain a husband with a glorious future ahead of him, and not bad looking, either. According to the *Knytlinga Saga*, "Cnut was very tall, strong and handsome, except that his nose was thin, long, and a little crooked. He was fair-skinned, with beautiful long hair and good eyes, which were both clear and sharp."

By all accounts theirs was a handfast marriage (in Old Norse, *handfesta*, to agree to a bargain by joining hands), unsanctioned by the church. That mattered not a whit in those days, when marriage, particularly royal marriage, was a contract between families, and none of the church's business. Handfasting or *troth plight*, "truth pledge," of longstanding tradition among the Germanics and Scandinavians, had legal standing and was so common the church, while neither liking nor recognizing it, referred to it as *more danico*, "Danish marriage." The details of the ceremony itself are largely lost today. Exchange of gifts, dowry and dower between Cnut and Aelfgifu were of no record and little import. She had no family to speak of, and little to offer other than her name, her looks and demeanor, and a willingness to bear royal children.

All that, it appears, was more than enough for Cnut. And Aelfgifu could certainly be happy with her new husband. According to his own saga, "He was a generous man, a great warrior and valiant, victorious, and of good fortune in both style and regality. He was not too smart, much like King Svein or [his grandfathers] Harald and Gorm, who were not always wise either."

As far as Aelfgifu was concerned, the perfect husband.

And what Olaf Haraldsson may have thought of the match, when word reached him far to the south, no one wrote down.

"Then he went to Oxford," records the *Chronicle* of Forkbeard, "and the people soon submitted and offered hostages. From there, Winchester."

Worcester added, "When he arrived there, the citizens, panic-stricken at his unending cruelty, immediately made peace with him, and gave him whatever hostages he demanded."

Having subdued the north and west, Forkbeard now finally drove toward London. He found it stoutly defended. According to the *Chronicle*, "When he came to the city, the people refused to submit. They manned the walls, ready for war, because King Aethelred was inside, and Thorkell too."

To attack the city from the south required crossing the Thames, but the only crossing point for many miles in either direction was London Bridge itself. Its southern end, called by the English *Sudweca*, and by the Danes *Sudvirke*, "Southern Works" (modern Southwark), had been heavily fortified. The Vikings did not excel at taking fortifications or have much patience for sieges. Forkbeard attempted to cross the river without using the bridge, and failed. A number of his men were swept away and drowned.

It was the first setback of the campaign, which had taken only about a month. Svein decided Aethelred could keep London, while he took the rest. He withdrew west to Wallingford, then Bath, as Wendover wrote, "like a mad dog, destroying whatever got in his way."

"When he had vanquished all," reports the *Chronicle*, "he returned north to his ships, and all the people fully accepted him, and thought of him as king."

"And, although all England had already bowed to his rule," added Malmesbury, "not even then would the Londoners have yielded, if Aethelred not failed to lead them."

Wendover accused, "King Aethelred lay in dull indolence in the city of London, fearful and suspicious, and not trusting anyone."

The Londoners had proved willing to fight for him, and Forkbeard had demonstrated his reluctance to lay siege to the city, but Aethelred decided now was the time to get out. Malmesbury scoffed, "Being a man so given to sloth, and through awareness of his own misdeeds, believing no one was loyal to him, and simultaneously wishing to escape the trials of a battle and a siege, he left town, abandoning his people to fate."

It may be that the real decision was Thorkell's. It is difficult to reconcile the various accounts of the Jomsviking's actions and conflicting motives in this period. Like Eadric Streona on the Anglo-Saxon side, and like the rest of the Jomsvikings, Thorkell is known in the histories for changing loyalties as the situation warranted, always playing both sides. He had invaded England on Forkbeard's behalf, joined Aethelred when it suited him, only to (perhaps) invite Forkbeard to return to England as well. Now, with Forkbeard in control of most of the country, he may have seen Aethelred's eventual defeat as inevitable, and sought favor with both by offering the English king an easy exit.

To his credit, Aethelred at least saw to his family's safety first. Worcester recorded, "Things being what they were, King Aethelred sent his queen, Emma of Normandy, to her brother Richard II, Duke of Normandy, together with their sons, Edward and Alfred."

The Duke of Normandy's motives and loyalties at this time are hardly less suspect than Thorkell's. Whether out of fear, greed or simply good diplomacy, it seems Richard was willing to entreat with whoever showed up in his harbor at Fécamp, whether Anglo-Saxon or Dane. It had been the Norman trade in Forkbeard's ill-gotten English loot that had provoked Aethelred's ire and necessitated the treaty of marriage with Emma in the first place. Richard would appear to have dissolved that agreement by his recent pact to resume business with Forkbeard. And now he was accepting the wife and children of Forkbeard's enemy into his own household. That could perhaps be excused by their Norman blood – they were Richard's kin, too – or just good Christian charity. Seemingly Richard wasn't called *le Bon*, "the Good," for nothing. Malmesbury certainly credited that he was "the equal of his father in good luck and good qualities, and even surpassed him in religious matters.... He was more focused on prayer and temperance than you would expect of any monk or hermit."

Richard was right to seek God's favor. The Normans were very much the junior partners in any dealings with Vikings or Anglo-Saxons. Carefully trying to remain on everyone's good side, Richard risked getting on the bad side of whoever won.

He could always claim to Forkbeard that he had shown Aethelred's grown children no such protection. It's thought the surviving *aethelings* Aethelstan, Edmund, Eadwig and the rest were still with the king in England. According to the *Chronicle*, Aethelred even spent the autumn with Thorkell the Tall on his ship at Greenwich, only just downriver from the city (so close that today it is part of Greater London).

A lot of good that did his subjects when Forkbeard came down from Gainsborough to complete his conquest. He had sent sixty ships under the Danish *jarl* Eilif Thorgilsson on a flanking maneuver up the Thames. Worcester admitted, "The Londoners sent him hostages and made peace with him, afraid his fury toward them was so intense that he would not only seize all their belongings, but have them blinded, or cut off their hands or feet."

Evidently Forkbeard and Thorkell reached some accord, for all winter the Jomsviking fleet lay at Greenwich. The Danes not only did not molest them, but joined forces to take whatever was not given. Worcester claimed, "The tyrant Svein ordered that his fleet be fully supplied, and that an almost impossible tribute be exacted. Jarl Thorkell gave the same orders to his fleet at Greenwich. Besides this, both of them launched raids to plunder as they liked, and committed great atrocities."

By then Aethelred was long gone. By different routes, according to the various sagas, he ended up on the old Viking haunt, the Isle of Wight. He lingered there through Christmas, perhaps seeking some miracle to restore his throne. Then, finally giving up all as lost, he boarded a ship to join Emma and their children in Normandy.

Hnefatafl. By the rules of the game, Aethelred had won. He had escaped off the board, lived to fight another day. But Svein owned the playing field.

Huntingdon admitted, "Svein was now recognized by the whole nation as king."

With the addition of England to his lands in Denmark and Norway, Forkbeard had made himself one of the most powerful kings in Europe. His empire made the North Sea a Viking lake, and was on a par with the Carolingian Empire, or even the Holy Roman Empire.

But Danes and English had fought each other too hard and too long to love one another. In 1014 Wulfstan, the firebrand priest who had incited the St. Bryce's Day Massacre twelve years earlier, and so done as much as any man to bring on Forkbeard's vengeance, foretold the end of days: "Beloved men, realize the truth – this world is hastening toward an end. Things go from bad to worse, and because of the people's sins must necessarily get much worse before the coming of Antichrist. It will then be dreadful and terrible indeed, far and wide across the world."

Truly it seemed to the Anglo-Saxons that both God and their king had abandoned them. Malmesbury wrote, "If they decided to revolt, they had no one to lead them. If they chose submission, they would have a harsh ruler over them. And so their public and personal property, along with their hostages, was taken away to the fleet, for he [Forkbeard] was not a lawful king, but the cruelest of tyrants."

But he added, "Yet God was too kind to leave England struggling too long in such acute pain."

And as the monks of Worcester put it, "Divine vengeance did not suffer the blasphemer to continue living."

───────

"The tyrant Svein," explained Worcester, "besides his neverending cruel atrocities both in England and other lands, assured his damnation by daring to exact a huge tribute from the town where rests the unsullied body of the dear martyr Edmund."

This Edmund had been king of East Anglia in the 9th century, when the Great Heathen Army invaded. The *Anglo-Saxon Chronicle* tells us, "In the winter [869–870] King Edmund fought them, but the Danes were victorious, and slew the king." It goes into no detail. (West Saxon writers gave little priority to the affairs of East Angles.) Some 150 years later, Edmund's story was written down by the Benedictine abbot Aelfric of Eynsham. According to that version of events, the Viking Ivar the Boneless, son of Ragnar Lodbrok, ordered Edmund to submit or die, but the king refused. Ivar had him seized and beaten with cudgels, then tied to a tree and whipped, but the king hewed to his faith, which drove the Vikings into such a fury that they shot him full of arrows, until his body fairly bristled with them. Still Edmund lived, and still proclaimed his trust in God, so Ivar had him beheaded. Head and body were buried at nearby *Beodericsworth*, Beodoric's Fort. Miracles were soon said to occur at his shrine. A cult grew up around it, pilgrims flocked to it, Edmund was canonized and the town renamed St. Edmunds Burh, modern Bury St. Edmunds.

In AD 1010, almost a century and a half after the saint's death, when another Danish army threatened the land, Edmund's body had been spirited to London for safekeeping. The cult of such an Anglo-Saxon champion could not be allowed to persist, and so King Svein Forkbeard made a special example of it. London was not his capital, and Edmund, he declared, was no saint. If tribute was not paid the Danes would burn the martyr's church to the ground, and all the city and citizens with it.

Even a king, however, should beware battling a saint. Wace shrugged: "It is true what the peasant says: 'A mad dog does not live long.'"

At the beginning of February 1014, Forkbeard was back in Gainsborough, addressing a *thing* meeting of all his lords from horseback. While he was thundering out more threats against the English, Worcester claimed, Svein saw a vision of the saint coming through the crowd at him. He called out in terror: "Help, comrades, help! Lo, St. Edmund has come to slay me." No one else, though, could see the apparition, much less stop it before it speared the king.

Forkbeard, who was about fifty years of age – relatively long-lived for a man in that day – in reality probably suffered a stroke or heart attack, or simply a fall from his horse. According to the Encomiast, he lingered long enough to pass along his crown. "So, feeling that death was upon him, he summoned his son Cnut to his side, and said that he must go the way of all flesh. He charged him with governing the kingdom and zealous Christianity, and, thanks be to God, passed the royal scepter to him, the most worthy of men."

Forkbeard's North Sea Empire had lasted just five weeks. On his death it sundered into two or three pieces. In Denmark, his eldest son

Harald went from regent to king. His *jarl* Hakon Ericsson, technically a Danish vassal, became for all practical purposes King of Norway.

And England was to be Cnut's. The Encomiast continued, "The Danes, over whom he now rightfully ruled, very strongly approved of this, and were glad that he was made king over them, while his father still lived."

Yet Cnut, it appears, was hardly up to the challenge. In his early twenties at most – and if his own saga is to be believed, not yet in his teens – he must have found his father's death a hard blow. There was hardly time for him to grieve, for a changing of kings is always fraught with danger, particularly in a newly conquered land. Barely had the young prince settled onto his father's throne at Gainsborough when word arrived from the south.

King Aethelred had returned.

———

In the north, the old Danelaw, people might have been happy to have the crown peaceably passed down from one Viking to another. On the other hand, the people of the south, whom Forkbeard had so relentlessly victimized, saw the hand of God in his abrupt death, and thought better of yet again bowing their heads so easily to the Danish yoke. Worcester wrote, "As one, the elders of all England quickly sent messengers to king Aethelred, declaring that they neither did nor should love any one more than their natural lord, if only he was willing to govern them more justly, and treat them with more kindness than he had done before."

Aethelred was not so certain of their loyalty that he was willing to risk returning in person. Instead, in an act of callow ruthlessness, he sent his eldest son by Emma, Edward, as his ambassador. Little diplomacy would have been required of the boy, who after all was only ten or so. In reality he was being offered as a token hostage, signifying the king's good will. The true negotiations would have been left up to the royal envoys among his escort, who assured the members of the *witan* that Aethelred would forgive all transgressions and betrayals against him and rule with more wisdom and justice than he had hitherto shown, if they would to a man declare for him.

To this the earls and other nobles had agreed.

During Lent, Aethelred made the Channel crossing. On landing he declared any would-be Danish King of England henceforth an outlaw. The English nobles, in the south at least, rose to his banner. Thorkell the Tall was apparently still with the ex-Jomsviking fleet at Greenwich. Aethelred paid him 21,000 pounds (according to the *Chronicle*; according to Worcester, 30,000 pounds), if nothing else to prevent him switching sides to Cnut. Aethelred didn't really need him, for the Jomsviking's young Norwegian protégé Olaf Haraldsson is thought to have wintered in France with Aethelred, and remained in his service on his return to England. He may have had no argument with Forkbeard, but definitely appears to have held a grudge against Cnut and Aelfgifu. According to *King Olaf's Saga*, later written about him, Olaf was "one who ever wanted to be the first, as suited him according to his birth and dignity."

The key to Aethelred's invasion was London Bridge. Though built of wood on piles driven into the river bottom, it was wide enough for two wagons to pass, and had always been the main connection between the two halves of England – Wessex and Mercia, Saxon and Dane, north and south. Aethelred had held it against Forkbeard, who had declined to attack it and tried to go around. His army had paid the price in drowned men. Now Eilif Thorgilsson held it for Cnut against Aethelred's return. The Vikings had strengthened the bridge defenses with barricades, towers and parapets. Besides the walled *burh* at the northern end of the bridge, at *Sudvirke* at the southern end, they had dug a moat, used the soil to raise an embankment, and topped it with a palisade of stone and timber. "King Aethelred ordered a massive attack," claimed the saga writers, "but the Danes defended bravely, and Aethelred could make no headway."

Archaeologists have turned up spearheads, axes and a grappling iron from the riverbed, dating from the Viking era and attesting to heavy fighting for the bridge. As long as the Danes held it, they could prevent Aethelred from moving any further upriver, and move warriors quickly from one side to another, wherever he attacked. In that sense, the bridge did not need to be captured, but simply destroyed.

It was Olaf the Stout who came up with a plan.

Downriver, where the old Roman docks and depots had once existed, were still villages of Saxon thatch-roofed, sunken-floor huts. Olaf ordered them knocked down, but their roofs of packed straw over wood framework kept intact and reinstalled over his longships. Thus covered, the crews put out on the river and rowed upstream toward the bridge.

As the ships came in range, the defenders sent arrows arching out over the water, but they would not have pierced the thatching, and if it was wetted even fire arrows would have been ineffective. Vikings were well acquainted, however, with catapults – ballistae and mangonels – and the impact of javelin-sized bolts and heavy stones soon took a toll of men speared through or crushed under collapsed roofing. Some of the ships returned downstream. According to his saga, however, "King Olaf, with the Northmen's fleet, rowed right up under the bridge."

While the furious defenders dumped more stones over the rail onto the longships below, Olaf and his men flung grappling hooks and lines around the bridge pilings and supports, and when they had a secure hold, rowed hard downstream. One can imagine the slack lines snapping taut out of the water and fairly humming as the longships, still being pelted with arrows, spears and stones, hung on the far ends like dead weight, with Olaf and his captains bawling at their men to put their backs into their oars, and men on the bridge frantically clambering down the sides of the bridge to hack at the lines. Too late.

The bridge pilings did not rest on rock, but in sand, gravel and clay. The combination of river current and the drag of the longships slowly pulled their feet out from under them. After that, according to Olaf's saga, nature took its course: "Now as the warriors thronged upon the bridge, along with many heaps of stones and other weapons, the piles under it loosened and broke. The bridge gave way. A great many of the men on it fell into the river, and the rest fled, some into the city, some into Southwark."

With the south riverbank cut off from support by Cnut's forces on the north side, Aethelred and Olaf were able to storm its walls from behind. And with Southwark taken, the English were able to move troops upstream past the city and disembark them at will. London would soon be cut off as well. Olaf's saga proclaims, "Now when the Londoners saw the Thames was mastered, and that they could not stop ships from moving upriver, they lost heart, surrendered the city, and accepted Aethelred as their king."

Because this episode is only covered in Scandinavian accounts and doesn't rate a mention in the English, including the *Chronicle*, some historians discount it completely. Yet to Anglo-Saxon annalists of the time, Olaf would have been just another nameless Scandinavian mercenary. It's not inconceivable that English writers chose to credit victory to their own king Aethelred, rather than to other Vikings.

Olaf Haraldsson, though, would go on to be a thorn in Cnut's side for years to come.

The ensuing campaign demonstrates what the Anglo-Saxons might have accomplished in years past, if only they had acted of one accord. Henry of Huntingdon recorded, "King Aethelred came with a great army and, taking the land by surprise, put it to the torch, and most of the provincials to the sword."

Then again, Aethelred was no longer going up against the veteran warfighter Forkbeard, but against his son who quickly proved not up to defending his father's lands. As the English closed in on Gainsborough, plundering, burning, and murdering at will, Cnut had difficulty raising men and horses from among the reluctant people of Lindsey, who must also have been rethinking their loyalties. According to his own saga, "After his father's death, Cnut tried to keep the royal scepter of the kingdom, but was quite unequal to the task, for he had too few followers. The English, because his father had unjustly invaded their lands, amassed all the forces of the kingdom in order to evict him, as he was just a boy."

Cnut finally lost his nerve. Leaving his consort Aelfgifu behind in his haste and confusion, he loaded his men and the southerner hostages delivered to his father by Oxford and Winchester aboard ship, sailed down the Trent, out the Humber, and down the coast to Sandwich. There, at least, he proved himself his father's son. As Malmesbury told it, "Defying all laws of God and man, he mutilated his hostages, young men of great nobility and grace, by cutting off their ears and noses, and some even their manhoods. Thus tyrannizing the innocent, and bragging about it, he went home."

Aethelred answered reprisal with reprisal, on the northerners who had capitulated so easily to Svein. "King Aethelred set upon them with a powerful army," wrote Worcester, "and having driven out Cnut and his navy, laid waste and burned the whole of Lindsey, putting as many of the people as he might to death."

Further north at Slessvik, Thorkell's brother Jarl Heming submitted as well to Aethelred, saving his life. (Probably that was also part of Aethelred's deal to keep Thorkell out of the fighting.) Aethelred did not capture all of Cnut's collaborators, though. The Encomiast confided:

A certain English matron had a ship readied. Taking the body of Svein, who had been interred in her land, and having embalmed it [which in those days meant immersing it in a barrel of vinegar, wine or honey, possibly with the internal organs removed] and covered it with palls, she put to sea, made a successful voyage, and arrived in Denmark.

Though unnamed in the *Encomium Emmae Reginae* – written on behalf of Emma of Normandy and pointedly ignoring details of Cnut's early life inconvenient to her – this "English matron" can only be Aelfgifu of Northampton. While Cnut was disfiguring English hostages in Sandwich, it's thought she smuggled his dead father out of England on a separate ship.* Risky business, and that wasn't all. The dates are uncertain, but by this time Aelfgifu may also have been carrying Cnut's child...or, at least, somebody's child.

More of that later. At any rate, Cnut could claim to have won his *hnefatafl* rematch with Aethelred, having escaped the board still alive, though that was surely not his idea of victory. England was English again, but alas, Aethelred would soon prove to be Aethelred again. As for his promise to rule justly over his English subjects, he would renege on that at the first opportunity.

*Though Gaimar says the body wasn't returned to Denmark for another ten years.

VI

SONS OF THE FATHERS

1014–1016

A swiftly spreading rumour suddenly reached the palace of King
Harald, that his brother Cnut had landed on his shores. The king
and his entire army pondered why, and though they could not be
sure, they had a feeling that he had met with bad luck.

Encomium Emmae Reginae

Across the North Sea, Cnut arrived at the court of his brother in
Roskilde with proverbial hat in hand. A military escort was sent
down to the dockside to welcome him to the hall of Harald Bluetooth,
Svein Forkbeard and now King Harald II. The *Knytlinga Saga* tells
of the brothers' embrace and mutual tears over their father's death.
Probably over copious amounts of mead, Cnut would have related the
whole sorry tale of his father's triumph and his own defeat, from the
conquest of the English to the treachery of Olaf Haraldsson, Thorkell
the Tall and the entire Anglo-Saxon *witan*, and finally being chased
out of his own kingdom like a whipped dog. The Encomiast claimed
he told Harald, "I have come, my brother, partly from my love for
you, and partly to escape the unexpected rebellion by those furious
barbarians. Not because I feared war, which I will fight again for my
glory, but so, with your advice and military support, I should return
certain of victory."

In the meantime he was a king without a kingdom, but of course
his loving brother could assuage that loss. In the *Encomium*, Cnut

puts it to Harald with a certain lack of tact: "But there is one thing first, if you will not begrudge me my glory, and that is to divide Denmark with me – my inheritance, which you now hold alone. Afterwards we will add England to our mutual inheritance, if we can do so together. Keep whichever you choose, and enjoy your success. I will keep the other."

This, as can well be imagined, came as a bit of surprise to Harald, in whose mind Cnut's failure to defend his half of their father's realm did not entitle him to half of the rest. "What you say about dividing the kingdom is a serious matter. It is my task to rule what our father gave me, with your approval. As for you, if you have lost a greater realm, I am sorry, but though I am able to help you, I will not have my kingdom divided."

Obviously, that was not what Cnut wanted to hear, but he was in in no position to make demands. He agreed to table the matter for the time being. His grief, regret and thirst for vengeance would have been mollified somewhat by the arrival of Aelfgifu with their father's body, and probably news of her pregnancy. Cnut the would-be king had a queen and, if things went well, an heir. All he needed was his kingdom.

Just who would inherit the English throne was made even more questionable that year of 1014. In June Aethelred's eldest son and heir to his throne, Aethelstan Aetheling, whether through disease or wounds sustained in the recent fighting, fell deathly ill. He was only about thirty. For England this was a tragedy of what might have been, for compared to his father, Aethelstan was not only more martially inclined, but he was also more just. His last will and testament, composed on his deathbed by special dispensation of the king to dispose of his worldly goods however he saw fit, still survives. Its very first declaration is that Aethelstan freed all his slaves. (Admittedly, it would have been better for posterity if he had never owned slaves in the first place, but in those days owning people was hardly out of the ordinary, especially for nobility.)

There follows a long list of lands, money, property and beneficiaries, including no fewer than eleven prized swords from

Aethelstan's personal collection. To his father Aethelred, a silver-hilted blade, given to Aethelstan by the formidable Ulfcytel Snilling, in whose hands it might have tasted Danish blood, and in his father's hands Aethelstan might hope would taste it again. To his surviving brothers Edmund and Eadwig (recall that Ecgberht, Edgar and Eadred had already gone to their rewards), more swords: another silver-hilted one for Eadwig, and for Edmund – present at his bedside – one even more prized, which had once belonged to King Offa of Mercia, the most powerful Anglo-Saxon king prior to Alfred the Great. As Offa died in AD 796, this blade was an heirloom over 200 years old. One might expect Aethelstan's brother-in-law Eadric Streona, now Ealdorman of Mercia, to have coveted the sword of Mercia's greatest king, but "the Greedy One" does not appear in the will. Also slighted were Aethelstan's stepmother Emma and his half-brothers Edward and Alfred, despite Aethelstan remembering even his lowest retainers and servants – an inlaid, though notched, blade to his personal *swurdhitan* (sword-polisher), and no less than a *stodes*, stud farm, to his *headeor hunton* (stag huntsman). Aethelstan went out of his way to mention the brothers Sigeferth and Morcar, *thegns* (ministers) of the Seven Burhs (thought to be the Five Boroughs conquered by Forkbeard, plus Torksey and York), who were of Danish blood, and suspected not so much of supporting Forkbeard as opposing Eadric. To rub salt in the wound, Aethelstan even remembered Eadric's kinsman: "And I grant to Godwin, Wulfnoth's son, the land at Cumtune [modern Compton, in Sussex] which was once his father's."

This was land Aethelred had confiscated back in 1008 as punishment for Wulfnoth Cild's supposed treachery, and evidently given to Aethelstan. The prince was going some way to correct his father's wrongs from beyond the grave. As a sign of the respect shown him by his would-be subjects, he was interred at the Old Minster in Winchester, the first non-king buried there in almost a century.

Aethelred apparently agreed to Aethelstan's last wishes, at least for the time being. The king was running low on sons. Of those by his first wife, only Edmund and Eadwig remained. However, his sons-in-law,

Eadric Streona and Ulfcytel Snilling, more than made up for the loss. Ulfcytel's hatred of Danes, and Eadric's general treachery, made them ideal allies of Aethelred and willing tools in fresh plots against those Vikings left behind by Cnut. In London Eilif Thorgilsson, and in the north Thorkell's brother Heming Haraldsson, were doing their best to get along with the Anglo-Saxons, even going to church unarmed. Now, with Forkbeard dead and Cnut exiled, had come the time – yet again – for the English to rid themselves of Danes.

According to the *Jomsviking Saga*, "Every winter around Yule, people went into town with wagons, loaded with goods for market. So it happened this winter. All the wagons were in place, according to the treacherous advice and instigation of Ulfkel Snilling and the brothers, Aethelred's sons."

Twelve years on, the English were planning another St. Brice's Day massacre, this time around Christmas, but they were not as successful at keeping the plot secret. In London, a Viking named Thord had an English *frilla*, who warned him not to go into town on the seventh night of Yuletide (seven days after the winter solstice, December 27), because Eadric Streona had organized the townspeople to murder the Vikings at church. "It is true," she said, "that people drove wagons into the city, pretending to carry goods, but there are no goods, only men in each wagon, and they are doing the same up north in Slessvik."

Thord reported this to Eilif and his men. Many found the story hard to accept, but some believed it and took up weapons. When they arrived at the churchyard, they were surrounded by the English and attacked. Eilif and a few of his men were able to cut their way out and flee to their ships – so few men, in fact, that only three ships were needed to carry them to Denmark. In the north, at Slessvik, Heming Haraldsson and his men were not so lucky. Ulfcytel Snilling organized this massacre, murdering them all. (Small consolation that the town later became known, and is known today, as Hemingbrough, Heming's Fort.)

"At that time a certain man rose to high station in this way," wrote Map. "Aethelred became lost during a hunt. It was winter [this would be 1014–1015], and, wandering alone by night, he came to a cowherd's farm, where he requested and received hospitality. There he met the herdsman's energetic son, a boy named Godwin, handsomer and finer than his ancestry warranted."

If Map is to be believed, this was the same Godwin, son of Wulfnoth Cild, the South Saxon *thegn* who had been accused of treachery in 1008, and then turned pirate, destroying Aethelred's fleet. It's thought Wulfnoth died in June 1014, about the same time as Aethelstan Aetheling, which may be what moved the prince to name the son in his will. (And, by the way, gives some credence to Map's story.) If Godwin was now living in the home of a humble herdsman, he had fallen about as far as he could go in Anglo-Saxon society. According to Map, he did not recognize the king, and probably his adopted father did not either, except as a nobleman, for the two classes did not mingle. Yet, as Map told it – exaggerating a bit for effect – Godwin showed himself to be a good lad, tending to his guest's horse, putting a goose on the fire for dinner (Map says ten) and a hen and salt pork too (Map says three of each). The point of the story is that Godwin so impressed the king that Aethelred took him into his own service: "The king, dull as he was, took note of everything, and, though himself lazy, approved of the lad's busy care and attentive service, as many praise what they do not practice."

The tale can be taken with a grain of salt – by this time Godwin should have taken receipt of the lands willed to him by Aethelstan, unless the king rescinded it – but bears repeating because it is Godwin's first appearance on the stage, and one of the few stories which reflects well on Aethelred. (And, for that matter, on Godwin.) Map described the boy very differently than other writers would describe the man: "Who would have thought a peasant could be free of all boorishness and redolent with such a sweet air of gentility?"

The next year, 1015, the king called a convention of the *witan* at Oxford. His purpose was not simply to reassert his authority over the delegates. Eadric Streona had secretly accused Aethelstan's friends Sigeferth and Morcar of treachery. With Aethelred's blessing, Eadric lured them to his chambers, got them drunk, and, as he had done with

Aelfhelm of York, had them murdered. Their estates and property were confiscated by Aethelred, and the widow Ealdgyth (though to which brother she had been married is uncertain; both brothers were married to Ealdgyths) was sent to be confined in the nunnery at Malmesbury Abbey in Wiltshire.

William of Malmesbury, naturally enough, attested, "I have read the history of this deed, which is kept in the church archives." He described this Ealdgyth as notable in both rank and beauty, which must have been true, as she was not long without a champion.

Edmund, until recently third in line to the throne, suddenly found himself heir apparent. Like his late brother, he seems to have been determined to right their father's wrongs, starting with the widow Ealdgyth. He contrived some reason to journey to Malmesbury and visit the abbey. If an *aetheling* showed up at its door, he represented the crown, a benefactor the abbey could little afford to offend. Edmund could simply have demanded entry and to meet with Ealdgyth. "Seeing her, he fell in love," wrote Malmesbury, "and falling in love, he took her for his wife."

There was more than romance involved. The authors of the *Chronicle*, writing to please their patron Aethelred (that year, at least) – and possibly to excuse the actions of their fellow priests at Malmesbury in losing custody of their charge – had it that "Edmund Aetheling seized her against the king's will, and took her to wife." Ealdgyth was surely seized against Aethelred's will, but hardly against her own. She had been more or less sentenced by the king to life imprisonment in the nunnery. She escaped that fate by marrying a friend of her late husband, and an *aetheling* no less – one who could restore her family lands, which Edmund promptly did. With the prince at her side, Ealdgyth became not only a free woman again, but the future Queen of England.

Edmund may have realized, though, that he had crossed a line and betrayed his father, which amounted to rebellion. Yet he was already thinking like a king. By marrying a lady of the Midlands, he secured a power base of his own against any future strife.

And in England in those days, strife was never very far off.

By the summer of 1015, Cnut and his brother Harald had spent the better part of a year together. Harald was still king of Denmark, but if Cnut had his way he would soon be king of England again, and in more than name. They had assembled a fleet, according to the *Jomsviking Saga* numbering 800 longships. The Encomiast claimed just 200, but waxed poetic in describing this Viking navy, its figureheads adorned with gilded and silvered beasts, its gunwales hung with the shields of many nations: "In this great expedition there was no slave, no freedman, no lowborn man, no old man. All were noble and of prime age, all ready for fighting, all so fleet of foot that they scorned horsemen."

Eilif Thorgilsson's brother Ulf, Jarl of Skane (modern Scania in southern Sweden), joined the crusade as well; he had recently married the kings' half-sister, Estrid. Their other sister Gytha brought in her husband, the Norwegian *jarl* Eric Hakonsson, one of the greatest and most experienced Viking warriors of any age. In the old days he had helped Svein defeat Olaf Tryggvason at the Battle of Svolder. He had fought and conquered all over the Baltic, Sweden, Estonia and Russia. He had long been Jarl of Norway, as now was his son Hakon. Every great Viking of the day was to take part in Cnut's crusade – all, that is, except for Cnut's foster-father Thorkell the Tall. The Encomiast admitted Cnut had told his brother, "Deserting us like he did our father, our former ally Thorkell has settled in the country [England], keeping many of our ships. I believe he will be against us, but for all that he will not prevail."

Yet as summer came and Cnut was strolling the Danish shore, doubtless looking wistfully across the water toward England, he beheld nine longships bearing in from the horizon. Rather than come in to port, they dropped anchor offshore and sent a small boat bearing a messenger, from Thorkell.

Probably in light of the treacherous murder of his brother Heming by Ulfcytel Snilling, the Jomsviking had reconsidered his loyalty to Aethelred, and his loyalty to Cnut. According to the *Encomium*, he asked his foster son's forgiveness, swore to serve him faithfully, and furthermore encouraged his return to England, "saying that he could easily defeat people whose land was familiar to them both. Specifically, he said that he had left thirty ships in England with a loyal army, who on their arrival would change sides, and would lead the fight through the length and breadth of the land."

Hard as it might be for modern readers to accept, particularly when Thorkell's promise of loyalty came with a promise to betray his former master Aethelred, Cnut welcomed him. With the Jomsviking's force added to theirs – and with a goodbye kiss for his queen Aelfgifu and their newborn son Svein, and perhaps on her swollen belly, for it's thought she was pregnant again – in August the Danish fleet weighed anchor and sailed for England.

After Cnut's hasty abandonment of the north the previous year, and the retribution it suffered in his absence, a fresh invasion there could expect a rough reception. The Danish fleet made the usual initial landfall at Sandwich, and according to the *Encomium* found a hot welcome awaiting them there, too. Scouts returned from ashore to report thousands of English eager for victory or death against the Danes. It seems the Kentish locals, by now tired of playing host to Viking invaders, were finally well prepared to drive them back into the sea.

It says something of Cnut's inexperience, hesitancy – or wisdom – as a battle leader that, rather than starting his campaign with a contested landing, heading up the coast or simply driving straight up the Thames, he took his fleet down around the Kentish coast to Poole. Even in those days this was one of the world's largest natural harbors, but also the shallowest, averaging less than two feet deep. That did not stop sea-skimming longships. The Danes ransacked the chapel and hermitage there and used it as a base from which to ravage the nearby villages. Then they went up the River Frome, thirty miles into the heart of Dorset and the village of Cerne Abbas – relatively fresh pickings, as it had grown up around Cerne Abbey, only just founded in 987. From there the Vikings probably could see the famous Cerne Giant, the 180-foot chalk-filled outline of a man cut into the hillside above the town, bearing a 121-foot club. (Long thought to be prehistoric in origin, recent archaeology has revealed the imposing figure was cut between AD 700 and 1100 – the Viking

Age – possibly as a billboard warning off raiders.) The Danes do not seem to have been intimidated.*

That autumn all of Wessex trembled before the Viking advance. Dorset, Somerset, Wiltshire, burned. The Danes drew uncomfortably close to *Cosseham*, "Cossa's home." (Rather than modern Cosham, suburban Portsmouth on the southern coast, this was more likely modern Corsham in Wiltshire, site of a royal estate.) There, King Aethelred himself lay ill abed, perhaps heartsick over the break with his eldest remaining son Edmund. The *aetheling* was still in the north, raising his army. With these two out of the picture, it was up to Eadric Streona to mount a defense of England.

The Greedy One, as might be expected, took a self-serving view of the situation: Cnut, on the march, with the odds in his favor; King Aethelred ill, perhaps fatally so; his heir Edmund far away and on the outs with the court; Edmund's only surviving full brother Eadwig, in his early twenties, probably susceptible to the advice – manipulation – of his elder brother-in-law Eadric. Then there was Edward, eldest son of Aethelred and Emma. He was young, and without his father would be all alone. Even without Streona's influence, his half-brothers would as likely see him dead as king. What was an ealdorman – one conceivably, if distantly, in line for the throne – to do?

Eadric called on Edmund for help against the Danes. The *aetheling* dutifully set aside his differences with his father and came marching down to his rescue. According to the Encomiast, "Eadric, his chief supporter, was a man skilled in advice but treacherous in spirit, yet Edmund gave him hearing in all affairs."

Streona eagerly awaited his arrival. Worcester reported, "When their forces were united, the ealdorman laid all manner of traps for the Aetheling, and plotted his death."

The objective of this scheme, whether to capture Edmund and hand him over to Cnut or simply murder him outright, is unrecorded, but the *aetheling* was not stupid and apparently anticipated it.

---

*Cnut's men probably did not see the giant as today's naked man with a 36-foot erection. It's now thought the figure was originally clothed, but in the 17th century, during the English Civil Wars, was "stripped" and endowed as a thumb-of-the-nose to Puritan dictator Oliver Cromwell. And to judge by vintage photography, its phallus was extended another six feet, up to the navel, by locals (for whom the Giant was even then a tourist attraction) in a 1908 re-cut.

Sure enough, the ruse was soon discovered and the trap went unsprung, yet the damage was done. Rather than carry the fight to the Vikings, Edmund had to determine who was the greater enemy, them or his own brother-in-law.

Eadric soon made that decision for him. He had finally gone too far to go back. As Malmesbury recorded, "Thinking it useless to hide himself, but that he could finally cast aside the mask, Eadric defected to Cnut with forty ships, and with him all of West Saxony, delivering hostages and surrenduring their arms."[*]

For the English, the defection of Eadric the Greedy to the enemy was a matter of no great loss, and good riddance. The loss of his men, though, and Wessex with them, was a catastrophic setback. Edmund was forced to withdraw, ceding ground to the encroaching Danes. The royal estate at Cosseham being indefensible, King Aethelred was put on a horse – or, depending on the severity of his illness, on a litter or in the back of a wagon – and pointed east. The walled *burhs* of Cicester (Chichester) and Winchester were closer, but the king had made London his capital, and his next appearance in the *Chronicle*, in early 1016, is there. The trip itself, of some hundred miles, is not described in the records, but must have been cold, wet and unhealthy.

But Cnut – and Streona – knew that London was not England. With the aim of separating it, and Aethelred, from the rest of the kingdom, in early May they followed an old Roman road to cross the Thames at Cricklade, far upstream near its headwaters. From there they drove into Worcestershire, Gloucestershire and Warwickshire. Known as the Hwicce, this former kingdom had been absorbed into Mercia in the 780s. Its ealdorman, Leofwine, might have been expected to follow his liege lord Eadric, but mixed loyalties split the family. Their names will figure later in our story: Son Northman followed Eadric, but other son Leofric followed Leofwine, and their domain paid the price. Cnut and Streona, according to Wendover, overran the Hwicce and "invaded Mercia with many horsemen, and burned many villages, carrying off everything and slaying everyone they met."

---

[*]This being a land campaign, the ships mentioned here might be a measurement of men – crews – rather than actual sailing vessels.

The Mercians looked to Edmund for salvation. The *aetheling* now bore the sword of their ancient king Offa, and we can be sure he rode about the countryside waving it overhead to stir the locals. The *Chronicle* attests, "An army was again summoned under strictest penalty, that every person, from however far, should come. They also sent to the king in London, and prayed him come to meet the army with whatever aid that he could bring."

"He lost no time in assembling an army," Worcester commended Edmund, "but when it was mustered, the Mercians refused to work with the West-Saxons and Danes, unless they were joined by king Aethelred and the Londoners."

Shades of the old days, when the Anglo-Saxons detested each other as much as the Vikings, but really, who can blame them? By this time, armies, both Viking and Saxon, had been marching back and forth and up and down the length and breadth of England for years, each time inflicting punishment on whatever unlucky locals got in their way, for having not sufficiently resisted the previous conquerors. Fyrdmen enlisted in the service of lords returned home to find wives raped, families murdered, farmsteads plundered, livestock slaughtered and fields burned by troops nominally on their own side. All this could be laid at the feet of Aethelred, who neither surrendered outright nor sufficiently defended his kingdom. At this point, if his subjects were to back him, they needed to see some show of equal dedication from their king.

As usual, the *Unraed* proved not up to the task. As Huntingdon recorded, "When vast troops had been gathered, the king heard that some were ready to betray him. So he disbanded the army, and retreated back to London."

According to Malmesbury, he never left town: "Used to hiding behind fortifications rather than attacking the enemy, he remained in London, never venturing out for fear, as he claimed, of traitors."

After years of Streona's trickery, it was a little too late for Aethelred to worry about treason. It may have been that the king was simply too ill to persevere, but for whatever reason, Edmund was on his own. Meanwhile, towns and villages were going over to Cnut, who kept busy making plans by night and fighting battles by day.

Edmund fell back on the Midlands, to the domains gained by him through his marriage to Ealdgyth. She was now pregnant or had perhaps already given him a son, and Edmund counted on her subjects – his new subjects – for their support.

Uhtred of Northumbria answered the call. This was much to England's regret, for rather than face each other in battle the two sides, as usual, vented their wrath on the helpless countryfolk to, shall we say, encourage their loyalty. That spring of 1016 Edmund and Uhtred devastated the West Midlands – Eadric's lands, Staffordshire, Shropshire and Leicestershire – for following the Greedy One's lead in siding with the Danes. Meanwhile Cnut and Eadric laid waste the East Midlands – Buckinghamshire, Bedfordshire, Huntingdonshire, Northamptonshire, Lincolnshire and Nottinghamshire – for loyalty to Edmund. The two armies circled each other counterclockwise, the Viking advance carrying them around the English, toward Northumbria.

That was a losing game for the *aetheling* and ealdorman. Edmund had no interest in defending the north, a bunch of Viking sympathizers. And Uhtred had no intention of abandoning his people for the south, who had proven again and again unwilling to defend anyone but themselves. They went their separate ways. Worcester recorded, "Edmund Aetheling gave up ravaging the land and hastened to his father's side in London. Ealdorman Uhtred hurried home and necessarily submitted, along with all Northumbria, to Cnut, giving him hostages."

Uhtred's submission gained mercy for Northumbria, but none for himself. Summoned into his new king's presence, Uhtred went with forty of his men. An old enemy of his, the Dane Thurbrand, called "the Hold" (a rank of nobility above a *thegn* but below a *jarl*), led an ambush in which Uhtred and all his men were killed.[*] Cnut appointed Eric Hakonsson in his place as Earl of York. Not ealdorman, for that was an Anglo-Saxon rank, and not *jarl*, for that was Danish. But as Eric had been Jarl of Norway for Svein Forkbeard, he was now Earl of York for Cnut, the first time we see this title.

Meanwhile, in London, Edmund found his father dying.

---

[*]One version of the *Chronicle* says this was done on Cnut's order, by the advice of Eadric Streona, but it's thought Uhtred's death was part of some northern blood feud that, as shall be seen, would go on for decades.

The manner of Aethelred's end is not recorded, except that it was not on the battlefield or in any other dramatic fashion, so it must be assumed he died relatively peacefully. His surviving family was likely gathered round his bedside, and though it's not specifically said so, that probably included Emma and her children. As soon as Aethelred regained his throne she would have returned to England, if only to look after her interests, and as soon as he was gone, she would need to look after her sons' interests. After all, her husband's power as king was her power as queen; without the first, she would lose the second. By this time Edmund's wife Ealdgyth had certainly given birth to both their sons, Edward and Edmund. He might well send Emma to a nunnery, or even banish her to Normandy for good, in which case her brother Richard would foist another husband on her. In either case, what then the fate of Emma's children?

But then, Aethelred's reign had started with an elder half-brother's murder....

As for Edmund, well, he surely had bigger concerns at the moment. It was not Aethelred who had borne the brunt of this war with the Danes, and it would not end with his death. This was no time for the *witan* to set the crown on a young son of Emma. England needed a war leader.

Aethelred himself made no recommendation as to a successor, or at least none that was written down. That was in keeping with the rest of his reign, which Huntingdon called "one of almost incessant toil and indecision."

Of the longest-reigning Anglo-Saxon king, the *Chronicle* says only, "He died on St. George's day [April 23], having held the kingdom in much struggle and trouble all his life."

"Aethelred, son of Edgar and Aelfthryth, on gaining the kingdom, mismanaged rather than ruled it for thirty-seven years," concluded Malmesbury. "His life story is said to have been murderous in the beginning, miserable in the middle, and despicable in the end."

He was buried at St. Paul's church, presumed to have stood at the highest point in the city where the modern cathedral stands today. (Both the original church and Aethelred's tomb were later destroyed in the Great Fire of 1666.) He was barely in the ground when the lords and nobles gathered in the city for the funeral proclaimed Edmund as their king. When the news reached the countryside, however, a different assembly of nobles from Wessex convened in Southampton. They agreed to send a messenger to Cnut, pledging their loyalty to him and advising him to take possession of London as king.

Immediately Edmund departed the city, bound for Wessex with an army in order to reclaim the loyalties of its wayward lords. Their loyalties, it turned out, lay with whoever held a blade to their throats, but Edmund's departure left London exposed. In the second week of May Cnut's Viking fleet made its way up the Thames, joined by Eric Hakonsson, who had sailed down from his new domain of Northumbria. London Bridge, having been repaired and strengthened, blocked the way further upriver. Rather than attempt to pull it down as had Olaf Haraldsson, Cnut had his men dig a channel around Southwark and row their ships past it. They disembarked upstream on the city-side bank and laid siege to the town, as Forkbeard's army had besieged Exeter, and Thorkell's Jomsvikings Canterbury. Cnut's tenacity is understandable. Queen Emma, it seems, resided within the city, the closest thing it had to a leader. If she was looking down on the fighting from atop the walls of London, she had to be wondering about Cnut's end goal. Her eldest son Edward, still in his early teens, is said to have joined the army of his half-brother Edmund. If Cnut won out, both their lives were at risk, and if they were slain, where would England be?

By this time there was extra incentive for Cnut to take the city, and with it all of the kingdom. Word would have arrived that, behind his back in Norway, Olaf Haraldsson, supposedly Cnut's old rival for his consort Aelfgifu's heart, was now a rival for the Norwegian crown.

After his victory at London Bridge – and when his partner Thorkell had crossed the North Sea to re-enlist in the service of his rival Cnut – Olaf had instead sailed across the Channel to Normandy to fight as a mercenary on behalf of Duke Richard, Queen Emma's brother. As a pagan, he admired the way in which the continentals, dating back to Charlemagne, had used the worship of the one Christian God to unify their people. It made a useful tool for his personal ambition. With Eric Hakonsson, Forkbeard's Norwegian regent, now in England fighting alongside Cnut, Norway was ruled by his son Hakon Ericsson and half-brother Svein Hakonsson. Neither of these was the equal of the legendary Eric...nor of Olaf. A Norwegian prince himself, he saw an opportunity to unite the Norwegians against them.

Before departing on his quest, Olaf was baptized as a Christian by no less than Duke Richard's brother Robert, the Archbishop of Rouen, and declared his to be a holy crusade. *King Olaf's Saga* proclaims, "When King Olaf Haraldsson landed in Norway the poor and commoners came together, and would have no one except Olaf as king over all the land, although later some thought his power left the people with no self-government, and went into self-exile."

On Palm Sunday 1016, in a sea battle at Nesjar in Oslofjord, Olaf had defeated Svein Hakonsson and driven him to Sweden, where he soon died, possibly of wounds sustained in the battle. Hakon Ericsson fled to England with news that Olaf had set the Norwegian crown on his own head. Olaf's saga sneers at Cnut, "He thought all Norway was his by right of inheritance, but his sister's son Hakon, who had held part of it, looked to have lost it with disgrace."

There was little to be done about Norway now. Anticipating and desiring a quick victory, the Danes instead found themselves bogged down outside the walls of London, which they were unable to overcome. They were doubtless relieved to learn that Edmund was raising an army to the west. Worcester wrote, "So, raising the siege for the moment and leaving part of the army to guard the fleet, they force-marched to Wessex, giving king Edmund Ironside no time to assemble his army."

But now Edmund began earning that nickname. At Penselwood, in Someset, the English made a stand on the site of an old Iron Age hill fort and turned the Danes back. On a Monday in late June, about thirty-five miles to the north in the Cotswold foothills, and only about five miles from Malmesbury Abbey, they came together again, at *Skorsteinn* or *Scorranston* (Scorran's Stone, possibly a boundary or border marker), modern Sherston in northwest Wiltshire. Cnut – who, it should be noted, was still a young man, and so far had personally done nothing braver than mutilate a few hostages at Sandwich after abandoning his wife at Gainsborough – seemed to be having somewhat of a crisis of confidence. According to the *Encomium* it was now that Thorkell the Tall promised to make good on his pledge to his foster son, by taking his place in battle: "I and my men will win this battle for my lord. Eager though he is, he should not fight, for he is yet young. For if I win, I will win on his behalf, but if I lose or run, it will not be an English victory, for the king will live to fight again, and perhaps avenge my loss."

On the other side of the field – ground of his own choosing – and with the advantage of numbers, Edmund became the Ironside the English needed. He arrayed his army with his best men in front. Reminding one and all they were fighting for their wives, children, homes and country, he signaled the advance. The English throng began to move.

According to the *Encomium* Cnut, or Thorkell, did the same: "The leader, relying on courage rather than numbers, sounded the trumpets at once."

Like opposing tidal waves, the two shield walls surged together in a cacophony of clashing armor, curses and death screams. Thorkell and Edmund, the sources claim, both fought in the front ranks. (Sherston tradition has it that a local English militia commander, John Rattlebone, fought at Edmund's side even after mortally wounded, staunching his bleeding by holding a roofing tile to his side.) It's said the English were near to victory until Thorkell reminded his men they were far from their ships, and that if defeated they would all die together. With that encouragement they pressed the Anglo-Saxons back again. Worcester wrote, "The battle was so contested and bloody that, too weary to maintain combat, both armies willingly stood down at sunset."

What can be said of men who went through that, retired for the night to bind terrible wounds and rest weary bones, then rose again in the morning to go right back at it? Nor did their kings shirk from the fighting. The *Chronicle* attests, "the leaders themselves met in battle."

Here Cnut finally showed himself at least willing to fight. The *Knytlinga Saga* gives Edmund credit for near-victory, plunging into the thick of the Danish horde to get within a sword's cut of the Viking: "King Cnut laid the shield forward over his horse's neck, and the blow hit the shield a little below the handle, so hard that it rent the shield to pieces, and cleaved the horse's neck in front of the saddle."

Clearly these were not the same English who had repeatedly folded at the mere threat of Viking onslaught, as when Eadric Streona was advising Aethelred. Eadric, for one, seemed willing to put their resolve to the test. Worcester claimed that at the battle's peak, he beheaded an English warrior who bore passing resemblance to Edmund and held the head up for all to see: "Men of Dorset, Devon, Wiltshire, flee quickly, for your leader is lost! Look, I hold here in my hands the head of your lord, King Edmund! Flee while you can."

According to Gaimar, even Prince Edward, Emma's son, fled. Malmesbury has it that all the English would have lost heart and given up had not Edmund, seeing the trick, spurred his horse to the nearest high ground and taken off his helmet for all to see. "Then brandishing a spear, he launched it at Eadric with all his might. Being seen and avoided, it missed him, and struck a soldier nearby with such violence that it even pierced a second."

Worcester wrote of the English: "As soon they realized the king was alive their courage returned. Charging the Danes harder than ever, they killed a great many, fighting with the utmost resolve until dusk, when the armies separated as the day before."

Malmesbury insisted the second day's battle at Sherston ended much like the first: a draw. "Nightfall ended the battle, the hostile armies withdrawing as if by mutual agreement, though the English had nearly obtained the victory."

The Encomiast, however, called it for the Vikings: "They ultimately won the victory they wanted, and buried what remains of their comrades as could be found."

And according to the *Knytlinga Saga*, "The whole English army was beaten and a terrible slaughter ensued, with the Danes chasing the fleeing enemy until nightfall."

This version of events bears strongly on our story, because even if the Battle of Sherston decided nothing, it should be remembered, if only for a chance meeting in its wake. The *Knytlinga Saga* resumes, "As usual Jarl Ulf pursued the enemy further than anyone. Come evening he found himself in a forest so thick that he was lost for the night. Seeing a well-grown lad herding some sheep across a clearing, Ulf greeted him, and asked his name."

The boy answered, "My name is Godwin."

The meeting of Godwin, son of Wulfnoth Cild, with Ulf Thorgilsson, brother-in-law of King Cnut, in the Viking saga bears so much semblance to Walter Map's story of Godwin meeting King Aethelred, a year and a half earlier, that some confluence can easily be supposed. What are the odds that one boy, living in disgrace because of his father's crimes, would have chance meetings with two of the leading figures of the day, and on opposite sides of a titanic struggle?

It's not impossible, of course. Assume the first story is true. On Aethelstan's death, and then Aethelred's, Godwin, with no more patrons at court, might well have returned to obscurity where Ulf stumbled upon him. The fact that this second version was considered important enough to be recorded in the saga of Cnut and his family – right down to the very conversation – gives it added credence.

The sight of a bloody-handed reiver emerging from the woods should have given any English shepherd good reason to run. According to the sagas, "Jarl Ulf was quick to temper, stiff, and unyielding, but everything he did and was done according to his orders went well, and he was a great warrior, of whom there are many tales."

Godwin simply asked Ulf, "Are you one of Cnut's men?"

(It's hard to say in what language this little chat might have been carried out. Having lived alongside each other for 150 years, Danes and English would have had passing familiarity with each other's Old Norse and Old English, which after all were similar Germanic tongues, and may have spoken some pidgin mix of the two. And as sons of noblemen – even if Godwin had fallen somewhat in station – they both may have been educated in Latin.)

Ulf had little to fear from a herdsman. He freely admitted to being a Viking, and inquired of the way to their fleet.

Godwin replied, "I do not believe you Danes will get much help around here. You deserve something very different."

"True, but I will be grateful if you help me find our ships."

"You have been headed in the wrong direction, far up into the forest. Cnut's men are not well liked in these parts, with good reason. In the villages the news is of the man-fall that took place yesterday at Sherston. I imagine you and the rest of Cnut's men will regret it if the peasants find you, and so will anyone who helps you. You might be a man worth saving, though, if you are more than the man you seem to be."

Jarl Ulf took off his gold armlet. "I will give you this if you take me to my people."

The *Knytlinga Saga* is thought to have been written in the 1250s, over two centuries after this scene took place, if it ever really did. The author almost certainly took some liberties in recreating the conversation, but in hindsight knew enough of Godwin's nature, and his future – and the future of England – to know that, if true, this was a critical moment in history, and to indulge in a bit of characterization. He has Godwin pause to think over Ulf's offer.

The old kings were dead, yet their sons refused to give up the dreams of their fathers, no matter the cost, no matter that those dreams were nightmares to the common folk. The people of the land cared nought for whose flag flew over which city, and wanted only to be left alone to tend their fields and herds, raise their families, and not have some lord's soldiery destroy their lives.

To be born in that chaos, to grow to adulthood in that anarchy, was to learn how fickle was royal whim, how worthless loyalty. It was men like Eadric Streona and Thorkell the Tall – treacherous, calculating, willing to change sides as the situation demanded – who gained and kept power. One misstep, though, like that of Uhtred the Bold – or Wulfnoth Cild – invited quick reversal, and even death.

No less than Edmund and Cnut, Godwin was his father's son.

"I will not take the armlet," he told Ulf, "but I will try to take you to your ships. If we succeed, I will accept your reward. If we fail, I won't deserve it. First, though, you must come home with me to my father."

According to the story, the two repaired to the family farm, said in the saga to be a nicely furnished homestead headed by a handsome couple. They provided Ulf with food and drink and entertained him all day, for it was evidently too dangerous for a Viking to travel alone by daylight in those parts. Come nightfall they furnished two well-appointed horses. The father took Ulf aside: "We bid you farewell, and trust our only son to you. We ask only that when you rejoin your king, if you have any sway over him, that you ask him to let the boy serve him. He can not stay here if our neighbors find out he helped you, even if we manage to save ourselves."

Factual or not, there is some sense here of the desperate nature of what was essentially a civil war, the difficult choices that had to be made, and the families it tore apart. The *Knytlinga Saga* specifically names the father as Wulfnoth. As stated before, Wulfnoth Cild is thought to have died around 1014. Whether the date is wrong, or the saga is wrong, makes little difference. An orphaned Godwin could have been fostered by a local family. The parents' choice was no less agonizing. They and their boy would likely never see each other again.

Godwin and Ulf rode through the night. In the morning they reached the anchorage where the Viking ships lay beached and, according to Encomiast, the Danes were celebrating victory. On Ulf's arrival his countrymen, who had been mourning him as dead, crowded around to welcome him back. The *Knytlinga Saga* reveals that this is the first time Godwin realized Ulf was a Danish *jarl*. As an Anglo-Saxon himself, he might have expected a quite different reception, yet according to the saga Ulf was not one to forget a debt: "The jarl raised Godwin to the high seat beside him and treated him like an equal, or like his own son."

Assuming the story has some grain of truth, the son of Wulfnoth Cild had taken his first step to power. Wulfnoth, Streona and Thorkell had shown how. The only way to avoid royal retribution was to play all sides, becoming strong enough to dare a king's fury.

And in the end to make oneself, in all but title, king.

VII

One King to Rule All

1016

Edmund Ironside, king of England, pursued the enemy with the army he had collected from the whole of England, and met them as they were retreating at a hill called Assandun.

Worcester

If Sherston was a Viking victory, as the *Knytlinga Saga* boasts, their king certainly didn't act like it. "Before dawn," wrote Wendover, "Cnut ordered his men to withdraw from the battlefield under the cover of darkness."

He fell back toward London, perhaps thinking that would be the easier fight after all. The Vikings took shelter within their city-encircling earthworks. Edmund did not come at them directly, but circled north of the Thames to launch a surprise attack out of the forest of Tottenham, today part of North London. The English poured into the enemy earthworks and drove the Vikings out of them. Cnut and his men took to their ships, moving upstream to the crossing at Brentford, today in West London. The 11th-century Icelandic skald Ottar *svarti*, Ottar the Black, in one of his poems lauding Cnut, said they destroyed the village there, but two days later, despite losing men drowned in fording the river, the English attacked again. According to the *Chronicle* they were victorious, but Ottar claimed Edmund was badly wounded, and his losses were so heavy that he could not hold the position. He withdrew westward to recuperate and replenish his forces.

For his part Cnut, unable to take London and in need of supplies as well, took his fleet down to the coast to raid into East Anglia and Kent. Edmund returned in time to intercept him there, at Otford on the River Darent. The English sent the Danes reeling back toward the Thames estuary, yet could not catch Cnut. Ironside's frustration with these inconclusive running battles was such that he was said by the Encomiast to have challenged Cnut to resolve the matter by single combat. The Dane refused: "I will choose a time better suited for battle, when with luck I shall be sure of victory. As for you, who desire to fight in the winter, beware. You might not live to fight come spring."

He had a better idea. Huntingdon has it, "Cnut and Eadric also laid plans for winning by treachery that which they could not gain by arms. Eadric undertook to betray King Edmund."

According to Malmesbury, "While Edmund was preparing to run down and utterly exterminate these raiders to the last man, he was prevented by the sly and treacherous Eadric, who once again worked his way into his favor. He had come to join Edmund at the instigation of Cnut, in order to betray him."

At Aylesford, about a dozen miles east of Otford, Streona came into Edmund's camp with an offer to switch sides, again. It seems incredible that anyone would still trust the Greedy One. Wendover spat, "He was the very scum of humanity, the disgrace of England, a double talker, tricky, a betrayer of secrets, a skilled deceiver, readily inventing lies. He was often sent to the enemy to make peace talks, but instead fanned the fires of war."

Yet Ironside halted his advance to hear Streona's proposal. Worcester lamented, "If the treacherous ealdorman, Eadric, had not dissuaded him from further pursuit at Aylesford, he would have won a total victory that day."

Huntingdon agreed: "Never had more fatal advice been given in England."

In trying to understand why Edmund would ever accept a man of such dubious loyalty back into his service, it should be remembered that Eadric never acted alone. Wherever he went, whoever he served, he brought with him the warriors of the Midlands: his loyal retainers, housecarls and other fighting men. After all these hard-fought battles against the Vikings, Ironside surely needed every warrior he could get. (Another ealdorman of doubtful loyalty, Aelfric of Hampshire, who had betrayed King Aethelred in 992 and 1003, was also fighting for Edmund.) He should have known better than to depend on such men, or to trust Eadric, whose first act was to urge peace, thereby talking Edmund out of victory and giving Cnut a chance to escape. Malmesbury backs this up: "Had the king but persisted, that would have been the Danes' last day. But, misled by the sly words of a traitor, who swore the enemy would make no further advance, he brought swift destruction upon himself, and all of England."

The *Anglo-Saxon Chronicle* admits, "No greater error of judgement was ever made," with at least one version scathingly using the word *unraed*, ill-advised, the very term that would come to characterize Edmund's father Aethelred. Poor judgment, it would seem, ran in the family.

Contrary to Streona, Cnut was not interested in peace. With his own forces depleted by battle, he rendezvoused with his fleet and escaped across the Thames estuary to plunder in Essex and Mercia. Worcester claimed Cnut urged his men to commit greater atrocities than ever before: "They butchered everyone they captured, burned a great many towns, wasted the fields and then, loaded with booty, went back to their ships."

The Danes were still raiding there in October. Meanwhile, the English took the long way around the estuary to the west. The *Chronicle* claims that while circling from Kent to Essex, Edmund had "levied all the people of England," which is the monks' way of saying this was probably the largest army he ever fielded. The roster included almost every remaining lord of the Anglo-Saxons. There was Ulfcytel Snilling, Ealdorman of East Anglia, who not far from this battlefield had nearly defeated the Danes in 1004, and had seen to the murder of Thorkell the Tall's brother Heming. There were the ealdormen of Hampshire and Lindsey, and Aethelweard, the son of the late Ealdorman Aethelwine of East Anglia. Monks and priests from nearby monasteries and abbeys arrived to bolster the troops' morale with the relics of St. Wendreda, or Wendreth, a 7th-century

East Anglian nun and healer. Together they caught up to Cnut and the Vikings at Assandun.*

Edmund is said to have set up his camp atop Ashingdon Hill, just south of the modern village. Worcester has him rallying the troops prior to battle. "He went round to each rank and file, reminding them of their former valor and successes, encouraging and exhorting them to defend themselves and his kingdom from the savagery of the Danes, whom they had previously beaten and would again."

Cnut had pitched his camp on another hilltop, said by the citizens of Ashingdon to be Canewdon Hill, about two miles to the east. There the Danes raised their famous raven standard. The *Encomium*, which goes on at length on behalf of its patron Emma and subject Cnut, confides, "Though woven of plain white silk, with no design on it, in time of war a raven was always seen as if embroidered there, in victory snapping its beak, flapping its wings, and stamping its feet, but in defeat very forlorn and drooping its whole body."

Now, it's easy enough to imagine a wily Viking commander always carrying two flags, a blank one for everyday use and one with a raven insignia to inspire the men on the day of battle. If so, Thorkell the Tall was in on the act: "Let us fight bravely, men, for we are in no danger. To this the bold raven on the prophetic banner attests."

After a year and a half of warfare, the Viking army had to have been whittled down to the hard core. Besides Cnut and Thorkell, there was Jarl Ulf and his new protégé, Godwin son of Wulfnoth, perhaps having set aside his single-edged English *seax* for a Viking broadsword, wondering if it would as easily pierce the mail of his countrymen.

It was about nine o'clock in the morning. Just above a ford in the River Granta near Ashdon the land levels out into what the locals call Red Field, where the digging of an 1850s railroad cut uncovered Viking-era weapons. Worcester reported, "Cnut led his troops by

---

*To this day historians quibble over whether this is modern Ashdon in northern Essex, or Ashingdon in southeastern Essex, about thirty-five miles away. Both towns lay claim, both have their proponents, both have a case. "Assandun," according to the monks of Worcester (or their Victorian translators), means "Ass's Hill." The Encomiast, in Latin, refers to the site as *Aesceneduno*, and gives its translation as *montem fraxinorum*, literally "mountain of ash," in the sense of trees, thus more accurately "hill of the ash trees." Notably, ash is not native to the area around Ashingdon.

slow march down to level ground. On the other side, King Edmund advanced rapidly in his ordered array and, giving the signal, fell suddenly on the enemy."

This is interesting, because very few medieval battle commanders on the defensive – as Cnut was at Assandun – would have surrendered high ground, as opposed to making the enemy climb it to reach him. If the Viking really led his army down off their hilltop, he may well have had good reason to expect the English to fold. And that reason was Eadric Streona.

"Then Ealdorman Eadric did what he had so often done before," declares the *Chronicle*, "betrayed his rightful lord and all the people of England."

According to the *Encomium* Eadric took one look at the oncoming Vikings, turned to his men and cried, "Let us flee, my friends, and save our lives from onrushing death, or else we will soon fall, for I know the determination of the Danes!"

With that the treacherous ealdorman and his warriors deserted the battlefield, drawing off to await the outcome.* That this is virtually the same trick Streona is said to have played at Sherston might be put down to a mixup by the chroniclers, but Eadric never seemed to miss an opportunity for betrayal. Even the pro-Cnut *Encomium*, which should have applauded the Greedy One for siding against the English (again), sneers, "And according to some, it was later plain that he did this not out of fear, but guile, and many claim that he had secretly promised this to the Danes in return for some favor."

At the sight of Streona and his Midlanders abandoning the field, a roar of triumph would have gone up from the Danish line, and a groan of dismay and terror from the English. From his position Edmund would have seen the tide of battle turning. The armies were now more evenly matched, with momentum behind the Danes. Cnut could well believe his pet ealdorman Eadric had won the battle for him. Yet the *Encomium* credits Ironside, true or not, with a speech to fire Anglo-Saxon hearts: "Englishmen, today you will fight, or surrender, as one. So fight for your freedom and your country, and

---

*There is a meadow near Ashdon called Traitors' Field, where according to tradition Streona and his men sat out the battle. To this day the locals claim it is unlucky to plow.

know that, truly, those who retreat in terror, even if they were not retreating, would only hinder the rest of us."

And he led by example, perhaps more than was wise. According to Huntingdon, Ironside deserted his position beneath the *draco*, the Roman-style dragon-mouthed windsock banner, and rushed the enemy: "He attacked like lightning, wielding a chosen sword suitable for a royal hand [perhaps the Sword of Offa] and, hewing a passage through the center, exposed himself and his followers to counterattack."

Malmesbury admitted: "A small number who, recalling former glory and cheering each other on, separated themselves, and were cut off to a man."

Worcester recorded, "Both armies fought desperately. Many fell on either side." The treacherous ealdorman Aelfric of Hampshire redeemed himself by dying on the field. Thorkell the Tall cut down Ulfcytel Snilling, thus avenging his brother's murder, and furthermore would claim his widow Wulfhild, daughter of King Aethelred, as his war bride.* Vikings came upon the English priests as they were saying Mass, slew them, cut their bodies to pieces, seized the relics of Wendreda and later carried them off to Canterbury, whence they never returned.

According to the *Encomium*, the battle went on all day, Danes and English grinding away at each other, *seaxes* and battle axes stabbing and hacking. No man could keep that up forever, but to turn aside for the man behind to come up in relief made an opening in a shield wall, a chance for a sword thrust or axe swing to strike home. The progress of battle was not measured in victory or defeat, but by the clutter of dead and dying men being trampled into the blood-soaked soil. The outnumbered Danes fought knowing that any retreat would turn into a rout. The English could see the Vikings were determined to conquer or die. By the time the moon came up, they were played out. In ones and twos, and then in droves, they turned and fled into the surrounding woods. Eventually Ironside was left no choice but to

---

*According to a Viking saga, it was Eric Hakonsson who killed Ulfcytel in the fighting west of London, but it was Thorkell who ended up with Ulfcytel's widow. Marriage by capture was a tradition dating back at least to ancient Rome and the Sabine Women. Northern European warriors carried on the tradition happily. Their widows, it is presumed, not so much.

follow. He conceded the field, whether Ashdon or Ashingdon, to the Vikings and slunk off into the gathering darkness.

Cnut, whom it must be remembered was still a young man, possibly only about twenty-one, had finally achieved a great victory. Malmesbury admitted, "On this battlefield Cnut gained the kingdom, the glory of England died, and the whole flower of the country withered."

The Danes, being unfamiliar with the local terrain, could not pursue by night. They camped on site, rising in the morning to bury their dead and to strip the bodies of the enemy, which they left as carrion on the field. Then, while their adversary was on the back foot, they marched for London.

Meanwhile the English survivors of Assandun regrouped to the west, in Gloucestershire, to decide a course of action. This was recommended to Edmund by none other than Eadric Streona. Aware that he was scorned for his withdrawal, according to the *Encomium* he somehow managed to persuade everyone that defeat at Assandun had been inevitable, that it was better to survive in one piece, and that in the end the whole English army had done no less. To avoid a repeat, he advised making peace with the Danes: "I think it better that our king should have half the kingdom in peace, rather than in spite of himself lose it all at the same time."

According to the pro-Cnut Encomiast at least, the English chieftains – those who were left – were in favor of his proposal. Their island had been divided between Anglo-Saxon and Dane before. Perhaps Streona was right – it was time to take the long view again, and look forward to ousting the Danes at some point in the indefinite future.

Ironside, feeling their resolve weakening, made a last-ditch effort to settle the issue personally. The kings parleyed at Deerhurst, about twenty miles south of Worcester. The story goes that Edmund demanded again to meet Cnut one-on-one, in a fight to the death. Perhaps he expected the Dane to again decline, shaming himself in front of his men, but Cnut's recent victory may have boosted his confidence. He agreed. (It should be said that the *Chronicle* makes no mention of single combat between the kings.)

With Edmund's forces gathered on the western bank of the Severn River, and Cnut's on the eastern, the meeting was to take place on neutral ground: in mid-stream on the island of Olanege, modern Alney. Boating across, the kings donned armor and took up weapons. According to Gaimar, Cnut offered peace before somebody got killed, but Matthew Paris insisted they fought it out.

He has them meeting first on horseback, splintering their spears on each other's armor.* The battle undecided, they dismount to settle the matter with swords. Cnut has more skill, but Edmund more strength, and as any good tale would have it – and as their people had been doing for years – they fight to a draw. Before either dies, it is Cnut who calls a halt. Paris gives him a pages-long speech, which Huntingdon pares down to a single quote: "Brave lad, why should either of us lose his life for the sake of a crown? Let us act as brothers and divide the kingdom as co-rulers, that I may govern your affairs, and you mine."

Various accounts give various divisions of England by the resultant treaty, but the way it worked out was that Ironside would retain Wessex, while Cnut would rule everything north of London. To this Edmund agreed – perhaps reluctantly, surely bridling at receiving the smaller fraction of the Island Kingdom, but with his own barons on the verge of following Streona's example and backing Cnut. The kings embraced.

Paris declared, "When they saw this, both peoples rejoiced without fear. English and Danes were one."

Gaimar wrote, "Now they reigned more equally than brothers or kinsmen. And they loved each other, I believe, as more than brothers."

That, however, was not Eadric Streona's idea of an ideal outcome.

Recall that a division of the kingdom had been the Greedy One's idea in the first place. There's no way to prove it, but it's certainly

---

*Neither the English nor the Vikings had a tradition of cavalry, but fighting from horseback was not exactly new, and Scandinavian nobles like Edmund and Cnut would have been trained in it. This might also be Paris depicting the fight in terms of the tactics of his own day.

conceivable that, before his most recent defection to the English, he and Cnut had schemed a way to get Edmund to desist with minimal loss of Viking life. That much was done. Now to finish the job. The *Encomium*, defending Cnut in most matters, makes no mention of treachery, much less murder, but his own *Knytlinga Saga* admits, "There was then a mighty man, named Eadric Streona, whom King Cnut bribed to betray King Edmund, and murder him."

Six weeks after the Battle of Assandun, Edmund had taken up residence in London. As king, he would have enjoyed the constant protection of a squad of housecarls and men-at-arms, who would have cut down any would-be assassin who so much as fingered a dagger. The problem for an assassin, then, was to get at the king in a private moment.

The English would have known of public latrines from their Roman days. In later times toilets were built into the sides of stone castles, with waste falling down a shaft or even the outer walls to the moat or cesspit, but stone castles would not come to England for some decades yet. Anglo-Saxon aristocrats and the wealthy could afford private latrines outside their manor houses.*

Malmesbury asserted that Streona enlisted two of Edmund's manservants to commit the (literally) dirty deed. Wendover and Huntingdon accused Eadric's own son, the latter reporting: "One night [November 30], this great and powerful king feeling the call of nature and retiring to the house suited to the purpose, the son of the ealdorman Eadric, at his father's command, hid himself in the pit, stabbed the king twice from beneath with a sharp dagger and, leaving the weapon stuck in his bowels, escaped."

Gaimar credited Streona with a modification to the latrine too diabolical even for Vikings. "Eadric caused a device to be made, a bow which would not miss. Once drawn, if anything touched the string, soon would one hear bad news…. The moment he [Edmund] sat down, the arrow struck him in the fundament, up into the lungs.

---

*In 2017 archaeologists on the southeast coast of the Danish island of Zealand discovered a two-meter-deep pit latrine dating from Viking times, complete with post holes where a shelter had been built over it – an outhouse. (Vikings would have called it a *garðhus*, yard house, *naða-hus*, house of rest, or *annat hus*, other house.) The Danes would certainly have brought such a convenience to England, if the English didn't have outdoor privies already.

Not even the fletching showed of the arrow within him, nor any blood."

Huntingdon intoned, "So perished King Edmund Ironside, having reigned one year. He was buried at Glastonbury, near his grandfather Edgar."

In Malmesbury's opinion, "He would have made up for his father's indolence, and his mother's low birth, by his own outstanding virtue, if only the fates had spared him."

On news of Edmund's death, Cnut journeyed to London and called a *witenagemot*, a meeting of the *witan*. Normally the nobles would have convened to choose a new king, but Cnut reminded them England already had a king. He and Edmund had been co-rulers. The death of one did not mean his half of the domain should go to any other, not even Edmund's brother Eadwig or his sons, the *aethelings* Edward and Edmund.

To this the Anglo-Saxon nobles agreed without question, as well they might, considering the chamber was full of armed Danes. Worcester jeered, "God knows they bore false witness and spoke foul lies, believing that he would show favor to them, and reward them well for their duplicity."

Cnut divided the country into quarters. Each of his *jarls* – his earls – received a portion. Earl Eric retained Northumbria, and Eadric Mercia. East Anglia went to Thorkell. And for Cnut himself, the traditional heart of Anglo-Saxon England, Wessex. In London he took his seat as the rightful and confirmed King of all England.

VIII

Under King Cnut's rule, profound peace was everywhere declared,
and flourished again throughout all the provinces of England.

History of the Abbey of Croyland

The young King of England had proven himself a conqueror. Now he had to prove he could rule as well.

His first task was to eliminate any threats from the bloodline of Aethelred. He publicly ordered Ironside's brother Eadwig Aetheling to be banished, but at the same time called upon the ever dependable Eadric Streona to devise a plan of assassinating him. Eadric, by this time knowing his sole remaining brother-in-law would never trust to come within his grasp, recommended a man, Aethelweard, trusted by them both. Cnut summoned this Aethelweard in turn and promised him wealth and honor if he would assassinate Eadwig. Aethelweard accepted but was secretly still loyal to the House of Aethelred. Eadwig was spirited into hiding in a monastery.

Streona also went after his nephews, Ironside's young sons Edward and Edmund, who were living with their mother, the former queen Ealdgyth. Streona delivered the princes to Cnut in London and advised the king to do away with them, but even Cnut balked at the idea of infanticide. The boys were sent to Sweden, where the king, Olaf Skautkonung, might be more inclined to eliminate the problem. He, however, likewise reluctant to murder children, merely passed them along to King Stephen I of Hungary, in whose court they would reside most of their lives as Edward the Exile and Edmund Aetheling.

They were out of Cnut's reach, but there were others of Aethelred's blood, closer to home. As it turned out, Cnut solved two problems at once: a surplus of princes, and the need for a rightful queen. The *Encomium* asserts, "Matters thus resolved, the king lacked only a suitable wife. He ordered one to be sought everywhere, in order to gain her hand lawfully, when she was found, and to make her the royal partner when she was won."

At this time Edward, Aethelred's son by Emma (said to have accompanied his elder half-brother Edmund on campaign in England) was back with his brother Alfred and sister Godgifu in their mother's home in Normandy. Emma's whereabouts are less certain. According to Cnut's own *Knytlinga Saga*, she had tried to escape to France: "King Cnut's men heard of Queen Emma's attempt. When she and her people were about to board, they seized the ship with all aboard, and took the queen to the king."

Jumièges, writing in Normandy only a few decades later, certainly believed she was held captive in London until summoned into Cnut's presence. He is backed up by the *Anglo-Saxon Chronicle*, which notes in its entry for 1017, "before the calends of August the king ordered the widow of the other king, Aethelred, the daughter of Richard [I, the Fearless], to be fetched to him for a wife."

But fetched from where? According to Emma's own version of events, the *Encomium*, theirs was a more fairy-tale romance. As her writers told it, she had already made good her escape, obliging Cnut to pursue her, all the way across the Channel to Normandy.

The fact that Cnut was already married, to Aelfgifu of Northampton, was a matter of little import. Whether still in Denmark or by now returned to England, Aelfgifu would have been thrilled at the news of Edmund's defeat and death, eager and fully expecting to assume a throne of her own beside her husband. The fact was, though, their handfast marriage was not recognized by the church and, as a daughter of a noble but disgraced family, Aelfgifu had little to offer Cnut other than their sons, Svein and Harold.

On the other hand Emma, as widow of dead king Aethelred and sister of Duke Richard II of Normandy, could still bring an international alliance to her wedding bed. The Normans might still be a people of minor note, but they were descendants of Vikings. They had carved a land of their own out of France, and might willingly lend Cnut troops to defend or expand his. And though she was in her early thirties, at least five or six years older than Cnut, Emma was still quite the catch – at least, as her Encomiast described her: "…a lady of the greatest nobility and wealth, but also the most distinguished woman of her time for delightful beauty and wisdom, and already a famous queen."

She had enjoyed a decade and a half or so on the English throne. Now she was a Norman widow but, lacking husbandly control over them, widows on both sides of the Channel had more say in their lives than their married sisters. The problem was, what did Cnut have to offer Emma if he could not force her into marriage?

As her Encomiast told the story, if anyone went to "fetch" her to Cnut, it was not Danish warriors but royal ambassadors, perhaps some she had known well in Aethelred's court. They crossed the Channel to woo her with gifts (Wace claims Cnut paid her weight in gold for her) and pleas to resume her royal position, only with a different king. The *Jomsviking Saga* puts Thorkell the Tall in charge of the delegation: "Thorkel led the way along the coast, and met Queen Emma on a ship, and he brought her home to the country with him. He urged King Cnut to court her."

One might think a widow would spurn the advances of her husband's enemy, but to take a dead foe's woman to wife was in those days hardly unknown, merely the spoils of victory. (Recall Thorkell the Tall marrying Wulfhild, widow of Ulfcytel Snilling.) Cnut had not personally slain Aethelred, and it's not as if her late husband had given Emma any reason to be loyal to his memory. He had been dead over a year. Emma's legally required period of mourning was at an end. Events had simply tipped her way. The hand of God was at work, and who was she to deny God's will? She who had been facing a lonely life as a dowager might once again be Queen of England. It was, in many ways, still her duty, even as a Norman noblewoman. If her brother Richard could not force her to marry, he could certainly encourage it.

Malmesbury certainly took a dim view of them both: "He married his sister Emma to the enemy and invader, and it is hard to say whether whose was the greater ignominy, he who bestowed her, or she who consented, to share the nuptial bed of that man who had cruelly driven her husband into the grave and her children into exile."

Importantly, those children were excluded in Emma's deal. She left them behind. Some might say, deserted them, but others might add, saved them. Wendover wrote, "Aethelred's sons Alfred and Edward, born of queen Emma, in light of Cnut's cruelty, remained quietly in Normandy with their uncle Duke Richard."

Probably Alfred, their sister Godgifu and particularly Edward, now about fifteen, had grown used to living in exile. If Emma had joined them there it was likely the first time, maybe the only time, they ever lived together as a family. Edward, having been raised in a monastery, would have found his uncle Richard's court reassuringly religious. Jumièges wrote, "Duke Richard, although distinguished everywhere by his most brilliant works, always remained a faithful servant of Christ, so much so that he was justly called the very loving father of monks and clerics, and the inexhaustible protector of the poor."

Emma willingly gave up that family to regain her throne. She, and she alone, would be the link between Anglo-Saxons, Danes and Normans in this new England. (It is worth noting that Gaimar has it that it was she who recommended that Cnut send the late Ironside's sons into exile.) England's only princes would be hers and Cnut's. She was well aware of the existence of Cnut's handfast wife Aelfgifu and her sons Svein and Harald, and had no intention of again entangling herself and any future children as another second-string family. She drove the same deal with the Danish king that she had driven with the Anglo-Saxon one. The Encomiast insisted, "She refused to ever become Cnut's bride unless he swore to her that, if it pleased God to give them a son, he would never raise the son of any other wife to rule after him."

That at least does not sound like a king forcing himself on a captured queen. The Encomiast concluded, "The king found the lady's demand acceptable, and the lady found the king's will acceptable, and so when the oath had been sworn, thanks be to God, Emma, noblest of women, became the wife of the mighty King Cnut."

There follows a royal wedding scene with great rejoicing on both sides of the aisle, English and Danish. "For the king was happy to have unexpectedly entered upon the noblest of marriages," insists the *Encomium*. "The lady, on the other hand, was inspired both by her husband's excellence and by optimistic hope of future children."

Somewhere up north, though, in Northumbria or even across the sea in Denmark, Aelfgifu of Northampton must have taken the news of the royal marriage with shock, dismay and even anger. (Much as Olaf Haraldsson might have taken news of her marriage to Cnut. In retrospect Aelfgifu's trade-up wasn't looking quite so clever as planned.) Leftover queens typically lived out their lives in a nunnery or in exile, their royal children taken from them to be raised elsewhere or even slain. (The fate of England's previous queen, Edmund's widow Ealdgyth, is unknown.) Yet Aelfgifu had been down before, and still risen almost to a throne. The bitter news was not accompanied by worse news, that Cnut had disavowed her. Therefore Aelfgifu bided her time, awaiting further events, nursing her young sons...and, doubtless, thoughts of revenge.

With Cnut dividing the Island Kingdom into four earldoms – Northumbria, Mercia, East Anglia and his own Wessex – Thorkell, Eric and Eadric held lands and power practically equal to his. It wouldn't take much for one of them to cook up a rebellion among the others. And everyone knew who among them was the schemer.

During the Feast of the Nativity (Christmas) in 1017, when all the earls gathered in London, Eadric saw fit to remind Cnut of murdering Edmund on his behalf. Accusation of mortal sin on a holy day did not sit well with the king. As Hector Boyce, the 15th-century Scottish historian and principal of King's College in Aberdeen, told it, "Even though Cnut did not completely regret his rival's death, he preferred to pay his killer a proper and just reward for his crime rather than thank him."

According to Wendover, Cnut replied, "As a reward for your service, I will today raise you above all the nobles of the realm."

The *Encomium* admits he summoned Earl Eric and said, "Pay this man what he is owed. Kill him, before he betrays us."

And Eric struck off Streona's head with an axe. Gaimar claimed Cnut wielded the blade himself, Malmesbury had it that Eadric was strangled, and Map that he was hung from the tallest oak, but as

Wendover put it, "However the traitor died matters little, since it is plain that he who had deceived so many by God's justice met with proper punishment." Eadric's head was mounted on the highest spike in the city, and his body dumped in the Thames.

While he was at it, Cnut took the opportunity to clean house. Those nobles who had been constant in their loyalty, even to Edmund, were spared. Those inclined to deceit and trickery were not. Aethelweard, who had promised to murder Eadwig Aetheling but instead hidden him in an abbey, and for good measure Eadwig himself, whom Cnut coaxed from hiding with a promise of clemency, were both executed. (Clearly Cnut himself was perfectly fine with treachery when it served his purposes.) Ealdorman Leofwine of the Hwicce, who with his son Leofric had remained loyal to Aethelred in early 1016, was awarded Eadric's earldom of Mercia, but his son Northman, who had joined Streona, was executed. Brihtric, Eadric's brother, who back in 1009 had accused Wulfnoth Cild of treason and forced him into piracy, was likewise put to death.

Yet Wulfnoth's son Godwin, who had deserted from the English cause to join the Viking *jarl* Ulf Thorgilsson after the Battle of Sherston, evidently came through this purge not only intact, but high in King Cnut's estimation as well. "Godwin," one chronicler attested, "was seen by the king himself as most cautious in advice and most audacious in war. Because of his even temperament, he was also very agreeable to both the people and the king. He was tireless in his dedication to work, and well-mannered with everyone."*

Cnut may have nurtured a man of English blood (unlike Queen Emma) to act as a go-between with the Anglo-Saxon commonfolk, for his Danes were not the most benevolent of conquerors. As Map told it some 150 years later, "Being stronger than the English, they made of them the lowest of slaves, even abusing their wives and daughters and granddaughters."

The annalists penning the *Anglo-Saxon Chronicle* entry for 1018, perhaps to avoid Danish retribution, make no mention of such

---

*Part of the reason for Godwin's rise, according to Malmesbury, was that he married Cnut's sister and even had a son by her. Alas, the boy accidentally died by drowning and the wife by lightning. It all happens implausibly fast, and Malmesbury, as shall be seen, probably got his royal sisters mixed up.

depredations, but they do account for the *gafol*, the Danish tax Cnut squeezed from his new subjects: 72,000 pounds, plus an additional 10,500 pounds from London itself. According to Wendover, Emma advised Cnut how to best spend his new wealth: "Serving as mediator between him and the English, she advised him to send his fleet and his mercenaries back to their own lands." This Cnut did, except for some forty ships and crews he kept for himself. He next convened a *witenagemot* at Oxford where he declared that all English and Danes should live together in peace according to the laws of Aethelred's father, King Edgar the Peaceful.

Some of Cnut's benevolence can certainly be credited to Emma. According to Wace, "Cnut loved the queen.... He regarded her dearly and she pleased him well." The increasing respect given her is measurable by her signature on successive royal documents, at first still as *thoro consecrata regio*, but then *eiusdem regis conlaterana*, consort of the king, and eventually – finally – as *regina*, queen. In the spring of 1018, about nine months or so after their marriage, she gave birth to Cnut's son. They named him Harthacnut, "Swift Cnut" or "Strong Cnut." Though the dates are uncertain, the timing was good, for around this same time the current King of Denmark, Cnut's brother Harald, passed away.

The cause of death is likewise unknown – in fact, very little at all is known about Harald II – but without a king, the Danish chiefs began to vie among themselves for supremacy, along with Denmark's neighbors. It was time for Cnut to assert his right to rule.

He now likely regretted sending part of his Danish army back home. To replace those warriors in his ranks, he called upon his English subjects, and to lead them he named Ulf's young English follower, Godwin, to a position opened by the death of the treacherous ealdorman Aelfric of Hampshire at Assandun: Earl of eastern Wessex.

That the boy was still only eighteen or nineteen mattered little. He was by now a veteran of several battles, and one did not have to be the greatest warrior in a medieval army to lead it, only be a man its greatest warriors would follow. To put a loyal Anglo-Saxon at the head of his Anglo-Saxon contingent further demonstrates Cnut's faith in his newly minted earl. As events would show, it was not misplaced.

Leaving his foster father Thorkell behind to rule England as regent, Cnut gathered his fleet and crossed the North Sea. As might be expected, there were some who saw his landing as an attempt to make Denmark part of England, and resented it. Among these were the Wends, the Slavic people living further east along the south shore of the Baltic. (Wendover claims it was the Swedes.) The power vacuum in the wake of King Harald's death had left room for them to raid into Denmark. If Cnut wished to be king of the Danes, it was his duty to take the fight to them. According to Huntingdon, at some point the Wends made a stand, but on the morning of the battle, the king awoke to find Godwin and his English allies gone.

Believing they had either fled or deserted to the enemy, Cnut nevertheless arrayed his Vikings and launched a (now more desperate) attack on the enemy camp. They arrived unopposed, on ground already bloody and littered with dead, the enemy defeated and scattered. Godwin, with the guile of the Anglo-Saxon, had taken it upon himself to launch a surprise night attack, slaughtering many of the Wends in their sleep and routing the rest. Far from being angry with his young earl for acting without orders, according to Huntingdon, Cnut gained new respect for him and his warriors: "He ever afterwards regarded the English with the highest honor, considering them equals of the Danes."

After this victory, Cnut's claim to his brother's realm was acknowledged by his Danish subjects as well. Presumably at Roskilde, the seat of his late father Forkbeard and of Danish kings going back 500 years, he assumed the crown of Denmark. It was one more step to reassembling Forkbeard's North Sea Empire. The third piece of the puzzle, Norway, was still under the sway of Cnut's rival, Olaf the Stout, but that would not be the case forever.

And for young Earl Godwin there was reward as well. Living in Denmark at this time was Gytha Thorgilsdottir, the sister of Godwin's patron, Earl Ulf. As man of the family, it was Ulf's duty to arrange his sister's marriage. The church's position that bridal consent took precedence, even over the objections of male relatives who might otherwise use her marriage to advance family interests, was in those days a matter of some contention, but probably not in this instance. For her part Gytha was netting a fine, up-and-coming husband, even if he was English. She would have been about twenty-one or so, perhaps a few years older than Godwin. It was high time both were married, and she very likely agreed to the match. (There may have been another reason she agreed, more of which later.)

This was Godwin's highest honor yet. Earl Ulf was the husband of King Cnut's half-sister, Estrid Sveinsdottir, so by marrying Ulf's sister, Godwin was essentially marrying into the Danish royal family. It's unclear what Gytha, as a nobleman's daughter, brought to the pairing other than prestige. According to the oldest Scandinavian law codes, the *Frostathing* and *Gulathing*, daughters were barred from inheritance while sons lived. Svein Forkbeard, however, had changed all that, and in Denmark at least daughters had legal right to inherit half as much as sons. Little matter; until very recently, Godwin himself had been nothing but a poor herdsman, for whom Gytha would have been far out of reach. Luckily an earldom came with property and income.

The *Chronicle* records that the king, his freshly extended family, and their retinues spent that winter in Denmark. On their return to England in 1020, Gytha bore Godwin a son, Sweyn. (The English spelling, also given as Swegen.) Forkbeard would have been flattered that all three young fathers, Cnut, Ulf and Godwin, gave their firstborn sons his name, but family gatherings must have been a bit confusing with the little Sweyn and the Sveins underfoot. Later that same year Queen Emma gave birth to Cnut's daughter, Gunhilde. The non-Viking party at court was strengthening its position relative to the king, and true to his word at Oxford, Cnut treated them all as equals. He and Thorkell even returned to Assandun and ordered a church built on the site of the battle in memory of the dead, which Cnut commended to his personal priest, Stigand.*

Not all was well, however, between the king and his foster father. In 1021 Cnut and Thorkell had a falling out. It was said that Thorkell's new wife Wulfhild had enlisted a witch to poison his son by his

---

*This does nothing to clear up the actual location of the battle, as there are stone minsters from this era at both sites, St. Botolph's near Ashdon and St. Andrew's at Ashingdon.

previous wife. (There is no record if the son died.) Thorkell swore her innocence, but she was found guilty. There may have been other factors involved. The *Heimskringla* gives us a clue: "Svein, son of King Cnut and Aelfgifu, daughter of Ealdorman Aelfhelm, was sent to govern Jomsborg in Wendland."

If Cnut was relieving his foster father of his command of the Jomsvikings in order to hand it over to his own handfast wife and son, Thorkell had good reason to object. Yet, given Cnut's inclination to kill anyone suspected of betraying him, their dispute must have been relatively minor. Thorkell was not executed, but banished to Denmark.

Even as Earl Thorkell's star sank, Earl Godwin's rose. Cnut expanded his earldom to include all of Wessex and Kent as well. As the chroniclers reported, "When Godwin came home, having done his duty well, he was appointed by him [Cnut] earl and official of almost all the kingdom."

That put Godwin on a higher pedestal than the earls Leofwine of Mercia and Eric of Northumbria, making him one of the most powerful men in England. From this point on, his name appears first in the list of lay witnesses to Cnut's royal decrees.

And the next year, 1022, Gytha gave birth to Godwin's second son. Harold.

IX

FORGING AN EMPIRE

1022–1028

*When King Cnut ruled over England and Denmark, Olaf
Haraldsson ruled over Norway.... Then there was discord between
King Olaf and King Cnut.*

Knytlinga Saga

The early 1020s were, finally, peaceful years in England, so much so
that the *Anglo-Saxon Chronicle* records little of note in those years
other than routine reports of deaths, promotions and various priests'
trips to Rome to visit the Pope, Benedict VIII. Unusually in those
days when almost half of all children died in infancy, the sons of Earl
Godwin and Countess Gytha not only survived, but thrived. Then
again, they were a nobleman's sons, so their lives differed from those
of peasants, and thanks to their Danish mother, probably from the
average Anglo-Saxon nobility as well. Child-rearing is better known
among the Vikings than the English of this period, but we can guess
that Godwin's half-Danish children were raised in the Viking manner.*

They would have been suckled by a wet nurse, or a series of them,
until age two, and thereafter largely raised by trusted servants. Rather
than a simple hut, they lived in a stately, though still wooden, hall,

---

*Notably, Sweyn and Harold were given Scandinavian names with English spellings. No Svein
or Harald appears in Godwin's known ancestry. Wulfnoth Cild's father was named Aethelmaer.

probably with a planked floor rather than rush-strewn packed dirt, perhaps under a roof of turf or even wooden shingles rather than thatch. (It's thought that although their churches clearly indicate a mastery of stone architecture, the Anglo-Saxon inclination to build their homes in wood reflects their Scandinavian reverence for forests.) Their playthings – hoops and balls, toy animals and swords – would have been made of brass, silver or gold rather than wood. They wore the finest clothing, though being children, more of linen than wool, as it was easier to keep clean. They drank the best ale, watered down, but enough alcohol remained to kill anything living in it. They had the best food – mostly vegetables, but also chicken, mutton and goat, plenty of pork and wild game; cod, herring, and Scandinavian-style salted fish; oysters, eel, lobster and crab; occasionally even beef, a luxury item on Anglo-Saxon menus. Instead of fingers, they ate with utensils: knives and, given the family's wealth, almost certainly spoons; although the dining fork was known, it was yet not popular in Northern Europe. Having an earl for a father had its perks. And Earl Godwin's power and influence was only growing. One by one, anyone standing between him and King Cnut was removed.

In Mercia, Ealdorman Leofwine died in or shortly after 1023, and was peaceably replaced by his son Leofric. In 1024 Thurbrand the Hold, who had organized the murder of Uhtred the Bold in 1016, was murdered in turn by Uhtred's son, Ealdred. Meanwhile Cnut had reconciled with Thorkell the Tall, not only appointing him as his regent in Denmark, but giving him custody of his son by Emma, Prince Harthacnut, then about five or so, to be raised in Thorkell's court, the way Thorkell had raised Cnut for Forkbeard. But Thorkell had died as well, some said by murder.* The old ex-Jomsviking's absence was a great loss to his respective foster sons. For Thorkell's former protégé, and Cnut's old nemesis, Olaf the Stout was ruling Norway as though he owned it, which in Cnut's opinion he manifestly did not.

Over the winter of 1024 Cnut sent a delegation to politely request that Olaf pay him homage as his vassal, along with tribute befitting

---

*The *Jomsviking Saga* blames the killing on Cnut himself. The king was said to be a guest in Thorkell's hall when he first beheld the beauty of the *jarl*'s wife Wulfhild, daughter of Aethelred. Thinking Thorkell had talked him into marrying Emma instead of Wulfhild, he ordered Thorkell killed.

that which the Norwegians had traditionally paid their Danish overlords. As might be expected, this did not go over well. According to his saga, Olaf told the emissaries, "I will defend Norway with axe and sword as long as I live, and will pay tribute to no man for my kingdom."

War was coming, but not until Cnut was ready. To replace Thorkell as regent for Harthacnut in Denmark, Cnut had sent Godwin's patron, Earl Ulf, and his brother Eilif. Now veritable rulers in the prince's name, they had let the power go to their heads. Further, it seems Ulf had developed a personal dislike for his king. Saxo Grammaticus had it, "Ulf had been inflamed with the strongest hatred against Cnut, because the king put so much wind on virtue and bravery. Since he could not safely let his enmity come to light, he hid his betrayal under the guise of jealousy in order to better spin his schemes."

According to the *Heimskringla*, Ulf and Eilif called a *thing* in Denmark at which they produced a forged document, complete with Cnut's royal seal, to the effect that he desired to give away Denmark to his son, for him to rule as an independent king.*

This was an inopportune time for a palace coup. The year is uncertain; the *Anglo-Saxon Chronicle* and *Heimskringla* date it at 1025, and Huntingdon goes along with that, but Roger of Wendover says 1024. Malmesbury makes no mention of the year, and Worcester makes no mention of the event at all. In any case, across the Kattegat, Olaf Haraldsson, ruling Norway, the Orkneys, Shetlands and even part of northern Scotland as King Olaf II, had acquired a queen of his own, Astrid, the sister of Sweden's king Anund Jacob.

Both Olaf and Cnut had been trying to strike an alliance with Anund. According to the *Heimskringla*, in 1026 Cnut had sent ambassadors to the Swedish court in Sigtuna with gifts and overtures of friendship. Too late. Olaf's envoys had gotten there first, warning that Cnut, having conquered England and Denmark, would soon be coming for Norway and Sweden, and that they had best ally for mutual defense. Anund sent Cnut's ambassadors home empty-handed, and he and Olaf set about defending their lands by attacking Cnut's, in Denmark.

---

*The 13th-century Icelandic historian, poet and politician Snorri Sturluson blamed this plot on Harthacnut's mother Queen Emma, claiming she desired a throne for her son and used the king's signet ring without his knowledge.

Ulf and Eilif raised an army and went to meet them, but whether to fight them or join them is an open question. Different versions of events have come down from different sources. *King Olaf's Saga* has the brothers calling on Cnut for help against the invaders, but the *Chronicle* declares Cnut went to war against Ulf and Eilif, and Saxo Grammaticus has Ulf switching sides and declaring war against Cnut, though he may have mistaken Ulf for Olaf.

Whoever he was about to fight, Cnut appointed Hakon Ericsson, his former regent of Norway and now Earl of Worcester, as second in command. He called up the combined English-Danish army and assembled the fleet. Hakon supplied the ship in which he presumably had escaped Norway, with forty oarsmen and a gilt figurehead. Cnut's *drakkar*, his dragon ship, was even larger, with sixty rowers. They led the fleet over the North Sea to Denmark and entered the Limfjord, the winding channel that separates the island of North Jutland from the rest of the peninsula, to use as a shortcut across to the Kattegat. According to Malmesbury, Cnut may have run into Ulf and Eilif there: "He initially fell into an ambush, and lost many men."

Godwin led by example, telling his English that it was their bad luck to have been conquered by Cnut, but would be a credit to their courage if they fought and won for him. (Wendover claimed this is when Godwin launched the surprise night attack which the king so admired.) In any case, Malmesbury has Cnut winning the battle: "He routed his opponents, and brought that nation's kings, Ulf and Eilif, to peace terms."

According to Snorri, Ulf, Eilif and their followers had a choice: throw themselves on the king's mercy or flee Denmark. They chose the former. Cnut easily forgave his son Harthacnut, who was scarcely old enough to have masterminded the plot, and he accepted his nephew, Ulf's son Svein, as a hostage against any further treachery. He could deal with Ulf later. For now, he needed the earl and his brother and their fighting men.

The delay, however, gave the Norwegians and Swedes time to prepare. Olaf had been plundering Zealand, the largest island in the Danish Straits, which included Roskilde and Copenhagen, browbeating the Danes there to accept him as overlord and make the island part of Norway. On news of Cnut's coming, though, he took to his ships and sailed east, around the southern coast of Scania into the Baltic Sea, where Anund and the Swedes had been raiding. They linked up in Hano Bay, off the mouth of the Helgea (modern Helge), "Holy River," their combined fleets coming to some 160 ships.

Again, accounts of the battle differ. According to *King Olaf's Saga*, Anund remained in the bay, preparing for a sea fight in the Viking fashion, binding his longships together into a giant raft. Meanwhile Olaf took his ships upriver. The land around the Helgea, today's Kristianstad Basin, is the lowest in Sweden, with some points actually below sea level and the whole area to this day subject to flooding. About ten miles upstream the river widens into Lake Hammarsjon. Snorri recorded, "At the riverhead they made a dam of timber and soil, and backed up the lake. They also dug a deep ditch, through which they led several streams, so that the lake swelled very high. In the riverbed they laid large timber logs."

Cnut's Anglo-Danish fleet, half again the size of the Norwegian and Swedish fleets together, sailed into the bay at dusk, too strung out and too late to attack. They occupied a small islet in the river mouth which is no longer there, having washed away in the 1770s. Saxo claimed that Ulf (Olaf?) occupied a neighboring island and goaded Cnut's warriors into crossing a tottery bridge connecting the two, which collapsed and drowned them in large numbers. The *Heimskringla* has it that Olaf received word from Anund of Cnut's arrival:

> Then King Olaf broke up the dam, and let the river run. The torrent came washing over them like a waterfall, carrying huge trees which plunged in among their ships, damaging all they hit, and the water covered all the fields. The men on shore drowned, along with many aboard the ships. All who could do so cut their cables so that the ships were loosed and driven by the current, and scattered here and there. The great *drakkar*, which King Cnut himself was in, rode before the stream, and as it could not be easily turned with oars, washed out among Olaf's and Anund's ships.

Olaf's fleet rode the surge downriver to join the battle. "Soon Earl Ulf too came up with his fleet," wrote Snorri, "and then the battle began, and King Cnut's fleet gathered together from all quarters."

Viking longships and *drakkars* excelled at missions of exploration, troop transport and raiding, but they were not weapons of war in the manner of ram-tipped, catapult-equipped Greek or Roman triremes or flame-throwing Byzantine galleys. Furthermore, in the less wealthy kingdoms of Northern Europe, ships were relatively more expensive, too valuable to lose. The goal, therefore, was not to sink enemy ships, but to capture them intact, by killing their crews or driving them overboard. There was little opportunity for strategic maneuvers or decisive tactics. Vikings fought sea battles the way they fought land battles, by lashing their boats together and boarding from one to the next, fighting ship to ship, man to man – slow, bloody work.

Swedish and Norwegian longships swarmed around Cnut's big *drakkar*, but its freeboard was so much higher than theirs that nobody could board. Even with so many vessels destroyed, the English and Danish were more than a match for the Swedes and Norwegians. Oddly, the *Anglo-Saxon Chronicle* claims Cnut was defeated, and perhaps he was, but only in the sense of not completing his enemies' total destruction. *King Olaf's Saga* has it that it was Olaf and Anund who abandoned the fight, drawing off to the east toward Anund's city of Sigtuna. In terms of *hnefatafl*, they escaped off board, and in that sense won the game. For Cnut, the Battle of the Helgea may have been a tactical loss, but it was a strategic victory.

He ordered the bodies of his drowned men to be recovered with hooks and nets for burial ashore and took his depleted fleet back to Zealand, blocking the Danish Straits to keep the Swedes and Norwegians bottled up in the Baltic. For their part, Anund gave up any dreams of conquering Denmark, and Olaf marched his men over the mountains to Norway. But this game of Viking chess was not over. As Adam of Bremen put it, "Between Cnut and Olaf, king of the Norse, the war went on, and did not end all the days of their life."

Earl Ulf was certainly happy to treat the battle as a Danish victory. According to Snorri, at Michaelmas (September 29) he threw a feast for Cnut at Roskilde. The king's procession arrived a day early. Cnut was not in a good mood. Ulf did everything he could to cheer him (doubtless drink was involved), but the king remained sullen. Finally he suggested chess – *hnefatafl* – to which Cnut agreed.

Clearly Cnut's mind was not on the game at hand, but still on the one at Helgea. When he made a move in error, Ulf took his piece. Cnut put it back on the board and told the earl to choose a different move. Now it was the earl's turn to anger. He knocked the board over and turned for the door. Cnut called after him, "Running away, Ulf, you coward?"

Ulf paused to remind him, "You did not call me Ulf the coward when I came to your aid as the Swedes were beating you like a dog." And he went out.

Both men went to bed, but Cnut at least did not sleep off his anger. While getting dressed in the morning, the holy day, he summoned a manservant and ordered him to kill Ulf. The boy returned in a little while, reporting that he had been unable to carry out the mission because Ulf was in church.

Cnut turned to one of his housecarls, Ivar *hinn Hviti* (the White). "You go kill Ulf."

This Ivar was a Norwegian who had fled the country when his father, Arnljot *Jarnskeggi* (Iron Beard), was killed for his pagan beliefs during King Olaf's Christian crusade. He had no problem murdering a man in the house of God, particularly one rumored to have sided with Olaf. Snorri recorded, "Ivar went to the church, and inside at the choir, thrust his sword through the earl, who died on the spot."

Their church defiled, the monks closed and bolted the doors. Cnut ordered it reopened and a high Mass sung to cleanse it, but knew that such a blatant crime called for restitution. On attending the service, he bestowed the church with land grants which would sustain it for generations to come, which naturally put him back in good standing with the priests.

With Ulf's kin it was a different story. His wife, Cnut's half-sister Estrid, demanded the king pay the *weregeld* – "man-price," blood money – although some whispered she had condoned her husband's murder on account of his betrayal of her brother. In atonement Cnut awarded her large holdings of land in Scania and Zealand. Now a rich widow, Estrid not only donated land to the priests of Roskilde, but she also paid to have the bloodstained wood-stave church torn down and a new stone edifice raised on the site, the progenitor of the brick cathedral which still stands to this day.

Ulf's boy Svein Ulfsson, whose patronymic changed to the matronymic Estridsson on his father's death, was only about seven or eight, too young to avenge him. The *Jomsviking Saga* claims Ulf's brother Eilif set out for Byzantium, where he would join the all-Viking Varangian Guard and die fighting for Constantinople. Their loss created an opening in Cnut's court, and their disgrace did not extend to the rest of the family. They had a cousin, Siward, like Olaf called *Digri*, the Stout, who would journey to England and rise far in the service of Cnut's family.

And of Earl Godwin of Wessex, whom Ulf had raised to high station and who was married to the dead earl's sister, Gytha, there is no mention. But Ulf's death and Eilif's departure left him as head of her family, responsible for blood justice.

And not long afterward, Ivar the White mysteriously vanished from the historical record and is presumed dead.

Given his proximity to them in Denmark, Cnut likely would have pressed his advantage against Olaf and Anund, but around this time was presented with an easier opportunity to raise his stature as king. Considering the upheavals that England had gone through in recent years, it says something of his confidence in his earls that he did not immediately go home, but went on something of a pilgrimage. Leaving Earl Godwin to rule England as his regent, Cnut traveled south to visit the Eternal City, Rome.

In those days the Holy Roman Empire, welded together over centuries of warfare and marriages out of a patchwork of kingdoms, bishoprics and duchies, covered what is now Germany from the Danish border in the north, down through what is now eastern France and Switzerland. In the spring of 1027 the German king, Conrad II, was to be crowned Holy Roman Emperor, and as a gesture of friendship he invited his neighbor and fellow sovereign Cnut to witness the event.

Of course, Cnut was far from the only guest. King Rudolph III of Burgundy was there to designate Conrad as his heir, thereby adding Burgundy to further expand the empire. (Not to be outdone, Cnut had brought his own wedding gift: his and Emma's daughter Gunhilde, then about seven years old, to betroth her in future marriage to

131

Conrad's eldest son and heir, ten-year-old Henry.)* In addition, four archbishops, twenty bishops, and a plentitude of dukes and noblemen, priests and clerics from some seventy imperial cities came to Rome for the coronation. For Cnut to be included among them was a sign that he was accepted as more than a barbarian usurper. He was a legitimate European ruler, an equal.

A trip to Rome – the holiest city in the West, the shrine of apostles, the seat of popes, the final resting place of myriad relics and saints – as to Jerusalem and to Compostela in Spain, counted as one of the great pilgrimages of the age. It's uncertain how much faith Cnut put in Christianity, whether he was truly a man of religion or simply used it as just another means to control his subjects. He favored some churches and churchmen, but disfavored others. Adam of Bremen credits him with sending many English missionaries to Denmark to proselytize to the pagans. Yet whatever his faith, the king went to Rome in part to seek the patronage of St. Peter, the keeper of the Keys of Heaven.

In the Middle Ages the Eternal City was quite different from what it had been in its glory days. Over the centuries since the fall of the Romans its once-magnificent temples and palaces had been deserted and steadily demolished by time, wars and by the locals themselves for construction materials. All that remained were those buildings too large for total destruction – the Coliseum, the Baths of Diocletian, the wreckage of the Forum – and those repurposed and restored by the church, like the Curia Julia, the former meeting house of the Senate. Pilgrims from the former barbarian regions could have known little of the great city's history, already shrouded in myth and legend. Still, the very grandeur of the ruins would have reminded them of what humanity had lost, and to what it still aspired.

The visitors had plenty of time to take it all in. The coronation ceremony lasted a week. Cnut made the most of his time, getting Pope John XIX to reduce the price English archbishops paid for their palliums, their ecclesiastical vestments. (He secured this, in part, by agreeing to a household tax of a penny per hearth – "[Saint] Peter's

---

*In 1024 Emma's daughter by Aethelred, Godgifu – "Goda" – then about twenty, had married Count Drogo of Mantes in Normandy and had since borne Emma a grandson, Ralf. The game of empire was played in the marriage bed as well as on the battlefield.

Pence," collected on the saint's feast day, August 1st – the proceeds of which were to be sent annually as alms to Rome. This payment, the *Romefeoh*, "Rome fee," or *Romescot*, "Rome tax," dated from the reign of the West Saxon king Ine in AD 725, but had lapsed under Viking rule. It behooved Pope John to re-establish his English income stream.) He got Conrad and Rudolph to guarantee the safety of Cnut's subjects on pilgrimages through their lands to and from Rome, and to reduce the fees and tolls paid along the way. According to Adam of Bremen, in return for Gunhilde's hand for Henry, Conrad even ceded the imperial territory of Schleswig, at the foot of the peninsula of Denmark, to Cnut. These were no mean achievements for a king from the hinterlands.

The event culminated on Easter Sunday, 1027.* The coronation took place in the 700-year-old Saint Peter's Basilica. Amid much singing, praying and chanting, the Pope bequeathed Conrad with the imperial sword and scepter, and then set on his head the Imperial Crown of the Holy Roman Empire.

Conrad was now more than a king; he was a king of kings. Cnut was no longer his equal. Back home in Scandinavia, though, an empire awaited the Dane as well: the North Sea Empire of his father, Forkbeard.

Cnut, King of England, realized it. For him it would be an epiphany, a turning point.

On the very day of the coronation, he was inspired to write, or dictate, a letter to his subjects, similar to the one he had written from Denmark those few years earlier. Dreams of imperial power were clearly on his mind, as he opened by declaring himself *rex totius Anglie et Denemarcie et Norreganorum et partis Suanorum*, "king of all England, and Denmark, Norway, and part of Sweden," although Olaf and Anund would have clearly disagreed with the latter half of that statement.

---

*The *Anglo-Saxon Chronicle* includes no entry for the year 1027, inexplicably dating Cnut's trip to Rome to the year 1031, and Worcester, Wendover and Huntingdon follow its lead. However, Conrad's chaplain and biographer, Wipo of Burgundy, who was present at the coronation, dates it to 1027, and expressly states that both Rudolph and *Chnutonis regis Anglorum*, "Cnut king of the English," attended. There is a gap in English royal charters between 1026 and 1031, which might indicate that Cnut was out of the country for most of those years. Possibly he made a second trip to Rome in 1031 before returning to England.

He wrote at length of his trip to Rome, of his religious inspiration, the negotiations he had made and the deals he had closed, to impress upon his subjects that the King of England was now a player on the world stage, an associate of other kings, an emperor and a pope. He apologized for past transgressions against his people and swore to rule justly in the future, and furthermore exhorted his administrators and magistrates – presumably including Earl Godwin and the rest – to do likewise. Finally, he advised that he was returning home via Denmark, "to conclude a firm treaty for a lasting peace, all the Danes agreeing, with those nations and peoples who would have taken my life and crown if they could, but were not able to accomplish, God bringing their strength to nothing."

If Cnut attempted any peace negotiations in Scandinavia, however, they were not with Olaf and Anund. Quite the contrary, it's thought that on his return to Denmark he launched a punitive raid up the Baltic to Anund's stronghold of Sigtuna, about twenty-five miles north of modern Stockholm on the shore of Lake Malaren. It may be that he even temporarily subdued or even ousted Anund.

This is not well recorded, but based on a few clues. Ottar the Black, who served as court poet to Olaf, Anund and finally Cnut, and so was in a position to know all three, referred to Cnut as *Svia þrengvir*, "Oppressor of the Swedes." He made this claim, however, in his *Knutsdrapa*, a praise poem and therefore not necessarily factual. Coins discovered to have been minted at Sigtuna bear the inscription "Cnut King (of the) Swedes." Of course, the argument against the Danes taking over Sweden is the fact that Anund reigned in Sigtuna until around AD 1050. So if Cnut ever ruled there, it was from afar, as a king of kings, with Anund as his vassal.

He returned as promised to England, but only long enough to raise a fleet of fifty ships full of fighting men, including English *thegns*. This time, to conquer Alba, modern Scotland.

Whether this expedition was accompanied, or merely supplied, by Earl Godwin is unknown. Judging by the birthdates of his next few children – son Tostig no earlier than 1023 and no later than 1028, and daughter Gytha circa 1025, but son Gyrth not until about 1032

– there's a gap in the sequence indicating the earl may have left home around the same time Cnut did. The *Anglo-Saxon Chronicle*, though again evidently getting the date wrong, records of the king, "The same year [1027], as soon as he came home, he went to Scotland," and Wendover follows along: "On returning, the most powerful king Cnut led a hostile expedition against the rebel Scots."

The Shetland and Orkney and, further west, Hebrides Islands – what the Vikings called the *Norðreyjar* and *Suðreyjar*, the Northern and Southern Islands – were all then considered part of Norway, the *jarldom* of Orkney. Just to the south, the *Katanes*, modern Caithness, the northernmost headland of Scotland, was a *mormaerdom*, a *mormaer* being the Gaelic equivalent of an English earl or Viking *jarl*. It was held as a fief of both Alba and Norway, a situation that led to constant feuds and murders among the inhabitants. The Scottish king was none other than Malcolm II, who had tried to invade Northumbria back in 1006 and had been rebuffed by Uhtred the Bold. Since then he had been kept busy at home, ruling the chieftains of the lochs and highlands by way of marrying his daughters off to rivals, making them in-laws and allies instead. Now he called them to account. In his view Scotland owed fealty to a rightful English king, not a Viking usurper.

The 14th-century Scottish priest and historian John of Fordun, whose *Chronica Gentis Scotorum* or "Chronicles of the Scottish People" was the earliest great work of Scottish history, wrote, "As soon as he returned from his pilgrimage to Rome, Cnut swiftly set out with a large army and, in easy steps, went to Cumbria to conquer it. The king, for his part, equally prepared for war, advanced to meet him with a strong force."

Wendover has it that Cnut "easily defeated Malcolm," but it might be more accurate to say the Dane easily gained the Scot's submission. They were, after all, perhaps family. Malcolm's queen is thought by some to have been Gunnor, a daughter of Duke Richard II of Normandy, and so Queen Emma's niece. The 11th-century Burgundian monk Rodulfus Glaber ("the Bald"), living in Italy at the time, was writing a five-book history of the era, and claimed the duke even interceded on their behalf to mediate the dispute. The task was made easier, according to Fordun, since Cnut made no great demands, other than the fealty of Malcolm and his son Duncan to Cnut and any future kings of England. The *Chronicle* records: "Malcolm, king of the Scots, submitted to [Cnut], and became his man...but he only remained loyal a little while."

That was good enough for the time being. Cnut hurried on to the next task.

He had learned that the Norwegians had grown dissatisfied with their king. Olaf forbade his nobles from raiding without his approval – meaning, without contributing his due cut of the profits – but failed to make up their loss of income. He also persecuted pagans with zeal. Even *King Olaf's Saga* concedes: "He punished powerful and weak with equal severity, which seemed to the chieftains of the land too severe, and hatred rose highest when they lost relatives to the king's justice, although they were in reality guilty."

Cnut's spies and agitators took full advantage, reminding everyone of the virtues of his former Norwegian regent, Hakon Ericsson. He sailed up and down the Norwegian coast, calling *thing* meetings at which he promised the great lords money, land and power, and accepted their hostages and oaths of fealty. His support evaporating, Olaf was forced to flee the country, to Sweden and (more evidence of Cnut's influence there) ultimately Russia. Even Olaf's saga admits, "King Cnut returned south to Denmark having conquered Norway without swinging a sword, and now he ruled three kingdoms."

With his regents Jarl Hakon ruling in Norway and Harthacnut in Denmark, Cnut had finally emulated the short-lived accomplishments of his father Forkbeard. The North Sea Empire was again a reality. And Cnut, like Conrad, had made himself its emperor.

X

KINGDOMS, DUKEDOMS, HEIRDOMS

1028–1030

*Since we have so far reported, without any claim to elegance of style,
the memorable actions of the first Dukes of Normandy, it seems
reasonable to us that those who have shone in our time receive the
honor due them, as we explore their careers.*

Jumièges

Compared to the ocean-spanning, empire-building wars sweeping
over England and Scandinavia in those years, the incessant squabbles
going on in Normandy might seem trifling. Then again, a warrior
slain in the service of a petty warlord instead of an emperor is just as
dead. Normandy having politically existed for only about a hundred
years, its people had not yet climbed out of that stage of cultural
development where the Jutes, Angles and Saxons had been in England
before the Viking conquest united them: incessant infighting to sort
out the pecking order. Brittany, Boulogne, Ponthieu, Flanders, Blois,
Chartres, Maine, even Burgundy and the kingdom of Francia itself
(as a state, younger than Normandy) were all elbowing each other for
territory, prestige and power, and within each state feudal warlords
jostled for supremacy, the Normans most of all. As Malmesbury
wrote of his father's people:

They are a race accustomed to war, and can barely live without it.
They are fierce in attacking the enemy, and where strength does

not achieve success, ready to employ guile, or to corrupt with bribery. As I have told, they live in large halls with thrift, envy their equals, desire to excel their betters and plunder their subjects, though they defend them from outsiders. They are faithful to their lords, though the slightest insult renders them deceitful. They weigh treachery by its chance of success, and change allegiances for money.

Emma's brother Duke Richard II, the Good, had died in 1026, but not before parceling out the duchy to his sons Richard and Robert, both about thirty. The eldest, as Richard III, got the dukedom and the younger, as Count Robert I, got the little county of Hiemois, modern Exmes, down on the border with Alençon.

The Anglo-Saxon *aethelings* Edward and Alfred still resided in exile at this Richard's court. They would have found their cousin's rule, like his father's, much to their ecclesiastical taste. Jumièges asserted, "Infinitely fit to bear arms in combat, he [Richard] was however entirely devoted to the Catholic faith, filled with kindness and leniency for the servants of God. He governed warriors with justice, and was pleased to enjoy an uninterrupted peace."

Though the duke had fought in his father's wars, none are recorded at this point in his reign, and Richard took his other duties seriously. He already had a daughter, Alais (Alice), and a son, Nicolas, by a mistress or handfast wife whose name is lost, but soon after assuming the ducal throne undertook a legitimate marriage to Adela, thought to be a younger daughter of King Robert II of France. The dynasty looked to be in fine fettle.

It was too good to last. Being Normans, Richard and his brother soon fell to quarreling. "Robert was not happy with his lot," wrote Wace, "and, believing he could take Falaise away from him [Richard], quickly entered the castle and supplied it with men and arms."

It seems Robert had good reason to hold Falaise. It's said that as he was walking the fortress ramparts the count beheld a young girl wading below. According to various versions of the legend, she was either washing clothes in the shallows of the River Ante, or dyeing or tanning leather in the courtyard. Seeing the duke looking down on her, she lifted her skirt, flashing him a bit more leg than necessary. As Wace put it, "She was still a virgin and she struck him as beautiful."

Robert immediately sent some of his men down to fetch her. She insisted on making her entry into the castle as a lady: via the front gate, in fine clothes, on horseback. That would give her official status, if only that of a concubine, but Count Robert couldn't resist. The girl got her wish and came into his life – into history – on her own terms.

Her name was Herleva, the old version of our Arlette, charmingly French. She was the daughter of, as the stories vary, a burgess (merchant), cloth dyer or leather tanner; at any rate, a commoner. No dull-witted one, though. If she was to be debauched by a lord, Herleva was determined to make the most of it.

"I wish to say nothing more about a man disporting himself with his beloved," Wace wrote primly, returning to the scene afterward, with the lovers still in bed. Herleva awakens with a start.

"I dreamed a tree emerged from my body, growing up towards the sky," she tells Robert. "Its shadow covered the whole of Normandy."

"All will be well if God pleases," he tells her.

"He comforted her and held her close," concluded Wace.

She could not know it, but Herleva the washing wench would be the mother of the modern English-speaking world.

The peace in Falaise was interrupted by Duke Richard. No Norman warlord could brook an insurrection, even by – especially by – his own younger brother. The duke and his knights laid siege to Robert in his fortress. Jumièges recorded, "After he had attacked it for some time, constantly playing with rams and catapults, Robert finally renounced his rebellion and gave him his hand. They rediscovered their old friendship, and parted company after making a solid peace."

It may be, however, that Robert had a different definition of peace than his brother. Wace put it delicately: "A little after this reconciliation Richard was in Rouen with many of his men. I know not what he ate or drank, but he fell ill and died, as did many of his companions and best barons. They had no idea who to accuse, despise, or blame, but they claimed and vowed...he had been killed because of envy."

The fact that many of Richard's men sickened and died with him would seem to indicate something in the food or water, but whether poison or simple contamination – always a possibility in those days

– remains an open question. That said, it was Robert who profited by his brother's death. Richard's young son Nicolas was hustled off to a monastery, and Robert assumed the ducal throne. For what it's worth, Wace certainly thought him a proper heir: "He cherished devout men, revered priests and clerics, and showed enormous compassion for the poor, especially lepers."

God seemingly rewarded Robert. Herleva soon gave birth to a son, there in Falaise. They named him after Robert's great-great-grandfather Longsword, the son of Rollo, who founded the Norman line: in Old Norse *Vilhjalmr*, in French, *Guillaume*, and in Old Norman, *Williame*.

In English – the language that this boy, grown to manhood, would change by force, along with everyone who would ever speak it – he would be called William.

Consider the word *bastard*, or in the French, *bâtard*. It's thought to have originated in Roman times, from the Latin *bastum*, pack saddle. Adding the medieval pejorative intensifier *-ard* (as in coward, drunkard, laggard, braggart) implied one was "conceived in the saddle," i.e., the bed of a passing stranger, to an unknown father. It was not necessarily a mark of shame. Children born out of wedlock were commonplace, particularly among aristocrats, both before and after marriage. Illegitimacy bore little social stigma if a lord acknowledged a child as his. Bastard became merely a term of distinction, during the Middle Ages a title borne by almost two dozen entirely noble sons. Many of them – perhaps compelled by their birth status – went on to great deeds.

It's said that the newborn bastard William of Normandy was laid in a bed of straw by the midwife. Tossing and turning, he soon covered himself in armloads of straw. On her return she exclaimed, "What a man you will be! You will conquer much and have much! You have quickly seized your rightful property with both hands and your arms are full."

Perhaps because his clever, willful mother Herleva saw to it, by all accounts the boy enjoyed the full acknowledgement and love of his father Robert. Wace reported, "The duke loved him no less than a legitimate son. He had him raised in luxury and just as nobly as if he had been born of his wife."

That said, William was not brought up in the ducal headquarters at Fécamp or Rouen, but in his mother's hometown of Falaise. It was no small village, but one of the biggest towns in Normandy. Furthermore, it was only about thirty miles north of Alençon, then also part of Normandy but held by the House of Bellême.

Bellême formed the bottom of Normandy's flattened U, lying against the counties of Maine to the south and Blois to the east, but this hilly country of critical roads and passes had always been contested. In the middle, the cities Alençon and Sées were part of Normandy, but in the west Domfront owed fealty to the counts of Maine, and in the southeast Bellême was claimed by Henry of France. Holding a family domain in the face of three overlords required devious, brutal men, and the House of Bellême did not disappoint. The current head of the family, also named William, was then approaching the age of seventy. He was only a lowly *seigneur* (lord), but styled himself *princeps*, prince. Wace recorded, "He was infamous as an evil traitor," and Jumièges wrote, "He was infinitely cruel and ambitious, and he had four sons, named Warin, Fulk, Robert and William, who were exactly like him."

No sooner had Duke Robert assumed his throne than Bellême rebelled against him. Robert laid siege to him in Alençon. As part of his surrender William was humiliated, forced to march out of his castle barefoot with a saddle on his back, no better than Robert's horse. The duke let him keep the castle, but Bellême would not soon forget the insult.

About this time, according to Wace, he was passing through Falaise when a local burgess called upon him to pay homage to Duke Robert's infant son. Presented with the baby, Bellême was said to have cursed him, aloud, three times: "For through you and your sons mine will be much humbled, and through you and your lineage mine will be greatly harmed."

William of Bellême would not be the last lord of Normandy to wish evil on William the Bastard. He may have been, however, the last to merely wish it.

Across the Channel, the children of Earl Godwin were growing up, enjoying the comforts and privileges of minor royalty, for their father was first among equals. The *Vita* records, "During the reign of King Cnut, Godwin thrived in the royal palace, enjoying pride of place among the highest nobles of the land. And as was proper, what he wrote everyone decreed should be written, and what he erased, erased."

Like all medieval folk, however, an earl's sons had obligations both upward and downward. The lowborn learned farming, animal husbandry and to bow to their betters. The highborn learned to manage servants and tenants who did the actual work, plus the necessities of aristocratic life: the handling of weapons, horses, ships and court politics. There being no such thing as a school, tutors would have been brought into the home to teach them reading and writing, in both Old English and Latin, including the runic and Roman alphabets.

Sister Gytha's path in life, like any noblewoman's in those days, was set practically from birth: marriage to some lord or another, making his family allies of the Godwins. Her brothers, however, could expect to follow different careers. Anglo-Saxons had passed along their earthly estates by partible inheritance, in which, although the eldest was given precedence, a father's property was divided among his sons. England, however, was now a Viking land, and Vikings preferred male-preference primogeniture, with the eldest son taking all. A generation earlier Sweyn and Harold would have been more or less equals. Now Sweyn, as firstborn, would likely become Earl of Wessex, with all the military and administrational skills that would require. As second son, Harold was more likely headed toward a career in law or the monastery, necessitating skills of mediation and planning. Tostig and Gyrth might expect to become their brothers' *thegns*, or perhaps another lord's or even the king's, their only reward being the scraps their betters might deign to toss them in passing.

Even at an early age, this expectation would have been known to the sons of Godwin. And, given how their lives played out, it's easy to think it colored their attitudes toward life.

Cnut's regent in Norway, Jarl Hakon Ericsson, was never as great a warrior as his legendary father Eric, Earl of Northumbria. (Recall that Olaf Haraldsson had once chased Hakon out of Norway.) As long as Cnut propped him up on the throne, though, Hakon seems to have been a worthy *jarl*, well liked by his subjects.

In the summer of 1029, according to the *Heimskringla*, he was of a mind to marry. Cnut arranged for him an English bride – his niece, Gunhilde – and Hakon sailed to England to meet her. They were betrothed, or even married, but late in the year he left her to return to Norway, apparently to prepare her new domain ahead of her arrival, and intending along the way to visit that remote part of his realm, Orkney. His ship skirted the Scottish coast and the Caithness headland, and was seen, on a stormy evening, entering the *Petlandsfjorð*, the "fjord of Pictland," modern Pentland Firth, which divides the Scottish mainland from the southern Orkneys.

In places no more than six miles wide, the Firth is a chokepoint between the North Atlantic and the North Sea, which makes for treacherous sailing in the best of conditions. To this day its bottom is littered with the wrecks of hundreds of ships, lost over the centuries to rocks, tidal rapids as fast as sixteen knots, and an infamous whirlpool, "the Swelkie," known even then to Vikings as *Svalga*, "the Swallower."

Communications lag being what it was, not until the end of the year or early 1030 was it realized that Jarl Hakon was not in the islands, nor England, nor Norway. He, his ship and his entire crew had simply disappeared. No trace of them was ever found. The *Heimskringla* laments, "All that can be said is, the ship vanished and no one survived...As of that winter Norway had no ruler."

After that initial delay, the news of Hakon's death traveled fast. All the way to Russia, then known as Kievan Rus, where Olaf Haraldsson had gone in exile. A Norway without a *jarl* was a Norway ripe for reconquest. The Norwegian people, Olaf believed, must surely be chafing under a Danish king ruling them from across the sea, and would surely welcome one of their own kind back to reign over them once more.

Over the summer he made the return journey, crossing the Baltic to land in Sweden. He raised an army of Swedish mercenaries, Norwegian expatriates, and even his fifteen-year-old half-brother Harald Sigurdsson. Together they marched over the mountainous spine of Scandinavia, recruiting more warriors along the way into what Olaf once again cast as a Christian crusade. In August they reached the little farmstead of Stiklestad, at the northern tip of Trondheim Fjord.

Olaf had expected the Norwegians to flock to his banner. Instead an army arose to oppose him: nobles and *thegns* right down to tenant farmers and slaves, all united against him and outnumbering his forces by some four to one. His invasion had been carried out so swiftly that Cnut could not be there to counter it, but the Norwegian lords who had suffered under Olaf's previous reign willingly led the people against him.

At Stiklestad there ensued a battle right out of myth, not least because it was fought partially under a near-total eclipse of the sun, a night fight in the middle of the day, an omen of momentous events to Christians and pagans alike. Olaf was slain, his army defeated, and even his little brother Harald, in his first battle, barely escaped with his life.

It would be decades before Harald returned to Scandinavia. For the time being he was just one among many boys of that age – Harthacnut of Denmark, Svein of Norway, Harold of Scotland, Edward and Alfred Aetheling, even Sweyn and Harold Godwinson – with claims to a piece of Cnut's North Sea Empire.

XI

SEEKING DELIVERANCE
1030–1035

Duke Robert ruled his domain well and determined to conquer all the lands which were rightfully his.

Wace

After humiliating William of Bellême, Robert had been further testing his influence in foreign affairs. In the east, he went to the aid of Baldwin IV, Count of Flanders, when his son Baldwin V rebelled against him, subduing the son and putting the father back on the Flemish throne. In the south, he gave shelter to Henry I, King of the Franks, when the queen mother Constance engineered a rebellion against him, enabling Henry to regain his throne. In the west, he fought a little border spat with his neighbor and kinsman, Duke Alan III of Brittany, laying waste the coastal Breton town of Dol and weathering a retaliatory attack on Avranches. That left only the north, across the Channel.

Robert still played host to two other kinsmen, Queen Emma's eldest sons, the young *aethelings* Edward and Alfred. Jumièges wrote, "These young men, thus residing at the court of the dukes of Normandy, were treated with great honor by the duke, who, having attached himself to them by the bonds of affection, adopted them as brothers."

Edward had never relinquished his claim to the English throne. Even in exile he signed Duke Robert's charters as *Regis Edvvardi* and *Rex Anglorum*. But what use were a pair of English *aethelings*, if not to make something of their claim?

"The duke sent word to King Cnut, who was married to their mother and held their father's estate," continued Wace, "telling him to yield their birthright to them. He had held the land long enough and it ought to be returned to them."

The response to this polite entreaty by the Emperor of the North was entirely predictable, to wit: *If they want it, tell them to come take it.*

"The duke was rather upset at this response," noted Wace with some understatement, and Jumièges continued, "Then the duke, animated by a very violent fury, summoned the nobles of his duchy, and gave orders to build a great number of vessels with all haste."

"He had all the ships in Normandy and the best warriors, steersmen and sailors, good footsoldiers and bowmen assembled at Fécamp," recorded Wace. "He intended to cross to England and take from Cnut the land he refused to hand back to the rightful heirs."

The best ships, helmsmen and mariners in Normandy perhaps, but – not for the last time – the Normans proved not up to the seafaring skills of their Viking forebears. The square-rigged sails of Northern European longships and cogs were just fine with a bellyful of wind behind them, but unlike Mediterranean galleys with their triangular lateen (Latin) sails, were not so suited to beating into the wind. The breeze was behind the Normans when they set out from Fécamp, but they were only partway across the Channel when it changed, gusting into their faces.

"The north wind, blowing hard, harried them so much they could neither reach land nor return to Normandy," recorded Wace. "Yet they kept close enough together that they landed on the island of Jersey."

That Jersey, the largest of the Channel Islands, is all the way over on the other side of the Cotentin Peninsula gives some idea of how far off course the Norman fleet was blown. Though today a bailiwick of England, it's only fourteen miles from the French coast, and had been part of Normandy since its annexation by Robert's ancestor William Longsword in the year 933. So Robert and Edward were not cast upon a hostile shore, but had not quite the landing Robert had envisioned. "They remained on this island for some time," allowed Jumièges, "and the contrary wind still continuing to blow, the duke was in despair."

All was not lost, however. With an invasion fleet and army eager to do some invading, and having arrived so near the Breton coast, Robert decided to make the best of the situation. He sent his ships and men (south this time, before the wind) to bully his cousin Alan some more. The Duke of Brittany finally conceded and swore fealty to the Duke of Normandy at Mont Saint-Michel.

So Duke Robert got something out of it, but Edward's dreams of conquest had to be put on hold, at least for the time being. Jumièges and Wace, ever the pro-Normans, both put the best face on things. As the latter put it: "God had arranged matters in this way, before worse happened, for there would have been very great slaughter before the land [England] was conquered."

It's uncertain if Cnut ever even knew of the Normans' attempted invasion. He had more pressing matters at hand, in Norway. When word came of Olaf's invasion, he had sent word from England to his long-departed consort, Aelfgifu of Northampton, and their son Svein at Jomsborg on the Baltic coast. For the better part of ten years the boy had served as a ruler-in-training. Now aged about sixteen, he was ready for the job. The *Heimskringla* reports, "There came word to him from his father King Cnut, that he should come to Denmark, and after that proceed to Norway, take that kingdom as his and assume the title of king."

Mother, son and little brother Harold journeyed up the Jutland peninsula to Roskilde. It must have been an uneasy meeting there with Harthacnut, the son of Aelfgifu's rival Queen Emma. Only about twelve himself, he was ruling Denmark as Svein was to rule Norway – both as frontmen for the adults behind their thrones, and all in the name of their father in England. The king probably intended them to ally with each other for a counter-invasion of Norway, had Olaf carried through with his conquest. Olaf's death at Stiklestad made that moot.

Cnut's grand vision, his father's North Sea Empire, had become reality. The *Knytlinga Saga* proclaims, "Then Svein, King Cnut's and Alfifa's son, came to Norway as arranged by his father, and was accepted as king over the whole country. Cnut named his son

Harthacnut to be king over Denmark, and his son Harald also ruled a large part of Scotland as king. Still, King Cnut was supreme over them all."

Cnut was in his forties now and, as many men do, mellowing with age. The prince who had once drenched England with blood, as king ruled it in tranquility. Though conflict had raged around it, England itself had been in relative peace for some fifteen years or more. On Malcolm of Scotland's death in 1034, Cnut had no more wars to wage. He left the management of his empire largely to his kingly sons and his earls – most predominantly Godwin of Wessex, Leofric of Mercia, and now Siward the Stout of Yorkshire – devoting himself less to secular matters and more to spiritual ones. "He became a true friend and familiar of churchmen," declares the *Encomium*, "to such a degree that bishops felt him to be a brother for maintaining of perfect faith, and to monks as well, not a layman but a monk, such was the temperance of his life of humblest devotion."

The emperor's humility, in the face of all the sycophants, flatterers and hangers-on that accumulate around every person of power, is demonstrated by the most famous story about him. Though apocryphal, there's nothing impossible about it. The tale of "Cnut and the Tide" was retold by Gaimar, Huntingdon and Wendover, and has passed into legend as a parable about imperial power. Though usually taken as an indictment of royal arrogance, it is actually the opposite. As Huntingdon told it, Cnut's intention was to rebuke the worshippers who likened his power to God's:

> When at the peak of his power, he ordered a throne placed on the seashore as the tide was coming in. Thus seated, he shouted to the waves, "You, too, are subject to my command, because the land on which I sit is mine, and no one has ever defied my commands with impunity. I command you, then, not to wash over my land, nor to wet your lord's feet and robe."

This is usually said to have taken place on the banks of *Porn-ieg*, Thorney Island, where the old rivers Tyburn and Westbourne entered the tidal Thames, upstream from London.* Cnut had built a royal residence on Thorney, which would eventually become the Palace of Westminster. As for the Tyburn and Westbourne, they are today part of the London city underground sewer system, which also says something of the king's point.

As the incoming tide raised the river in defiance of his command, he is said to have jumped up and, as Wendover put it, remonstrated with his courtiers: "Let all the people of the world see that royalty is finite and ephemeral, and that no one is worthy of the name of king besides Him whose eternal laws the heaven, earth, the sea, and all things in them, obey."

It was said that Cnut never again wore his imperial crown but set it on a *rood* (the Old English for pole, but meaning a life-size icon of Christ on the cross in a medieval church; the word *crucifix* doesn't enter English for another hundred years or so). The Encomiast wrote, "For he had not forgotten the nature of living, that he was to pass from this world, and to leave behind whatever can be wanted in mortal life. And so while still living he gave with honor to God and his holy places the wealth which, dying, he would not take with him."

According to the Norman chroniclers, this generosity extended even to Edward and Alfred, the first sons of his queen Emma, across the Channel. Jumièges claimed, "Behold, emissaries from King Cnut approached Duke Robert, telling him that this King wished to restore to the sons of King Aethelred half of the kingdom of England, and to make peace with them during his life, seeing that he was overcome with a very serious bodily illness."

If true – and, as shall be seen, the Normans would acquire a habit of claiming English kings had promised them the world – it was too little, too late. Duke Robert, now about thirty-five, was less interested in Edward and Alfred's inheritance than his son William's.

---

*Although, reminiscent of the towns of Ashdon and Ashingdon in Essex contesting who hosted the Battle of Assandun, Bosham on the southern coast and even Svein's capital of Gainsborough on the River Trent also claim to be the site of Cnut's demonstration.

William de Bellême and his family were to the Normans what Eadric Streona had been to the English, times five. "They never kept their word," attested Wace. "Much harm his four sons caused, whom he raised and trained.... There were no greater betrayers in any kingdom."

The oldest, Warin, decapitated one of his own knights, apparently for no other reason than because he could. Somebody soon strangled or poisoned him for his trouble. William sent the next eldest, Robert and Fulk, on a pillaging raid through Normandy, but they were caught red-handed by Duke Robert's riders. Fulk was slain and Robert, wounded, barely escaped. It was said their father died from the shock. Robert took over the house and continued to war on Normandy and Maine. In 1031, while raiding the people of Le Mans, he was captured and lay in a dungeon for two years before his captors bashed his head in. The estate then passed to the youngest, William, called Talvas (from either *talevas*, shield, or *talevassier*, a warrior who lives on plunder; either was applicable). Jumièges claimed, "This one showed himself, by all sorts of crimes, even worse than all his brothers." When his wife, the mother of two of his children, wanted no part of his odious doings, Talvas had her strangled on her way to church.

And that was just one family. Another of Robert's warlords, one Roger of Tosny, had fought the Saracens in Spain, earning a reputation as *Mangeur de Maures*, the "Moor Eater." To rule over men like these would test any Christian's faith. Duke Robert was called the Magnificent, but also *Deable*, "the Devil." The constant bloodletting around him would have forced the noblest, most well-intentioned of men to turn hard-hearted and ruthless.

But this wasn't just true of Normandy. Europe was an anarchy of such warlords, turning on each other at the slightest opportunity, dotting the landscape with fortified keeps from which their armed brigands rode out to wage private wars, respecting neither sanctuaries, nor clergy, nor holy days. On top of that, 1034 was the third year of a severe famine in France. Combined with the constant petty conflicts rending society, many common folk feared God had abandoned them. The unrest and fervor culminated in a mass movement, a precursor to the one that launched the Crusades later in that century, in which crowds gathered to view relics, acclaim miracles, and proclaim peace in God's name. A papal synod at Elne in the Pyrenees Mountains in 1027 had proclaimed the *Treuga Dei*, the "Truce of God," demanding the cessation of all warfare from noon on Saturday until Monday morning, on pain of excommunication. The Normans did not yet adhere to it, but the movement was spreading northward and Robert would certainly have heard of it. Perhaps, like Cnut, he was becoming concerned for his own salvation. Malmesbury had it that the death of his brother Richard – his murder – was weighing on Robert's soul. How else to explain that, around 1034 or so, he found God?

He convened a gathering of his abbots, bishops, barons and lords at Fécamp and announced his desire to visit the Holy Land, barefoot and dressed as a pilgrim, to atone for his sins by praying at the Holy Sepulcher in Jerusalem.

This revelation met with predictable effect. "All were extremely astonished at these words," wrote Jumièges, "fearing that his absence would cause all sorts of troubles in their country."

That was putting it mildly. Robert's men begged him not to go. The Burgundians and Bretons, they pointed out, were just waiting for an opportunity to invade and conquer. Without an iron hand to hold them together, the Normans would quickly turn on each other.

Not to worry, Robert told them. They could all unite behind his heir, eight-year-old William: "He is little, but he will grow up and, God willing, become strong. I recognize him without reservation and consider him my son."

The boy would not have to be a battle leader, but merely a figurehead, a symbol of the dukedom. That said, the idea seems incredibly shortsighted. Whoever held young William would in effect hold the dukedom.

To this Robert's vassals, each probably already sizing himself up for the ducal throne, agreed. "They swore many oaths and vowed loyalty and allegiance to him [William]," wrote Wace, "as is proper for barons and vassals to do for their liege lord."

Duke Robert appointed his uncle Robert, Archbishop of Rouen, as regent. The two had not always seen matters eye-to-eye. The younger Robert had a taste for expropriating church properties, to which the elder Robert naturally objected. In 1028 the duke had besieged and driven the archbishop into exile, and in retaliation was excommunicated by him. They had reconciled, however, and Archbishop Robert had even negotiated the peace treaty between Duke Robert and his cousin, Duke Alan of Brittany, at Mont-Saint-Michel. Duke Robert now appointed Duke Alan as one of William's guardians, along with another cousin, Count Gilbert of Eu and Brionne. Robert took William to present him as his heir to the Frankish king, Henry I, who accepted the lad as his vassal and, in July 1035, confirmed him as Duke of Normandy.

The record of other boy rulers of the day is decidedly mixed. Cnut's sons, Harold in Orkney and Harthacnut in Denmark, were apparently doing fine – at least, as far as recorded. In Norway, however, all was not going well for the eldest, Svein. Or perhaps better to say, not for his mother, Aelfgifu of Northampton. As recorded in the *Heimskringla*, "King Svein, Cnut the Great's son, reigned over Norway for a few years, but in both age and understanding was still a child. His mother Alfifa [her Norse name] ruled, and the people of the land were her worst enemies."

English Aelfgifu had married into a Viking royal family, but Danish, not Norwegian. Of blood twice removed from that of her subjects, as far as she was concerned, they were a conquered people, hers to do with as she wished. And she wished to inflict on them forced labor and military service, excessive taxation and property confiscation. In legal matters, one Dane's word counted for more than ten Norwegians'. No one was permitted to leave the country without royal permission, which was rarely given.

Svein tried to be a good king. When, in 1033, a pretender claiming to be the son of Olaf Tryggvason raised a rebellion, many of the Norwegian lords declined to fight for Svein, who, to his credit, led an army without them and defeated the rebels. It did not raise his standing among the Norwegians, who held his mother responsible for their ills. The Icelandic skald Sigvat Thordarson, who had sailed with Thorkell the Tall, Olaf and Cnut, wrote of those days in Norway, "The young man will long remember the time of Alfifa, when we ate cattle feed, the way goats eat peeled bark. It was different when Olaf, the warrior, ruled the land."

That was the conclusion to which ever-greater numbers of Norwegians were arriving. The problem was aggravated by a cult of Olaf that had elevated the late king to the status of a martyr. Miracles were attributed to him by those who prayed at his tomb. Olaf was even declared a saint. His holiness aside, the chieftains who had rebelled against him to fight on behalf of Cnut had come to regret their decision. They had expected high honor and recompense for their efforts. Instead they were lackeys to a Danish prince and his English mother. Feeling betrayed, they began to look around for an alternative.

Olaf's half-brother Harald having by this time journeyed from Kievan Rus down to Constantinople to join the Byzantine Empire's all-Viking Varangian Guard, they settled on Olaf's bastard son Magnus, born of one of the king's serving wenches, but acknowledged by him as his heir. He was only about ten or eleven, and living in exile in Kiev, but one boy ruler was as good as another. A few Norwegian lords slipped out of the country and fetched him back, whereupon he was welcomed as king.

Any remaining support for the other boy king, Svein, and his mother Aelfgifu melted away. The *Heimskringla* records, "No sooner did the warriors of King Svein, the son of Alfifa, hear that King Magnus Olafsson had come to the country, than they bolted in all directions and hid, so that no resistance was offered to King Magnus."

Svein and Aelfgifu fled across the Skagerrak to Denmark, taking refuge in the court of his half-brother Harthacnut. The first block of Cnut's grand edifice had fallen. Norway was now the realm of King Magnus Olafsson.

Even from beyond the grave, Olaf Haraldsson was still bedeviling Cnut the Great.

———

Duke Robert of Normandy set out for Jerusalem, though hardly as the barefoot penitent to which he claimed to aspire. Wace snorted, "With him he had many warriors, chamberlains and servants, quartermasters and hirelings who led the horses and pack horses."

The procession traversed the Alps to visit young Pope Benedict IX in Rome. It crossed the Balkans to visit Byzantine emperor Michael IV in Constantinople. The journey was then delayed for two weeks when the duke fell ill. Unable to mount a horse or even walk, he had himself borne onward in a litter. "He persisted nevertheless," wrote Malmesbury, "not stopping, but safely traveling the whole way, and purchasing entry at a high price [from the ruling Saracens, who charged Christian pilgrims admission], barefoot and tearful, he worshipped at that Christian glory, the Holy Sepulcher."

His mission accomplished, his soul cleansed, Robert undertook the journey back to Normandy to reap his reward. At the beginning of July, in Nicaea in northwestern Anatolia (modern Iznik, Turkey), he fell sick again, and died. His death, like his brother Richard's, was attributed to poisoning, perhaps his final atonement.[*]

The sorrow was greatest, of course, in Normandy. The loyalty of the counts and barons was as fickle as their trust in each other. As soon as word spread of Robert's death they went their separate ways, building forts, stocking up on supplies, and looking for the first opportunity to rebel against the boy duke. "William his son, still very young, was grief-stricken," wrote Wace. "He had many warriors, but few friends, for he found many of them quite hostile."

Mourning was pervasive that last half of 1035. In Denmark, King Harthacnut was sheltering his half-brother, the former king Svein and his mother Aelfgifu while they planned the reconquest of Norway. Their schemes were cut short when, late that year or early in 1036, Svein died.

The cause of his death is unrecorded. Svein was only about nineteen or twenty but, as has been shown, youth and vitality were not proof against the endemic diseases stalking medieval Europe: typhoid, scarlet fever, various poxes, dysentery and more. The greater tragedy is that Svein never got the chance to become his own man. Even in death he was overshadowed by his father.

If grieving Aelfgifu sent missives across the North Sea to inform Cnut of his son's death and for instructions regarding Norway, they

---

[*] Also dying this same year on pilgrimage, and perhaps on this same one to the Holy Land, was Count Drogo of Mantes, husband of Queen Emma's daughter Goda and father of her son Ralf, more of whom later.

went unanswered. In early November 1035, at Sceptesberie (modern Shaftesbury in Dorset), Cnut the Great himself passed away.

According to his own saga the king died of *gulusot*, "yellow disease," jaundice, a buildup of bile in the skin and whites of the eyes. Typically that's just a symptom of a greater malady – liver disease, blood disease, hepatitis, pancreatitis, even cancer. Both the Encomiast and Jumièges alluded to the king, months earlier, feeling unwell; symptoms of jaundice include abdominal pain, fatigue and weight loss. A sense of impending doom is perhaps why Cnut had tried to settle accounts with the *aethelings* Edward and Alfred in Normandy. That certainly would have done nothing to soothe the dread of his courtiers. The idea of the conqueror of England and Norway, the emperor of Denmark, the overlord of Sweden, Scotland and the Isles, lying abed with his skin and eyes gone yellow, feverish and vomiting, had to be as upsetting to his queen Emma, his court, and – upon receiving the news in Denmark – his former consort Aelfgifu, as the knowledge that one of their sons must soon take his place. But which? Both situations were literally life and death.

Before it comes to that, let us turn to the two medieval accounts closest to Cnut the Great for his epitaph.

The *Knytlinga Saga*, the chronicle of his dynasty, declares, "He was of all the kings who have spoken the Danish tongue, the mightiest, and the one who ruled over the greatest empire."

The *Encomium Emma Reginae*, the account commissioned by Queen Emma on his behalf, opines, "So let kings and princes learn to emulate the deeds of this lord, who lowered himself to the depths that he might be able to scale the heights, and who gladly gave away earthly riches in order to attain heavenly ones."

XII

POWER GAMES

1036–1037

In the monastery in the honor of the Saint [Peter], the lady Queen
Emma was now alone in the kingdom, bitterly grieving the death of
her lord, and fearful for the absence of her children.

Encomium Emmae Reginae

Curious thing about *hnefatafl*, Viking chess: there were no queens in the game, only pawns and kings. Around the North Sea there was now a plethora of kings – boy kings, petty kings – but only two queens. So in early 1036 the question was, which one of Cnut's wives would run the board?

Emma and Aelfgifu found themselves in an odd position. Each had a son with a claim to the throne of Cnut the Great, but each queen lived in the domain of the other's son. Aelfgifu resided in the court of Emma's son, King Harthacnut, in Roskilde. Meanwhile, across the North Sea in England, seeing to her husband's funeral at Winchester, Emma could only look with growing apprehension on the arrival of Aelfgifu's son, Earl Harold, coming down from his domain in Orkney. Not for nothing was he called Harefoot. She sent urgent missives to Harthacnut to quickly sail for England and claim what was his.

Harthacnut could not. Across the Skagerrak in Norway, King Magnus, feeling secure on his new throne, was making noises of war against the by now ancestral enemy of his subjects, Denmark. Unable to claim the English crown without jeopardizing the Danish, Harthacnut was obliged to act like a king, to stay and defend his realm.

So it was up to Emma to assert her youngest son's claim, even over his elder half-brothers, Edward and Alfred in Normandy. She could fall back on the deal she had struck with Cnut as the price of her hand in marriage, that a firstborn son of theirs should be designated over all others as heir to the throne. It may well have been that Cnut had always intended for Harthacnut to succeed him as king, since his handfast marriage to Aelfgifu was not recognized by the church, nor the offspring of it, Svein and Harefoot. Emma went so far as to claim Cnut, on his deathbed, had designated Harthacnut to succeed him. Then, according to her own *Encomium*, she took it a step further, planting (or at least repeating) the story of Harefoot not only to be a "son of a certain concubine of King Cnut, but many people assert that this same Harold was secretly taken from a servant who birthed him, and put in the chamber of the concubine, who was indisposed, and this can be taken as the more truthful account."

Even a thousand years ago, politics was a dirty game. The story had legs, however. The *Chronicle* records, "Harold claimed to be the son of Cnut by Aelfgifu of Northampton, but that was not true," and by a hundred years later Worcester was claiming that both Aelfgifu's sons may have been counterfeit, that Svein was the son of a priest and Harefoot the son of a cobbler: "For our part, since there are doubts on the topic, we cannot be certain of the parentage of either."

Rumor became legend, perhaps, but Emma's stories evidently didn't play so well at the time. In England the choosing of kings was not up to queens, or even kings, especially if there was no king to do the choosing. It was up to the *witan*, the *thing*, the gathering of nobles, at Oxford.

They soon separated into two factions, headed up by the two most powerful earls in the land. On the side of Emma and Harthacnut was Earl Godwin of Wessex, whose loyalty was to the widow of his late king. For Godwin, Harthacnut was the legitimate and rightful heir. Malmesbury asserted, "The greatest stickler for justice, at this point, was earl Godwin. Positioning himself the defender of the fatherless, and with Queen Emma and the royal treasures in his safekeeping, for a while he restrained his foes by the sheer power of his name."

He was opposed, however, by Earl Leofric of Mercia, who with his late father Ealdorman Leofwine had remained loyal to Aethelred when Godwin was going over to the Danes. Leofric had prospered under Cnut, true enough, but he had a good Midlands distrust of Wessex, and much of England felt the same. Aelfgifu of Norway had once been Aelfgifu of Northampton, and her son Harefoot was Jarl of Orkney. Many northerners were Aelfgifu's kin, and probably Leofric's as well. And if the crown was to pass to a half-Viking prince, let it at least go to one half-English, rather than one half-Norman.

Godwin's was the most powerful earldom in England, but – for for the time being, at least – not powerful enough to stand against all the rest, not when they had a prince to unite them. The throne might be rightfully Harthacnut's, but the throne was in England, and Harthacnut was not. Harefoot was. The proverb "possession is nine-tenths of the law" dates only to the 16th century, but the principle must have had a corollary in Old English. The *Chronicle* records, "Earl Godwin and all the chieftains of Wessex held out as long as they could, but in the end they were unable to oppose it."

Still, Godwin had enough power to prevent total defeat. The men of the *witan*, in true Anglo-Saxon fashion, elected to take both sides. According to the *Chronicle*, "At a council of all the nobles at Oxford, Earl Leofric, and almost every *thegn* north of the Thames, and the naval contingent in London, chose Harold to be regent of all England, for both he and his brother Harthacnut in Denmark."

Harthacnut might be King of England in title, but Harefoot would rule in fact. Malmesbury scoffed, "He was chosen by the Danes and the London citizenry, who from long dealings with these barbarians had almost entirely adopted their way of life."

"But it was resolved," added Huntingdon, "that Queen Emma should reside at Winchester with the household of the late king, and hold all Wessex on behalf of her son, with Godwin as commander of her army."

That mattered little to Harefoot, who wasted no time establishing who held power in England. Worcester wrote, "Harold, however, on assuming the royal authority, quickly sent his men to Winchester to tyrannically seize the greater part of the treasure and riches which king

Cnut had given to Queen Emma, and having robbed her, permitted her to continue living at Winchester."*

So much for holding Wessex for Harthacnut. Emma was lucky to not end up banished to some nunnery, or worse. That Harefoot's men got away with this much while Godwin was in charge of Emma's security is proof of the earl's weakness against Harefoot and his supporters. Critically, however, Emma had other backers, including Archbishop Aethelnoth of Canterbury, the only man who could crown and confirm a king of England. He should have had no great loyalty to Cnut – he was a brother of Aethelweard, whom Cnut had executed back in 1017 – but he also had been the king's chaplain. (He is also thought to have been Godwin's uncle.) The *Encomium* records that when Harefoot went to him, demanding to be crowned, Aethelnoth refused to crown anyone except a son of Queen Emma: "I lay the scepter and crown upon the holy altar, and I neither refuse nor give them to you. But by my apostolic authority, I forbid any bishop to remove these things, or give them to you, or to consecrate you. As for you, seize what I have commended to God and his table, if you dare."

Neither bribes nor threats could sway him. This so enraged Harefoot (again, according to the *Encomium*) that he turned against the church, not only skipping services but running his baying hounds outside the cathedral during prayers. "The English beheld his conduct with sorrow, but as they had chosen him for their king, they were reluctant to criticize him."

The *Brut Chronicle*, a 13th-century collection of medieval tales of English history, declares: "This Harold had nothing of the bearing and manners of his father King Cnut, for he set little value on chivalry, courtesy, or worship, but only on his own will."

By this time Aelfgifu had arrived from Denmark and, as she had managed her other son Svein's court, was giving banquets and gifts and offering bribes and making threats to organize the pro-Harefoot faction in England, with the goal of making his reign permanent. Having lost a third of Cnut's North Sea Empire, she cared little if the remaining two-thirds, England and Denmark, became two separate kingdoms.

---

*She resided at Goudbeyete Manor, an estate granted her by Aethelred in 1012. *Goudbeyete* means "goods-getter," probably the site of a trading post or market house before she acquired it. Today the site is occupied by God Begot House on High Street.

England was the bigger prize, and who was to say that Harefoot might not eventually launch an invasion of Harthacnut's realm?

Then again, the Danes weren't Emma's people either. An England united under Aelfgifu might pose a greater threat to her ancestral home: Normandy.

In truth, a concerted invasion of Normandy might have toppled the dukedom, which was falling into anarchy. Many of the late Duke Robert's vassals had quickly rebelled against his son William. Jumièges wrote that the Moor Eater, Roger of Tosny, "in his pride disdained to serve him, saying that a bastard was not made to command him and the other Normans."

He wasn't the only one to feel that way. Jumièges wrote, "A great number of Normans, renouncing their loyalty, erected defenses in several places, and built themselves very solid fortresses. While, in their audacity, they put their faith in these fortifications, there soon arose between them all sorts of quarrels and dissent, and the dukedom was everywhere given up to cruel conflicts."

According to Henry of Huntingdon, at this time William did not even reside in Normandy. His mother Herleva had borne Duke Robert a daughter, Adeliza, but had long since – perhaps even before the duke's departure for Jerusalem – gone on to marry, legitimately this time, a minor Norman lord, Herluin, Vicomte de Conteville, and borne him two sons, Odo and Robert. However, the safety, and control, of Herleva's eldest son was beyond her new husband's power. For his own security William was spirited away to be raised in the court of King Henry in Paris.

The problem was, none of the Norman barons wished to be ruled by any of the others, yet none of them had a better claim to the ducal crown than William. The houses of Normandy quickly fell to fighting among themselves, some in the name of the new duke, many against. "Each built a castle or fortress according to his wealth," recorded Wace. "As a result, wars sprang up and there was destruction of land, great conflicts, great animosity, great thefts and great challenges...they paid hardly any attention to the duke's wishes."

Archbishop Robert of Rouen, as regent, along with the boy's guardians, Duke Alan of Brittany and Count Gilbert of Brionne, assembled something of a pro-William faction with the goal of bringing the rebel barons to heel.

Roger de Beaumont, called *la Barbe*, "the Bearded," was William's second cousin once removed, kinship distant enough that he might have stood aloof from the fighting, but he would be one of Duke William's staunchest supporters.

Old Duke Robert's seneschal (steward, or senior retainer) Osbern fitzArfast, called "the Peacemaker," was a nephew of William's grandmother Gunnor. He became the young duke's steward as well, and his personal bodyguard.

William's cousin and close friend Guy of Burgundy was a younger son with no inheritance, sent to be raised as part of William's household in hopes of making his fortune there.

Arrayed against them, in what was basically a family quarrel, were others of William's kin. William of Arques, legitimate son of Duke Richard II, felt the dukedom should have passed to him, and was backed in this by his brother Mauger.

Archbishop Robert's son, Ralf, was a lowly lord of Gacé in lower Normandy, with even less claim to the ducal throne, but he evidently hoped to increase his holdings by opposing Duke William.

Lord Roger de Montgomery had been named Vicomte of Hiémois, where William had grown up, but had illegally acquired church properties. He had been compelled to give them back and pay restitution, lost his rank, and was forced into exile by Osbern.

The whereabouts in all this of the two outcast English *aethelings*, Edward and Alfred, has gone unrecorded. Though William's kinsmen, they were of only minor concern to the battling warlords. As nephews and former wards of Duke Robert, they might have been expected to lend their support, such as it was, to Duke William, for if he was killed, there would be no one of Emma's family left to protect them. The previous year their widowed sister Goda, whose husband had died on pilgrimage to the Holy Land, had remarried to Eustace II, Count of Boulogne, and in 1036 their half-sister Gunhilde followed through on her betrothal to King Henry III of Germany. Alfred and Edward might soon have resorted to seeking shelter in those realms, becoming a pair of vagabond princes like Ironside's sons Edmund and Edward in Hungary.

Then, that summer, they received a letter from England.

The provenance of this letter is still disputed. In the *Encomium*, Emma's propagandist later claimed it was a forgery crafted by Harefoot, and by extension his mother Aelfgifu: "The usurper was secretly laying traps for the queen, since as yet he dared not act openly, and nobody allowed him to hurt her."

Considering the way things turned out, though, it makes sense that Emma would want to put the blame on somebody else.

The letter informed the princes that Harefoot was going about the realm, tightening his grip on what should be their kingdom through threats and cajolery, bringing the nobles to his side even though they would prefer an *aetheling* to rule. He even had a young heir, Aelfwine, to inherit the throne if he died. Emma, the letter said, was summoning at least one of her sons (the letter did not specify which) to join her at her Winchester estate, where they could all decide what to do about it.

"They read this concoction in innocence," continued the Encomiast, "and alas, too trustful of the lies, they foolishly replied to their mother that one of them would meet her, and set a day, time and place."

If the letter indeed came from Emma, it amounted to treason, and furthermore completely overstated the loyalties of the *witan*, for whom the *aethelings* were not such a popular choice to rule. According to Malmesbury, "Almost everyone held Aethelred's sons in contempt, more from the memory of their father's sloth, than the might of the Danes," and of either of them regaining the throne even the *Chronicle* admits, "the powerful men in this land would not allow it, because popular opinion favored Harold, although it was not right."

And why wouldn't popular feeling be in Harefoot's favor? Aethelred's long reign had meant nothing but warfare and misery for England. His successor Cnut, Viking though he was, had brought almost twenty years of peace. And after their long exile, Aethelred's sons, now in their early thirties, might be more Norman than English.

Their claim to the throne through Emma, however, was more legitimate than Harefoot's through Aelfgifu. And being half-brothers to Harthacnut, not through a dead father but through their very alive mother, they would be more amenable to a peaceful relationship with Denmark. Who is to say Emma didn't even envision a reunification of Cnut's North Sea Empire – this time, perhaps, under a unifying queen mother, a *de facto* empress?

As usual, the various accounts of what happened next differ in detail, but all seem to agree that, whether as part of a two-pronged invasion or to beat each other across the Channel and onto the throne, the brothers journeyed separately to England.

This is where 11th-century Norman priest, historian (and onetime soldier) William of Poitiers takes up the story. Like Jumièges, he actually has Edward hurrying across the Channel without any mention of a letter from his mother: "As soon as they heard of Cnut's death, Edward crossed the sea, taking forty ships [probably left over from the abortive invasion attempt with Duke Robert a few years past] packed with warriors to Southampton, where he found a very great number of English lying in wait to kill him."

They knew he was coming. Edward had barely stepped off the boat when he was met with a hostile reception. There was a fight. The Normans gave a good account of themselves, but the longer it went on, the more English arrived to take part. Given all the fighting going on in Normandy, and his history with Edmund Ironside, this was probably not Edward's first combat, but it was likely his first command. Wace recorded, "Edward saw that he could not win his birthright without great losses...he himself, if he were taken, would be killed without ransom...he could do nothing more, so he returned to Barfleur."

The hoped-for rendezvous with Emma never happened. Edward's expedition was so inconsequential – or so embarrassing – that it didn't even rate a mention in his mother's *Encomium*.

Yet Edward's landing went better than his brother's.

Unlike Edward, Alfred intended to land at Sandwich in Kent, stopping off in Flanders and Boulogne to enlist mercenaries along the way, fifty ships' worth. Like Edward, however, there were men waiting for him to land.

(The fact that both *aethelings* are said to have met with organized resistance on arrival does give some credence to Emma's claim that Harefoot and/or Aelfgifu sent the letter to bait them across the Channel. The returning messengers would have given the reception committees precise intelligence as to the time and place of the princes' arrival. An invasion force of forty or fifty ships would not have been stood off by anything less than a medieval *fyrd*, but no sizable army could be assembled without plenty of time to prepare. To have two armies waiting, in two separate locations, would have required advance knowledge and planning.)

To his credit, Alfred spotted the ambush, sailed off without a fight and, having evaded the trap, landed unopposed further down the coast. From there he struck off inland, toward London. The *aetheling* had not set foot on English soil in over twenty years, having passed into exile when he was only eight. How strange to hear Old English again, from travelers as they passed and villagers along the way. Doubtless Alfred informed one and all that, despite his brother's failure, the sons of Aethelred had returned. England would have an English king again.

Again, details vary among the accounts, but at some point they were met on the road by armed men. Expectation of battle would have been relieved by the newcomers' welcome. It was Queen Emma's protector, Earl Godwin.

He persuaded Alfred to bypass Harefoot and London, and instead, like Edward, head for Winchester to link up with his mother. With Emma's support, the countryside would harken to the *aetheling*'s banner, giving him a much more persuasive argument when it came time to confront Harefoot, whether diplomatically or in battle.

Though Alfred's route overland to Winchester was much longer than Edward's, it was much smoother going then than it is now. Today in places little more than a hiking path, modern Harrow Way – *Harweg* in Old English, "the Old Way" – was then a major religious thoroughfare connecting Canterbury Cathedral to that of Winchester. The road paralleled the chalk ridges of the North Downs all the way from Dover to Farnham, where a lefthand fork continued on to Winchester as the Pilgrim's Way.

John Brompton, the 15th-century Cistercian abbot of Jervaulx in Yorkshire, compiled a chronicle of English history from AD 588–1199 based on earlier accounts, some included here, others presumably lost. He has the procession cresting the ridge at the western edge of the Downs called *Guldesdowne*, "Guild-down," today called the Hog's Back, where Godwin turns to Alfred: "Look below, right and left. Behold what a realm will be yours."

"Alfred thanked God," wrote Brompton, "and swore that if he was ever crowned king, he would enact only laws that would be pleasing and agreeable to God and man."

That evening the party reined up at *Gyldeforda*, the "Golden Ford" over the River Wey, modern Guildford, about thirty-five miles from Winchester. Alfred's men split up to billet themselves among the townspeople. "But after they had dined and drank, and being tired, had gladly taken to their beds," wrote the Encomiast, "behold, men of the most abominable tyrant Harold appeared."

In early 1929 a gardener working a plot alongside the Harrow Way, on the summit of the Hog's Back overlooking Guildford, uncovered human remains. The bodies, buried right on the chalk of the ridge only a foot or two beneath the surface, appeared to have been cut up by farmers' plows over the centuries, and were so old that all traces of clothing had deteriorated to a thin film of carbon over the bones.

Archaeologist A.W.G. Lowther of the Surrey Archaeological Society was called in to uncover what turned out to be a medieval burial site. Judging by the grave furniture – the brooches, beads, buckles, finger rings, knife and spear blades found with the bodies – there were three main interments. Thirty-six people, mostly women and children, dated to the pagan days of the 6th century, and others to the late 11th, but the vast majority – there were 222 in total – were male, dated to circa AD 1040.

This was curious. When the Anglo-Saxons converted to Christianity in the 7th to 8th centuries, they began burying their dead in churchyards. Only criminals were buried in unconsecrated ground.

But then, these dead were not Anglo-Saxons. Anglo-Saxons had long skulls and stout, long leg bones. These bodies had round skulls and slim leg bones, more typical of the Gallic type from across the Channel, in France.

Many were found with their wrists together behind them, as though bound at the time of death, although any binding had long since rotted away. Some had their arms, legs, feet and heads severed. One's back had been broken before burial; another, his neck. Several had their heads placed between their legs.

The Guildford finding was a horrid precursor to the discovery of the mass graves of the St. Brice's Day Massacre: graphic evidence of Anglo-Saxon vengeance on invaders.

———

Alfred and his men, taken completely by surprise, were bound and forced to their knees. The 12th-century monk Richard of Devizes, in his account of events, claimed they sat in a circle, with Alfred tied to a stake in the center where he could watch as they were variously tortured – scalped, their eyes and noses and hands and feet cut off and hung in the trees – before execution: speared through, beheaded. By most accounts they were decimated, in the reverse Scandinavian style (nine out of ten executed). Huntingdon added, "But when all except the tenth man were slain, the English were unhappy that so many still lived, so they reduced them by a second decimation, so that very few escaped indeed."

As for Alfred, he was marched off to London along with his leading men, to face the king's mercy. Poitiers continued, "Harold rejoiced to see Alfred in chains and ordered his closest friends to be beheaded in front of him, and that Alfred should be blinded. Harold then had him tied, shamefully naked, on a horse, and had him taken to the marshes, so that he could be tortured in lonely starvation on the Isle of Ely."

Some of the monks of Ely were the very same who had raised Alfred and Edward as boys. The *aetheling* would need someone sympathetic to care for him. Before he was handed over, the rest of the sentence was carried out. The Encomiast, writing for Alfred's mother Emma, spared her no detail: "Two men each took an arm, with one on his chest and one on his legs, in order that the punishment might be more easily carried out. He was held fast, and after his eyes were put out was most wickedly slain."

Poitiers would have it that the prince's death was not intentional, but the work of clumsy torturers: "He could not survive long, because while they were popping out his eyes with a dagger the point pierced his brain."

The *Chronicle* has it that Alfred lingered, blind and brain-damaged, until February of 1037, and was finally put out of his misery, perhaps by even more horrific means. "Indeed," wrote Brompton, "some say that the start of his bowels were drawn out through an opening at his navel and tied to a stake, and he was driven around it with iron goads, until the last bits of his entrails were extracted. And thus through the treachery of Godwin, Alfred died at Ely."

The incident was so heinous that some versions of the *Chronicle* go to the extent of lamenting it in verse: "No more horrible deed was ever done in this land."

However, not all accounts of the "Guildford Massacre" in the *Chronicle* are so damning. One, compiled at Abingdon Abbey in Oxfordshire a few years after the event, puts the blame for the event squarely on Godwin, by name. The version written at Worcester Abbey in the mid-11th century does not name Godwin as the perpetrator, but leaves the reader to surmise his involvement. The edition maintained by the monks of Peterborough Abbey in Cambridgeshire was destroyed in a fire in August 1116 and recopied from the beginning from the Winchester chronicle, but with a later viewpoint. It actually skips over the massacre entirely. By then, the deaths of a minor Anglo-Saxon *aetheling* and his men were not worth even a footnote. These differences reflect the prevailing attitudes at the time they were written. As the various players went in and out of power, they recast events to their benefit or erased them from the record.

Still, the latter view is a remarkably charitable one, given that Alfred's landing amounted to nothing less than an invasion by an exiled, outlawed prince at the head of a foreign army, against a lawfully chosen King of England. In that context Harefoot's conduct is, while shocking to a modern audience, at least understandable to his contemporaries. Many other medieval kings, and even later kings of England, would have done no less. Edward would think twice about pursuing any claim to the throne while Harefoot sat upon it. Poitiers wrote, "He delighted in making his enemy's life more onerous than death. At the same time he intended to terrify Edward with his brother's suffering."

It was Godwin who came in for particular blame for Alfred's murder by later pro-Norman writers. In Jumièges' opinion, he "received him at first in good faith, but in the same night he fulfilled the role of Judas the traitor to him."

"Godwin loved Danes more than the English," declared Wace. "What deviltry, great treachery and great crime he committed! He was a traitor and committed treason."

"One might wish to forget this inhuman crime and never speak of it," judged Poitiers, "but, since horrible events occur over the course of history, we believe they should not be erased from the written record, so that repeat of such deeds may be forbidden."

Really, though, what else was Godwin to do? For Wessex to betray a duly chosen king – to oppose all the rest of England – would mean plunging the island back into civil war. Godwin had already made and lost the case for Harthacnut with the *witan*. Harefoot surely already distrusted him. Godwin needed to gain the new king's favor. Walter Map, whom we last saw describing the youthful Godwin in the most flattering manner, described the adult in terms tempered by events: "I do not say he was a good man, but a man capable of much good and much evil."

Devizes, describing Godwin as "a man of as much cunning as power," even accused him of being some kind of evil mastermind, who sent the letter to the *aethelings* in the first place to lure them into the trap and get them out of the way, "for he had sons intended for the government."

Whether Godwin's eldest sons, Sweyn and Harold, even bore witness to any of this, let alone took part, is not recorded in the annals. They would both have been in their mid-teens, old enough to learn the gritty side of the family business. They would have been no strangers to the sight of blood, of animals butchered on their father's estates and perhaps criminals executed, but not likely the sight of hands and feet, heads and eyeballs scattered on bloody ground and hanging from trees. Blood justice, however, was the way of their world. The main lesson to be learned from these sordid episodes was that Sweyn and Harold would be, if they weren't already, players in this deadly game, in which the only objective was to survive and rise above the vagaries of court politics. That required power, the attaining and keeping of it. And if achieving power required treachery, then treacherous the Godwins would be.

Godwin had proven his loyalty to Harefoot. With none opposing him, and with Harthacnut still dithering in Denmark, in 1037 the *witan* finally designated the prince as Harold I, the full, lawful King of England. Not regent, not king of the north, King.

And he did not need two queen mothers.

For her part Emma was struck with shock at her sons' treatment, and grief over Alfred's murder, and alarm at the betrayal by Godwin. Some at the time questioned why she did not take her own life, but that was not Emma of Normandy's way. She still had a royal son in Harthacnut. To kill herself now would mean deserting him and his rightful cause. She had to look to her own salvation. Without Godwin's support, it was only a matter of time before she was accused of treason, taken prisoner and subjected to Harefoot's – and Aelfgifu's – justice. Her only chance to win this deadly game of *hnefatafl* was to escape off the board.

The problem was, it wasn't even safe for her to go home.

XIII

Nadirs

1037–1040

The barons warred with each other and the strong overran the weak...they burned and destroyed towns, imprisoned and robbed peasants and caused much harm.

Wace

Normandy was indeed no place for an exiled queen. Beset with assassinations, pitched battles, sieges and general anarchy, it was hardly yet safe even for its young Duke William. His kinsmen Alan of Brittany and Gilbert of Brionne had so far managed to prevent the rebel barons from tearing the duchy to shreds, but they lost a loyal supporter in Archbishop Robert of Rouen, who died in 1037. To maintain his family's support, William's kinsman Mauger was named archbishop, even though he was only eighteen, and his elder brother William named Count of Arques. They were sons of the dead Duke Richard II first, however, and neither had any great love for a bastard son of their cousin Robert I.

Even Henry I, King of the Franks, William's suzerain and supposed protector, took advantage of the situation. The presence of a Norman keep at Tillières on the Avre River, the border with France, had long irked him. As a condition of his continued protection, he demanded that William have it torn down. The duke's barons decided that the king's support was worth more than a border fort, and advised him to accept...all except one, Gilbert Crispin, to whom Tillières had been given by Duke Robert. Wace admitted, "He blamed the duke and thought his barons cowardly and treacherous."

So William and his loyal Normans found themselves allied with the army of France, laying siege to one of their own, in his own castle. "What more can I say?" shrugged Jumièges. "Conquered at last by the duke's prayers, Gilbert gave up the castle with regret, and soon afterwards he had the cruel chagrin of seeing it delivered to the flames under the eyes of all."[*]

Just to make it clear who owed allegiance to whom, Henry warned William not to have the keep rebuilt for four years, then promptly proceeded to raid the Norman county of Hiesmes, modern Exmes, which had been William's father Robert's seat when he was still only a count. The French burned the town of Argentan and, returning by way of Tillières, rebuilt the fortress for Henry. From now on it would guard the border of France from Normandy.

With even friends having become his enemies, William could trust no one.

For Emma, to return to this hotbed of intrigue and violence was fraught with danger. In addition to being the young duke's aunt, she was a proven meddler in court politics and might be assumed to be aiding his succession. She would make a prime target for kidnapping and ransom, or worse, become a brood mare for some warlord or another. Her protection would require fighting men whose absence would weaken William's forces. For that reason, probably not even the duke's supporters wanted her around. Malmesbury wrote, "Believing Normandy unsafe, as her brother and nephews lay dead and disgust with the rule of a deserted orphan created great dangers, she crossed over into Flanders."

Flanders had recently come through its own succession crisis, with Baldwin V having rebelled against his father Count Baldwin IV in 1035. The family had reconciled before the old count had died, power transitioned smoothly from father to son, and Flanders' peaceful cities, Ghent, Ypres and most importantly Bruges, on the Channel coast a little north of the Dover Strait, were well on the way to making it a financial powerhouse of Western Europe.

---

[*]Recall that most Norman castles at this time were motte-and-bailey designs, a wooden palisade surrounding a wooden tower atop an earthen mound.

By his wife Adela, sister of King Henry of France, Count Baldwin V had three children of his own, sons Baldwin and Richard and daughter Mathilde. In addition, his stepmother Eleanor of Normandy – daughter of Duke Richard II, and so Emma's niece – had borne the old count a daughter before he died, Judith. Both she and Mathilde were to play prominent roles in years to come, and there can be no doubt that Emma helped their mother prepare them for it. She was welcomed among them as part of the family, and allotted a house and waitstaff of her own in the city.

This warm atmosphere probably encouraged the former queen to reestablish what was left of her own family. One of Flanders' other benefits, from her perspective, was that it was halfway between Normandy and Denmark. Having settled in, Emma sent word south, calling on Edward to come to her.

The last time the *aetheling* had received such a summons he had narrowly escaped with his life, and his brother had paid with his, but Edward obeyed. Despite the danger of a cross-country ride through the war-torn land, he was probably just glad to have somewhere to go, for his usefulness to his Norman hosts was no longer obvious. Duke William had his hands full trying to stay alive, and having to accommodate an English *aetheling* was more hindrance than help. On the other hand, it had been made plain to Edward that he was no better loved in England, nor much of a military leader either. Many of his Norman supporters lay dead there, and the rest would not be inclined to make a return trip on his behalf, or his mother's. Any claim he had to the throne could no longer be anything more than a dream, best forgotten. "When they began their talks," records the *Encomium*, "the son declared his sympathy for his mother's misfortunes, but that he was unable to help, since the English nobility had sworn no loyalty to him."

Such complacency would not have been very welcome in the house of Emma. This, after all, was not the first time she had come to the mainland as an exile from England. The last time she had returned to become its queen. She was well-practiced at making comebacks. Yet a queen, even a dowager queen, needed a king at her back.

Edward was not that man. His childhood, far down the line of succession in the monastery at Ely, and his adolescence in exile at the peaceful religious court of Richard II, with even less chance of ever attaining a throne, had rendered him more monkish than warlike.

And Edward's faults as a son could be marked down to Emma's as a mother. She had always been a queen first, a mother second. This was most likely the first time she and her firstborn had so much as met in twenty years. If she suddenly desired a son at her side, her Encomiast asserted rather acidly, Edward advised her to turn to Harthacnut.

It's worth remembering, though, that the *Encomium* is Emma's account of events. It's just as probable – more, even – that Edward rode all that way to seek his mother's help in regaining his crown, only to be brutally rebuffed, and for the exact same reason: He was not kingly material.

In any case, their parting was apparently unpleasant, so much so that Edward felt he was better off amid the deadly dangers of Normandy. He promptly returned there.

The reunion with her eldest son having not gone quite according to plan, Emma did not take long to follow his advice and reach out to her youngest. (She had nowhere else to turn. Her daughter by Cnut, Gunhilde, wife of Emperor Henry III of Germany, had reigned as queen only two years before passing away in 1038.) The *Encomium* minces no words. "After her son left, she sent word to her son Harthacnut, king of the Danes, of her exceptional sorrow, and begged him to come to her as quickly as possible."

In Roskilde, Harthacnut was finally secure on his own throne. The long-anticipated war with Magnus of Norway had never come to pass. Both countries had assembled armies and fleets and sailed for battle, but too many men on either side remembered each other from the old days, and prior to combat feelers were put out to see if there was another way of resolving the dispute. The kings were yet boys – Harthacnut around twenty-one, and Magnus only about fifteen – and all the noises about war were coming from an excess of manhood on their part. Their respective advisors arranged a summit of sorts, where it turned out the two had something in common: resentment of their fathers' ex-lover Aelfgifu and her misbegotten sons. In Magnus's view they had usurped Norway; in Harthacnut's, England.

The enemy of an enemy is a friend. Magnus's saga records the outcome: "At this meeting a treaty was proposed: a brotherly union under oath to maintain peace between them as long as they lived. And if one of them died without leaving a son, the other would succeed to the combined lands and people."

In effect, two-thirds of Cnut's North Sea Empire was reconciled, even if under different kings. (Which, after all, was how they had been ruled under Cnut.) It was up to Harthacnut to see to the remaining third, and now that he could safely turn his back on Norway, he could do something about it. To make sure Magnus hewed to their agreement, he appointed Svein Estridsson, son of Jarl Ulf, as Jarl of Denmark. Svein was about twenty-one now, had done some fighting for King Anund of Sweden, and apparently held no blood-oath against Harthacnut, whose father had after all ordered his father's murder. (Svein had two younger brothers, Beorn and Osbeorn. Their whereabouts are unknown at this time, but judging by their later appearances Harthacnut may have kept them with him, as insurance against betrayal by Svein.) Leaving Denmark in his hands, Harthacnut went south to meet Emma. "For his heart burned to avenge his brothers' injuries," wrote the Encomiast, "and even more to obey his mother's summons."

By this time the maelstrom in Normandy was nearing a murderous peak. Malmesbury wrote, "The country, once flourishing, was now rent with internal strife, and divided up among plunderers, so one could justly say, 'Woe to the land of a child sovereign.'"

Years later Duke William is said to have remembered, "My closest allies and relatives, who should have defended me with everything they had against all adversaries, frequently conspired and rebelled against me, robbing me of almost all my father's birthright."

His very birthplace of Falaise had been stolen out from under him. It had been gifted, as part of the Hiémois, by his father Robert to his *vicomte* Roger de Montgomery, but after Roger's exile the castle was handed over to a new *vicomte*, Thorstein le Goz. He was of Danish blood – his name translates from the Old Norse as "Thor's stone" – and, seeing how the duke of the Normans was so easily cowed by the king of the Franks, thought better of his own loyalties. "He treacherously abandoned the duke," wrote Wace, "fortifying Falaise, of which he was master, and importing mercenaries from France, good footsoldiers and fine archers. His intent was to hold the castle in spite of the duke and he did not stoop to offer him service for it."

It got worse from there. While besieging a rebel castle at Vimoutiers, William's guardian Duke Alan of Brittany abruptly died, according to 12th-century English monk and chronicler Orderic Vitalis, poisoned by his own Norman allies. Not long afterward William's guardian Gilbert, Count of Brionne, was assassinated while riding, on the orders of Ralf de Gacé. William and his dwindling retinue lived on the run, taking shelter with whatever sympathetic count, baron or peasant would take them in, their safety never assured. Decades later, according to Orderic, William recalled, "Many nights, for fear of my own relatives, my uncle Walter [of Falaise, his mother Herleva's brother] smuggled me in secret from the castle bedchamber to the cottages and bolt-holes of the poor, to keep me from discovery by traitors seeking my death."

The duke's tutor, Thorkell of Neuf-Marche, was murdered. William and his guardian, Osbern the Steward, were asleep in a village south of Rouen when a killer burst into their bedchamber and slit the Peacemaker's throat in front of the boy. William, probably not yet a teenager, escaped, and may not have been the intended target – the killer was William de Montgomery, son of the ex-*vicomte* Roger, exacting vengeance for his father's exile – but though physically unharmed the duke acquired emotional scars so deep he still lived with them decades later: "Such acts taught me the true depth of my people's loyalty."

Like Edward Aetheling (who at this time must have been living a similarly furtive existence in Normandy), and Sweyn and Harold Godwinson in England, William was learning the hard lessons of medieval life. In their world a man's heart needed to be hard as his armor, his wits honed as sharp as his sword, and his goals as pointed as the tip as his spear.

And the Bastard's goal, for now, was simply to stay alive.

The Danish fleet assembled for war against Magnus of Norway was kept in preparation for war with Harefoot of England, but it would not do to bring the whole lot down the Channel in full view of English spies lining both shores. Harthacnut sailed with just ten ships, down to Bruges to meet his mother Emma.

"There are no words for the sadness and happiness of their meeting," declared the Encomiast. "There was great pain when his mother imagined the face of her lost one [Cnut] in her son's, but she greatly rejoiced at seeing him safe."

The King of Denmark took up residence in Emma's home while the two plotted a new game of *hnefatafl*. An invasion of England could no longer be undertaken as easily as when the divided Anglo-Saxons had ruled it. Aethelred had given Forkbeard virtually no opposition, but their sons Ironside and Cnut had fought practically to a standstill. And even if Anglo-Saxons still made up most of the aristocracy, England was a Viking country now.

But Harefoot had not been required to conquer it. Everything he had, he had been given, or had taken with minimal resistance. He had never had to fight for his crown. Even Alfred's invasion had been foiled by Godwin, who had once favored Harthacnut and might do so again. Alone, Wessex could not stand against the king and the other earldoms, but with a Danish army at his back, might Godwin be enticed to switch sides?

The *Chronicle* confirms that England's fleet was down to just sixteen ships. Harthacnut had mustered sixty for his war with Norway. Taken as a measure of manpower, the odds would seem to have favored the Danes. Faced with an invasion by fellow Vikings, Harefoot might well fold and flee, be slain, or even be taken alive.

"And not long afterwards," wrote the Encomiast, "while the son tarried with his mother laying invasion plans, messengers arrived with happy news: Harold was dead."

Among the kings of England, Harold Harefoot has garnered some of the worst press, but also the least. Most of what we know of him comes from the people who wished him ill: Emma of Normandy and her sons. "He was neither courteous nor very smart," sniffed Matthew Paris, "but he did not reign long."

Other than the incursions by Edward and Alfred, which in the grand scheme were hardly of note, Harefoot's reign was uneventful. The *Chronicle*, which often bewailed high taxes during Cnut's reign, makes no complaint of them during Harefoot's. There were a couple of border wars, with the Welsh to the west and the Scots in the north, but Harefoot was by and large a peaceful king.

He passed away on March 17, 1040, but apparently he had been ill for some time. There is no record of the cause of his death. Among the last people to see him were some church fathers seeking to sort out a land dispute. A record of the visit notes, "The king was then lying at Oxford, very sick and fearing for his life...the king lay and grew black as they spoke." That might seem to imply gangrene, but the word in question, *asweartode*, to blacken, darken or obscure, might simply refer to his mood, that Harold was angered or obfuscating. What killed him was simply *aelfscot*, elf shot, random chance, from which no one – like his brother Svein – was immune.

His son Aelfwine was probably ten years old or less, not yet of age to rule, though the boy's grandmother Aelfgifu doubtless lobbied hard for him, arguing to be his regent as she had been Svein's in Norway. (His mother, possibly also named Aelfgifu, is otherwise unknown and can be assumed to be the king's *frilla*.) This time, however, the men of the *witan* were united in their choice. Wendover wrote, "The English and Danish nobles then, with one voice, sent messengers to Flanders for Harthacnut king of Denmark, who was living there with his mother, and invited him to England to wear the crown."

The nobles of the *witan* were undoubtedly aware of Harthacnut's Viking invasion fleet amassed across the North Sea. England had passed almost a quarter century under Danish kings; an entire generation of English had known no other. Easier, then, to invite yet another to the throne, rather than plunge the country back into war over it. In his dealings with Magnus of Norway, Harthacnut had proven himself willing to yield power for peace; now let him rule England in the same spirit.

On hearing the verdict, Harefoot's mother Aelfgifu promptly got out of the city, presumably taking her grandson Aelfwine with her, and apparently fled to the Continent. Aelfwine is thought to have grown up to become a monk at the Abbey Church of Sainte-Foy in Aquitaine, on the pilgrim's path to Compostela in Spain, but save for one apocryphal mention yet to come, Aelfgifu of Northampton vanished from history. By the rules of *hnefatafl*, she had escaped off the board with her life, and would have to count that as a win.

Emma of Normandy's victory, however, was complete.

XIV

HARTHACNUT

1040–1042

In this same year came King Harthacnut to Sandwich, seven days
before midsummer, and he was quickly acknowledged as king by the
English and Danes, though later his advisers grievously regretted it.

Anglo-Saxon Chronicle

The beach at Sandwich was where, in 1014, Harthacnut's father
Cnut had mutilated his English hostages before fleeing to Denmark.
Presumably none of those unfortunates attended the welcome of
England's new king in 1040, when Harthacnut arrived there with fifty
or sixty ships. Archbishop Aethelnoth of Canterbury, who had refused
to crown Harefoot, had since passed away, but his replacement,
Archbishop Eadsige, had been King Cnut's personal priest and gladly
bestowed the crown and scepter on his son.

Attending the coronation, Earl Godwin, for one, must have felt
himself on thin ice. He had opposed Harefoot's reign in the first
place, which should have stood him in good stead with the new king.
His treatment of Alfred Aetheling, though, was cause for misgivings.
Godwin was to learn that the new king held his various half-brothers
in quite differing regard.

Harthacnut's first act as king was to send men – according to
Worcester, headed up by Godwin himself – to deal with Harefoot.
Boyce reported, "He did not even let his brother's ghost rest in peace.
He had the body dug up and beheaded, as he did with the living who

had insulted him and his mother. Then he stuck his head on a spike at a conspicuous spot in London to be mocked, and had the headless body thrown into the river Thames."

Harefoot's corpse ended up in the nets of local fishermen. They gave it to some sympathetic Danes, who had it secretly re-interred at St. Clement Danes, today on the Strand in the City of Westminster, but back then a Viking enclave on the riverbank, outside the city.

As for his other dead half-brother, Harthacnut had a different kind of vengeance in mind. In casting about for perpetrators of Alfred Aetheling's brutal murder, it was revealed to him that Earl Godwin had carried out the initial arrest.

By now well experienced with the capriciousness of kings, and with Alfred's mother Queen Emma having returned and doubtless simmering with hate, Godwin did not wish to be found washing headless down the Thames. He quickly made restitution: a warship with a gilded prow and fittings, and 800 soldiers with gold-trimmed arms and armor. In addition, the earl swore an oath before the king and the *witan* that Alfred's blinding and murder had not been his doing.

I was just following orders is an excuse relied upon throughout history for all sorts of despicable acts, but when accompanied by a sufficiently large bribe can absolve anyone of guilt. Yet Godwin was wise to make amends to Harthacnut, who held all Anglo-Saxons in low regard. "He also enacted a law that whenever an Englishman should happen to meet a Dane he should remove his hat, bow, and salute him as master," recorded Boyce, "and if an Englishman and a Dane met on a bridge, the Englishman should wait at the end until the Dane had crossed."

Earl Eadwulf of Bamburgh had unwittingly overstepped this line. He had been the beneficiary of the ongoing blood feuds among the northerners, succeeding to his earldom after the murder of his elder half-brother Ealdred, in which he may have had a hand. Back in 1038 he had instigated a war with *Donnchad*, "Dark Chieftain," King Duncan I of Scotland. Eadwulf overlooked, however, that his fellow earl Siward of Yorkshire was (we think) King Duncan's father-in-law, *and* son-in-law to dead Earl Ealdred as well. And via Earl Ulf and Cnut, Siward was also (again, we think) a distant kinsman of Harthacnut – not a good combination where Eadwulf was concerned.

Lax Harefoot had done nothing about Eadwulf's warmongering. Harthacnut, already looking dimly upon the northern Anglo-Saxons for their support of his late brother, was more open to the Dane Siward's complaints. In 1041, he invited Eadwulf to come explain himself, but as one version of the *Chronicle* records, "Having guaranteed his safety, Harthacnut betrayed Earl Eadwulf, and thereby made himself an oath-breaker."

Symeon of Durham wrote, "When he came to be reconciled with Harthacnut, he was slain by Siward, who afterward assumed whole province of Northumbria."

This was more evidence, for Earl Godwin and his sons, that treachery could be either brutally punished or well rewarded. And that his fellow earls were not above their own personal gain.

Neither was Harthacnut. He had brought with him a much larger fleet than Harefoot's, of course, and its crews needed compensation. It was only fair to pay them the same wages as had Cnut and Harefoot: eight marks each.* Harthacnut's fleet, however, combined with his brother's, came to over four and a half times as large, requiring a commensurate rise in taxes. It was time to reinstate the *gafol*, the Danish tax, the payment of tribute. In the king's estimation, the amount due came to over 11,000 pounds for the ships, and almost twice that for the army – over 33,000 pounds total. Since the payment was not technically to Danes, but to the king to support his housecarls, this annual tax was henceforth to be known as the *heregeld*, "army gold." It was to become a double strain on the common folk, because of course the cost of it all was passed to the consumer. The *Chronicle* records that the price of a sester of wheat (about eight bushels, a horse load) that year rose to almost two ounces of silver.

All England groaned under this imposition, to the point that the royal housecarls were required to collect it. Wendover recorded, "Harthacnut, king of England, sent his men throughout the kingdom, accepting no excuses in collecting the tax which he had enacted, to supply his pirates with necessities."

---

*A mark equaled 100 pence, at approximately a gram each, so each rower would receive a little over twenty-eight ounces of silver, and the steersmen over forty-two.

There was a mint and two moneyers in Worcester (*Weogornaceaster*, "Camp of the Weogorans," the "People of the Winding River"), making it a prime source of revenue. Its citizens were first to revolt. In May 1041 two royal tax collectors were forced to seek refuge in the town priory, to no avail. The citizens chased them to the top of the church tower, and there murdered them.

Harthacnut, in the manner of bloody-handed Viking kings of old, determined to make an example of the city. He ordered it to be *harried*, from the Old English *hergian*, to lay waste, to ravage, to devastate.

The monks of Worcester compiled their histories in probably the same abbey where the royal tax collectors were slain, and only a few decades later, so that they very likely knew citizens who took part in the revolt. As they told it, to avenge the deaths of two housecarls the king sent practically the entire English army, including the earls Godwin of Wessex, Leofric of Mercia, Siward of Northumbria and the rest, with all their men, "with orders to kill everyone they could find, plunder and burn the city, and lay waste the entire province."

It was not until November, however, that such a massive army could be assembled to march on the town, a hundred miles northwest of London. Worcester commanded a ford over the then-tidal River Severn. It had been fortified since Roman times with an earthen bank, and later, as one of King Alfred's *burhs*, with a wall of red sandstone blocks, bastions and a water-filled moat. As the earls topped the steep hill where the London road began its descent toward the riverbank town, they doubtless expected to lay siege. They would have instead been astonished to find the city walls deserted, the gates open, the streets, markets, churches and even the homes empty. The entire populace, on news of the army's approach, had vacated the town and scattered into the surrounding countryside.

Nevertheless, the earls carried out their orders. They looted Worcester of everything worth carrying and burned the rest to the ground. Meanwhile they discovered the whereabouts of many of the townsfolk. They had taken refuge on Beverege Island (modern Bevere), about three miles upriver. Possibly they threw themselves on the earls' mercy; technically, Worcester no longer had any inhabitants to slaughter. The earls judged the town's sack to be sufficient punishment. The monks wrote, "On the fifth day, with the city burnt, everyone marched off loaded with loot, and the king's anger was sated."

That did little, however, to improve their view of King Harthacnut: "During his reign he did nothing worthy of royalty.... He became thoroughly hated by those who at first were most eager for his arrival," and Wendover agreed: "He made himself odious to everyone who had once hailed him as king."

"Meanwhile," wrote Jumièges, "Duke William grew, by the favor of God, in age, strength, and wisdom."

"William grew up strong," agreed Wace. "He heard many tales which broke his heart, but at the time he could do nothing about it. The barons fought among themselves and in spite of him refused to stop."

Having (barely) survived his first years as duke, and as a result of the violent deaths of his various guardians, William of Normandy was forced to take charge of his own destiny. As Jumièges put it, "Considering how much the Normans had, in acting out their fury, devastated the entire land, he drew from his heart, still a boy, a man's determination. Recalling his father's greatness, he applied himself to win them to his side, demonstrating by his prayers and his command how to avoid every untoward act."

A new generation of Norman leaders accrued to him: William fitzOsbern, bastard son of the late Steward Osbern, Roger "the Bearded" de Beaumont, even Roger de Montgomery, the Great, son of the exiled *seigneur* and brother of Osbern's killer. William bestowed his cousin and friend Guy of Burgundy with Brionne, on the Risle River, and Vernon on the Seine, the dominion of the late Count Gilbert. He even talked over to his side Ralf de Gacé, son of the late Archbishop Robert, said to have masterminded Gilbert's murder. That William could win over these nobles, who rightfully should have been calling for each other's blood, shows a hard-earned level of diplomacy and command beyond his years.

Unfortunately, his diplomacy and command could not unite all the feuding barons. In 1042 he, or more properly those nobles loyal to him, managed to call the rest together to at least consider adhering to the Truce of God. The Truce movement had been gaining influence in the south, and now extended beyond Sundays to include the days commemorating Christianity's great mysteries: Thursday (the Ascension), Friday (the Passion), and Saturday (the Resurrection), plus the holy days of Advent and Lent, and the feasts and vigils of the Blessed Virgin and the twelve apostles and selected saints. One would think limiting war, outlawry and predation to the typical Monday, Tuesday and Wednesday would give the bickering warlords the better part of the workweek off in which to refresh and rearm, but they were not yet ready for such a radical idea, and declined to abide by the Truce. "Some people preferred to enjoy their usual liberties," shrugged Poitiers, "keeping tight grip on their own holdings and seizing others' at their whim."

Whatever Duke William required of his vassals, he would have to make them do by force. Years later he was said to describe them thus: "If the Normans are checked by a just and firm hand they are capable of great valor, achieve the most difficult tasks and, demonstrating their worth, strive to defeat all foes. But without such guidance they tear each other to shreds and destroy themselves, for they lust after rebellion, love sedition, and indulge willingly in treachery."

Harthacnut had already learned much the same of his new subjects. He had used the stick; now it was time for the carrot. For the king was not only willing to defile and destroy in the Viking manner; he was willing to revel like a Viking too.

Henry of Huntingdon wrote: "He was of childlike enthusiasm, and treated his followers with generosity born of naivete. Such were his spendthrift ways that tables were spread four times a day with royal lavishness for his entire court, and leftovers were to be thrown away after the diners were sated, rather than retained for the uninvited."

When such fine repast was far beyond the reach of his average subject, Harthacnut set an example that Marie Antoinette, centuries later, would be hard-pressed to follow. Huntingdon would later sniff, "In our time it is the convention, whether from cheapness, or as they claim, frugality, for rulers to provide only one meal a day at court."

183

Meanwhile Harthacnut's half-brother Edward Aetheling was reaching the pit of despair, almost totally alone. "A proper death had taken his father, a hostile death brothers," wrote his biographer Aelred of Rievaulx. "He was an exiled patrician of royal honor, living bereft of help, full of terror. He feared traps, doubting both friends and enemies."

His mother was queen again in England, and her son by a man other than Edward's father was sitting on the throne that was rightfully Edward's. His kinsman William was too busy battling his own barons to ensure his safety. He knew too well that he was constantly watched by both English and Norman spies, and that any moment he might be kidnapped and held for ransom, or worse. His only comfort came from his priest, Robert Champart, the abbot of Jumièges Abbey, who had become one of his closest advisors. If there was ever a time for Edward Aetheling to place his trust in God's hands, this was it. He is said to have vowed to St. Peter that if returned to England he would make a pilgrimage to Rome, where the saint had been martyred.

And Peter answered. A letter arrived from England.

The last time Edward had received such a letter, it had come from his mother. He and his brother had obeyed it, as a result of which Alfred had died, and Edward had given up any hope of ever seeing England again.

This letter was not from Emma. It was wax-sealed with an emblem even Edward, across the sea, recognized: the seal of the *witan*, the noble leadership of England.

He was being summoned home.

It's interesting to compare the accounts of the *Vita Aedwardi Regis*, written on Edward's behalf, and the *Encomium*, his mother Emma's account, for their take on his return to England. The Encomiast wrote of Harthacnut, "Given recent events, he arranged all his affairs in a moment of peace, and in the sway of brotherly love, sent messengers to Edward requesting him to come rule the kingdom at his side."

That's putting a rosy spin on the Waster of Worcester. Yet, having demonstrated himself willing to crush all resistance in the merciless Viking manner of his grandfather Forkbeard, perhaps Harthacnut had taken another lesson, from his half-brother Harefoot: that it was best to have any pretenders to his throne close at hand, rather than plotting against him across the sea. Then again, he may have been busy enjoying himself at court, carousing and debauching, and simply preferred to leave the hard work of actual ruling to his stern, monastical, elder half-brother.

It's Edward's *Vita* that has the letter coming from the *witan*, and specifically from Earl Godwin, who "urged most strongly that they should welcome their king to the throne that was his birthright. And as everyone regarded Godwin like a father, his opinion carried weight in the *witenagemot*."

Taken at face value, this is even harder to understand. The only reason Godwin would want, let alone encourage, Edward's return was as an appeasement – or offset – to Queen Emma, who had good reason to distrust the Earl of Wessex and even see him harm. Whether she was for or against Edward's return we can't know without knowing her true feelings for her eldest. The only evidence we have of that is inconclusive: that in their mutual hour of need, when they met in Flanders, she and Edward had failed to reconcile.

It's also important to recall, however, that the author of the *Vita* is thought to have been sponsored by Gytha, daughter of Earl Godwin. It wasn't just Harthacnut and Edward being propagandized here.

That said, the various versions of the *Chronicle*, which might be taken as neutral in this case, have Edward arriving early in 1041, residing in Harthacnut's court, and even being designated as his royal heir. Neither man had children, or so much as a woman of note. (Or a male favorite for that matter, though any such might have gone unspoken.) Given that Svein and Harefoot had both died young – and Alfred too, though not by natural causes – Harthacnut was thinking not only of his future, but the realm's.

By naming Edward as his heir, though, Harthacnut reneged on his agreement with Magnus of Denmark: that, lacking children, whichever of them died first would inherit the other's kingdom. It may be that, as an autocratic Viking ruler in Denmark, he had not realized that in England such a decision was rightfully the *witan*'s, but once King of England he should have known better. This would not be the last time an English king promised his throne to more than one man, but it may be how Edward learned the trick.

There was, however, an unforeseen complication to Edward's return. He came as a package deal. After his last experience in England, he had no intention of returning alone, and if he was to serve as co-king, he needed his own court. The *Vita* records, "When King Edward of holy memory returned from France, quite a few men of that nation, and they of noble birth, accompanied him. And as master of the whole kingdom, he kept them with him, enriched them with many honors, and made them his personal advisors and administrators of the royal palace."

Lacking written evidence of their presence at this time – signed documents and the like – we must take the contemporary chroniclers at their word that these Norman arrived with Edward. They might equally have arrived later, but it stands to reason that, even if they weren't yet of such status as to sign papers, Edward would want his closest friends and advisors with him. They included his sister Goda's son, Ralf of Mantes, but foremost among them was Edward's priest, Robert, abbot of Jumièges. As shall be seen, Robert had his own agenda, and was no proponent of either Emma or Godwin.

But that was in the future. In one of his last passages, Emma's Encomiast painted a glad picture: "Here there is loyalty between sharing kings, here the bond of motherly and brotherly love is indestructible. All this were granted by Him, who causes dwellers in a house to be of one mind."

Having failed to convince his barons of the benefits of peace, Duke William resolved to show them the detriments of war.

He began with his birthplace, Falaise. The *vicomte* Thorstein le Goz held it by virtue of the manpower, and possibly the blessing, of Henry, King of France. For William that would not do. Jumièges recorded, "As soon as he heard of this malevolent man's intentions, the duke assembled the legions of Normandy on all sides, and laid siege to the castle."

Ralf de Gacé, having been granted by William some of the authority he desired – and perhaps thinking himself in charge of the dukedom by having taken charge of the duke – now led the Norman knights in William's name. Their attack was so fierce that they managed to pull down a section of the castle wall (again, at this time probably not stone, but a wooden palisade at the top of the hill, which some grappling hooks and heavy medieval horses might have uprooted). Only nightfall prevented a general slaughter. Thorstein, looking down from his tower keep upon the broken wall and the newly united Normans preparing to kill him in the morning, abandoned his claim. Wace recorded, "He requested permission to leave the castle and was granted truce to depart."

The former *vicomte* fled, like his predecessor Montgomery, into exile in France. In a display of political suavity that William would display throughout his life, he granted the town and castle to Thorstein's son, Richard le Goz. Richard would go on to marry the duke's half-sister Emma, and in gratitude faithfully serve him for the rest of his life.

William de Montgomery, son of the (previous) exiled *vicomte* of Falaise, brother of the duke's lieutenant Robert and murderer of Osbern the Steward, met a less generous fate. Jumièges decreed, "William was not long in receiving from God the just retribution for the crime he had committed." That, however, was not Duke William's doing. One Bjarni of Glos-la-Ferrière, formerly Osbern's vassal, avenged his lord's death in most appropriate fashion, by assembling a number of like-minded accomplices, breaking into Montgomery's house at night while he slept, and murdering him and all his men. Around this same time another rebel paid the fatal price. The Moor Eater, Roger of Tosny, had been waging a private war on his neighbors for control of the Risle River valley when Roger the Bearded brought him to battle and slew him and his eldest sons in the bargain.

Notably, William did not himself lead in these victories. He was still only about twelve or thirteen, by Norman standards not yet a man. He was growing up fast, though – a fact both friends and foes would soon be forced to recognize.

———

Edward was in England at most only a few months when Harthacnut died. It was sudden and without warning, at a wedding feast in Lambeth, now a borough of London but then called *Lambehitha*, the "landing place of lambs," where sheep were loaded for shipping up or down the Thames. The bride was Gytha, daughter of Osgod

Clapa, Osgod the Rough, "a man of great wealth," according to Worcester. Her new husband was Tovi Pruda, Tovi the Prudent, but usually translated as Tovi the Proud. Worcester called him "a noble and powerful Dane." (All three are worth mention, as their names will appear again later in our tale.) Actually both men were Danes. Each had served as a *staller*, a high official of the court, going back to Cnut's days, and Osgod was, if not in title, in practice the earl of East Anglia. They had likely known Harthacnut since he was a boy, and the wedding of one's daughter to the other – old Tovi was gaining a much younger wife – was an occasion for fellow Vikings to reminisce about the old days and, as the drink flowed, celebrate their final, total domination of Anglo-Saxon England. (Osgod, for one, had even been opposed to the succession of Edward.) Worcester described Harthacnut as "carousing, full of health and good cheer, with the bride and the rest."

"As he stood drinking," records the *Chronicle*, "he suddenly fell down in a tremendous convulsion. Those nearby helped him up, but after that he spoke not a word."

An optimist might guess the king had suffered a stroke. A pessimist would suspect he had been poisoned. Nobody at the time made any accusations, but somebody certainly stood to gain. Whether Emma and Edward were present at the event is unrecorded, much less their reactions to the king's plight. Both had Danish blood, and given their positions both would probably have attended a marriage of wealthy, powerful Danes – leading citizens of the royal court – just to maintain appearances. Or alibis.

There is an alternate explanation, however – admittedly farfetched, but rumored back in the day and so worth mentioning now. The *Morkinskinna* (Moldy Parchment), a saga of Scandinavian kings compiled in Iceland around AD 1220, tells the story of Harthacnut's fate quite differently. It claims that during their peace negotiations King Magnus of Norway visited him in Denmark. They were served by none other than Alfifa – Aelfgifu of Northampton – then not yet a foe of both kings. According to the story, she poured wine for Magnus first, as guest, but he insisted that Harthacnut, as host, take precedence. "So she gave the horn to Harthacnut and he drank from it, crying, as he cast the horn aside, 'shouldn't have,' but he got no further and gave his death rattle. This was proof of Alfifa's treachery toward King Magnus because she intended him to take the fatal drink. But she vanished so instantly she could not be prosecuted."

The story has so many holes – the date, the location, the attendees – that it can be discounted almost completely. Almost. After a thousand years even rumors of the time are worth examining. If we indulge ourselves, crediting Aelfgifu of Northampton, as Saxo Grammaticus did, with a premarital affair with a young Olaf Haraldsson in 1010, then it's at least an entertaining flight of fancy to imagine she perhaps had not fled England in 1040, but had gone into hiding or simply returned in 1042 to strike one last blow at her enemies. She certainly couldn't have served anyone at the wedding personally; as former queen mother, on setting foot inside she would have been recognized. But might she have found or placed someone in the kitchen or wine cellar still loyal to her and Harefoot? There was nobody attending the wedding feast who was a friend of Aelfgifu; as far as she was concerned, they could all die. And the venue was right on the banks of the Thames, offering a quick escape route. Once she was across the Channel, her story might have been repeated across Scandinavia and even Iceland, the facts getting mangled as it went, even while the tale remained unknown to English chroniclers. It's highly unlikely, but not impossible.

If we can be sure of anything, it's that Queen Emma and Edward Aetheling – soon now to be Edward, King of England – did not partake of the wine at that particular wedding.

XV

Their Just Rewards

1042–1043

At last a happiest day dawned magnificently for all who wished and eagerly awaited peace and justice. Our duke, more mature in his grasp of honor and in bodily strength than his age warranted, was armed as a knight.

Poitiers

The awarding of arms was a Northern European warrior tradition going back a thousand years. As early as the dawn of the first millennium the Roman historian Publius Cornelius Tacitus wrote of the Germanic tribes, "Before the council one of the chieftains, or the young man's father, or some relative, bestows on him a shield and a spear. These weapons are what the 'toga' is to us, the first honor awarded youth." The Germans passed this tradition down to the Franks, and the Franks to the Normans, which is how, as liege, King Henry I of France came to bestow his vassal Duke William of Normandy with the arms of manhood.

The year is uncertain – Norman chroniclers had some sort of aversion to exact dates – but most historians settle on 1042. That William was only fourteen or fifteen that year should not put anyone off the idea of him becoming a man. The more rigid feudal system of turning boys into warriors – page at age seven, squire at fourteen, knight at twenty-one – would not develop until the higher

Middle Ages. The very idea of knights and knighthood was only just beginning to take hold. The French and Normans and even Anglo-Saxons, like the Vikings before them, took a much looser view of manhood rites. According to Malmesbury, Alfred the Great himself invested his grandson Aethelstan, still only a child, with "a red cloak, a diamond-studded belt, and a *seax* with a gold scabbard." Recall too the Viking lads who first embarked on their raids and slew their first men when not yet in their teens, and how Olaf the Stout was called king by his men when still only a landless boy.

The details of the ceremony in this time probably varied among peoples and are not well documented. It was likely not yet the *accolade*, the *adoubement* or dubbing as in later medieval times, imbued with religious ritual and climaxed by the touching of sword to shoulder or even a slap to the cheek. Being "armed as a knight" would seem to imply the aspirant would wear, or don, or be awarded, garb fit for a warrior: a suit of mail, shield and helm, sword and spear. Much of this was fantastically expensive – a mail hauberk might require a thousand man-hours to manufacture – and may have been handed down from father to son as far back as the Normans' Viking ancestors, for much of it was unchanged since those days. The centerpiece of the ceremony, though, the *raison d'être*, was the *taking of the sword*, the *girding with the sword*, the *tying on of the sword*. Armed with a sword, a boy became a man, ready at last to conquer those who defied him.

William of Poitiers, born in Normandy about 1020 and in 1042 a soldier, apparently in the ranks loyal to the duke, described the service as though he attended it: "It was a sight both gladdening and awe-inspiring to see him take the reins, girded honorably with his sword, his shield gleaming, impressive with his helmet and spear. For striking as he was in looks when clothed as a peaceful prince, wearing armor against enemies suited him perfectly."

Jumièges described the moment as a turning point: "The duke, shining with all the splendor of the finest youth, began to devote himself with all his heart to the service of God, avoiding the company of ignorant men, taking the advice of the wise, mighty in the art of war, and endowed with great wisdom for the affairs of the time."

Harthacnut lingered until June 8. "He was king of all England ten days short of two years," records the *Chronicle*, "and he is buried in the Old Minster at Winchester with King Cnut his father."

Harthacnut's pact with Magnus of Norway – that if either he or Harthacnut died childless, the other would succeed to his kingdom – was not worth the parchment it was written on, as far as the *witan* was concerned. The nobles had made no such agreement. Harthacnut had arguably not been King of England when he made it, and at any rate no longer had a say. To claim England, Magnus would have to come through Denmark, for on news of Harthacnut's death, Jarl Svein Estridsson had likewise decided he was not bound by any agreements, and declared himself King of the Danes. Cnut's North Sea Empire had fallen apart, and there were no more sons of his to put the pieces back together.

Or were there?

Godwin's eldest, Sweyn and Harold, had reached their twenties. By that age their father had already become an earl and married, perhaps for the second time. They must have been eager to step out from his shadow and claim renown of their own. Sweyn, perhaps, a little too eager. The rash eldest son, most like his father, is widely held to be his favorite as well, whereas circumspect Harold, more like his mother Gytha, was hers, though that might have been Sweyn's own fault.

The *Liber Wigorniensis* (Book of Worcestershire) is a record of rents and charters compiled by the monks of Worcester Abbey (though probably a generation prior to our chroniclers John and Florence). Judging by the handwriting, five scribes recorded the various transactions. Most date from the 10th century, but some cover the 11th and even 12th. The earliest known such record in medieval English history, it was likely used as evidence against the losses of property at the hands of noblemen, including Eadric Streona and even King Cnut, in the lawsuits to regain said properties. Sweyn Godwinson would eventually make the list, and the monks went to some effort to disparage his reputation: "He was so devoted to vainglory, so lazy, so driven with pride, that unfortunately he would deny being the son of Earl Godwin in every way. He pretended to be of the race of Cnut, the most vigorous king, and that he was his father, and falsely testified that he was born of no other."

The date of this incident is not recorded in the cartulary, but there would be no better time to make such a claim than while Harthacnut lay dying, and before the *witan* designated his successor.

The monks do not say that Sweyn accused his mother Gytha of adultery, of cuckolding his father with her brother-in-law King Cnut. The implication is that back in 1019 Cnut had lain with Gytha, sister of Earl Ulf, when she was still unmarried, and got her pregnant.

This in itself did not need to become a scandal, especially for a king or even the girl, if the noble did the right thing and took responsibility for the deed, as Duke Robert of Normandy had done by Herleva of Falaise in acknowledging their son, the future Duke William. If Sweyn Godwinson's accusation was true, Cnut (who already had two wives by that time) had only taken responsibility to the extent of pawning his lover, and his unborn son, off on another man: his new young earl, Godwin of Wessex. Whether Godwin entered the arrangement in full knowledge or ignorance, the truth – if indeed there was any truth in it – might have eventually come out, only to become a family secret. That is, until Sweyn decided to claim his birthright. It could have been – indeed probably was – an out-and-out lie. Certainly the rest of Sweyn's family certainly treated it as such.

For her part his mother Countess Gytha vehemently denied everything, and convened a party of her peers, noblewomen of Wessex, to vouch for her. This sounds like a *compurgatio*, a "making clean," a trial by oath, a very legal process in those days by which a defendant swore an oath of innocence, and a sufficient number of respected witnesses, typically twelve, likewise swore their belief in it. (It would form the basis of the modern jury system.) In essence, according to the chartulary, Gytha "swore with great oaths that she was his mother and that Godwin was his father, and that evidence proved it."

If that was not enough for the *witan*, also going against Sweyn's claim was that, even if he spoke the truth, Cnut had never acknowledged him as his son. Sweyn might be a bastard, but could never be *The Bastard* in the manner of William of Normandy. His claim to Cnut's throne was dropped, not worth bringing up even in the *Chronicle*, which was followed by most subsequent medieval historians. We can give the monks of Worcester the benefit of the doubt in that they would not have made up such a story, but since the wasting of their town they harbored a grudge against the earls and may have willingly repeated a vicious rumor. Even a rumor, though, coming from one of their own, would have shaken the family of Earl Godwin to the core. Sweyn had shamed them and made himself look foolish, all in one stroke. Little brother Harold in particular, not even expecting an earldom for himself, must have been shocked to see what Sweyn – raised to command – was willing to do, and to sacrifice, to attain the kingdom. Having heard his parents swear to it, he had to believe the story could not be true.

Recall, though, that it hadn't been long after the wedding of Earl Godwin and Gytha Thorgilsdottir that her brother, guardian and Godwin's patron, Earl Ulf, had suddenly developed an abiding hatred of his brother-in-law King Cnut.

Even ruling out Sweyn, for the *witan*, including the many Danish nobles among them, Edward could only have been a default choice to rule, not a popular one. He was, after all, the son of one of the worst kings in memory, and after all his time in exile practically a foreigner, more Norman than English. The various earls and bishops must have been shouting each other down across the meeting chamber. Any one of them might lay claim to the throne by sheer right of might, and then what?

For his part Edward was probably chewing his nails off, awaiting the *witan*'s decision. Yes, he had been designated heir by Harthacnut, but Harthacnut was dead. Edward might count himself lucky, as with his last venture to England, to get off the island with his head still attached. To survive, much less attain the crown, meant recognizing certain political realities. As Jumièges asserted, "At this time, the proud and clever Godwin was the most powerful earl in England, and vigorously occupied a great part of that kingdom, which he had conquered either through the nobility of his family, or force, or his own perfidy."

According to Malmesbury, Edward swallowed his enmity for his brother's killer. He arranged a meeting with Godwin, at which he begged the earl's help in returning to Normandy before he met the same fate as Harthacnut.

Godwin, the story goes, took full advantage. Better for a son of Aethelred to rule England, he told Edward, than to die exiled and forgotten. The crown was Edward's by right of birth. He ruled England in name already. All he needed was proper backing.

In effect Godwin offered Edward the crown, but at a price. The power behind the throne would remain Godwin's. His sons were to have their share of it in perpetuity. According to the *Chronicle*, there was virtually no debate. Harthacnut was dead, and the country needed a king. "Before he was in the ground, all the people chose Edward for king."

With Harthacnut's death, the long line of claimants to the throne of Aethelred ahead of Edward, both foreign and domestic, from Forkbeard and Cnut and their dozen sons starting with Aethelstan Aetheling and including Ironside's exiled sons Edward and Edmund, had finally been removed from contention. God had swept the board clean. Edward was the last man standing, the culmination of the line of Anglo-Saxon kings, the sons of Wessex, going back almost a hundred and fifty years to Alfred the Great and beyond. The coronation ceremony could come later, after suitable arrangements were made, dignitaries invited, nobles assembled and fealties declared. That was all mere formality. Edward son of Aethelred was King of England.

The *Chronicle* exalts, "May he hold it the while that God shall grant it to him!"

PART TWO

THE ANGLO-SAXONS

AD 1042–1065

When I gained the love of strangers and a fine home,
Love returned nothing but sorrow, as I have now proved.
Still it is best, when a man cannot change his fate,
that he endures it well.

"The Exile's Prayer"
Anglo-Saxon, late 9th/early 10th century

XVI

EDWARD REX

1042–1045

All that year the season was in numerous ways very severe, both from the inclement weather, and the loss of crops. More cattle died this year than any man could remember, either from various diseases, or from the severe weather.

Anglo-Saxon Chronicle

King Edward's reign did not get off to an easy start. At home, all that prevented famine was the surplus of dead livestock. Across the North Sea, Magnus of Norway had chased the upstart earl-turned-king, Svein of Denmark, out of the country to Sweden (though not for the last time). While there was a lull in the fighting, Magnus took time to pen a letter to England, politely inquiring whether Edward intended to honor Harthacnut's pact: "As a result of this agreement, I now rightfully own England as well. It is my will, therefore, that you hand over the kingdom. Otherwise I will invade, from both Denmark and Norway, and whomever fate gives victory may rule the land."

Edward had to take the threat seriously. The Danes had conquered the English more than once, and Norway was a much bigger country than Denmark. If the Norwegians could conquer the Danes in turn, they would constitute an even bigger threat to England.

But Svein Estridsson was running interference for Edward. He had been neither captured nor killed, and while he lived Magnus could not afford to turn his back on Denmark. And possibly under the influence of Earl Godwin, that most Viking of Anglo-Saxons, the English army was no longer a bunch of pushovers – in fact, it was said that one English housecarl was worth any two Vikings. To his credit, Edward replied in the same manner Magnus's father Olaf had replied to Cnut over who should rule his kingdom: like a king. "I will not renounce my title while I live…. He shall only get to take England when he has taken my life."

Brave words from one who reigned only by his earls' permission. Godwin of Wessex was nearly as big an impediment to Edward's reign as Svein was to Magnus's. Godwin had taken the enemy's side in the past, and if Magnus invaded there was every expectation he might do so again. Edward had made a deal with the devil and, having gotten what he wanted, was evidently intent on extricating himself from the rest.

He had used the months since assuming his title to shore up his support among the other earls, many of whom resented Wessex's power. In the past, united in opposition, they had been able to overrule Godwin, as when they chose Harefoot as king. With their support, Edward could not only renege on his deal with Godwin; he might disavow him and his sons, for someone still had to pay for the murder of his brother Alfred.

Edward's *Vita*, written in hindsight, makes nothing of the charge, sweeping it under the carpet. A hundred years later, Geoffrey Gaimar told a different tale. According to him, Godwin was not going to let Edward wriggle out of their agreement so easily. He has the earl sailing his fleet up the Thames, making a show of force before making his case to the king. He awards lavish gifts to the other nobles of the *witan* to encourage their support, hoping things will come to nothing more than compurgation, a trial by oath. Feeling sure of himself, Godwin pledges to accept the king's judgment.

Edward is not inclined to mercy. "The king himself rose," wrote Gaimar. "He angrily accused him, saying that his brother died because of him, that he betrayed him like a felon and robber, and if he declared himself innocent of all that, he must prove it."

"I totally deny what you have said," declared the earl. "Word by word I deny it. I give you my oath. I demand a trial, let a trial be granted. Between your accusations and my answer, let all these barons declare what is right."

In those days the *witan* comprised twelve earls, plus the various *thegns* and clergy, more than enough for compurgation. The most powerful among them, earls Siward of Northumbria and Leofric of Mercia, were not great friends of Godwin, no matter how grand his gifts. They must have seen his fleet, his fighting men, tied up at the London docks, and knew the choice it implied. Nobody wanted another civil war in England. Yet they had to be just as wary of giving King Edward too much power. Being a son of the notorious King Aethelred, he might soon acquire a taste for it, in which case they would need Godwin as a counterweight. Edward himself, a virtual stranger in his own court with few friends to back him, could hardly expect to overrule a *witenagemot* by decree. "But they held their peace," recorded Gaimar. "None moved until the king ordered that they should pronounce judgment."

Siward the Stout was a kinsman of old Earl Ulf, and so of Ulf's sister Gytha, Godwin's wife. He might have been expected to take Wessex's side, but his support is lukewarm. "He makes bold denials to the king," he said of Godwin. "He might receive the benefit of the doubt, but he denies felony, treason and perfidy. From these a man should defend himself and accept judgment. A king's accusation is serious. It will come to trial, I wager, by fire, or by water, or by battle. One of these three will not fail."*

Then Leofric has his say. "This is nothing to do with battle. An oath is not sufficient, nor fire, nor water, nor ordeal. We will not judge in such manner. He who wishes to bring another to the iron or make him float in water should require an eyewitness. Let us make a decision without such a trial, together."

He suggests that Godwin outfit himself, his sons, his kin and their men, to the number of sixty, with the finest arms and armor – hauberks, helms and shields trimmed in gold as befit a royal bodyguard – then give it all to the king, along with oaths of loyalty and hostages to guarantee it.

If true – and though Gaimar doubtless supplied the dialogue, the logic is entirely reasonable – this was clever politicking on Leofric's part. If Godwin failed to win a trial of whatever sort and was

---

*Here Gaimar dates himself a bit. Trial by combat was not an option under Anglo-Saxon law.

removed, there would be nothing keeping his troublesome son Sweyn from making a play, not just for Wessex, but for the kingdom itself. Edward's only real power at court were the few Normans he had brought with him, but fighting men could always be found to wear Godwin's fine armor and carry those arms on behalf of the king. In effect, this restitution would supply Edward with his own housecarls, his own personal security team – protection from the earl who had as good as slain his brother, and at Godwin's own expense, too. From Leofric's view it had the added appeal of weakening a rival at court. Earl Godwin must have gritted his teeth at the idea, but after all it was basically how he'd bought off Harthacnut's anger, and for the same offense. It was cheaper than going to war.

"To this all agreed," wrote Gaimar. The *Vita* claims Godwin gifted Edward a magnificent warship capable of carrying 120 warriors, its prow in the form of a golden dragon and its sternpost a golden lion, with a purple sail embroidered with the sea battles of English kings.

And that should have been the end of it.

On Easter Sunday of 1043 Edward was crowned at Winchester. After Holy Communion, hymns were sung, and the king prostrated himself before the altar as a gesture of submission. Amid suitable prayers, he made the Threefold Promise to his subjects:

> In the name of the Holy Trinity, I vow three things to my Christian subjects. First, that God's church and all Christians in my kingdom preserve true peace. Second, I forbid robbery and all unrighteous acts to all. Third, I promise and order justice and mercy in all judgements, in order that the kind and merciful God may grant us all his eternal mercy, who lives and reigns.

Then came the anointing with consecrated oil, accompanied by its own special prayer, in part, "May your most sacred unction flow upon his head, descending inwards and penetrating the most secret parts of his heart."

Now a king in the eyes of God and man, Edward was seated on his throne and invested with the royal regalia: the signet ring, as the seal of the kingdom; the sword, its might; the crown, its justice; the scepter, its righteousness and strength; and the rod, its virtue and equity.* The attendants then acclaimed their new monarch: *Vivat rex feliciter in sempiternum!* "May the king live happily for eternity!"

For a queen there would then have come a separate, simpler benediction, prostration, anointing and investiture. In 1043 that was not necessary, as Edward had no queen, yet.

But England did. A dowager queen: Emma of Normandy.

She would have been present, of course, for her firstborn's coronation, and happy, one would think, to finally be rid of her arch foe Aelfgifu of Northampton and have a son sitting uncontested on the throne of England. Yet Malmesbury accused her of "transferring her ingrained hatred of the father to the son, for she had both loved Cnut more in life, and honored him more in death."

The ghost of Edward's father Aethelred still haunted them both. Perhaps Emma still saw the *Unraed* in her son. And Edward would have known how Aethelred's reign had suffered under his own mother Aelfthryth's interference.

He would not repeat that mistake.

———

There is an old English expression, "to give a Roland for an Oliver," referring to two of the main characters of *La Chanson de Roland*, "The Song of Roland," about the Battle of Roncesvaux Pass in AD 778 between the Moors (actually the Basques) and the forces of Charlemagne. One of the first chivalric romances, the Song is thought to have been first composed in France around AD 1040, and may have already become known in England. Since then, "to give a Roland for an Oliver" has come to mean a *quid pro quo*, an exchange of equal values, like the exchange that now took place between King Edward and Earl Godwin.

It began with Godwin's son Sweyn, the very same who had sought the crown for himself. Apparently he had reconciled to some extent

---

*Today's other symbols – spurs, bracelets, orb – were incorporated later, separately, over ensuing centuries.

with his parents, but it would not do to have him lurking about the court, probably with an entourage of like-minded young malcontents. If he didn't get what he felt was his right, he and they might try to take it.

The solution was to give him what he wanted, or at least a small taste of it: power. He was to be made an earl. In theory this made him an equal with his father Godwin, Leofric of Mercia and Siward of Northumbria. In practice, there were great earldoms and those not so great. Sweyn's was the latter.

He would be lord of five shires: Gloucestershire, Herefordshire, Somerset, Oxfordshire and Berkshire. Together they made up a not inconsequential dominion. Berkshire, in the east, ran right up to the banks of the Thames and included a royal manor, later to become Windsor Castle. And Oxfordshire, just across the river, was where the *witan* frequently met, King Edward had been born, and Harefoot had been chosen as king. To the west, however, Sweyn's earldom bordered on Wales.

King Gruffydd ap Llewelyn – Griffin son of Llewelyn – of Gwynedd and Powys (roughly, northern Wales) was no friend of the English. Or the Irish. Or even other Welsh. His own wife was the widow of one of his rivals. The Welsh *Brut y Tywysogion*, "The Chronicle of the Princes," boasts only a bit when it proclaims, "He, from start to finish, pursued the Saxons and other nations, killed and destroyed them, and vanquished them in many battles." While laboring to conquer the rest of Wales, Gruffydd sometimes took time out to rampage over Offa's Dyke, the 150-mile-long earthwork wall the Mercians had built in the latter half of the 8th century to keep the Welsh out. It was his army who had surprised, defeated and killed Earl Leofric's brother Edwin in battle in 1039.

Now Gruffydd was to be Earl Sweyn's problem. And Sweyn's earldom, pinched between Wessex and Mercia, could be held in check by his father and Earl Leofric. Sweyn would be kept too busy for designs on the throne. Getting him settled into his new earldom may be why the king and his earls were in Gloucestershire later that year, when the time came for the next Roland for an Oliver.

"And this year, two weeks before St. Andrew's Mass," records the *Chronicle*, meaning November 16, "the king was advised to ride out of Gloucester, with Earl Leofric, Earl Godwin, Earl Siward and their followers, to Winchester, to surprise the Lady."

Recall that "Lady," *Hlæfdige*, was the Anglo-Saxon term for queen. In England in early 1043 there was only one such: Emma, *mater regis*, the king's mother. In Winchester she probably resided at Goudbeyete Manor, the estate bequeathed to her by Aethelred twenty-one years earlier. It was to be her retirement home. Now about sixty years old, she could have lived out her remaining years in peace and luxury, but apparently she could not resist meddling in politics. From Gloucester to Winchester is near ninety miles, a two- or three-day ride. For Edward, his three most powerful earls and their housecarls – a small army – to make such a trip in order to surprise the queen indicates they had more than well wishes in mind. "The king was advised," as stated in the *Chronicle*, would seem to imply that someone had convinced Edward that his mother was up to no good.

It may have been the king's Norman bishop, Robert of Jumièges, who on arrival in England found himself going up against the queen mother's priest, Bishop Stigand. Stigand had been Cnut's chaplain and advisor as far back as 1020, and had served both Harefoot and Harthacnut, and now Emma, in the same capacity. His Scandinavian name implies that he was one of the last Danes left in high position, and may have owed that position to the queen. On his coronation day, as the first episcopal appointment of his reign, Edward had relegated Stigand to the relatively poor diocese of Elmham in East Anglia. Stigand could only have looked on this as a demotion, and resented his replacement as royal chaplain by Bishop Robert, who may in turn have looked suspiciously on this survivor of the old regimes, and by association the queen.

Then again, the informant may well have been Earl Godwin. For him to be reconciled with Edward would have given Emma all the more reason to resent him, not only for Alfred's death and her exile to Flanders, but for not making the kind of restitution to her that he had made to the king. And she was Norman, yet the one most estranged from those in Edward's court, estranged and powerless. Reason enough for Godwin, as the most powerful Anglo-Saxon in the land, to see her removed.

The charges against Emma were almost certainly trumped up, and ignored by the *Chronicle* – too unbelievable – or simply hushed up. For the inside story we have to turn to other sources, not above such gossip. The Flemish-born monk Goscelin of Canterbury, who was born about 1040, moved to England before the Conquest and wrote about Emma's disgrace years after the fact. According to him she was an embezzler.

The royal treasury – gold, silver, jewels, saintly relics – had traditionally accompanied Anglo-Saxon kings on their travels, the better to keep it from becoming a stationary target for Viking raiders. With Magnus of Norway and Svein of Denmark busily occupied with warring on each other, the Viking threat had subsided. Now the treasury resided at Winchester, rather conveniently for the queen. Malmesbury snorted, "Stockpiling riches however she could, she had hoarded it, caring not for the poor, to whom she gave nothing lest it diminish her wealth."

The hoard had been commandeered by Harefoot upon Emma's exile in 1037, but replenished by Harthacnut's heavy taxation. Embezzlement was difficult to prove in those days – accounting and record-keeping was more a Norman thing – but nobody needed to prove anything, only insinuate it. Goscelin claimed Emma had pilfered funds to help finance an invasion by none other than Magnus of Norway.

It sounds ludicrous on its face. Magnus was a Norwegian, the son of Cnut's old enemy Olaf the Stout. Why would Emma favor him when there was the Dane, Svein, son of Earl Ulf, right across the water, still battling Magnus in the name of her late son Harthacnut? Svein had a claim to the English throne himself, by blood. After all, he was Cnut's nephew, and Emma's as well, by marriage...but Earl Godwin's too. Who could say whose side he would take if he gained the throne of England?

Then again, Harthacnut had made that treaty with Magnus, whereby if either of them died without issue, the other would inherit his part of the old North Sea Empire. England and Norway would make an even more powerful alliance than England and Denmark. What Emma's position in such an empire might be is hard to say, except that she would be ruled by an emperor who owed his power to her, rather than a king – even a son – who despised her. Hard as it might be to believe Emma would honor that above the wishes of the *witan*, relations between her and Edward had evidently deteriorated to the point of hatred. Malmesbury admitted, "His mother had long mocked her son's neediness, without ever assisting him."

It would not have mattered to Edward, nor the *Chronicle*, for what his mother intended to use the money, only that she had used the money. He had come to get her fingers out of the till. As king, he needed no excuse, only the backing of his earls. The Dowager Queen of England was not offered trial by compurgation. Wendover did not mince words. Edward "stripped his mother, Queen Emma, of all her gold and silver and other wealth, because before he was king she had never given him anything that he had requested. Still, he ordered that she should not lack for necessities while she lived at Winchester."

Small comfort. Emma was basically confined under house arrest at Goudbeyete, left nowhere else to go. The *Chronicle* continues, "Soon after this the king determined to confiscate all his mother's lands."

If Emma still held title to the city of Exeter, it reverted to the crown, along with whatever other estates and properties she had accrued over the years, including lands in Northamptonshire, Devonshire, Suffolk and Oxfordshire and almost 32,000 acres in Suffolk. Her disgrace and loss extended even to her closest associates, as the *Chronicle* notes: "Soon after this Stigand was deprived of his bishopric, and they took everything he had for the king, because he was his mother's closest advisor and men believed she acted according to his direction."

Emma's disgrace did not last long. The story goes that she was visited in a dream by St. Mildreth, whose remains she and Cnut had moved from little Minster Abbey in the marshes of Kent to glory in St. Augustine's Abbey in Canterbury. The saint promised to help her. Emma donated twenty shillings to St. Augustine's, and seemingly Edward's heart was changed. According to Goscelin's *Life of St. Mildreth*, "When the queen did as commanded, the king saw fit to set right his mother's injury and restore her former dignity. He recalled her, and begged her forgiveness." Emma returned to court in 1044, apparently chastened, never again to wield the power she once had.

Edward had more to worry about than his mother's feelings. That was a tense year in England. The famine went on unabated. A sester of grain cost over two ounces of silver. Though Svein of Denmark still battled Magnus, the threat of a Norwegian invasion of England was ever present. At one point Edward took the English fleet to Sandwich in apparent anticipation of attack. Thankfully it never came, because Edward – like his father Aethelred – could not trust his own earls.

This time the ruckus only peripherally involved Godwin and his sons. The trouble was in East Anglia. It had been an earldom under Thorkell the Tall, but since his exile had languished. That had been all right while Cnut and his sons ruled, but the return of an Anglo-Saxon king had caused some discontent. The *staller* Osgod Clapa, Osgod the Rough, at whose daughter's wedding Harthacnut had his fatal seizure, had not favored Edward's succession. He had friends of the same mind. Two of these were Thorkell's son Harold, a Danish *jarl*, and his wife Gunhilde, widow of the Norwegian regent Eric Haraldsson who had drowned in the Pentland Firth, and niece of the late King Cnut. All three of them might be assumed to be members of a pro-Danish, or pro-Norwegian, or simply anti-Edwardian faction. Were they linked to Emma's supposed Magnus plot?

The timing may be coincidental. The details are not well known. In 1042, the year Harthacnut died and Edward took the throne, Harold Thorkelsson departed on a pilgrimage to Jerusalem. In November, on his return via Denmark, he might have asserted a claim to that throne in the name of his father. Perhaps to prevent that, King Svein ordered his assassination. In 1044 Edward banished Gunhilde as well, who took her sons Heming and Thorkell with her to Bruges. Osgod himself soon overstepped his bounds. While accompanying the king on a visit to Bury St. Edmunds, he got drunk and barged into the sanctuary with his gilt-inlaid axe in hand, an affront to the saint. He apparently passed out before he could do any damage, but Edward would soon outlaw and exile him too.

Osgod had good reason to be surly. The earldom that might have been his was to go to another. East Anglia, though further from the continental coast than Sandwich, was a prime landing place for Viking raiders – say, under Magnus of Norway – either moving up the coast after crossing the Dover Strait or down from Scotland. Osgod, and before him Thorkell the Tall and Ulfcytel Snilling, had served as buffers against invasion. Now Edward needed his own man between him and any invaders.

The exact date is unknown – recall that Anglo-Saxon years overlapped according to the writers' personal dating preferences – but on a will dated to 1044, Harold, younger son of Godwin, is first listed as *dux*, duke, earl. King Edward named him Earl of East Anglia.

For Harold, still in his early twenties, it was a life-changing moment. Up to this point, as recorded on royal charters, he was titled *ministri*, *nobilis*, not unimportant but no better than a myriad of other minor officials. Now, like his father, his elder brother and their counterparts Earls Leofric and Siward, he was one step away from the throne, the king's representative to a large part of the realm. It was his duty, among others, to keep the peace, to render legal decisions in the king's name, oversee taxation, and summon and lead the warriors of East Anglia in battle, and also to attend upon the king at court. There were only about two dozen men of such power in the entire kingdom, and at this same time Harold's cousin Beorn Estridsson, son of old Jarl Ulf and brother of King Svein of Denmark, was named Earl of the southeast Midlands. (Beorn's younger brother Osbeorn was probably a captain of the Danish mercenaries in the English fleet.) With Godwin in Wessex, Sweyn in the western shires, Harold in East Anglia, and Beorn in the middle, the family now dominated the south lands, and was the most powerful of all.

The only territory in England left for them to conquer, as the *Life of King Edward* admits, was the king's bed. "It was decided a wife worthy of such a husband should be sought among the daughters of the nobility. One alone was found in that class, inferior to none, superior to all, recommended both by the entitlement of her family and the striking beauty of her exceptional youth: the eldest of the daughters of the most illustrious Godwin, Edith."

XVII

COMEUPPANCES

1045–1046

*Godwin in foresight thought that he would make a great alliance
in giving his daughter to the king. Through her own goodness, her
common sense and learning, she would make an excellent queen,
and also put to rest the hue and cry of his murders.*

Rievaulx

As has been seen, May–September marriages were quite common
among 11th-century Scandinavians, particularly the nobility. King
Aethelred had been the better part of twenty years older than his
second wife, Emma of Normandy. Emma and Aethelred's son
Edward was almost a quarter-century older than his bride, Gytha
Godwinsdottir.

Now about eighteen or nineteen, Gytha had been educated at Wilton
Abbey, a Benedictine convent in Wiltshire. A sheltered upbringing,
certainly, but she emerged from it speaking several languages
and known for her piety. The *Vita* proclaims she was "famed and
respected for her verse and prose, and in spinning and embroidery
was another Minerva." Wendover and Malmesbury agreed she was "a
woman whose breast held all liberal wisdom, but little understanding
of worldly matters."

Decades later Ingulf, the abbot of the Benedictine abbey of Croyland
in Lincolnshire, remembered her:

In my boyhood I often saw her when I went to visit my father, who worked at court, and many times when I met her coming from school, she questioned me about my studies and my verses. Most readily passing from the rules of grammar to the loftier studies of logic, in which she was particularly skilled, she would astonish me with her subtle reasoning. She would always give me three or four pieces of money, counted out to me by her handmaiden, and then send me to the royal larder for repast.

In the late 19th century, the *Croyland Chronicle* attributed to Ingulf was shown to be a later forgery, drawing on sources that could not have existed at the supposed time of its writing, with the intent of supporting the abbey's property claims. Lately, however, its value is being reassessed. Ingulf was a real person, whose memoirs could have been used as a source for the chronicle. The details expressed therein certainly don't all lend themselves as proof in property disputes, as when the abbot calls Gytha "a young lady of outstanding beauty, very well-versed in literature, a maiden of faultless purity of conduct and manners, and of religious humility. In no way did she join in the barbarous ways of her father and brothers, but was shy and modest, honest and honorable, and an enemy to no man."

Malmesbury, who wasn't born until twenty years after her death, likewise did not refrain from singing Gytha's praises, both cerebral and physical: "On seeing her, you would have been amazed at her intelligence, but would certainly have also been attracted by her modesty and physical beauty."

In Godwin's view Gytha was the perfect match for a monkish, middle-aged, unmarried king. Certainly Leofric, Sigurd and the other earls and the nobles of the *witan* saw through his designs. "He had many opponents, because Godwin was a known traitor," claimed Matthew Paris. "But the maiden is so beloved, of proven goodness and wisdom, that no one can oppose her, since nothing can be said of her but good."

They were wed on January 23, 1045, and Gytha was anointed as Queen Ealdgyth, Edith. Not *hlæfdige*, lady, but *cwen*, queen. The *Vita* speaks at length of the celebrations of the court, the music, singing and dancing, the men fighting mock duels for the amusement of the royal couple, and of the rich clothing, gold and jewelry awarded to the new royal. Earl Godwin and his sons had reason for joy. A royal heir could not be far in the future – a union of the blood of the House of Godwin and the line of Anglo-Saxon kings running all the way back through Alfred the Great to Cerdic, the semi-mythical 6th-century King of Wessex. It would be a new Anglo-Saxon dynasty, rising even as the age of the Vikings waned.

Yet all was perhaps not so cheery among the sons of Godwin. A story has been passed down which, like some others in this account, might want for veracity. Aelred of Rievaulx told it, and it appears, illustrated, in Matthew Paris's biography of Edward. It may well have happened at another place or time, or never have happened at all. But, as it took place at a royal feast, in which the sons of Godwin were involved, the story is no less worth the retelling, and this seems like the most appropriate time to tell it.

"The king sat at dinner one day," goes Paris's version. "The queen's father was there, Godwin the rich and famous earl. He sat at the king's side, as one who was of the highest station in the land. And he had two very handsome sons, valiant and brave boys."

The sons are Harold and his younger brother Tostig, playing a game. *Hnefatafl*? "So hotly do they play that both are very angered. One gives the other such a blow that it strikes him down and quite stuns him."

Their ages at this point were left unsaid. Paris depicted them as small boys, but the earliest this could have been was 1042, when Edward was sole king. Harold would then have been about twenty, and Tostig as young as thirteen. It is said that Harold was the bolder and stronger of the two. Seizing Tostig by the hair, he dragged him to the floor, punching him and gouging his eyes until he was covered in blood. "He would have throttled him had he not been rescued, he was that wrathful, raging, and vicious."

King Edward took all this in, but hesitated to speak. The *Vita* claims he was foreseeing the future. Finally he turned to Godwin. "Earl, do you not see your sons' struggle?"

"Yes, lord, they are at play," replied the earl. "It is a quarrel, cruel and violent, but expect neither ill nor danger from it."

The king sighed. "Earl Godwin, I tell you, if it please you to hear it, the meaning of this is not simple child's play. Heaven has made it known to me. When they mature and have greater courage, the stronger one, through envy, shall rob the other of life. Yet the vanquished shall soon be avenged. The elder shall soon be defeated. Their lives will not be lasting, nor their power endure."

Edward would become known for his visions and premonitions, but a biographer looking back on past events, particulary one embellishing his subject for posterity, might be inclined to create such a passage to make a point. Paris is thought to have written his account about 200 years after the fact. By then it was possible only to look back in hindsight and try to find, in a seemingly minor incident, some cause, some reason for the great tragedy that was to befall them all.

Amid the wedding festivities the newly minted Earl Harold Godwinson of East Anglia would have done his share of dueling, dancing, singing and drinking. He had personal cause for good cheer. His sister would not have been the only noblewoman at the royal wedding named Edith, and Harold's affections for this other Edith were decidedly more than brotherly. Her name, in the gruff Old English of her day, was *Eadgyð* or *Eadgifu* or *Ealdgyð Swann Hnesce*, "Edith the Gentle Swan," which over the centuries has morphed into Edith Swanneshals, Edith Swan-Neck. She is remembered by no patronymic, like Harold Godwinson, or even a matronymic like King Svein Estridsson, which is unfortunate, because try as they might historians have been unable to shoehorn this Edith into a definitive ancestry. An Ealdgyth is mentioned as a daughter in the will of Wulfgyth, an East Anglian matron who passed away circa 1047, and either was, or was the daughter of, Wulfhild, daughter of King Aethelred who married Ulfcytel Snilling. (This Edith had brothers Aelfketel and Ketel.) That would make Edith the daughter or granddaughter of Ulfcytel, or even Thorkell the Tall, and at the same time Aethelred's granddaughter or great-granddaughter, as well as either a niece or great-niece of King Edward – all in all, certainly a fine catch for an up-and-coming earl of her homeland. Yet unlike Wulfhild and Wulfgyth, which had similar meanings (both *hild* and *gyth* translate as "battle"), the names Ealdgyth, Eadgyth and Eadgifu differed in meaning ("honored battle," "profitable battle," "rich gift").* The Normans, in Latin or their own tongue, later wrote of an Eddid, Eddiva, Eddive or Eddeva *Pulcra, Faira* or *Dives*, "Edith the Fair" or "Edith the Rich," but neither is there solid evidence linking that Edith to this one. Some even equate this Edith with Ealdgyth of Mercia, granddaughter of Earl Leofric, but at this time that Edith was probably little more than a child; her part in our story comes later.

No matter. In many ways the name "Edith the Gentle Swan" tells us all we need to know about Harold's Edith. He was certainly smitten with her, and she with him, for as Jumièges told it (likely without ever having met Harold), "he was exceedingly brave and daring, very handsome in his whole person, agreeable in his manner of expression, and affable with everyone." They were soon wed, though in the *more danico* style, without church approval. That might argue against royal blood on Edith's side, or that Earl Godwin, though himself married to Harold's mother Gytha in the same manner, urged his son to hold out for a church-recognized (and perhaps more politically advantageous) wedding in the future, or simply that the family cared little for church oversight in their personal lives. It says something of Harold, and Edith's feeling for him, that she (or her unnamed nearest male relative) agreed to such a match.

It's easy, though, to imagine Earl Godwin late at night, alone, bent over a *hnefatafl* board, playing both sides, giving each piece a personal name and thinking a half-dozen moves ahead. Harold's marriage to Edith was just one more step in the game.

Yet some of the game pieces had a mind of their own, and did not play according to Godwin's intent. It was soon plain that the earl's fervent wish for a royal heir of his own blood would not come to fruition. The reason was not well known at the time, but Paris would

---

*It should be noted that the Anglo-Saxons, particularly the East Anglians, had a penchant for transmuting names well into the 13th century when the language itself was changing from Old to Middle English. The extant version of Wulfgyth's will is a 13th-century copy of the original, but some historians question whether a competent cleric recording important documents would make such a change.

have it that as early as their wedding night King Edward and Queen Edith made a pact: "When they lie down at night, the king makes to the queen, by mutual consent and agreement, a firm promise and contract, of which they name God as witness and protector, that never on any day of their lives will they give up the honor of their virginity."

By Malmesbury's time this was well known: "The king conducted himself so primly, that he neither ousted her from his bed, nor knew her in the manner of a man."

Decades later the view, according to Wendover, was even more cynical: "Whether he did this out of hating her father, a convicted traitor, and all her family – which he wisely hid at the time – or from love of chastity, is unknown. It is strongly believed, however, that the pious king was unwilling to beget heirs from the blood of a traitor."

It should have surprised no one that a lord and lady raised in monastical seclusion would take vows of chastity, particularly if they were covering for the inability of one of them to beget children. Yet, even in their day, to carry that vow to the marital bed was a topic of note and rumor – some might say scandal – and as time went on it became apparent that something in the marriage was amiss. Edward's biographer Paris, overeager to see his subject sanctified, called it slander and treason when it was whispered that Edward was too simple and timid to approach his own wife, or that he had no wish to beget children by a daughter of the treacherous Earl Godwin. Rather, his uncouth subjects should look to a king living with his queen as a brother lives with a sister as an example, and a royal sacrifice: "So it is with holy King Edward. As wood which will not burn in fire, by his vanquishing of fleshly lust he ought well be called a martyr."

Whatever the cause, Edward's chastity indeed thwarted Godwin's goal, the union of the bloodlines. The king's two predecessors had died at half his age. If he died childless, who would inherit the kingdom?

To complete the joke on Godwin, about this same time, 1045, his wayward eldest son Earl Sweyn became a father himself. Small consolation. Sweyn apparently did not deign to marry the mother, an unnamed *frilla* of such little note that she is completely lost to history. Their son's first name, Hakon, hints at a Viking ancestry. His surname, Sweynson, means his father at least acknowledged him.

But everyone knew the chances of a bastard achieving real power were next to nil.

———

"William grew and gained strength and set to work on several fronts," wrote Wace. Now bearing the arms of manhood, Duke William sought to lay down the law to his fractious nobles. Poitiers, who soldiered in his ranks, declared, "He began with the greatest zeal to patronize the churches of God, to defend the weak, to impose just laws, to make judgments which never deviated from equity or moderation. Above all, to stop murders, arson, and robberies. For, as we have shown above, there was license everywhere for illegal deeds."

Duke William could take some comfort from the fact that his warlords were too busy fighting each other to gang up on him. Attrition gradually winnowed their ranks. The survivors began to look upon their duke as the biggest threat. Yet to keep William in his place – or to remove him from it – required a united front, an opposition leader and a plan. Evidently somebody realized the opportunity missed when William de Montgomery had murdered Osbern the Steward in the duke's bedchamber and neglected to kill the boy as well. The opportunity to correct that mistake came when William, feeling it safe enough to indulge himself in some hunting, overnighted in Alauna, modern Valognes in the Cotentin Peninsula.

This was near where the *vicomte* Néel I of Saint-Sauveur had annihilated King Aethelred's invaders back in the year 1001. He had since died, passing his fief to his son, Néel II. This Néel and his fellow *vicomte* Ranulf of the Bessin, the area around Bayeux, had become familiars of William's young cousin and companion, Guy of Burgundy. The duke could lay his head on his pillow that night thinking he was among friends.

He was awakened in the middle of the night, however, by a banging on his door. According to Wace, to whom this story is owed (and who embellished it into legend; most historians regard it as overly dramatic, but for all that it's worth the retelling), it was Gallet, William's court fool. "Open up! You will all be killed. Wake up, wake up!"

William must have thought it was another of his jester's pranks.* According to tradition Gallet, also called Gollet or Goles, had been residing outside town when he overheard men plotting to kill the duke. He told William, "If you are attacked here, you will be slain. Your enemies are taking up arms. If they find you, you will never escape the Cotentin. You will be dead by morning."

There was no telling how close the assassins already were, and William was not inclined to await their arrival. He could hardly have forgotten William de Montgomery breaking into his own bedchamber to murder Osbern the Steward. Wace wrote, "He was in breeches and chemise. He pulled a cloak around his shoulders, quickly grabbed his horse and set off."

Into the night rode the Duke of Normandy, alone, unarmed and of uncertain fate. An attempt on his life meant at least some of the barons, perhaps all of them, no longer valued him even as a symbol of the dukedom, but meant to take it all for themselves. And if that was the case, to whom could William turn?

---

*Contrary to popular depiction, jesters were not all objects of ridicule, but important and valuable members of the court who often provided a counterpoint to the approved wisdom of nobles, and could become minor nobles themselves. Edmund Ironside is said to have awarded his fool, Hitard ("Hit-hard"), with an entire town, Walworth in what is now south London, for his income, which he retained right through the reign of Cnut and his sons and Edward the Confessor. His Norman successor, Berdic, is titled in the Domesday Book as *joculator regis* and owner of three towns and 600 acres of farmland.

XVIII

OUTCASTS

1046–1047

The Cotentin and the Bessin were then in great confusion. Very terrible news about William, who had been betrayed, quickly spread all around the regions. That night he was thought to have been murdered. Some said he was dead, others that he had been imprisoned, and many said he had fled.

Wace

That must have been the longest night of William's life. He had been caught on the wrong end of Normandy's flattened, U-shaped peninsula. Valognes is actually closer to England than to Fécamp. The shortest route was by boat, across the Bay of the Seine, but that was more easily said than done, especially at night. The harbor towns – Carusburg (modern Cherbourg), Barfleur, even Avranches on the southwest coast – would surely be watched, and it would take time to find, hire and ready a boat for sail. Better to lose himself in the maze of marshes and dirt tracks of the Cotentin.

By now the killers would know they had missed him and would be riding hard in pursuit. William did not spare the horse under him, but raced south, hooves clattering on the cobblestones of the old Roman road from Valognes to Bagias, modern Bayeux. His only hope was to reach the Baie des Veys, twenty miles down the coast, before high tide. The Bay marked the border of the Cotentin and

Bessin (and, nearly 900 years later, between the Utah and Omaha landing zones of the World War II Normandy invasion). A broad estuary where the Aure, Douve, Taute and Vire rivers empty into the sea, at low tide it is a vast mud flat, carpeted with oyster beds. At high tide it is under water.

In those days there were two *veys*, fords, across the bay. The *Grand Vey* led across several outlets of the Taute and the Vire, and the *Petit Vey* across the last of the Vire. By sheer luck – or Wace's good storytelling – Willam reached them just before the tide came in: "In great fright and anxiety he crossed over the Vire by night."

The waters rose behind him. Any pursuers would have to take the long way around, fording all four rivers upstream, or wait six hours for the tide to go back out. Wace declared that William did not even stop to thank God: "He nodded to the monastery [by tradition the chapel of St. Clément in Géfosse-Fontenay, about a mile and a half on the far side of the fords] and fervently prayed God to guide him, if it pleased him, and let him pass in safety."

From there the route, still known to locals as *La-voie-le-duc*, "the Duke's Way," led east, along the coast, another twenty-five miles. Assuming it to be a center of the rebellion, William skirted Bayeux, the seat of Ranulf of the Bessin. By dawn he had reached Rigia, modern Ryes, about six miles northeast of Bayeux, and could go no further. According to Wace, Hubert de Ryes, one of Ranulf's *petits seigneurs* (little lords), looked down from his gate on his weary, ill-dressed suzerain and his worn-out horse. "Why you are traveling, good lord?"

"My enemies are searching for me and speak of murdering me," William confessed. "I will not hide anything from you. Some men, I do not know who, have sworn to kill me."

Evidently Hubert did not know them either, or he might have chosen a different loyalty. He took the duke inside his keep and furnished him with a fresh horse and his three sons as guides and guards: "Escort your lord until you reach Falaise."

That was another forty miles away. Hubert warned them to stay off the main roads and avoid villages – there was no telling who was mixed up in this plot – and sent them off. Wace has him standing on his drawbridge when William's pursuers ride up, demanding to know if he had seen the duke, and which way he went. "He did come this way, not long ago. You will catch him soon!" Hubert assured them. "I will lead you and strike the first blow."

He promptly took the pursuers off in the wrong direction. "He talked a lot about this and that," wrote Wace, "and then went back home."

Once safe in Falaise, his home ground, William could finally take a breath and try to make sense of events. It did not take long for the rebels and traitors to reveal themselves by their depredations. Néel of Cotentin. Ranulf of the Bessin. Baron Hamon, called *Dentatus*, "Toothy," of Creully, east of Bayeux. Baron Grimoult of le Plessis, south of Bayeux. Baron Raoul Tesson of Thury, northwest of Falaise. (William could surely take his luck in riding through all this rebel country untouched as a sign of God's blessing.) They had all been drawn into conspiracy against their duke by none other than his childhood companion, Guy of Burgundy.

As a legitimate grandson of Duke Richard II, Guy felt he had a better claim to the dukedom than his bastard cousin, and had come to resent him. "Guy," wrote Jumièges, "seduced by his pride, began, like Absalom, to divert many nobles from their fidelity to the duke, and to drag them into the abyss of his perfidy."

Decades later, Orderic Vitalis attributed a long deathbed speech to William. He would never have heard it in person, being only about twelve at the time, but may have heard it from sources later lost, or at least captured the duke's character in Shakespearean style. He has William recall, "I generously took him in [Guy] when he came to me from afar, honored him like my only brother, and gave him Vernon and Brionne and a large part of Normandy. Yet he talked and behaved without respect and slandered me faithlessly, calling me a bastard and declaring me low and unfit to rule. What more can I say?"

Guy had promised the rebels independence if they would support him in deposing William, while he would keep only the lands William had bequeathed him. Together they commanded practically two-thirds of the duchy. Having failed in their attempt to murder the duke, they had only one recourse: to conquer the rest. Malmesbury accused Guy, "With these followers, this most daring raider, driven by vain determination of gaining the dukedom, was laying waste the whole of Normandy."

Poitiers concurred. "The rebels killed whatever innocent people they could not convert to their cause, or recognized as major threats to their plot. They ignored everything right and regretted no wrong that would gain them power. Sometimes there is only the blindness of ambition."

The counts and barons might have envisioned themselves as mutual overlords. The reality would be that they would all soon fall into the kind of warring lawlessness that William had been trying to end. It would mean the end of Normandy as a continental power. Worse, with what remained to him, William could not hope to defeat Guy.

"Then," wrote Jumièges, "the wise duke, abandoned by many of his subjects, who labored constantly, and vigorously, to battle him from their forts, and fearing that they might deprive him of his dukedom and put his rival in his place, was compelled by necessity to find Henry, king of the Franks, to ask him for help."

———

Unruly vassals were a problem on both sides of the English Channel. Earl Sweyn, son of Earl Godwin, was making more trouble for King Edward than he was worth. Having been posted to the western marches to provide a buffer against the Welsh, he had taken it upon himself to involve England in their incessant wars. The north of Wales, Gwynned, was ruled by Gruffydd ap Llewelyn, and the south, Deheubarth, by Gruffydd ap Rhydderch. For a generation their families had been battling each other for control of the peninsula, to no conclusion. In 1046, as William had called upon French King Henry for aid, ap Llewelyn brought in English Earl Sweyn.

Why Sweyn would choose to support this Gruffydd, whose army had been responsible for killing the brother of his fellow earl Leofric in 1039, is something of a mystery. That Sweyn's assistance was rendered on King Edward's orders is doubtful. It was to England's advantage to have the two Gruffydds battle each other, rather than one of them take dominion of all Wales, after which he might well turn eastward and send his minions rampaging across Offa's Dyke once more. If anything, Edward needed an earl who would prosecute a war against

Gruffydd. That very year, 1046, Bishop Ealdred of Worcester had led a mixed-force *fyrd* on a punitive expedition against the Welsh, but was betrayed by some Welsh mercenaries in his own army and defeated.

Perhaps Sweyn hoped to forge an alliance to strengthen his paltry shires against what he saw as opposition from the English king and earls, including his father and brother. Or, perhaps, he was simply seeking a battlefield on which to glorify himself. In any case, Sweyn's assistance to Gruffydd paid off. Their combined armies rampaged over Deheubarth. The *Chronicle* records, "This year [1046] went Earl Sweyn into Wales with Gruffydd, king of the northern men, and hostages were given him." The Welsh *Brut* admits, "all South Wales was laid waste." However, any pretensions Gruffydd had to become *Tywysog*, Prince of the Welsh, would be dashed the next year when the southern *uchelwyr*, nobility, revolted and slew 140 of his household guard. The Welsh battled on.

By that time Sweyn was on to his next big adventure. It being the mark of a successful warrior, like Gruffydd and Thorkel, to take a wife whether she willed it or not, on his way back from Wales he stopped off in Herefordshire to kidnap a nun. Not just any nun, either: Eadgifu, the abbess, the mother superior of Leominster Abbey, the local Benedictine convent.

Details on this scandal are few – the *Chronicle* says only, "On his way home, he ordered the Abbess of Leominster fetched to him, and kept her as long as he desired." Even less is known of this Eadgifu, including whether she was a victim in her abduction or willing participant. How the story is told depends on the teller's view: taken against her will and threatened with marriage to hand over control of the convent's lands to Sweyn, or a lady of the church seduced into throwing it all away for a forbidden love with a returning war hero.

Sweyn was likely only in his late twenties, probably younger than an abbess, but old enough to know better. The abbey's chief benefactors were said to be Earl Leofric of Mercia and his wife Godiva. They were well known for their support of the church (most notably St. Mary's Priory in Coventry, where Godiva by this time may have already made her famous, though probably fictitious, naked ride). The earl and his lady would view such an affront, even by a fellow noble – especially by a son of Earl Godwin – most unfavorably, as would the other dignitaries of the church. The monks of Worcester, who had looked so dimly on Sweyn's claim to be the son of Cnut, recorded in their chartulary that he was "touching blood with blood, adding iniquity to iniquity, with pride and vainglory he also served the temptations of the flesh with a certain devotion of the soul." According to them the church fathers threatened the earl with excommunication. Edward's position on the matter is not plain. He apparently forbade any wedding. Eventually Sweyn set Eadgifu free and went into exile. Worcester claimed it was self-imposed, "because he was not able to marry Eadgifu, abbess of the monastery of Leominster, whom he had disgraced."

That winter Duke William found King Henry of France at Poissy, today a suburb of Paris but back then a separate town about fifteen miles northwest of the city. There William threw himself on his king's mercy.

The relationship of king and duke has been a matter of contention among historians, even from their own time. Norman writers vilified Henry as a treacherous overlord, citing for example his destruction, reclamation and basically theft of the castle at Tillières. At best they saw him as an equal of the Duke of Normandy, his most powerful vassal. In fact Henry was a strong ruler, but of a weak realm. The kingdom of the Franks was not yet the France that in centuries hence would come to dominate European politics. Like England and its earldoms, it was a conglomeration of feudal counties and dukedoms, among them Normandy, Burgundy, Blois and Aquitaine. The House of Capet, of which Henry was a son, only directly ruled the area around the Île-de-France and Orléans, and – as William might politely have reminded him – Henry only ruled that much because William's father Robert had sheltered him when his family had driven him from his throne. It behooved the king to keep the duke in his place, but also to support him rather than let his dukedom slide into anarchy. A rebellion against a vassal was a rebellion against his king.

Accordingly, Henry called up the army of the Franks, and in the spring of 1047 marched at their head, into Normandy.

XIX

Val-ès-Dunes

1047

*When the vicomtes of the Cotentin and the Bessin heard that
William was coming, intending to fight and bringing the King of
France, with whom he expected to defeat them, because of the bad
advice they had received and their innate arrogance they neither
restored his property nor sought peace nor accepted it.*

Wace

The rebels summoned their own vassals and marched to meet
William and Henry. The Normans loyal to the duke, from Rouen and
Évreux and eastern, upper Normandy, mustered to his banner. They
converged on August 10.[*] The allies forded the Muance River from
the east and the rebels the Orne from the west, meeting on a field
near modern Conteville called Val-ès-Dunes. The name would seem
to derive from the rather incongruous Old French or Gaulish "Valley
of Hills," but that notwithstanding, it was and still is today a flat
expanse on the Plain of Caen. Wace, a cleric in Caen some hundred
years later, doubtless visited the battlefield in person, and wrote, "The
plains are vast and wide, lacking hills or valleys…there are no woods
or rocks, but the land slopes [very gradually] down toward the east."

---

[*]A traditional date, lacking hard evidence. A few medieval chronicles even date the battle to
1046. Like the English, some Norman chroniclers began the new year at Christmas, or even
Lady Day, March 25.

That is a description of prime cavalry country, and this being an exclusively Norman-French affair, almost everyone at Val-ès-Dunes was on horseback. The old sources make no mention of infantry, but then medieval chroniclers typically concerned themselves primarily with their sponsors' glorious deeds, regarding the doings of footslogging commoners as beneath notice. The only mention of numbers is by Wace, who recorded that Baron Tesson had brought "six score and six" men of Thury. A barony was among the lowest, but most numerous, rank of nobility. How many men fought in the rebel army then depends on how many barons joined the rebellion, which is unknown. Rebellious western Normandy was larger and could presumably field more troops than loyal eastern Normandy, but with France backing the east, we might assume the armies were more or less evenly matched at a couple thousand men per side, or altogether. We might perhaps cede a slight numerical advantage to the rebels, as does Poitiers when he mentioned that "William, the leader of the avenging party, did not tremble at all to see so many swords."

Henry and William arrayed their troops with the French on the left and the Normans on the right. They could observe the enemy forming up as well, across the field, the Cotentinais before the French and the warriors of the Bessin facing William's Normans. Henry pointed out an enemy contingent, pennons flying from the tips of their upraised lances. "They are magnificently equipped," he told William. "What do you know of their plans? Whoever those men fight for will win the day."

William said, "My lord, I believe all of those men will fight for me. Their lord's name is Raoul Tesson. He has no dispute or issue with me."

Across the field, Baron Tesson was coming to the same conclusion. Guy of Burgundy and the *vicomtes* of the Cotentin and Bessin had drawn him in with their promises. He had sworn on holy relics to strike William on sight. Prior to that, though, in front of his men and his father, he had publicly sworn loyalty to his duke. A man who violated that pledge forfeited any claim to his fief or his honor. Wace recorded, "From the midst of his men he rode off, spurring his horse and shouting 'Thury!'"

His horsemen followed. Both allies and rebels must have thought he desired to lead the attack, but he reined in short. Riding up to

William alone, he pulled off his leather gauntlet and slapped the duke with it, laughing. "I swore to strike you on sight. I have done so in order to fulfill my oath."

William understood completely. He thanked Tesson, who joined the allied ranks with his men, honor intact. Honor was everything to men of that age, and it did not require throngs of men to die on the field if their leaders could resolve things by single combat, as Edmund Ironside and Cnut the Great were said to have done. That is why William next rode across the sward himself to call upon the rebel *vicomtes* Néel and Ranulf to meet him personally. They did not accept his invitation, but it says something of them that their own men pointed them out to the duke for his personal attention in the battle to come.

"There was great activity across the field," wrote Wace, "horses curvetted, javelins were raised, spears brandished, and shields and helmets gleamed."

At some point the two great lines of horsemen started toward each other. Slowly at first, at the walk, to spare the mounts. There is no record of massed archers or archery on the field at Val-ès-Dunes, as there would be three centuries later at Crécy, Poitiers or Agincourt. We can assume the riders were able to conduct their charges at leisure, without having to race through a shower of arrows. Only when the distance closed to within javelin range, about fifty yards or so, were spurs given and horses leaped into the gallop. Men shouted their war cries. "There was a tremendous noise when they crashed together," recorded Wace. "The entire earth shook and trembled."

In that bedlam of cursing men, screaming horses, metal ringing on metal and clattering on wooden shields, the main thing was not to be unhorsed, for that meant going down under all those churning, milling hooves. "The king himself was hit and knocked off his mount," reported Wace. "An unknown Norman had come up in their midst. He thought that if the king fell, his army would soon retreat, so he struck him sideways and unseated him, and had he not worn a good hauberk, I believe he would have been killed."

Henry's assailant is thought to have been no less than toothsome Baron Hamon of Creully. He never got the chance to finish off the king, either with his horse's hooves or by pinning him to the ground with his spear, before he was knocked out of his own saddle, ridden down and trodden underfoot. Henry, though, had gone down amid friends, who held off the press long enough for him to remount. Back in the saddle, the king showed himself to his men to encourage them to fight on.

Duke William made for Ranulf of the Bessin, but one of the *vicomte*'s housecarls blocked his way. "William rushed him, sword in hand," reported Wace, "and with a well-aimed blow drove the sharp steel into him below the chin, between the throat and the chest, where his armor did not save him. The body tumbled backward to the earth, and the soul passed out of him."

That was enough for Ranulf. He threw down his spear and shield, wheeled his horse and fled to the rear. At the sight, his men lost heart and followed.

Néel of the Cotentin was braver. "If everyone had fought like him," declared Wace, "the French king would have had a bad day, for his men would have been defeated and conquered." In the thick of the fighting, taking and dealing blows, his men dying around him, the *vicomte* fought on until it became plain the battle was decided. Then he, too, chose discretion over valor. "And Néel at length quit the field, to his life's greatest regret."

Seeing their leaders ride off, their men realized the day was lost. If taken prisoner, the wealthy among them might hope to be ransomed. The rest could only hope to escape with their lives. They fled west, toward the ford over the Orne. Poitiers wrote, "William hounded them for miles, punishing them harshly."

The orderly river crossing they had made earlier was forgotten in the mad effort to escape William's retribution. Jumièges reported, "Those not brought down by the sword, stricken with terror by God himself, fled and rushed into the waters of the Orne."

Anyone who hadn't thrown off their armor along the way (and mail hauberks are not the easiest things to get off, especially while under attack) regretted it on reaching the water. Of them Poitiers wrote simply, "The river Orne sucked down many horsemen with their steeds." Wace reported that so many drowned that mills downstream ground to a halt, clogged with corpses.

Guy of Burgundy, wounded in the battle, apparently did not take his chances with his army. His county of Brionne, which William had given him, was to the east, on the far side of the allied forces. He must have circled away, let the pursuing allies pass him by and run for home. William would deal with him soon enough. For the time being he had to see to his men, tending the wounded, celebrating victory with Henry.

Even at the time Poitiers recognized Val-ès-Dunes for what it was: "This one-day battle, far-reaching indeed and to be renowned for centuries, set a terrible example, wielding the sword on heads raised too high and the ramparts of the wicked, bringing down many fortresses with the victor's fist, and halting civil war among us for a long time."

As William had learned the hard way, in the medieval world a lord's grip on his realm was often only as good as the respect – the fear – he induced in his subjects. Treason was one of the most egregious of crimes, calling for the most brutal of punishments, but often only for commoners. In Normandy men of noble blood, even rebellious vassals, were spared such indignities. Ranulf of the Bessin capitulated, was forgiven, and William permitted him to retain his viscountcy. But Néel of the Cotentin refused to submit, and so was driven into exile in Brittany until he could reconsider. Only Grimoult de Plessis, as the architect of the murder plot at Valognes – and as the lowest-ranking conspirator – was imprisoned at Rouen, his lands forfeit to the church. Under God only knows what methods of persuasion, he confessed his guilt, but was shortly afterward found dead in his cell. His body was buried in its chains.

Meanwhile Guy of Burgundy had locked himself inside his castle at Brionne. This is not the current Château de Brionne, a stone keep built later in the century, the ruins of which still rise atop a hill above the town. As Wace revealed, "In those days the fortress stood on an island in the river Risle." Poitiers, though, did maintain that Brionne was no wooden bailey, but a prototype of the later, more imposing Norman keeps: "The site appeared impregnable, both from the lay of the land and its construction. For unlike other fortifications built for war, it has a stone hall for the combatants and is surrounded on all sides by the unfordable river Risle."

"The king having returned to France," wrote Jumièges, "the duke hastily set off in pursuit of Guy, besieged and blockaded him within the enclosure of his castle, and erected fortifications on the two banks of the Risle." The river being impassable from within as well as from without, William simply took command of either side to prevent his cousin from getting off his island, and sat down to wait. Guy held out as long as he could.* It was not the besiegers, but starvation that forced Guy out. William relieved him of his rank and reclaimed his dominions for himself, but spared him any further punishment except house arrest. Eventually he permitted Guy to return to Burgundy, where he made ineffectual trouble for that side of the family before fading into obscurity.

"Then all the nobles who had turned from their fidelity," wrote Jumièges, "seeing that the duke had taken away or rendered unapproachable any place of refuge for them, gave hostages, and bowed their haughty heads before him as their lord."

With such examples made, it was sufficient for William that the rest of the rebels should be compelled to obey him. That October of 1047, while he had them all together at metaphorical sword point, he convened them at Caen. Wace reported, "And when the priests and relics and barons came together on the agreed day, he made them all vow on the relics to declare peace and keep it from sundown on Wednesday to sunup Monday."

This was the same Truce of God which the barons had rejected five years earlier. With Archbishop Mauger (the duke's kinsman) as their witness, and excommunication as the penalty for breaking their oath, they agreed to limit their warring to three days a week. The castles and keeps they had raised all over Normandy, from which to terrorize the countryside, were to be torn down. That William and King Henry, as overlords, were not bound by any such restrictions and could descend on any violator at any time in a repeat of Val-ès-Dunes was surely extra reason to obey. Fear, not only of God, but of their duke, was to be the cause of peace in Normandy.

---

*Orderic Vitalis claimed three years, which hardly seems credible. He tended to count by years instead of months, meaning if the siege began in late 1047 and ended in early 1049, one year became three years.

"From then on the clergy rejoiced, because it was possible to celebrate the divine mysteries in peace," wrote Poitiers. "The merchant exulted that he could go safely wherever he wished. The farmer was happy that it was safe to work the fields, to scatter seed, without having to hide on sighting soldiers."

As always, Poitiers panegyrized on behalf of his duke. Though Normandy seemed secure, William's troubles were only starting. He was a head of state now, in fact as well as in title, a player on the world stage. Years later, according to Orderic, the duke recounted, "From childhood many dangers have always threatened me, but by the grace of God I have escaped them all with honor. And so I became an object of hatred and resentment to all my neighbors, but none could ever defeat me, for I always placed my trust in God, who was my strength."

XX

The Godwins

1047–1049

In England Godwin was quite wealthy. He was a great landowner,
and bore himself proudly. Edward had wed his daughter. But
Godwin was wicked and a deceiver, and caused many evils in the
land. Edward feared and loathed him because he had betrayed
his brother, decimated the Normans, and had plotted many other
crimes. And so great discord rose between them in both words and
deeds, which was never properly healed.

Wace

The latter half of the 1040s is a particular muddle in the *Anglo-Saxon Chronicle*, with the different versions recording the same events in different years from 1046 to at least 1050. It seems to have been a time of disasters both natural and manmade. There was at least one severe winter. An earthquake rattled the island. A plague killed many, both men and livestock. A wildfire raged in Mercia, killing more. Yet all that was nothing compared to the political upheaval.

After his exile former earl Sweyn wintered across the Channel in Bruges, possibly sulking, possibly seeking to throw his lot in with Count Baldwin V of Flanders. That realm, which had played host to Queen Emma before her disgrace, was turning into something of a hotbed of English discontents. It was now the residence of banished Gunhilde, daughter-in-law of the late Thorkell the Tall, and outlawed Osgod Clapa too, both with grudges against King Edward and

Earl Harold – not good company for an English earl if he valued his reputation. On top of this, Count Baldwin was at the time involved in his own war, in league with his brother-in-law Henry of France against the Holy Roman Emperor Henry III. Either Henry would have liked to pull England in on his side.

It was probably Earl Godwin who, having been unable to prevent his son's exile, at least saw to it the void left behind was not filled by Mercians, Northumbrians or Normans. Sweyn's earldom was divided up between his brother Earl Harold and cousin Earl Beorn, son of Jarl Ulf and brother to King Svein of Denmark. It's thought Beorn was next in line because he was a bit older than next-eldest brother Tostig, then about eighteen. Being a nephew of Godwin and his wife Gytha, Beorn's earldom only increased Earl Godwin's power, but it was not yet enough. Worcester recorded that when King Svein sent ambassadors to petition Edward for a fleet to aid Denmark against Norway, "Earl Godwin advised the king to send at least fifty ships full of soldiers, but as earl Leofric and the rest objected to the proposal, he did not send any."

Clearly Godwin still favored his Danish kin – there is a view that Sweyn, who soon left Flanders for Denmark, did so on his father's orders, to support his cousin Svein – but Edward wished to keep clear of foreign wars, and with the other earls' support he could still overrule Wessex.

It left King Svein with his back to the wall. Magnus of Norway had acquired a new ally, his uncle Harald Sigurdsson, the very same who as a boy in 1030 had narrowly escaped being killed on the battlefield at Stiklestad, along with his half-brother, Magnus's father Olaf Haraldsson. Since then Harald had made a fortune as a mercenary in Byzantium, taken a Russian princess as a bride, and returned to buy into the Norwegian throne, ruling as co-king with Magnus.* Together they had driven King Svein almost completely out of Denmark, but just on the point of total victory Magnus suddenly died, *aelfscot*.

Matthew Paris claimed Edward, sitting in church in England, had a vision of Magnus's death, attributing it to God striking down his

---

*Harald was later to become famous as *Hardrada*, the Hard Ruler. For much more on his remarkable life, see *The Last Viking* (Osprey, 2021) by the same author.

enemy and playing up this miracle as, in addition to his chastity, more evidence of Edward's sanctity. Even Jumièges, writing across the Channel, heard, "He often had mysterious and divine visions and made several prophecies, which were subsequently proven true by events."

For his part Harald, now sole Norwegian king, was careful not to antagonize the English and Danes at the same time. Worcester recorded that he "soon sent ambassadors to king Edward, offering peace and friendship, which were accepted."

Even as the heat turned down on the Denmark front, however, it turned up in Flanders, literally. Count Baldwin had burned Emperor Henry's imperial palace at Nijmegen, on what is now the German border. As a result of this insult, in early 1049, the entire weight of the empire, including allies Pope Leo IX and Svein of Denmark, was brought to bear on Flanders. Lacking England's assistance, Svein had sought and received it from the emperor instead, obligating him as a vassal to put his army and fleet at Henry's disposal. The allies soon had Baldwin backed up against the North Sea. The emperor ordered Svein to prevent his escape by ship, and furthermore requested Edward of England to do likewise.

Peaceable Edward had been attempting to wind down the fleet. He had granted trade rights and profits to what would become the Cinque Ports of England's southeast coast – Hastings, New Romney, Hythe, Dover, Sandwich – in order for them to step up and supply ships, twenty each, with crews of twenty-one apiece (*lithsmen*, sailors, and *butsecarls*, naval troops) fifteen days out of the year, as a first line of defense against invaders. Now, in one of the few instances in which Anglo-Saxon England took part in continental European politics, Edward ordered the fleet into the Channel to intercept Baldwin if he took to the water. Cornered, the count was forced to capitulate.

There's a little side story in all this that should be told. It's a bit spurious, but so are many of the tales that come out of 11th-century England, which can be retold without undue belief. Parts of it are true, and those are the parts that are important. It has a role to play in our greater story, and since it involves Emperor Henry and his dealings with England, this is a good place to tell it.

It concerns Earl Harold. Some versions say it happened during his childhood, some say not until the 1060s, but all agree that at some point he came down with a paralysis. As the 12th-century *Vita Haroldi*, the "Life of Harold," tells it, "Harold, suddenly laid low by this illness, became an object of extraordinary sorrow. Everyone grieved for him, especially the King. For the latter, as if by some premonition of future events, loved Harold, and regarded him above all others, though it is said he looked on other members of that family with a certain amount of suspicion and hatred."

The king's own doctors were unable to remedy Harold's malady. Upon hearing of this, sympathetic Emperor Henry is said to have sent the learned physician Adelard of Liege to England to attend him. Adelard, being unable as well to resolve the issue, advised Harold to pray to the Black Rood of Waltham.

According to the 12th-century *De Inventione Sanctœ Crucis Nostrœ*, "The Discovery of Our Holy Cross," better known as the *Waltham Chronicle*, the Rood was a life-size crucifix of black stone, unearthed years earlier at Montacute in Somerset, on the estate of Tovi the Proud. It was said to contain a fragment of the True Cross on which Christ died, by which it worked miracles, and became an object of veneration. King Cnut had bequeathed land to Tovi in Essex, at Waltham, *Weald Ham*, "Forest Home," north of London, where Tovi had a hunting lodge. He had raised a church to house the Rood, which became a destination of pilgrimages from across England. He clad the stone figure in silver and girded it with his own sword. His wife Gytha, Osgod Clapa's daughter, decorated it with a crown, gold bands and jewels.

Harold, following Adelard's advice, visited the shrine and prayed for salvation. "Soon his bodily pain and weakness lessened, but as his strength returned his love and devotion for the Holy Cross increased."

Believe it, don't believe it, explain it away, disregard it, it doesn't matter. What's undeniable, and matters, is that Harold's reverence for Waltham Abbey and its Black Rood would continue all his life.

With Count Baldwin having perhaps lost his fondness for English exiles, even the outlawed Gunhilde and Osgod Clapa thought better of residing in Flanders and, like Sweyn Godwinson, moved to Denmark. But Sweyn, according to the *Chronicle*, "ruined" his chances with the Danes through some unknown offense. In 1049, with eight ships, perhaps what was left of those he'd taken to Denmark, he came home, intending to petition Edward for forgiveness.

Presumably flying English colors, they made it through Edward's naval dragnet to a Godwin family estate at Bosham on the West Sussex coast. From there Sweyn traveled to Sandwich to meet the king. Accounts are confused, the only clear conclusion being that by now both Sweyn's brother Earl Harold and his cousin Earl Beorn had become quite fond of their parts of Sweyn's former earldom, and declined to return them – probably bucking Earl Godwin's wishes, but perhaps ingratiating themselves with the king.

Sweyn's case was not improved by the fact that his erstwhile ally Gruffydd ap Llwellyn, as feared, now felt secure enough in Wales to enlist some Irish pirates and come raiding up the Severn and Wye rivers. As he had in 1046, Bishop Ealdred of Worcester took command of the *fyrds* of Gloucestershire and Herefordshire – Sweyn's old earldom – and once again was badly beaten for his trouble. The earls Godwin, Beorn and Tostig, now of fighting age, took their fleet around the south coast to intercept Gruffydd. (Harold is conspicuous here by his absence. Recovering from paralysis, perhaps?) Either becalmed or because the Welsh had already retreated, they put in at Pevensey, where Sweyn caught up with them. Having made no headway with his immediate family, he focused his efforts on cousin Beorn, who agreed to accompany him back to see the king and plead his case.

What happened next is the most confused passage of all. Whether by road or by boat, they traveled not east but west, to Bosham where lay Sweyn's little fleet. Once aboard his cousin's ship, Beorn was tied up and taken prisoner. Sweyn raised sail, again not east but west. Was he attempting to round the Cornish coast, link up with his old ally Gruffydd, and hold Beorn hostage for the return of his earldom? Nobody knows, because they only made it as far as Dartmouth on the Devon coast. "There they murdered him," wrote Worcester, "and tossed him into a deep grave, and covered him with dirt."

Why? There is no reason, no logic to the crime. Did Sweyn think that murdering his cousin would leave England short an earl, allowing him to simply step back into his role? It's easier to think Beorn refused, even when threatened with captivity or death, to surrender his earldom or otherwise aid his cousin's cause, or that after his exile from Denmark Sweyn nursed some lingering grudge against Beorn's brother King Svein, and, either way, that rash, impetuous Sweyn slew his cousin in a (possibly drunken) fit of rage.

Adam of Bremen, on hearing of these events from afar, and after spending time in the court of King Svein, thought little of Earl Sweyn and his entire family. It was his opinion (and probably King Svein's) that the sons of Godwin conspired to remove the sons of Ulf as threats to their own power. "For they, having formed a conspiracy against King Svein's brothers, who were leaders in England, immediately killed Beorn, and banished Osbeorn with all his people from the land. And they held England as their domain, allowing Edward his life and the mere title of king."

Given the various atrocities committed over the years by the English against foreigners residing in their land, that might seem a reasonable conclusion at the grief-stricken court of King Svein. The crime was on a par with the murder of the *thegns* Sigeferth and Morcar and Ealdorman Aelfhelm by Eadric Streona, of Alfred Aetheling by Harefoot, or of Alfred's Norman mercenaries by Godwin himself. There was no covering it up. Six of Sweyn's crews deserted him on the spot. Two more ships were captured by locals and their crews put to death, the *butsecarls* of Edward's new coastal fleet now earning their pay. As the luck of the damned would have it, Sweyn escaped back to Flanders with two ships, and Count Baldwin, now reckoning him as a fellow antagonist of England, once again gave him shelter.

Baldwin was in a bit of a spot. Surrounded on all sides by greater military powers – England, Normandy, France, Denmark, the Holy Roman Empire – Flanders needed friends. Taking in English strays risked the ire of King Edward, but even at Emperor Henry's bidding and with a ready fleet Edward had not shown himself willing to cross the Channel and make war because of it. (More likely he was glad for such troublemakers as Sweyn and Osgod Clapa to have a place to go.) Normandy, on the other hand, was an ally only because Duke William was a vassal of Count Baldwin's brother-in-law, King Henry. The duke had no personal reason to support Flanders.

It was time to give him one.

XXI

William the Bastard

1049–1051

*Already the duke, having passed from adolescence, shone with
all the strength of a young man, when his nobles began to speak
seriously with him about perpetuating his race.*

Jumièges

Having proven himself a champion in battle and secured his ducal
throne, William of Normandy had attained a spot on the world stage.
The attention of his fellow potentates was drawn to this upstart
bastard who had tamed the unruly warlords of Normandy, both as
a power to be reckoned with and as a possible ally. And in medieval
times the best way to make an ally of an unmarried lord was to furnish
him with a wife. Poitiers, who by this time had given up soldiering
to become a priest, declared, "Kings from afar would willingly have
given their only dear daughters to this husband."

Now in his early twenties, William was already past due for
matrimony. Certainly a youth spent on the run from assassins and
rebels was not conducive to married life, but there is no record of
even a passing tryst with a lady fair, let alone any women of note at
his side. Perhaps it was simply a lack of opportunity, but in those
days – as with King Edward of England – such celibacy was cause
for whispered rumor, doubtless propagated by the duke's enemies.
"Besides his other virtues he, since in his youth, observed chastity,"

confided Malmesbury, "so much that it was often claimed that he was impotent."

That would be well excusable in a boy raised among fighting men and in constant fear for his life, to whom the ways of the supposed gentle sex were as alien as those of mythological beasts. Yet such rumors were of political as well as personal import. In the eyes of his fellow warlords, a man who could not beget children was not a man. Enemies both local and foreign would begin to look on William as weak, and weakness soon invited war. Naturally his friends and advisors urged him to take a wife.

"There is therefore," wrote Poitiers, "a difference of opinion in regard to his marriage, as disparate characters and opinions are wont to conflict, especially when the matter is discussed in a crowded court." As duke, William could have his pick of any woman in Normandy. To marry the daughter of a vassal, however, would strengthen his ties only to that house, and perhaps even aggravate tensions with the rest. William's name was already tainted with the stain of bastardy. He needed a noble wife to raise his stature among his peers and re-legitimize the line of his family going back to Rollo. The pool of available daughters was not large, and made even smaller by William's desire that any marital alliance should not be made with some far-flung principate, as Poitiers explained: "He desired, for good reason, to have neighbors as kinsmen."

Luckily, there was just such a candidate, and practically next door. Jumièges wrote, "Baldwin, count of Flanders, had a daughter, named Mathilde, descended from a royal family, very beautiful of body and generous of heart."

This Mathilde – in English, Matilda – certainly had the required pedigree. Her mother Adela was a princess, the daughter of King Robert II of France, sister to King Henry and Duke Robert of Burgundy. On her father's side the counts of Flanders traced their lineage back to Charlemagne the Great, father of French kings and Holy Roman emperors alike. (Matilda's very non-Flemish name, meaning "mighty in battle," reflected the Teutonic side of the family.) Furthermore, back in the mid-890s their ancestor, the margrave (*markgraf*, count of the border marches) Baldwin II, had married Aelfthryth of Wessex, youngest daughter of King Alfred the Great of England. Practically all the royal blood of Europe flowed through Matilda of Flanders.

She was probably in her late teens, but unlike her Norman suitor was no stranger to passions of the flesh. Very recently she had become quite smitten with the English ambassador, one Brihtric, a wealthy *thegn* of Gloucester but for all that still her social inferior. He was probably a decade or more older than her and already married – his wife, Godiva, would be recorded by name in the Norman *Domesday Book* – but that did not stop Matilda from risking her virtue, reputation and station for him. An anonymous scribe who continued Wace's account recorded that she, "as a virgin, loved a count of England named Brictric [*sic*].... To him the virgin sent a messenger for his pure love."

In those days no women, not even – in fact, particularly not even – wealthy aristocratic women were permitted to choose their life partners. Their marriages were affairs of state. There were protocols to be followed. Rather than cause an international incident, Brihtric wisely rebuffed the girl's advances and returned home. Matilda's fury, and her ability to carry a grudge, would prove legendary. Six hundred years later the 17th-century historian Sir William Dugdale recorded that decades after her rejection, when she had attained power, Matilda reportedly still remembered Brihtric's insult and was finally in position to do something about it. The former ambassador was arrested and thrown into prison, where according to Dugdale he "died and was buried there, leaving no children."

Duke William would have considered such a woman a fine catch, with her good looks, unsullied virtue (if not for lack of trying on her part) and prominent ancestry guaranteed to raise the station of any European nobleman. The old chroniclers were united in their praise of her: "endowed with beauteous face, high birth, education, good character, and – what is and will ever be worthiest of praise – strong faith and ardent love of Christ" (Orderic); "a singular reflection of prudence in our day, and the perfection of virtue" (Malmesbury); "very beautiful and noble" (Wace).

None of them, however, could ever have met Matilda. Jumièges may have. His comment about her "beautiful body and generous heart" can be taken as the most dutiful flattery. Poitiers may not have known her in her youth, but in his later capacity as Duke William's chaplain would certainly have known her well. Yet, curiously, he did not describe her except in terms of her nobility: "You must know that her mother's father was King Robert of Gaul, who, son and grandson of kings, begat kings, whose acclaim for his devotion and governance of the kingdom will not be silenced in any language of the world."

Probably out of respect for, or fear of, their noble duke, neither Jumièges nor Poitiers made mention of Matilda's most unique feature: her short stature.

Both William's and Matilda's tombs were opened and desecrated during the French Wars of Religion, 1562–1598. Only one of the duke's femurs survived. Matilda's skull and some other bones went missing, but enough remained of the duchess – assuming the remains were hers – that in 1819, when her casket was reopened, her height was estimated at under five feet. In 1959 it was opened again, and her height given as four feet two, a fact widely bandied about for its sheer novelty, but a misreporting. The scientists of the *Institut D'Anthropologie* at Caen, who conducted the exhumation, subsequently confirmed her height by measurement of her femur and tibia (the long bones being the most accurate predictors of total height) at 154cm, exactly five feet. Recent studies of grave remains have proved that people of the Middle Ages, due to better nutrition and warmer temperatures as compared to their Baroque and Industrial Age descendants, were of the same average height as people today, so even by the standards of her time Matilda was short. William, celebrated by Jumièges as "great in body and strong, tall in stature but not ungainly," by the same bone measurement, stood five feet ten.

Matilda's physical attributes mattered less to William than the status she would bring to his house. Jumièges recorded, "The duke, after having taken the opinion of his family, sent deputies to her father, and proposed marriage to her."

This was probably during, or not long after, May of 1048, when William and Baldwin are on record together at Senlis, the royal city northwest of Paris, witnessing a charter for King Henry. The count proved most agreeable to this proposal, which would only strengthen his alliance against the Holy Roman Empire. The problem arose when he took it to his daughter.

Norman, French and Flemish accounts of what happened next, most dating from the 13th century, differ in detail and probably embellish actual events. As the chronicler Baldwin of Avesnes told it, "she answered that she would not have a bastard for a husband."

The vast majority of 11th-century Anglo-Saxons lived in humble thatch-roofed shacks no bigger or better than these recreations at West Stow village in Suffolk, England. (Midnightblueowl)

In 1013, with Viking Svein Forkbeard on the verge of conquering the Island Kingdom, the English king Aethelred sent his wife Emma of Normandy and their children to safety with her Norman kin. Illustration by Matthew Paris, 13th century. (Cambridge University Library)

In 1016 Forkbeard's son Cnut and Aethelred's son Edmund Ironside agreed to rule England as co-kings. (Getty Images)

In this illustration from the *Encomium Emmae Reginae*, the anonymous author presents Queen Emma with the book, as her sons Harthacnut and Edward the Confessor look on. (Bridgeman Images)

King Cnut and his queen "Aelfgyfu" donate a golden cross for the altar of the New Minster at Winchester. Aelfgifu was Queen Emma's regnal name, but also the name of Cnut's first, handfast wife. (The British Library)

In this 13th-century illustration by Matthew Paris, King Harold Harefoot orders the blinding of his rival Alfred Aetheling, while his housecarls bully the English. (Cambridge University Library)

"Where Harold made an oath to Duke William." Whether by trickery or coercion, William claimed Harold Godwinson swore fealty to him on holy relics. Scene from the Bayeux Tapestry, 11th century. (Getty Images)

N

Orkney Is

NORWAY

Dee

Tay

Firth of Forth

DENM.

NORTH SEA

Northern Europe, at the time of the death
of Edward the Confessor, 1066. England
was divided into great earldoms, with th
House of Leofric in the midlands and nort
and the House of Godwin holding the sout
Gyrth also controlled Oxfordshire. Siwar
of Northumbria's son, Waltheof, had recen
been given his own earldom. William of
Normandy's neighbours posed no threa
to the Duke at this time.

Durham

BRITAIN

Tees

MORCAR

Swale

IRISH SEA

Ouse

York

Humber

Lincoln

Chester

EDWIN

Nottingham

Trent

FRISIA

Leicester

Ouse

GYRTH

WALTHEOF

Severn

Wye

Gloucester

GYRTH

LEOFWINE

Thames

London

Rochester

HAROLD

Canterbury

Dover

Exeter

Winchester

Hastings

Calais

FLANDERS

Aix la Chapelle

Pevensey

Boulogne

Rhine

THE EMPIRE

ENGLISH CHANNEL

Somme

PICARDY

Rouen

Bayeux

Coutances

Caen

NORMANDY

Mantes

Paris

CHAMPAGNE

Meuse

Mosel

Falaise

Dol

MAINE

KINGDOM

BRITTANY

Rennes

Le Mans

OF

Yonne

ANJOU

FRANCE

BURGUNDY

Loire

Marne

Seine

Anglo-Saxon England was twice the size of Normandy, even including its dependencies.
To invade required William to leave his duchy defenseless against the Continental
enemies surrounding it. (The Map Studio)

The Norman invasion fleet first sailed at night, following a lantern at the masthead of Duke William's flagship *Mora*. However, they did not complete the crossing until the next day. (Artwork by Steve Noon © Osprey Publishing)

Legend has it that at Stamford Bridge one Viking warrior single-handedly held the entire English army at bay, killing 40 of them with an axe before he was himself slain. (Artwork by Peter Dennis © Osprey Publishing)

The height of the Battle for the Island Kingdom. At Hastings, Norman knights charge the Anglo-Saxon shield wall. On the Bayeux Tapestry both Duke William and his half-brother Bishop Odo are shown wielding a *baculus*, a wooden club symbolic of religious or royal authority but also a weapon. (Painting by Tom Lovell)

The famous "arrow in King Harold's eye" on the Bayeux Tapestry is thought to have originally been a spear upraised by an Anglo-Saxon housecarl, shortened and fletched by a later embroiderer to better depict the legend. (Alamy)

King Harold's body was said to be so mutilated that his handfast widow Edith Swanneshals was brought to search the battlefield for it, identifying it by marks known only to her.
(Getty Images)

Senlac Hill. On October 14, 1066, the Normans and their Continental allies made repeated charges from this position, up the slope toward the Anglo-Saxon line across the crest. King Harold Godwinson is generally thought to have made his stand where Battle Abbey was built.
(Ealdgyth)

The French *Chronicle of Tours* – notably satirical and anti-Norman – claims, "On hearing this, William hastened secretly with a few men to Bruges [Avesnes says Lille], where the girl was staying, and as she was returning from church [Avesnes claims he broke right into her bedchamber in her father's own palace], he beat and chastised her with his fists, spurs, and heels."

An even more obscure and possibly spurious *Chronicle of Inger* or *Ingerius* claims, "William was so infuriated by the scorn with which Matilda treated him that he waylaid her in the streets of Bruges as she was returning from Mass, beat her, rolled her in the mud, spoiled her rich array, and then rode off."

Misogynist, we might say, abuser. And, assuming the story is true, we would be right, but we would be looking at it through a modern lens. The Normans and French of the day told the story of William's "rough wooing" with approval. To their mind, he was merely righting a wrong done him. No real man could brook such a slight on his honor, especially if it came from a woman, even one above his station. Flanders could consider itself lucky Normandy didn't declare war over it. As the story goes, even Matilda approved. When Count Baldwin tried to console his sorrowful daughter, assuring her he would find her another husband, she is said to have replied "that she would have no other than William, Duke of Normandy."

A woman tamed, or determined to tame her man? Consider that in the 13th century, when these stories appear, the violent earlier sagas of Dark Age warriors reveling in bloody deeds were transitioning to tales of the High Middle Ages, of chivalric romance and courtly love, in which a knight-errant goes on adventures and overcomes travails and hardships to win his lady's hand. Clearly William's biographers hadn't quite kept up with literary trends.

Unfortunately, Matilda's was not the only objection William had to overcome on the way to the altar. In September of 1049 Pope Leo IX convened a church council at Reims in northeast France. One of the decrees that came out of it concerned the betrothal of William and Matilda. Leo forbade their marriage, not because of William's illegitimacy, but on the grounds of consanguinity.

At this time the church prohibited marriage between relatives – less to prevent inbreeding than to regulate the inheritance and accumulation of property, and power, by ambitious noble families – to the seventh degree in the longer line, meaning a couple sharing just one of their 128 great-great-great-great-grandparents on either side, 254 total, was committing incest. Duke William was a seventh-generation descendant of King Robert I of West Francia (r. 922–923). Matilda of Flanders was his fifth-generation descendant, making her William's third cousin twice-removed. Too close for the church.

Almost certainly this had something to do with William naming his half-brother Odo as Bishop of Bayeux that year. The lad was probably not yet twenty, perhaps as young as fourteen, but then William's kinsman Mauger had only been eighteen when named Archbishop of Rouen. Best to have two blood-kin priests in one's pocket when a foreign pope took it upon himself to meddle in one's wedding plans. Of course, neither Odo nor Mauger had the power to overturn Leo's decrees, and Rome and Flanders were not Duke William's only problems. His family's old nemesis, the House of Bellême, was still stirring up trouble.

After all his transgressions, William Talvas had been driven out by his late son Arnulf. With no one willing to support his claim to the family holdings, he wandered the countryside as a vagabond. "Finally," reported Jumièges, "he went to [Duke William's vassal] Roger de Mont-Gomeri, spontaneously offered him his daughter Mabille, and also made him a concession of all the property he himself had lost as a result of his perversity and cowardice."

Inheriting the family properties, Mabille was embarking on what would be a long career of her own in the finest Bellême family tradition, as a land-grabber and poisoner. For the time being, with her husband keeping her and her humbled father in check, the House of Bellême should no longer have been a problem for Normandy.

Unfortunately, Roger de Montgomery's seat as *vicomte* of the Hiemois was to the north, along the River Dives in central Normandy. He ruled Bellême as an absentee overlord. And Bellême bordered on Maine. Like Normandy, Maine had been ceded to Rollo's Vikings in the early 900s; like Normandy, in recent decades it had been rent into near anarchy by bickering warlords. The counts of both Blois, to the east, and Anjou to the south had designs on it. It was the latter, in the person of Count Geoffrey II of Anjou, who could not resist an attempt to take it.

Geoffrey, called *Martel*, "the Hammer," lived up to his name. Of him Poitiers wrote, "Beyond the borders of Anjou he had no power, and considered this helplessness shameful. In expanding his territory, he accomplished much in a remarkable manner, with trickery and every resource." In 1051, when Count Hugh IV of Maine died, Martel moved in to take possession of both his capital at Le Mans and his young son Herbert II, and did not stop there. His men not only took over the fortress of Domfront in Maine, but also Alençon in Bellême. Poitiers snorted, "He believed he had increased his glory at the expense of the Duke of Normandy's."

At this time William might well still have been occupied with his cousin Guy at Brionne, but the duke was to prove adept at managing multiple wide-flung sieges at the same time. He assembled his lords, including Montgomery, his steward William fitzOsbern, and his uncle William, Count of Arques. In the autumn of 1051 they marched to take Domfront and Alençon back from Count Geoffrey.

The keep at Domfront was situated on a steep, rocky bluff above the Varenne River, impossible to assault. The duke, as at Brionne, satisfied himself with blockading the defenders inside. Wace reported, "William raised three castles nearby and took away their means of support."

Leaving Domfront to wither, William rode to Alençon to settle matters there. Unlike Domfront, Alençon lies on a plain ringed with hills at the confluence of the Sarthe and Briante rivers. Boggy marshland surrounded the town fortress. The Angevins had further fortified one end of the crucial bridge over the Sarthe with a ditch and palisade. "Brattices were raised around it, made from strong wood and crenellated," reported Wace. "There were warriors and men-at-arms there, hostile and abusive."

There follows one of the most famous scenes of William's life, in which he finally overcomes the stain of his bastardy. The story is not without contention, mostly based on (mis)interpretation of the original texts, but is illustrative of how his legend grew. Poitiers, who may have been there, skips it entirely. Jumièges recorded only that the Angevins defamed the duke: *posito quosdam se conuiciis subsannantes reperi*, "he found that some of them were falsifying their opinions."

It was Orderic Vitalis who, working from Jumièges' text four decades after the fact, started the controversy by embellishing it with the claim that the defenders "beat hides and pelts to insult the duke and contemptuously called him *pelliciarius* because his mother's parents had been *pollinctores*." The Latin terms are not exactly synonymous. A *pelliciarius* was a furrier, a trader in skins and hides, hardly insulting in the days when both sexes and all classes wore clothing lined and trimmed in ermine, sable, fair (squirrel) and budge (lambskin). On the other hand, *pelliciarius* could also mean leather tanner, a trade notorious for the stench of urine used to remove hair and dog feces to ferment and soften leather. This is the most common interpretation of the scene. Wace, writing about a century after the event, put words in the defenders' mouths – "The tanner's hide, that is his stock in trade!" – using the Old Norman *parmentier*, tanner. To further complicate matters, the 12th-century French poet Benoît de Sainte-Maure, in his *Chronique des ducs de Normandie*, used *peletier*, sometimes (but in the manner Benoît seemed to intend) tailor, but more often pelter, skinner. That's the version that stuck. By the 19th century translators were using the modern French *marchand de peaux* (Old French would have been *mercheant*), meaning "hide merchant."

But Orderic also used the term *pollinctor*, which in Classical Latin means "embalmer."

Now, it could be said that tanner, furrier and embalmer are related occupations – someone who preserves, in whole or in part, dead remains, animal or human, for burial or resale – and the skills and job descriptions may have even been interchangeable back in the day. Medieval businessmen were not exactly specialists. In a similar vein, around AD 1000 is when barbers often began doubling as surgeons – cutting hair and amputating limbs are *sort* of the same thing – and it's not inconceivable that Herleva's father Fulbert of Falaise had a dual career, or even owned two businesses.

The short version is, the Angevins maligned not only the duke, but his ancestry too. Tailor, tanner, embalmer – commoner – the insult itself matters less than how William took it. As Matilda of Flanders might have told them, the answer was, not well.

Wace reported, "The duke, hearing all this, swore by God's splendor – that was often an oath of his – that, if he caught them [the Angevins], they would pay for such talk. They would be trimmed of their limbs, left no hands or feet, and blinded as well."

He was as good as his word. The Normans launched an attack on the redoubt, but only as cover. "The roofs, the braces, the beams and whatever else was handy was piled in the ditch. Then they lit it on fire."

The wooden stockade burned. The attack broke through. The Normans were victorious. According to Orderic, William had thirty-two Angevins dragged before the keep so the defenders could watch as he had their hands and feet cut off, and to maximize the effect he catapulted the appendages into the fort. As Wace put it, "The duke swore on holy relics that they would get the same treatment if they did not immediately surrender. He added that if they did surrender, they would be free to depart with their limbs and bodies intact."

With a full gross of Angevin feet and hands littering their courtyard, and the donors presumably outside scrabbling blindly about on their bloody stumps, the fortress garrison quickly recalled who was Alençon's rightful lord. Tower and town reverted to Normandy. To ensure its future loyalty William left behind a detachment to both protect and occupy them, and returned to Domfront.

By now the defenders there were in a panic. Wace wrote, "They all knew well that if the duke took them alive the only ransom he would accept would be the one he exacted from the defenders of the Alençon bridge."

Word was sent to Geoffrey Martel. He rode to the town's relief with a substantial force of foot and horse. William sent a delegation of his barons, among them Roger de Montgomery and William fitzOsbern, to meet him under truce as intermediaries, and spies. Wace gave the duke voice:

You know how to count fighting men. Find out how many Martel has. He is putting everything he has into Domfront. Tell him I block the gate and will battle whatever he brings. I am defending my own land. He will be wise to leave me to it. He has defeated the people of Touraine and Poitou and taken what he wants from them. Tomorrow he can try the Normans, either army to army or in single combat, his choice. We are ready here and now. Let him know he shall not pass, and more than a thousand men will die to prove it.

Geoffrey replied that he intended to personally relieve Domfront the next morning, and if Duke William so wished he could recognize him on the battlefield by his white horse and gilded shield. The Norman envoys replied there was no need to go to such pains, for Duke William would be happy to meet the Hammer then and there, describing his horse, clothing and arms in turn. Norman tradition has it that the count politely declined – "Geoffrey, overwhelmed with sudden terror before he had even seen the opposing lines, fled to safety with his entire army" – but news may have arrived that, with Henry of France advancing from the east, the Angevins faced a dual attack. Geoffrey left comparatively unimportant Domfront on its own to face the bigger threat.

In any case, Martel was not the only combatant to prematurely vacate the battlefield. According to Poitiers, it was at Domfront that the duke's uncle William of Arques decided he had had enough of his nephew's ambitions: "He slunk off furtively, like a deserter, without asking permission. Afterward he withdrew his service as a vassal, behind which he had so far hidden his hostility."

Why Arques chose this moment to abscond can only be surmised. Jealousy certainly had something to do with it. "From the beginning of the boy's leadership," wrote Poitiers, "he was unfaithful and opposed to him, although he had sworn allegiance and obedience. He stirred up trouble, sometimes resisting boldly and openly and sometimes by clandestine tricks."

We don't know how sincere was Arques's religious faith – as has been seen, Norman lords professed love of God while committing the most wicked of sins – but that William had continued his pursuit of Matilda's hand in spite of Pope Leo's forbiddance might have been the straw that broke Arques's back. His brother Mauger, Archbishop of Rouen, would have been the one to transmit Leo's decree to the duke. That William was endeavoring to defy it, Arques may have taken as a familial insult.

He would have to be dealt with eventually. For now William made the most of his advantage over Anjou. "He razed the castles with which he had besieged Domfront to the ground," recorded Wace, "using the brattices to build a fort at Ambrières to annoy Count Geoffrey."

This was modern Ambrières-les-Vallées, fifteen miles over the border in Maine. William might have imagined that acquisition as being merely his due, but in reality it was an overstep, if not in power then in authority. It made Normandy not just a defender but an aggressor, an invader, on a lesser scale but with the same guilt as Anjou. The balance of power in northwest France was tipping, and King Henry took notice. He had shown in the past that, unlike his various western dukes and counts, it was to his advantage to have his vassals quarreling so that none of them ever grew strong except in the king's service. Geoffrey the Hammer was learning that lesson, and the time was coming for William the Bastard to learn it, too.

XXII

*But because, as we have said above, the pious king was more
inclined to listen to the rival party in those days, the earl's attempt at
power was defeated.*

Vita Aedwardi Regis

By the midpoint of the 11th century the earls of northern England
– Leofric of Mercia, Siward of Northumbria and the rest – must
have looked on with dismay as the court of King Edward of England
divided into two armed camps.

The family of Earl Godwin was down by two members, exiled
Sweyn and murdered Beorn, and had lost a corresponding bit of their
holdings, income and power as well. Meanwhile King Edward was
filling his court with expatriate Normans.

He assigned Beorn's Midland shires, and possibly some of Sweyn's
former dominion of Herefordshire on the Welsh border, to Ralf of
Mantes, son of his sister Goda and her first husband Count Drogo of
Mantes, who had died on pilgrimage to the Holy Land back in 1035.
Ralf, probably in his early twenties, had spent his formative years in
the Vexin, the contested area between France and Normandy, and
used that experience of keeps and castles to begin raising a couple in
his new shire.

Meanwhile Earl Beorn's ships were struck from the navy list. "King
Edward decommissioned nine ships," reports the *Chronicle*, "and the

crews went off with them, leaving just five ships behind, for which the king ordered twelve months' pay."

Some historians have seen this as an oversight on Edward's part, a weakening of the forces loyal to him, but more likely his intent was to thin the ranks of Beorn's leftover Danish mercenaries, who might be more loyal to the Godwins. About this same time the king abolished the hated *heregeld*, the Danish tax supporting the army, probably for the same purpose. If there is no money to pay them, mercenaries will seek employment elsewhere. Godwin and his sons Harold and Tostig did not, or could not, take them into the family service. Their pockets had been lightened by the loss of Sweyn's and Beorn's properties and incomes, as well as the tensions with Flanders, which took away the prime wool market for their earldoms of the south and east. (It may be around this time that Godwin and Baldwin of Flanders arranged a marriage of Tostig to Baldwin's half-sister Judith, as a way of preserving their bond.)

Matters were aggravated by a rash of deaths among church elders who might have mediated the struggle, including Archbishop Eadsige of Canterbury, who had been King Cnut's priest and who had threatened Earl Sweyn with excommunication. To succeed him the priesthood preferred Aethelric, a monk of Canterbury and a relative of Earl Godwin's. They urged the earl to intercede with the king on Aethelric's behalf.

Edward was by this time building on his reputation as a man of God. The *witan* had only talked him out of fulfilling his vow to St. Peter and making a pilgrimage to Rome by securing a special dispensation from Pope Leo IX, who admonished the king to use the funds for the expedition to instead raise a church. Just outside the London city walls stood a little monastery of St. Peter, just barely getting by on its congregation's alms. The site, on the sunny Thames riverbank, appealed to the king as an ideal place for him to spend eternity. Using a tithe of the royal income, he ordered it to be rebuilt in the Romanesque style popular on the Continent.* The work would go on throughout Edward's reign, but the cathedral, next to King Cnut's Westminster palace, was to

---

*The current Gothic abbey was raised on the same site beginning around AD 1245.

be known as Westminster Abbey, and would be the center of the church in England for the next millennium.

Such a pious king naturally took an interest in who succeeded to the highest priestly position in the land. Edward's choice was not a kinsman of Earl Godwin. It was one of his Norman favorites, the Bishop of London, Robert of Jumièges. Some seventy-five years later Malmesbury wrote, "Today the English revile this man and his ilk, as being the accuser of Godwin and his sons, the sower of strife, who bought the archbishopric."*

Robert straightaway set to working against the interests of Earl Godwin and his family. The *Vita* records, "His ambition finally satisfied, from the high office he had attained the archbishop provoked and opposed the earl with everything he had."

At issue were church properties of Canterbury and Kent which had of late fallen, along with their incomes, into the hands of the Earl of Wessex. Robert's efforts to retrieve these lands would have taken the profits directly out of Godwin's pocket. The earl, however, managed to foil the archbishop's efforts in court. So Robert and his fellow Normans undertook a campaign of rumor, whisper and slander, implying Godwin and his sons were disrespecting the king, calling him simpleminded, and aspiring to be his equals.

By all accounts Godwin and his sons declined to rise to the bait. In truth, and as would soon be proven, the family was not up to a struggle with the king. Godwin had to be satisfied with the crumbs Edward threw him, including (for what that was worth) the return of Sweyn.

Bishop Ealdred of Worcester, while returning from a trip to Rome (possibly with the Pope's release of Edward from his vow of pilgrimage), had come across the exiled earl on the Continent and taken pity on him. As an Anglo-Saxon bishop of a see too near the Welsh border, he would have preferred an Anglo-Saxon earl to defend

---

*Robert's replacement as Bishop of London was an Anglo-Saxon, Spearhafoc ("Sparrowhawk"), the former abbot of Abingdon and a renowned goldsmith, whom Edward immediately put in charge of the gold and jewels necessary for the crafting of a new royal crown. Spearhafoc was also an ally of Godwin, which may be why Archbishop Robert refused to consecrate him, citing charges of simony (selling church offices and roles). More of Spearhafoc later.

him, rather than the king's Norman nephew Ralf of Mantes, who around this time was acquiring the nickname "the Timid."

(Despite his very Norman impulse to dot his domain with castles, the Welsh had made inroads into Ralf's earldom and even built a keep of their own in Herefordshire. Malmesbury wrote that Ralf "was both shiftless and cowardly. He had been defeated by the Welsh, and left his county and its city, along with the bishop, to be sacked by the enemy.")

On his return to England Ealdred interceded with Edward on Sweyn's behalf. The king probably waved off the killing of a cousin as an in-house, family matter. He had, reluctantly, let Godwin off the hook for the murder of his own brother Alfred; now let Godwin deal with a son for the murder of a nephew. Sweyn was given back his earldom.

There matters might have rested, had not the court received visitors that summer of 1051 from across the Channel.

———

A little north of Fécamp, just across the Dover Strait from England, is France's Côte d'Opale, Opal Coast. Its gray clay promontory, Cap Gris-Nez, is where the Continent makes its closest approach to England, just twenty-one miles from Dover, where each coastline is plainly visible to the other. Just to the south, modern Boulogne-sur-Mer was then the old Roman seaport of Bononia (from the original Celtic *bona*, of uncertain meaning). Its Count Eustace II – known as *aux Grenons*, "Eustace with the long mustaches" – had married King Edward's sister Goda, mother of Ralf the Timid and widow of Drogo of Mantes. Around 1049 the marriage had ended (whether through divorce or her death is unknown), but in 1051 Eustace saw fit to visit his former brother-in-law, at the very least to keep up good neighborly relations. The *Chronicle* says only that he "went to the king, and said to him what he would, and set off for home."

Count Eustace's business in London, though, is less important than what came afterward. "When he came east to Canterbury," reports the *Chronicle*, "he and his men rested before proceeding to Dover." Dover was the natural launch point for a crossing to Boulogne. It's Eustace's prior stop at Canterbury, however, that raises suspicion.

The new archbishop, Robert, would surely have had words for his fellow continentals. A warning, perhaps? They were in the country of the Earl of Wessex, a friend of Flanders, but a foe of Normans and perhaps of Boulonnais as well. The *Chronicle* continues, "When he [Eustace] was about a mile or so from Dover, he donned his armor, as did all his men, and they proceeded to Dover."

Rather than sail immediately for home, Eustace and his men elected to stay the night, which meant billeting themselves in some of the locals' homes. The villagers might be expected to meekly submit to their betters, were they English, but the coastal folk had suffered generations of being put upon by seaborne foreigners and might not have been so accommodating. And the fact that the count and his men donned armor before coming to town might indicate they expected trouble, possibly of their own making. At any rate, it seems one of them got a little too domineering for his hosts' liking. As usual, versions of the story differ. Whether the visitor was struck first, or struck first himself, both guest and host soon lay dead. As Worcester heard it, "At this the count and his men were enraged, and put many men and women to the sword, trampling their babies and children under their horses' hoofs."

But the townspeople fought back, with the result that some twenty men were slain on each side. Some of the Boulonnais holed up in Dover Castle, while Eustace and the rest – Malmesbury had it that there was only one other – fled the town. Not to sea, but back the way they had come, until they reached King Edward at Gloucester. On hearing of the incident, he was inclined to make an example of Dover the way his brother Harthacnut had made an example of Worcester. "The king was very angry with the townspeople," continues the *Chronicle*, "and sent Earl Godwin to Kent with orders to subdue Dover, for Eustace had told the king that the townsmens' guilt was greater than his."

Rather than lay waste to Dover – as Earl of Kent, his own property – in the same way he and his fellow earls had harried Worcester, Godwin counseled restraint. He recommended that the town fathers be summoned to explain themselves and atone as necessary for any wrongs they had done. "And the earl would not consent to the foray, because he was reluctant to harm his own people."

It was a direct refusal to obey a royal command, the equivalent of treason, rebellion. Card games had not yet arrived in Europe, much less poker, but Godwin was likely running a bluff, figuring Edward, even with the housecarls the earl himself had contributed to him, was powerless to enforce his verdict. That gift of housecarls, however, had not healed the old wounds. Archbishop Robert was quick to take advantage. According to the *Vita*, Robert, "adding to his madness at every opportunity, turned the king's mind against him, and persuaded him to believe that Godwin secretly intended to attack the king, as he had once attacked his brother."

Edward was not powerless. He summoned the northern earls, Leofric and Siward and even Ralf, along with all their soldiery, to his side. Not backing down, Godwin called up his own troops, and Sweyn and Harold theirs. They assembled this army at Beverston, some fifteen miles south of Gloucester. The situation was rapidly getting out of control. Malmesbury reported a rumor that Edward planned to strike first: "Godwin, hearing this, spread the alarm to his men, telling them that they should not purposely defy their king, but if it came to a fight, they should not retreat without giving a good account of themselves."

Yet nobody wanted war, as the *Chronicle* records: "It was not wise that they should clash, for among the two armies was there almost every nobleman in England. So they avoided this, rather than leave the land open to attack while fighting amongst each other."

Godwin demanded that Eustace and his men, including those occupying the fortress at Dover, be handed over for trial. Edward, with reinforcements on the way and time on his side, refused. In his view it was Godwin who should stand trial. He ordered that the entire English army, including Godwin's men, should assemble at London for the *witan* to decide the matter. The earl, still seeking to avoid confrontation, obeyed, but perhaps his reputation for double crosses now came back to haunt him. Many of his *thegns* were having second thoughts about rebelling against their king. As the opposing forces marched down both banks of the Thames, not a few of them deserted to Edward, empowering the king and weakening the earl.

The two sides ended up at opposite ends of London Bridge. Bishop Stigand served as mediator, though perhaps not a neutral one. Like Edward's mother Emma, he had been allowed back in the king's good graces. Malmesbury didn't trust him, calling him "a priest of notorious ambition, too eager for honors, and who, through desire of a higher rank, deserted the bishopric of Sussex and took over Winchester as archbishop."

Nevertheless, he dutifully crossed back and forth over the bridge. From the Southwark side, Godwin demanded safe conduct and an exchange of hostages, offering his grandson, Sweyn's son Hakon, and his own son Wulfnoth, then about eleven. From the north bank, Edward, now answering from a position of strength, received Godwin's hostages, but offered none of his own. He again declared serial offender Sweyn Godwinson an outlaw, and that Godwin and Harold should hand over command of their remaining forces to the king. And Godwin was not to be brought before the *witan* for trial. The *Vita*, Queen Edith's version of events, claims that Stigand wept as he delivered the king's final verdict to the earl: "He could only hope for the king's peace when he returned his brother alive, and all his men dead or alive, and everything that had been stolen from them."

Godwin's entire family was outlawed. Leaving the hostages Hakon and Wulfnoth behind with Edward – to be the source of yet more trouble down the road – they split up. Godwin, his wife Gytha (and presumably their three youngest children, son Alfgar, perhaps ten, and daughters Edgiva and Gunhilde), Tostig and his wife Judith, and Sweyn and Gyrth, all made for the south coast. They loaded a ship with as much of their household wealth as they could pack and set sail for the Continent, reportedly just ahead of their arrest, or murder, on Archbishop Robert's orders.

Meanwhile son Harold, with his younger brother Leofwine, about sixteen, and presumably his wife Edith the Gentle Swan, rode hard in the other direction. Lucky for them their pursuers were led by a different churchman, Bishop Ealdred, treading a fine line between loyalty to his king and loyalty to the Godwins. He managed not to catch them before they reached *Brycgstow* ("the place at the bridge" in Old English, modern Bristol). The fugitives escaped down the River Avon and Severn estuary, into the Bristol Channel, the Irish Sea and freedom.

Earl Godwin had been a power at the court of four kings of England – Cnut, Harefoot, Harthacnut and Edward. Even the *Chronicle* admits, "No one in England would have believed it, if told such would happen. For Godwin had been raised so high that he ruled the king and England. His sons were earls, and the king's favorites, and his daughter married to the king."

But the Earl of Wessex had escaped England with his life. Like Aethelred, Emma and Cnut before him, according to the rules of *hnefatafl* he and his sons had won, just by living. And they would return to play again.

XXIII

Heir to the Throne

1051–1052

The troublemakers thus finding themselves either rejected or overthrown, all of Normandy rested in the shade of a gentle peace.

Jumièges

While the sons of Godwin sought safety far from home, in Normandy Duke William labored on in the face of danger. Ignoring the Pope's edict against it, he had gone ahead and married Matilda, daughter of Count Baldwin of Flanders. Baldwin of Avesnes, continuing his ribald tale of William's rough wooing of his bride, contended that at the wedding Count Baldwin asked Matilda why she had agreed after all to a suitor she had once scorned. "I did not know the duke as well then as I do now," she said. "Only a man of great courage and determination would dare to come beat me in my own father's house."

Not everyone was happy with the match. The duke's own uncle, Archbishop Mauger of Rouen, thought little of the ducal marriage, and did more about it than just lecture his nephew. He excommunicated both William and Matilda.

He surely wasn't exceeding his authority. As has been seen, Pope Leo issued excommunications so often that they became a hollow threat to the nobility. It must have been even easier for William and Matilda to disregard theirs if it came from Mauger, for though he was the duke's kinsman, in matters of religion he was even more of a hypocrite than the average Norman. Having been granted the archbishopric at age eighteen, rather than coming up through the ranks to earn it, he had spent fifteen years acting as though born to it, spouting contradictory edicts, appropriating church property for his own use, and generally defiling his office. He had never actually been invested with an archbishop's pallium because even the Pope thought him unworthy.

Nothing could be done about Mauger, however, without offending his older brother, Count William of Arques. He had spent the years building his fortress at Arques, modern Arques-la-Bataille, in the lake country just three and a half miles from the English Channel. The ruins of a magnificent 12th-century stone castle still rise from the site, on the peak of a narrow, steep, chalky outcrop above the Varenne River, but Count William's original was a simple, typical motte-and-bailey, making the most of the natural crest.

Duke William had summoned his uncle to answer for his desertion at the siege of Domfront. Count William had declined to appear. The duke sent a detachment of his own men to garrison the castle at Arques. They soon went over to the count, who made the betrayal worth their while. They used Arques as a base of operations from which to pillage the surrounding countryside, not caring who knew it. "It causes great misery in the entire province," admitted Poitiers. "Strife, pillage and rapine, unchecked fury, the constant threat of devastation. The fortress is supplied with weapons, men, food, and everything necessary for such raiding. The ramparts, already strong, are reinforced. There is no peace or rest anywhere. In short, a most dire rebellion is expected."

But the Count of Arques had more than walls and cliffs to support him. He had allies.

His wife, Beatrice of Ponthieu, was sister to Enguerrand II, who became Count of Ponthieu as of his father's death in March 1052. Enguerrand had been wed to Duke William's sister Adeliza until 1049, when Pope Leo had likewise dissolved their marriage on the grounds of consanguinity, and Enguerrand had not remarried. That left his closest familial alliance through his sister, to her husband William of Arques.

For Duke William, to have his next door neighbor Ponthieu side with the rebel was bad enough, but the rebellion had also come to the attention of his former ally, King Henry of France. Arques's rebellion presented a perfect opportunity for him to keep his ambitious duke occupied. He promised to support Arques against William.

The duke was at the other end of Normandy, in the Cotentin, when he got word of the rebellion. He soon arrived to lay siege to Arques. Normans – notably, rebellious ones like Arques and Guy of Burgundy – were of necessity advancing the science of castle-building toward its medieval apogee. Duke William, however, was becoming a master of proving that walls capable of keeping attackers out also penned defenders in. In the valley below Arques's hill he built a fortress of his own and manned it with his best warriors. With the rebel keep invested and the surrounding countryside loyal to the duke – if necessary, made so by force – there was nowhere for Arques to go, no way for him to resupply. It was only a matter of time until starvation forced his surrender.

Apparently, and rather curiously, about this time Duke William felt there were more important matters requiring his attention, as his biographers rather cryptically recounted. Jumièges, Wace and Poitiers all record that he left the siege to his men, and utterly disappeared for some while. True, rebellion and war had become more or less the normal state of affairs in Normandy, and sieges were becoming routine for William. Still, none of these scribes wrote down, or perhaps even knew at the time, why the duke departed the siege of Arques, or where he went.

In hindsight, William may have had good reason to keep his business secret. Even facing rebellion at home and threats from abroad, chances are he had departed the Continent entirely.

─────────

With the exile of the Godwins, the change in the English court amounted to a Norman invasion. (Not that such a thing could ever happen.) The new power behind the throne, Archbishop Robert, immediately set about restructuring the entire political makeup of the country, beginning with the last Godwin left (literally) untouched:

Queen Edith. At Robert's urging, King Edward repudiated her. Edith's lands and wealth were confiscated, and she was sent to live out her life in a nunnery.

No one in the anti-Godwin camp spared her any tears. They were too busy reaching out with both hands for every scrap they could get of her family property. Ralf of Mantes got Sweyn's earldom back again. Two other Normans who had tagged along with Edward were rewarded for it. Osbern, called "Pentecost," received lands in Herefordshire on which he built one of the first motte-and-bailey castles in England. And Robert fitzWimarc, who was related to both King Edward and Duke William, raised another at Clavering in northwest Essex.

To be fair, though, it wasn't only the Normans at court who benefitted from the Godwins' loss.* Earl Leofric's son Aelfgar, then probably about fifty, was bestowed with Harold's earldom of East Anglia. A big piece of Godwin's Wessex – Somerset, Dorset, Devon and Cornwall, basically the entire Cornish peninsula – went to another newly minted earl, Odda of Deerhurst. Odda was an old-timer Anglo-Saxon, but appears to have gotten along well with whoever was in charge; his name appears on charters dating from the reigns of Aethelred, Cnut, Harold Harefoot and Harthacnut. That he too was a distant kinsman of King Edward could not have hurt his standing. Edward doubtless felt keenly the lack of close kin, particularly his lack of an heir. Now, with the Godwins out of the picture, he could freely address that issue as well.

Wace wrote, "So for the honor of his good kinsman, with whom he had been raised, and because of the worthiness of Duke William himself, he decided to make him heir to the realm."

In the spring of 1051, Archbishop Robert had journeyed to Rome to secure his pallium from the Pope. On the way back he had

---

*The royal goldsmith and unconsecrated Bishop of London, Spearhafoc, fared better than might be expected. Before Archbishop Robert got around to him about his simony, he gathered up all the fees he had taken for the sale of offices, plus the gold and jewels that were to go into Edward's new royal crown, escaped with it all across the Channel and vanished into history.

evidently stopped off in Normandy to visit with Duke William, and perhaps (possibly even on Edward's orders) sound him out on the issue. Naturally William, even though still engaged in securing his dukedom, would have been willing to hear out an English offer about securing himself a kingdom. To their mutual point of view, Edward was practically a Norman king already. His mother was Norman. Norman blood ran in his veins. His father and his brother would surely not have survived if not for the support and shelter they had received over the years in Normandy. For much of his life Edward had been better treated by his Norman relatives than the English, and nobody could blame him if he thought of himself as Norman. In the Norman view, a Norman heir to the English throne could not be ruled out – was, in fact, even appropriate. That heir was logically, rightfully, inevitably, Duke William.

Of course, Earl Godwin and his sons would not have seen it that way, but as exiles their opinion mattered not at all. In fact the events of 1051 might be seen as a great game of *hnefatafl* to chase them off the board: In the spring, Archbishop Robert got tentative interest from William in the succession, was involved in sparking the violence in Dover by Eustace in the summer, and used it to outmaneuver and remove the Godwins by the fall. A window had now opened in which Edward could act without Godwin's blessing, and the timing was right. So the reason William mysteriously departed his siege of Arques may very likely have been a trip across the Channel to meet King Edward.

It must be pointed out, though, that some historians doubt such a visit ever took place, largely because none of the Norman writers mentioned it at this time. Only afterward, in hindsight, to justify later events, did Wace: "The duke went to visit Edward and learn his intentions, and when he crossed over into England Edward welcomed him with great honor, and gave him many dogs and birds, and whatever other good and worthy gifts he thought suited a man of such standing." The only contemporary Anglo-Saxon mention appears in the Worcester Cathedral version of the *Chronicle*, for 1052, and even that might have been a later interpolation. It claims only that once Edith had been banished, "Soon after Duke William came from across the sea with a large retinue of Normans, and the king entertained him and as many of his companions as he might, and saw him off again."*

If we assume this to be true – and not all historians doubt it – that must have been a happy reunion in Westminster Palace, which Edward had recently completed. The two heads of state were at least temporarily relieved of the stress and demands of duty – Edward because his troublesome underlings were in exile, William because he had for the time being left his troublesome underlings behind. As a pair of triumphant survivors, the two might have recalled the old days in Normandy, sharing jokes and chatting in Old Norman behind the backs of Leofric, Siward and the other Anglo-Saxon earls at court. Queen Edith was banished to the nunnery and Duchess Matilda evidently not in attendance.† King and duke could speak together as kinsmen, and kinship was surely a topic of discussion. Doubtless Archbishop Robert was there to remind them to think not only of their shared past, but of a shared future.

To say the succession was the prime topic of discussion, however, can only be a good guess. No one knows what, if anything, Edward and William decided. They might have discussed a divorce of Edward from Edith and marriage to William's newly single sister Adeliza. (Though it's hard to see pious Edward agreeing to that. Pope Leo would have annulled such a marriage as well, for as Edward's first cousin once-removed Adeliza was even more closely related to him than William was to Matilda. William, though, had shown he cared little for the Pope's opinion of marriage, and King Edward had received papal dispensation before.) They might certainly have discussed Norman military support for England in the event Godwin

---

*As has been noted, the English annalists' dating in this period overlapped and is not to be trusted. The Worcester *Chronicle* has Eustace's visit, the Godwins' exile, Edith's expulsion and William's mission in 1052, the Abingdon Abbey edition has everything but the ducal visit happening in 1051, and the Peterborough Cathedral edition in 1048. (The Peterborough monks, reconstructing their copy decades later, evidently recognized their error and skipped entries for 1049, 1050 and 1051 to get caught up.) The consensus among historians is that William's visit took place in late 1051, but there's no reason it could not have occurred early in 1052, about the same time the duke took time off from his campaign against the Count of Arques.
†On his return to England years later William would leave Matilda behind in Normandy, but then he would be on a different kind of mission. She delivered their first child, son Robert, about this time, and may not have been up to traveling.

and his sons staged a comeback. There was also the matter of the surviving English *aethelings*, King Edmund Ironside's sons Edward and Edmund. It is thought Edmund may have by this time died, but Edward was still alive in exile, and certainly had a stronger claim to the English throne than William. Yet the whole point of Archbishop Robert's mission was to put a Norman on that throne. The straightest path to the desired result was for William to be named Edward's heir, regardless of what the Godwins or the exiles thought.

As an autocratic ruler of a feudal state, William may well have come away with the impression, as his biographers later proclaimed, that the English crown would be his. (One would think, though, that such a momentous event would have been widely touted at the time.) The duke may not have understood – or if he understood, might not have cared – that English kings did not choose their heirs; they recommended them to the *witan*. With Godwin and the sons of Godwin off the island and the *witan* packed with the king's supporters, Edward's recommendation would carry weight.

Yet Edward could not have failed to learn from Harthacnut's broken pledge to Magnus of Norway years earlier: that kings, particularly English kings, could pledge succession to whoever they liked, never worrying they would be held to it.

XXIV

THE RETURN OF THE GODWINS

1052

*The famous Earl Godwin was welcomed by Count Baldwin with
great esteem, partly because of their former alliance, partly in
recompense for the many boons he had received from the earl.*

Vita Aedwardi Regis

Baldwin of Flanders had taken the Earl of Wessex into his household
in Bruges much as he had sheltered Queen Emma in 1037, and the
earl's son Sweyn just a few years past. After all, they were family now,
Harold's brother Earl Tostig being the count's brother-in-law. They
were all enemies of King Edward.

The question was, what to do about it.

The answer was, fight back.

Baldwin's war with Emperor Henry was in temporary abeyance.
Earl Beorn's Danish mercenaries, whom Edward had released from
service, would have come to the Continent seeking a war, in the ships
he had let go. Flanders was overrun with unemployed fighting men.
As far as Baldwin was concerned, the sooner they found someplace
else to fight, the better. Godwin had the money to pay them, and as
spring became summer he learned he had the sympathy of his former
subjects as well.

Things in Godwin-less England were not going as swimmingly as
King Edward and Archbishop Robert might have hoped. The insular

English soon had their fill of foreigners. Without the Earl of Wessex to keep them in check, the new Norman aristocracy quickly became overbearing. The *Chronicle* attests, "The foreigners had built a fortress in Herefordshire in Earl Sweyn's lands and inflicted all the abuse and indignities they possibly could on the king's men there." This can be none other than Osbern Pentecost's keep at Ewyas, on the Welsh border.*

The Normans were the worse for failing to defend their new holdings from the Welsh. King Gruffydd was taking advantage of the lack of Godwins to raid Herefordshire. The locals, with Norman backing, tried to resist him, to no avail. The Welsh defeated English and Normans alike, killed many of them, and went home rich with plunder.

The Norman party at court suffered another loss that spring. Queen Emma passed away in Winchester on March 6, 1052.

Edward, one way or another, certainly seems to have resolved his differences with his mother.† Queens were normally buried in the nunneries where they had spent their retirement. Emma, however, was not buried in Winchester's *Nunnaminster*, but the Old Minster, and next to her husband Cnut and son Harthacnut, the first English queen so interred since Ealswith, wife of Alfred the Great.

Decades later the prior of Winchester Abby, Godfrey of Cambrai, eulogized her in verse:

She had kings as sons and kings as husbands.
She stood out for the glory of her issue of kings
Unsurpassed in virtue even by the ranks of her glorious ancestors.

By midsummer Earl Godwin was ready to make his return to English soil, though he would have to do it without his contrary eldest son. Instead of joining his father's comeback, Sweyn opted to go on a pilgrimage. It's true that he had a plethora of sins to repent, and like

*The name comes from an old post-Roman Welsh kingdom in the area. The motte of Osbern's castle still rises thirty feet above the rural countryside.
†The legend of "Queen Emma's Ordeal" – of Edward ordering her to walk over nine white-hot plow blades to expiate a supposed unchaste affair with Bishop Aelfwine of Winchester – is rather obviously a romantic fiction, originated 200-odd years after the fact, and can be disregarded.

many nefarious men of that age, he may have had a sudden attack of conscience. It may have been, though, that Godwin felt bringing Sweyn back to England with him would have cast his return in a bad light. It's hard to claim oneself to be in pursuit of truth, justice and all that is right with a known debaucher and murderer at one's side. Sweyn's return would doubtless have been a source of ill will on the part of his brothers Harold and Leofwine, to say nothing of the earls Leofric and Siward, King Edward and the rest. Whether by choice or at his father's command, Sweyn stayed behind, and ultimately set off for Jerusalem.

On June 22 Godwin sailed with a small fleet from the mouth of the Yser River, where the city of Nieuport is today, and landed on the point of *Dengemersc*, modern Dungeness, the southernmost point of Kent. It did not take long for the earl to learn his former subjects there, and in Surry and Sussex as well, had already had enough of arrogant Normans and were eager for his return. He sounded out the seamen and *butsecarls* of the port towns, whom Edward had cultivated into something of a navy, about sailing and fighting for him instead, and found them agreeable.

Anticipating the earl's return, King Edward had reassembled a small fleet of his own, putting his new earls Ralf of Mantes and Odda of Deerhurst in command. These two soon proved why they depended on royal favor for their appointments. When they reached Dungeness, Godwin had already gone to Pevensey. When they attempted to follow him, they were put off by bad weather. In 1009 Godwin's father Wulfnoth Cild had taken advantage of a storm to destroy the royal fleet, but Godwin wasn't yet ready to take that step. Having learned what he wanted of Edward's defenses and local support, he simply doubled back to Bruges.

Nobody at Edward's court tried to claim that as a victory. In fact, they soon aggravated the defeat. The *Chronicle* admits, "It was ordered that the fleet should return again to London, and that other earls and other captains should be put in command. But it was delayed so long that the soldiers aboard all deserted and went home."

Poor planning. Bad leadership. Weak will. Edward's skill at war, or lack thereof, would seem to be hereditary, handed down from his father Aethelred. Nobody above a certain age in England could fail to remember the bad old days. And the bad old days were about to get worse.

As soon as he heard the southeast of England was undefended, Godwin sailed again, this time in force. He landed at the old Viking lair the Isle of Wight, harrying the locals just enough to squeeze provisions out of them before moving west to do the same to the Isle of Portland, very carefully not laying waste the countryside and not stirring up resistance.

His sons Harold and Leofwine were not as gentle.

Like Godwin, they had gone in search of fighting men, in their case to Ireland. After a storm-tossed voyage across the Irish Sea, they had arrived in the land of King Diarmait mac Máel na mBó of Leinster. Like Baldwin in Flanders, he was prosecuting his own war, against the King of Dublin. In 1052 he won it, which left him with ships and fighting men to spare.

Probably according to plan, whether prearranged with their father before their exile or during it, Harold and Leofwine sailed back up the Bristol Channel with their new army of Irish mercenaries to land at Portloc, modern Porlock on the Somerset coast. They met more resistance than had their father. To the Devonshire and Somersetshire locals, having suffered the depredations of the Welsh and Gaelic raiders in recent years, this army was just another bunch of Irish pirates, and Harold no longer an earl to be obeyed. For his part, Harold had been Earl of East Anglia; these were not his people, and he showed them no sympathy. According to Worcester, "Harold defeated them with the loss of more than thirty noble thegns, and many others. He then returned to his fleet with the booty, and sailed round Land's End."

The two navies linked up on the southern coast and proceeded eastward, recruiting yet more ships and troops from the port towns, rounding Kent and sailing up the Thames toward London. On September 14 they dropped anchor at the southern end of London Bridge, facing Edward at the northern end, in virtually the same position they had been the year before, but now with their situations completely reversed. As Wendover put it, "King Edward had assembled a large army and ample fleet at London, to battle Godwin and his sons by sea and land. But the English, whose sons, nephews, and kinsmen were with Godwin, refused to fight them."

Godwin and Harold might have stormed the crossing, invaded the city and driven the king off his throne. They did not. Negotiations simply resumed where they had left off, with Archbishop Stigand again wearing a footpath back and forth across London Bridge. By this time he could surely feel the wind blowing in the other direction. The abuses of the Normans were fresh in everyone's mind. Public sympathy was with the Godwins, who petitioned the king to restore their earldoms to them. The *witan* convened to consider their demands. Every moment's delay risked Godwin's horde of mercenaries and pirates storming the bridge and running wild in the city. In the end the earl did cross the bridge, but with only enough men to ensure his safety. The *Chronicle* attests, "There Godwin defended and justified himself before his lord King Edward and all people of the land, that he was innocent of the charges laid against him and his son Harold and all his children."

Edward must have been biting his tongue through all this, but ultimately the decision was not his. It was, as always, up to the *witan*, men like Earls Leofric and Siward. The king was, again, nothing more than an instrument of their will. And their will was that England was to be Anglo-Saxon again. Godwin, Harold and the rest of the family, including Queen Edith, had their titles, wealth and property restored. On the other hand, Archbishop Robert and the Norman party at court, for fomenting the troubles between the Godwins and the king, were outlawed.

Probably even before the decree was announced, Robert of Jumièges was on his horse. He and his fellow Normans rode hard for the coast, just as Godwin and his sons had done the year before. The difference was, Robert had hostages: the boys Wulfnoth Godwinson and Hakon Sweynson. According to Wace, this was done on the king's command: "Edward sent them to Duke William in Normandy, in whom he placed great trust, to keep them safe till he should himself recall then. This looked, people said, as if he wished William to keep them forever, to secure the kingdom for himself in the event of Edward's death."

Before anyone could stop them, the Normans caught a boat for home and were gone, in such haste that Robert left his pallium behind. (Stigand claimed it for himself and was named Archbishop of Canterbury in his place.*) Not all the Normans went to the

---

*Robert would take his grievances all the way to Rome, but Pope Leo IX could do little other than castigate Stigand from afar. Robert returned to Jumièges and died there not long after. The two boys Wulfnoth and Hakon, though, still had a role to play in future events.

Continent, however. Osbern Pentecost escaped to Scotland. Though he had given the fugitives shelter in his castle during their escape, Robert fitzWimarc, probably by virtue of being kin to King Edward, stayed on at court as the king's *staller*. Odda of Deerhurst, being Anglo-Saxon and also a kinsman of Edward, lost his earldoms of Dorset, Devon, Somerset and Cornwall to the Godwins but was compensated with a new earldom in Worcestershire, and doubtless glad to have it. Ralf of Mantes – Ralf the Timid – was Norman, but retained the earldom of Herefordshire, not so much because he shared the blood of Queen Emma and King Edward, but because Earl Sweyn left a vacancy, having died in September that year on his way back from Jerusalem.

The turnabout was as complete as it had been sudden and bloodless. The once-again Earl of Wessex, Godwin, and Harold, Earl of East Anglia reassumed their rightful places. Riders were sent to fetch Queen Edith back from the nunnery to her rightful place as well. Her *Vita Aedwardi* would have it that everyone was happy with the outcome: "Thus, after such great evil had been averted without bloodshed through the earl's wisdom, there was rejoicing both at court and across the whole country."

Wace, however, struck a different note, that of a king reduced once again to nothing but a figurehead: "On these terms, the king suffered Godwin to remain in peace."

XXV

Asserting Power

1052–1053

King Henry, hearing the man he supported and advised was under
siege, hastened to help, to that end bringing a large number of
armed men and plentiful supplies for the besieged.

Poitiers

Through the rest of 1052, Duke William's ongoing game of *hnefatafl*
with his uncle William of Arques was at a stalemate. The count was
penned in his castle, surrounded, like a playing piece on a game
board. No food or supplies could get in. By the rules of the game, he
had already lost. He simply didn't know it yet.

But *hnefatafl* is a game of two players. Not three.

King Henry of France had begun to look with dismay on his little
side project in Normandy. Count William was supposed to have kept
Duke William occupied. Instead the duke was so confident of victory
that he felt free to leave the siege to underlings and attend to other
matters, apparently more important. That would not do.

Yet to support Arques, so near the Channel coast, from France
meant marching right across upper Normandy. To do so against Duke
William's wishes amounted to an invasion, an act of war. Having
fought alongside his duke at Val-ès-Dunes, Henry had to be aware
that this was not the same boy from whom he had confiscated the
border castle at Tillières a dozen or so years before. In a one-on-one

match Normandy might even prove the superior. As a consequence Henry spent a year putting together an alliance against it.

By that summer he and Geoffrey Martel of Anjou had fought to a draw. William's aggression against Maine had them realizing the duke was a threat to both of them. In a surprising twist they now agreed to work together to put him back in his place. And the loyalties of Count Enguerrand II of Pontheiu, former brother-in-law of Duke William and now brother-in-law of William of Arques, had changed along with his marital status. Arques was closer to Ponthieu than to most of Normandy. By aiding his new kinsman against his old kinsman, Enguerrand would establish a buffer zone, and prevent Duke William from encroaching on his territory the way he had against Maine and Anjou.

Anjou to the south, Pontheiu to the north, France to the east. King Henry would force Normandy's back to the sea, the way Emperor Henry had forced Flanders'. And the recent return of the Godwins to England, and the expulsion of the Normans from it, might even cause the Island Kingdom to join him as well.

But England never pursued its Norman enemies across the Channel. Fate intervened.

———

Over the winter of 1052–1053, Earl Godwin of Wessex was, for all practical purposes, the ruler of England. As long as he and Harold were not too overbearing about it, Leofric and Siward and the other northern earls were content with the status quo. England was in harmony. There was still the matter of a lack of a royal heir, but with the troublemaking Sweyn and the Normans out of the picture, the choices left to the *witan* would be few: if not Godwin himself, then a descendant. By this time Harold was a father, perhaps three or four times over. (His sons Godwin, Edmund and Magnus are all thought to have been borne of Edith Swanneshals in the late 1040s or early '50s.) If it came to it, Harold himself, now about thirty, would make a fine king. Godwin could rest assured that he had finally surrounded Edward's *hnefatafl* piece on all sides.

But like Forkbeard and Harthacnut before him, Godwin's time at the top was brief, and his end unpleasant.

"In this year the king was at Winchester for Easter," records the *Chronicle* of 1053, "and Earl Godwin with him, and Earl Harold his son, and Tostig. On the day after Easter [April 12] he was sitting with the king at table when he suddenly sank down against the foot-rail, deprived of speech and all his strength."

That sounds like a stroke, but Malmesbury, writing three generations later, reported Godwin's last conversation with the king turned on the death of Alfred Aetheling: "I see, O king, that on every mention of your brother, you give me an angry look."

Wendover has Godwin holding up a bit of bread. "I know, O king, that you suspect me in the death of your brother, but, as God is true and righteous, may this morsel of bread choke me if ever your brother died or was harmed by me or by my counsel."

"So saying this," concluded Malmesbury, "he choked on the piece he had put into his mouth, and closed his eyes in death."

Worcester wrote, "His sons, Earl Harold, Tostig, and Gyrth, seeing this carried him into the king's chamber, hoping that he would soon revive. However, his strength failing, he died in great pain."

The whole story of the bread was certainly contrived after the fact by writers anxious to cast Godwin in a bad light, to wring God's justice from a simple case of choking or stroke. Dramatics aside, the similarities of Godwin's passing to King Harthacnut's – feasting hale and hearty one minute, suddenly keeling over the next – are obvious. No one accused Edward of poisoning either man, but in both cases he certainly had motive, and he did use Godwin's death to royal advantage. As everyone no doubt expected, he nominated Harold to replace his father. As was perhaps not expected, he used the promotion to weaken Harold's position. According to the *Chronicle*, "Harold succeeded to the earldom which his father previously held [Wessex], and Aelfgar succeeded to the earldom which Harold held [East Anglia]."

Whereas before England had two earls from Wessex, Godwin and his son Harold, now there was only one, and two from Mercia: Leofric and his son Aelfgar.

Maybe Edward was better at playing *hnefatafl* than anyone imagined.

By the autumn of 1053 King Henry was ready to march to the relief of Arques. Count Enguerrand of Ponthieu and his forces had circled around the border with Normandy to link up with the French. In October they set off together up the valley of the Scie River.

The invasion caught William completely by surprise. He was not even in the vicinity, having returned to Valognes in the Cotentin Peninsula, for about this time there was trouble brewing across the border in Brittany. In 1047 the late Duke Alan's son Conan II had reached his majority and was ready to claim his inheritance. Unfortunately his uncle and regent, Count Odo of Rennes, had grown comfortable on the ducal throne, and refused to give it back. With their other neighbor Geoffrey Martel of Anjou taking interest in the matter, it behooved William to keep a close eye on things and be prepared to intervene. As both Odo and Conan were William's kin, he had a vested interest in Breton affairs. (Which may be the reason he had cut short his visit with King Edward. As Wace put it, "He did not stay long, but returned to Normandy, for he was occupied with the Bretons, who were at that time troubling him.")

While William's back was turned the allies arrived with a large supply of grain and wine at Saint-Aubin-sur-Scie, about two and a half miles west of Arques.* Henry realized that to get it into the stronghold would probably involve a fight. He organized a caravan of packhorses and a contingent of cavalry to escort it.

For his part William had recruited some local kinsmen, Walter Giffard I of Longueville-sur-Scie and William de Varenne, to keep charge of the siege.† They had heard about the caravan gearing up in Saint-Aubin, and were not going to sit about waiting to be attacked. Giffard and Varenne were locals. Both knew the lay of the land around Arques, and though they were elite warriors a thousand years ago they were no less skilled at their task than special forces of today. The road from Saint-Aubin-sur-Scie to Arques-la-Bataille runs along a valley floor, even today wooded and in places quite steep-banked, ideal for what modern military manuals call a linear ambush.

---

*There are sixty-six Saint-Aubins in France, all named after the 6th-century Gallo-Roman abbot and bishop Albinus of Angers. There is another, Saint-Aubin-le-Cauf, about the same distance to the east of Arques-le-Battaile, but it's on the banks of the Bethune River, not the Scie.
†They were both related to the duke through sisters of his Danish great-grandmother Gunnor.

According to Jumièges, Giffard and Varenne "sent some of their own to try to lure some men of the King's army in pursuit, who would then be attacked by their hidden companions."

On October 25 Count Enguerrand led the relief effort out of Saint-Aubin. The horsemen of France and Ponthieu, having come a long way and forced by their wagons to slow-march, would have been itching to get to grips with the enemy. Imagine their eagerness on first sighting a handful of Norman riders on the road ahead, shouting in alarm and wheeling to escape. Jumièges wrote, "Having approached the king's army, they drew a considerable portion of it in pursuit and, fleeing before it, dragged it into the snare."

Spurring their mounts, leaving the supply wagons behind, the French chased the enemy into the defile. They had not yet gotten through when the Normans wheeled again, their own swords drawn. As Wace put it, "When they had gone through the ambush laid by their own men, they turned to face those who were chasing them, shouting insults, and attacked the French."

Today such an ambush would light off with an initial blast of automatic weapons fire or antipersonnel mines from hidden positions alongside the road, to slaughter half the enemy before they knew what hit them. Back then, it would have meant a deadly sleet of arrows and crossbow bolts, screaming horses and warriors tumbling from the saddle, all before the attackers even burst from cover.

Cavalry was most effective when acting as one monolithic block of hurtling flesh and armor. When horses, unable to scale the slopes of the embankment, were left milling, slipping and tripping in the bodies and blood of their stablemates with their riders struggling for control, they were very vulnerable to infantry, spearmen stabbing from all sides. As Jumièges told it, the Normans "began to massacre their enemies vigorously."

Wace claimed the advance force was nearly wiped out. "The French, who had strayed far from their army, were neatly tricked. The Normans surprised them, capturing and killing many."

Count Enguerrand was slain. Those of his men who weren't killed were captured. By the time Henry came on the scene it was all over. The Normans had retreated to their siege tower. The king, eager to avenge his loss and relieve Arques, attacked, but the Normans, by now expert at laying sieges, were equally good at defending against them. Their siege works were impregnable, and, after all this time, they were well provisioned. Henry did manage to get some men and supplies into Arques' castle, but he had come to lift the siege, not conduct one himself. The longer he tarried in Normandy, the sooner Duke William would unite the duchy against him, and his best men lay dead on the road to Saint-Aubin. While he still could do so on his own terms, he withdrew.

By the time Duke William reached Arques, things had settled back to normal. "The duke was delighted by events, about the great embarrassment suffered by the French and about their prisoners too," wrote Wace. He was not concerned that Henry had managed to slip some men and supplies into the rebel stronghold; extra mouths soon consume extra food. He simply waited, as Poitiers wrote, "like a man at ease with plenty of time," using hunger as a weapon. Poitiers evidently witnessed the final surrender: "It was a sad spectacle, a pitiful fate. The French horsemen, known to have fled the Normans, come out unarmed, with as much dishonor as hunger, their heads bowed, some of them clinging to starved mounts, whose dragging hooves barely stir the dust. Others wearing boots and spurs, unaccustomed to marching, carry their heavy saddles on their bent backs."

Count William's life was included in the deal. Jumièges confided, "He left with his wife, sister of Count Enguerrand of Ponthieu, went to Count Eustace of Boulogne, received food and clothing in the latter's house, and remained there in exile until his death."

That left just one traitorous uncle for William to deal with: Mauger, Archbishop of Rouen. In light of his poor conduct, the duke prevailed on the church to have him deposed. Wace would have it that Mauger, banished to Guernsey in the Channel Islands, soon sank into dissolution and madness, to the extent of dabbling in necromancy and making a pact with the devil. What is fact is that in 1055 he would die by drowning, but that wasn't William's doing. By medieval standards the duke was more than merciful.

As for King Henry, he wasn't yet finished with William. Supporting rebels was evidently not enough to keep the duke occupied. The loss of Enguerrand was a blow, but did not mean the loss of Ponthieu. Enguerrand's brother Guy took over his countcy, and the war went on. It was time for Henry to bring the full weight of his alliance to bear against the Duke of Normandy.

XXVI

Wars in the North

1054

Thus King Henry, greatly annoyed by the warnings, or rather by the dubious claims of his friends, about the power of the duke, advanced to attack Normandy with two armies.

Jumièges

At Val-ès-Dunes, Duke William had needed King Henry's help to retain his dukedom against rebellion. At Arques, he had shown himself capable of subduing Norman rebels himself, even those aided by outsiders, and of fending off foreign support. At Domfront, Alençon and Ambrières, he had prevailed in a border war. Now, however, Normandy was to face its greatest threat: an all-out invasion.

With plenty of allies and their forces at his disposal, King Henry devised a double-pronged attack, up both sides of the River Seine. He put the first contingent in the charge of his young brother Eudes, the *Enfant* of France, along with the royal chamberlain Count Renaud I Clermont-en-Beauvaisis, and the late Enguerrand's brothers, Count Guy of Ponthieu and Waleran, according to Wace, "a very strong and valiant knight." Their orders were to strike north, back toward Arques, laying waste the land as they went. He himself, in alliance with Geoffrey Martel, would advance up the south side of the river. If all went according to plan, they would approach the Norman capital of Rouen from two different directions. The army of Normandy would not be able to oppose both. Poitiers wrote, "No wonder the French, their rashness and pride thus encouraged, had considerable hope that our duke would either be overwhelmed by sheer numbers, or escape in shameful flight, leaving soldiers to be killed or captured, towns razed and villages burnt, some put to the sword, others plundered, and finally the whole land reduced to an abominable wilderness."

Contrary to Henry's expectation, however, William did divide his forces. In the north, Giffard, Varenne and Count Robert of Eu, from the borderlands aside Ponthieu, would have to handle matters. In the south, William carefully avoided battle, instead adopting a campaign of scorched earth. This was midwinter, February of 1054. He knew the French, needing to live off the land, could be defeated by privation as well as by force of arms. "He would, he said, keep very close to the king and camp near him, alert for foragers," recorded Wace. "They would not gather much food without taking losses. He had everything edible removed from the king's path and had the livestock taken into the woods and hidden by the peasants."

Giffard and Varenne, who after the ambush at Saint-Aubin were proving themselves excellent guerilla fighters, likewise stayed out of the enemy's way. They and Count Robert kept to the woods, concealing themselves so effectively that Odo and Count Guy believed themselves unopposed, that the Normans were all over across the river with Duke William.

"The French were very arrogant, cruel and destructive," accused Wace. "Wherever they passed, they destroyed everything, laying waste towns and estates, burning houses, capturing booty and prisoners, violating women and keeping those they wanted."

When they arrived at Mortemer-en-Brai, a little farming village about twenty miles southeast of Arques, they took over the local keep. (Today the outline of some sort of hill fort or ringwork still tops the rise above Mortemer, and down in the valley stands what's left of a stone tower, but which, if either, of these stood in 1054 is not known.) The castle was evidently not large enough to accomodate them all, so the French army basically made the town their own.

"They remained in Mortemer where there were good lodgings," Wace continued. "By day they devastated the land and they spent nights carousing, demanding wine, killing livestock and eating and drinking in safety."

Overnight, in a kind of medieval commando operation, the Normans converged their forces on the village, surrounding it, infiltrating it. Come dawn, they set it on fire. Wace reported, "The flames burned up one house after another, and the fire spread throughout the town. Then you would have seen terrified people, a town in confusion and a bitter fight."

Caught in their commandeered beds, the hungover French rolled out reaching for weapons and horses, only to find the doors and streets blocked by murderous Normans. "They attacked them immediately," recorded Jumièges, "and the fight continued on both sides until the ninth hour, and during all this time it was a continual massacre."

The French leaders made good their escape. Poitiers sneered, "When Eudes and Renaud, taken by surprise, saw their army being destroyed without mercy, they abandoned both their command and their swords and chose the safety of their horses' speed."

Their underlings were not so lucky. The fighting went on all morning, littering the pathways and nearby fields with dead and dying. Count Guy's brother Waleran was killed and Guy himself was captured, along with any number of rich nobles. "There was hardly a lowborn groom who did not take French prisoners and capture fine horses, even two or three, in addition to gear," boasted Wace. "There was no prison in all of Normandy that was not full of Frenchmen."

Jumièges recorded, "The Normans immediately sent fast messengers to the duke to announce this news."

Poitiers took up the triumphant tale: "The moment he heard of this victory, Duke William dispatched a herald in the middle of the night, carefully instructed to proclaim the full details of the victory from a treetop near Henry's camp."

Wace gave him voice. "Frenchmen, Frenchmen, get up, get up! Get moving, you have overslept! Go bury your friends who have died in Mortemer!"

Jumièges recorded, "The king's sentries asked him who he was, and why he was shouting like this at such an hour. The messenger replied, so it is said: 'My name is Raoul du Tosny, and I bring you bad news.'"

(This Raoul was none other than the son of Roger de Tosny, the Moor Eater. At some twenty-seven years old, *seigneur* of Conches-en-Ouche on the River Eure in lower Normandy, he was serving as his lord's flagman and herald, the bearer of his tidings, the voice of Duke William.)

While the king and his councillors were trying to decide if he spoke the truth or Norman lies, a messenger arrived with confirmation. Half their army was destroyed, many of their friends dead, most of the rest prisoners. Henry lost heart. Jumièges wrote, "The king, having learned of the defeat of his people, gave up as quickly as possible to devastate the territory of Normandy, and, saddened by the death of his Gauls, withdrew in all haste. This battle was fought in the year 1054 of the Incarnation of the Lord."

For his part, William had achieved victory without so much as a skirmish. "If the duke had wished to attack," insisted Wace, "he could have done the king great harm, but he did not wish to shame him any further. He had, he said, already enough cause for grief."

From Paris, Henry offered William a truce. William could keep the land he had taken from Geoffrey Martel (though the Hammer might yet have something to say about that). In exchange, the many French prisoners being held in Norman pens forfeited their horses, armor, weapons and other gear to their captors, and had to pay restitution for their upkeep while they were held, but were free to return home alive.

Duke William of Normandy had defeated his sovereign lord, a king of a major European power, twice in less than six months. And he had done it almost without lifting a finger, proving himself not just a great warrior, but one that great warriors would follow. Men like Walter Giffard, William de Varenne and Raoul de Tosny were joining with the old stalwarts like Roger "the Bearded" Beaumont and William fitzOsbern to form the hard core of what would become a near-legendary cadre of warriors centered around their duke. Like Cyrus the Great's Immortals, Charlemagne's twelve Paladins, or even Christ's Apostles, they would become the force that made Duke William great: his Companions.

As Poitiers put it, "Afterward almost all the Norman nobles began to regard him with great respect, striving (much as they had up to now resisted him) to prove that their fealty to him was total."

Meanwhile, back in England, as Earl of Wessex, Harold Godwinson proved much more levelheaded and diplomatic than his father had been. Partly that might have been his upbringing as a second son, schooled for the church or law, rather than as a sword-swinging near-Viking with distrust of authority. His sister Edith's *Vita Aedwardi* concedes, "he wielded power even more actively than his father, and walked in his footsteps with patience and mercy, and with kindness toward men of good intention. Yet this champion threatened thieves and robbers with the ferocity of a lion."

Hers was a flattering and certainly biased view of her brother, of course. The fact was, Harold had to be diplomatic. His earldom of Wessex was outnumbered, by Earl Leofric's Mercia and his son Aelfgar's East Anglia. With them behind him Edward had not been able to face down Godwin and Harold, but he certainly held the upper hand over Harold alone. Not even the earl's sister in the royal bed had been able to tilt that balance of power. If the king died now, his successor would likely come from the Midlands, or even Normandy, not Wessex.

It does appear, however, that no one but Edward seriously entertained the idea of Duke William on the English throne, nor would anyone else have stood for it. The king himself agreed to pursue other options. There were his nephews, his sister Goda's sons Ralf, Walter and Fulk, but by his poor handling of the royal fleet against Earl Godwin during the recent unpleasantness, and of his earldom of Hereford against Gruffydd of Wales, Ralf the Timid had proven himself not kingly material. His brothers, Fulk and Count Walter of the Vexin, weren't English, had never set foot in England, and had their own *comtés* to rule; even Duke William would have been a more likely heir.

Then there was the *aetheling* Edward, King Edmund Ironside's surviving son, still out there somewhere, whether in Hungary or Russia, nobody was sure. As king his father had been much more beloved than Edward's, and his descent through the male line made his a stronger claim than Ralf's through Emma and Goda. His mother, Queen Ealdgyth, had been a daughter of the north and may have been kin to Leofric and Aelfgar. The *aetheling* even had children, two near-teenaged daughters and an infant son, Edgar.

To find him and bring him home, an embassy to the Holy Roman Empire was put together under Bishop Ealdred of Worcester, who had experience in traveling the Continent as a diplomat on Edward's behalf (in 1050, to get papal dispensation for the king's pilgrimage, though his return with Earl Sweyn in tow had to count as something of a failure).

This trip would also be a tacit admission of failure on the part of Earl Harold and Queen Edith. By agreeing to it, they conceded that a scion of Godwin would never sit on the throne of England.

But, as their father could have told them, there is more than one path to a crown.

Wessex had one advantage over England's other big earldoms: it did not face foreign enemies on its borders. As the *Vita* puts it, "For example there rose, almost simultaneously, Gruffydd, king of the Welsh, on one side and on the other that king of the Scots with the outlandish name."

To the west in Wales, or more properly Gwynned (North Wales), King Gruffydd ap Llywelyn, as has been shown, presented an ongoing menace to Mercia and the western shires. Only his continuing struggle with King Gruffydd ap Rhydderch of Deheubarth (South Wales) prevented him from launching another war against Earl Leofric in Mercia, the way he had killed his brother Edwin in 1039. In the north, the "king of the Scots with the outlandish name" was Mac Bethad mac Findlaích, Macbeth son of Findlay. He was not the paranoid tyrant depicted by Shakespeare, having slain his predecessor Duncan I in 1040 in battle rather than by murder, but his mere existence was a perennial irritant to Earl Siward of Northumbria.

Since its days as the Danelaw, Northumbria had been England's most remote earldom, both geographically and politically. Earl Siward, himself a Viking, and his troops had dutifully come down to answer King Edward's call against Earl Godwin's insurrection in 1051, but for the most part his attention was turned north, not south. King Duncan's widow, Suthain, is thought to have been a kinswoman of Siward, perhaps even his sister or daughter, and on her husband's death fled south with her young sons. The eldest, Malcolm, about nine years old at the time of his escape, is said to have been raised in the court of King Edward. The king would certainly have empathized with a young prince in exile and, as his own uncle Robert of Normandy had done with him, may have pocketed Malcolm for future use. The fealty of Scotland to England, sworn by old King Malcolm to King Cnut, had expired with the former's death in 1034. Duncan had been no particular friend of Northumbria, having unsuccessfully laid siege to Durham in 1039, and if his marriage to Suthain had been part of the peace, that too expired with his death. Macbeth had sheltered Osbern Pentecost and his outcast Normans after the Godwins' return, which made him no friend of Earl Harold's either.

Settling things with Scotland had been put on hold while England ran through its own series of kings, but now that the matter with the Godwins was resolved, neither Edward nor Siward was averse to seating a puppet on the Stone of Destiny, the rock on which Alba's kings were crowned. This disagreement being mainly between Scots and Scandinavians, the various versions of the *Anglo-Saxon Chronicle* make little mention of it, and some not at all, but the consensus is that "This year [1054] Earl Siward went with a large army against Scotland, consisting both of *butsecarls* and land forces."

According to Huntingdon, Siward was "a giant in stature, whose vigour of mind was equal to his bodily strength." He was getting on in years, though, probably his mid-fifties at this point, too old to go trudging up and down the Scottish Highlands. To lead the expedition he called upon his son Osbeorn, called *Bulax* (said to be from the Old Norse for "Poleaxe," although such weapons were not invented until the advent of plate armor).

Dunsinane Hill in Perthshire, a thousand-foot peak rising 175 feet even above its surrounding highlands, and with cliffs halfway around, is traditionally said to be the site of Macbeth's castle, though the earthworks ringing the hilltop date from the Iron Age. A thousand years ago the ramparts would have been more prominent, perhaps topped with a wooden stockade. That would have been insurmountable, but given the divided loyalties of Macbeth's men it's likely some enemy sympathizer threw open the gate. The battle was a bloody one. The 15th-century Irish *Annála Uladh*, the "Annals of Ulster," claim 1,500 English and 3,000 Scots dead, plus a small number of Norman mercenaries, including Osbern Pentecost. (Contrary to Shakespeare,

Macbeth survived the Battle of Dunsinane.) Earl Siward's nephew, also named Siward, and his son Osbeorn lay among the dead. According to Huntingdon, on hearing of the latter's fall, the earl asked, "Was his death-wound received from the front or back?"

The messengers replied, "Front."

"I am content," said Siward. "No other death was fitting either for him or me."*

Malcolm was named King of Scotland, at least by the English, though not recognized as such by many Scots until after Macbeth was dead. All this might seem a needless digression from our story, but it turns out to bear directly on England's destiny.

Because the heirs of Earl Siward of Northumbria all died at Dunsinane.

And about six months later, death claimed Siward as well, leaving his earldom to fate.

---

*Huntingdon dated the battle to 1052, and has Siward still in Northumbria on hearing the news, only invading later to conquer the Scots with no mention of Malcolm or Macbeth. All the old accounts must be weighed against the others.

XXVII

THE GODWINSONS

1055–1056

*This year died Earl Siward at York, and his body lies in the minster
which he had himself ordered built and consecrated in the name of
God and St. Olaf, to the honor of God and all his saints.*

Anglo-Saxon Chronicle

Earl Siward was not *aelfscot*. He was struck down by the bloody flux,
in modern terms dysentery. It was a most undignified death for any
fighting man, let alone an old-school Viking. Siward called for his
arms and armor, with his shield and gilt battle axe, in order to at least
die dressed as a warrior. He was buried in the church he had built on
the high ground of York, later known as Earlsborough, Earl's *Burh*,
his fortified residence. The church was dedicated to Olaf Haraldsson,
the onetime nemesis of King Cnut. Since his death under the solar
eclipse at Stiklestad in 1030, Olaf's cult had spread across the Viking
world. Siward, the last great Viking earl of England, was not immune.

His death left a political quagmire in its wake. The Scottish problem
might be resolved, but a new one had been created for England.
The three great earldoms of England were Mercia, Wessex and
Northumbria. Any two of the three had always been able to keep the
third in check. Siward's death kicked a leg out from under the tripod.

He had a surviving son, Waltheof, with the blood of earls – his
mother Aelfflaed was a daughter of the late Ealdred, Earl of Bernicia,
and so granddaughter of Uhtred the Bold, Earl of Northumbria – but
he was still a boy, probably not yet six or seven. His mother would
have to serve as regent, the way Aelfgifu of Northampton had served

her sons Svein of Norway and Harold Harefoot, and everybody remembered how well that had worked out. The Northumbrians, still half-Viking themselves, needed a strong hand on their reins. (Recall the decades-long blood feud that had resulted in the murder of Ealdred, and Siward's rise to the earldom. That had been a spat between noble families; imagine the violence that went on among the commonfolk.) Without the Scots to occupy them, they might decide to take the north for themselves or, worse, hand it back to the Vikings. Across the North Sea the kings Svein of Denmark and Harald of Norway were still tearing at each other. Either might regard taking over half of England as an easier option. Northumbria needed an English earl.

There were few choices available to the *witan*. The royal nephew, Ralf the Timid, was barely in control of Herefordshire and would not be up to the challenge of Northumbria. The mission to fetch home Edward the Exile, son of Ironside, had failed. Bishop Ealdred had gotten as far as the Holy Roman Empire, and ascertained that Edward was alive and residing in the Kingdom of Hungary, but Emperor Henry III had then been on the outs with King Andreas I and refused Ealdred permission to go any further.

Between them, however, the families of Godwin and Leofric had plenty of sons eligible, indeed expectant, for earldoms. Earl Harold's sons Godwin, Edmund and Magnus were not yet of age – the eldest about ten or less – but his brothers Tostig, Gyrth and Leofwine were in their early to mid-twenties. In their view, they had already been passed over for an earldom, when Harold succeeded to Wessex and his earldom of East Anglia reverted to Aelfgar. But Aelfgar, having lost East Anglia to Harold in the first place, could justify his own family claim to Northumbria. He was older than Harold and had sons, Edwin and Morcar, of eligible age. They could argue that as Midlanders they had been raised closer to Northumbria and were better qualified to rule it.

King Edward surely pondered the problem over his *hnefatafl* board. To give Northumbria to Aelfgar or one of his sons would create an alliance of Mercia, East Anglia and Northumbria, a geographic two-thirds of England in one family's hands, a family of no kin to King Edward. But Earl Leofric was an old man. His earldom of Mercia would pass to another soon enough, and if kept in the family, would leave the power balance unchanged. A son of Godwin in Northumbria, on the other hand, would be another royal brother-in-law in power, and on the other side of Mercia and East Anglia, from where he could come down between the two or, if necessary, attack them from the rear. And the next-oldest son of Godwin was Tostig.

Tostig Godwinson is one of the most enigmatic figures of the era. Even contemporary accounts disagree about him. His sister's *Vita Aedwardi* devotes more description to him than to Harold, which might indicate Queen Edith's fondness for the younger brother, or that she felt more need to excuse his behavior. (Just as Sweyn was said to be their father's favorite, and Harold their mother's, Tostig was supposedly his sister's, and the king's.) Edith's writer positively tiptoes around her brother's qualifications, or lack thereof: "Earl Tostig was indeed of great and wise restraint, but sometimes unthinking in pursuing evil – a manly endeavor – and of unshakable determination." He does, however, allow that, "sometimes he was so devoted in these matters, that his actions exceeded his planning."

Overzealous, inflexible, acting before thinking, quick to jump to conclusions, with a bit of a temper: that's the Tostig known to history, more like his late brother Sweyn than Earl Harold. "He was tall and strong, scowling-browed, a big talker, and very warlike," claims a Viking saga of him. "He had not many friends."

According to one story he was called *Trespjot* – Tree Spear, Wooden Spear – because, learning that brother Harold coveted King Edward's ornate spear, Tostig took the metal point off his own spear, carved the shaft to a point and showed it to the king, seeking royal pity: "See, lord, my spear, which has no iron on it."

Edward was not fooled. "I will give you my spear and this name along with it. You will be called Tostig Wooden-Spear, and I think it likely that you will not lack envy if you see others more powerful than yourself."

If Tostig was Edith's favorite, that might be why he is also said to be King Edward's. Unlike father Godwin and brother Harold, Tostig had been too young to ever dictate terms to his king. He had a noble and pious wife in Judith of Flanders, and by all accounts was true to her. With his brother and sister backing him, Edward's choice for Earl of Northumbria was made easier. The *Vita* proclaims, "With the support of friends, but above all, and deservedly so, that of his brother Earl

Harold and his sister the queen, and with the king acquiescing because of his many services faithfully performed, Tostig assumed his earldom." Earl Aelfgar disagreed. Strongly.

Even during the recent rebellion, the family patriarchs Leofric and Godwin had always managed to avoid open conflict. Possibly their sons did not feel so obligated. And Aelfgar, at least, may have been careless in whom he let know it.

As a result, at a meeting of the *witan* at London in mid-March, Aelfgar was outlawed. The various editions of the *Chronicle* disagree on the sequence of events and guilt. The version compiled at Abingdon Abbey, generally hostile to the Godwins, makes no mention of Tostig. It admits Aelfgar was outlawed but claims he was innocent of any wrongdoing. The Worcester *Chronicle* has Tostig named earl first, then Aelfgar outlawed, "having done little to deserve his fate." The version from Peterborough Abbey in Cambridgeshire – the one recopied a century later, after the original was lost in a fire, and viewing events in hindsight – claims Aelfgar was "charged with treason to the king and the whole nation. He admitted his guilt before everyone assembled there, although the confession escaped him inadvertently."

In any case, the tables had been well and completely turned. Just a few years earlier, it had been Godwin and his sons who were cast out, while Leofric and Aelfgar looked on. Now old Leofric could only stand by helplessly as his son went on the run. Mercia, even allied with East Anglia, could not hope to conquer Wessex and Northumbria combined. There were other allies available, though. Earl Leofric doubtless aided, or at least did not impede, his son's escape across England to sanctuary at the court of Gruffydd ap Llywelyn.

Early this same year, 1055, Gruffydd had finally succeeded in catching and killing his archenemy, the other King Gruffydd, Gruffydd ap Rhydderch of Deheubarth, thereby making himself King of Wales. That gave him a surplus of fighting men with no fighting to occupy them. And Aelfgar knew where to find more – the same place Earl Harold had found them, in the course of his rebellion.

Ever ready to make trouble for his neighbors, Irish king Diarmait mac Máel na mBó backed Aelfgar as readily as he had recently backed

Harold and Leofwine. Since his recent victory the Irish called him *tigerna Gall*, "Lord of the Foreigners," the expatriate Vikings who then populated Dublin. Many jumped at the chance to go to England as mercenaries. Aelfgar returned to Wales with eighteen ships and convinced King Gruffydd to support him against King Edward.

The plan was to strike England where it was weakest – coincidentally, that part closest to Wales that was not Mercia. The *Brut y Tywysogion*, the Welsh "Chronicle of the Princes," records that "Gruffydd, son of Llywelyn, raised an army against the English, and convened his forces at Hereford."

Herefordshire was still the earldom of King Edward's nephew, Ralph the Timid, whom Worcester called "the cowardly son of king Edward's sister." Rather than repair Hereford's defenses, damaged in the recent incursions by the Welsh, he had raised a Norman-style keep within the city limits. Then, instead of making use of it, he chose to go out and meet the enemy on the field of battle.

On October 24 the armies came together about two miles outside of Hereford. The *Brut*, being the Welsh account, glorifies the Welsh king: "Gruffydd immediately attacked them with well-arrayed troops."

English accounts attribute the results more to the actions of Earl Ralf. "Before a spear could be thrown the English fled," admits the *Chronicle*, "because they were on horses."

The wording is unfortunate. Worcester took it to mean Ralf, in the Norman fashion, ordered the English, "contrary to custom, to fight on horseback," but modern historians are divided as to whether it was the Welsh or English in the saddle. The Welsh were not known as cavalrymen, and the Anglo-Saxons, like Vikings, preferred to fight on foot. At any rate Earl Ralf's defeat on land, as it had been at sea, seems to have been entirely due to his inability to lead, except to the rear.

"Just as the battle was about to commence," wrote Worcester, "the earl, with his French and Normans, was the first to flee. The English, seeing this, followed their example, and with nearly the entire enemy army pursuing, four or five hundred of them were killed, and many wounded."

Ralf's castle was on the banks of the Wye at the southern end of the modern town. He evidently did not return there, because he survived the sack. Many did not. Aelfgar and Gruffydd, chasing the enemy survivors ahead of them, seem to have overridden the defenses and got inside before the gates could be shut against them. "Gruffydd chased them into the fortress," proclaims the *Brut*, "which he depopulated and demolished, and then burned the town."

Hereford's cathedral had stood for some two and quarter centuries. Its clerics attempted to defend it. They were murdered for their trouble, and the church looted of its ornaments and relics, then burnt, along with the rest of Hereford. Laden with treasure and dragging captives away into slavery, Aelfgar and Gruffydd withdrew over Offa's Dyke, home to Wales.

"On news of this calamity," wrote Malmesbury, "the king [Edward] immediately ordered an army to be raised from every part of England, and when it was assembled at Gloucester, gave command to the brave earl Harold."

Harold's leadership is no surprise. Brother Tostig had his hands full, cracking down on the feuding and banditry in his new earldom in Northumbria. As at least part of Aelfgar's earldom had been bestowed on him, younger brother Gyrth would be doing the same in East Anglia. And old Leofric could hardly have been expected to pursue his outlaw son with enthusiasm.

Harold must have led a substantial force nonetheless, for he advanced over the border well into Welsh territory without meeting any opposition. Aelfgar and Gruffydd retreated before him, but Harold pursued only a little way. He left most of his army there in Wales to hold them at a distance while he returned to Hereford to do what Earl Ralf had not – repair the city defenses, including having a trench dug around it.

"Meanwhile," Malmesbury continued, "after an exhange of messages, Gruffydd, Aelfgar and Harold, with their attendants, met at a place called Biligesteagea [probably modern Bilsley in Gloucestershire], and peace being proposed and accepted, they entered into a firm alliance with each other."

Here we see Harold's upbringing as a second son – his early training for the church or law, or diplomacy – at work. His younger brother Tostig would have dealt with the Welsh as harshly as he was even then dealing with the Northumbrians. "Both had the advantage of being distinctly handsome and graceful, similarly strong, as they showed, and equally brave," claims their sister's *Vita*. "But the elder, Harold, was taller, well practised in endless work and going without sleep and food, and blessed with calm temper and a quicker understanding."

For Harold, domination was not the goal. The goal was to forestall any more raids, to resolve the crisis, and above all break up the alliance of Aelfgar with Gruffydd. If he could achieve that diplomatically, peaceably, so much the better.

By the terms of the treaty, Aelfgar would not receive Tostig's Northumbria, but would regain East Anglia from Earl Gyrth. Aelfgar's Viking mercenaries, content with their loot, drew off down the River Dee, and King Gruffydd could go home boasting of having defeated the English again. Harold's peace could be seen as capitulation, an appeasement, amounting to a reward for aggression. By not defeating Gruffydd and Aelfgar in the field and inflicting punishment, he practically invited them to further violence. Nor did he appease the people of Hereford, whose blood absolved Aelfgar of his outlawry. The deaths of commoners were of small import – there were always more commoners where those came from – but the townspeople felt compelled to mount their own expedition into Wales to seek retribution. The Welsh quickly fell on them and wiped them out.

Still Harold sought a diplomatic solution. Before the war could flare up anew, Harold brought in Edward himself to make peace with Gruffydd. As Walter Map told it, the two kings arrived on opposite banks of the Severn River between Austclive (August Cliff, modern Aust) and Beachley, now a tidal island but then a peninsula of Wales. The river there is a mile wide. The royal envoys had a job of work just rowing back and forth between the two kings, neither of whom would initially concede to cross to the other.

In the end, Edward agreed to cross, and in return Gruffydd is said to have waded out waist-deep to meet him and carry him on his back to shore. The *Chronicle* records, "Gruffydd vowed that he would be a steady and true viceroy to King Edward."

His word given to the king, however, was worth little more than that he had given to the earl. From all this Harold likely drew a lesson about the limits of diplomacy. "This was an excellent beginning of peace," concluded Map, "but, in the Welsh manner, it was maintained only until opportunity arose to do harm."

XXVIII

WAR AND DIPLOMACY

1057

Geoffrey Martel hated the duke. He was very annoyed because he heard that all was going well for him and that he had attained peace with the king.... He who does not bother to defend his own rights has little hope of taking someone else's.

Wace

King Henry of France was right: If William of Normandy had no wars to busy him, he would go looking for one. In the three years since the Battle of Mortemer, and having retained the territory gained prior to it, the duke had returned to his original goal of expanding his dukedom at the expense of his neighbors.

On the death of Count Hugh IV of Maine in 1051, Count Geoffrey of Anjou had more or less imprisoned the rightful heir, young Count Herbert II. Five years later Herbert had escaped and claimed asylum in Normandy. Duke William drove a hard bargain for it. According to Poitiers, Herbert – or his advisors; he was only about nine or ten – pledged to marry one of William's daughters (giving Herbert plenty of time to grow into the idea, because the eldest, Cecilia and Adelize, were barely toddlers) and betrothed his sister Marguerite, then about twelve, to William's son Robert, three or four. Finally, Herbert agreed that if he died without issue, his *comté* of Maine was to become part of Normandy.

The only man standing between them was Count Geoffrey.

290

The next castle beyond the Norman outpost at Ambrières, about six and a half miles to the south, was a Carolingian-era stone keep on a granite outcrop above the River Mayenne. The local baron, also named Geoffrey, had married Count Herbert's sister. According to Wace, "He had long opposed the duke, often waged war on him, and caused him much harm. His kin who were barons supported him."

Like Bellême, Mayenne had always relied on its neighbors Maine, Anjou, France and Normandy to keep each other in check, but Normandy had grown in power to the point it was willing to take on all the others put together. This Baron Geoffrey knew simply because Duke William told him so, giving Mayenne forty days' notice of his coming.

The way Herbert had gone running to Duke William, Baron Geoffrey went running to Count Geoffrey, and like the duke, the count simply needed an excuse for war. According to Poitiers, he told the baron, "You may reject my sovereignty completely for being a sorry and dishonorable lord, if these things you fear come to pass while I do nothing."

This time lacking the support of Henry of France, Martel put together his own alliance of Normandy's neighbors, who had also looked on the rise of Duke William with apprehension: William VIII, Duke of Gascony, and Count Odo of Rennes, nominal regent of Brittany (although in dispute with his nephew, Duke Conan II). They and the two Geoffreys set out in force to strike first, with the Hammer taking the lead. Wace accused, "He greatly ravaged the land, burnt and destroyed many towns, looted, took peasants captive and caused misery to men and women."

They laid siege to Ambrières. Poitiers, who may have heard about it from the defenders or been one himself, wrote of attackers trying to tear down the palisade under a shower of rocks and spears, their battering ram breaking on impact with the wall. Meanwhile Duke William, on hearing reports of the assault, stepped up his schedule. Assembling his army, he marched to the rescue of Ambrières. "Martel knew the duke would soon arrive, and that he could not take the castle," recorded Wace.

As Poitiers told it, faced with Normandy the combined might of Gascony, Brittany and Anjou packed up and ran without a fight: "On seeing his approach, the three above-mentioned nobles departed with their huge armies with surprising speed, or one might say terrified flight."

With his protectors abandoning him, Geoffrey of Mayenne had no choice but to remember Martel's vow. He renounced his fealty to Anjou and swore it to Duke William. Mayenne, like Ambrières, became part of Normandy.

———

In October of 1056 Holy Roman Emperor Henry III had died, not yet forty years of age. His son Henry IV was only about six, so the late emperor's widow Agnes of Poitou took the imperial reins as regent. (His first wife, Cnut and Emma's daughter Goda, had died in 1038, leaving only a daughter, Beatrice.) Agnes's position was not strong, and she was eager to create alliances, even with her husband's enemy, Andreas I of Hungary, to whose son she engaged her daughter Judith. With those two countries' relations on the mend, a road suddenly opened from England to Hungary, from King Edward to his nephew Edward Aetheling, the Exile.

"King Edward growing old, with no children himself, and seeing the sons of Godwin growing in power," wrote Malmesbury, "sent messengers to the king of Hungary, requesting him to send over Edward, his brother Edmund's son, and his family, intending, he said, that either he or his sons should inherit the kingdom of England, and that his own lack of children should be rectified by that of his kin."

It's thought this time Edward sent Earl Harold, fresh off his diplomatic experience in Wales, to lead the embassy. The earl's presence in Flanders, at least, is attested in November 1056 by his signature on one of Count Baldwin's charters. Baldwin was then on his way to Cologne to secure his own treaty with the empire, and Harold may have accompanied him for his own reasons. Although the paper trail dries up in St. Omer, Harold's collection of sacred relics would include items from Ghent, Aachen, Cologne, Worms, Metz and Rheims, which would seem to indicate travels in Germany, and according to the *Vita Aedwardi* he visited Rome around this time, expanding his diplomatic experience to include continental politics.

Harold may have had quite a job to convince Edward the Exile to come home. Spirited to the Continent as an infant, having spent his entire life in eastern courts, he may not even have spoken English. He had made a good life for himself in exile. "There he gained favor with the nobility, as God willed, and it suited him," records the *Chronicle*, "so that he was given the emperor's cousin in marriage, and fathered her children. Her name was Agatha."* His daughters Christina and Margaret were nearing their teens. His son Edgar was probably about five.

This sheltered upbringing had not created Edward in the image of his father Ironside. "He was neither valiant, nor of great ability," sniffed Malmesbury. Still, in Hungary, Edward would never be anything more than a foreign prince. Here was an opportunity to become a king.

He made the journey home in the spring of 1057, probably with his family. (There's no actual evidence that they accompanied him, but they are known to have arrived in England at some point.) It's unlikely that they, even more foreign than he, would have come later, because almost as soon as he set foot on English soil, and before he even had a chance to meet his uncle, on April 19, 1057 Edward the Exile died.

Aelfscot? The rash of sudden death in high places in these decades – Forkbeard, Svein son of Aelfgifu, Harefoot, Harthacnut, even Earl Godwin – raises suspicions in the modern mind, but nobody at the time seems to have brought up poison, and in the Exile's case it's particularly hard to see who would have profited by his murder. King Edward could easily, simply have left him out of the succession by making no effort to bring him home. And if Earl Harold had wanted the *aetheling* dead, it would have been easier and less suspicious for him to have seen to it before his return to England. In the end, the Exile's death did not remove an heir to the throne; it simply created another: his young son, Edgar. All King Edward had to do was live long enough for the boy to achieve his majority.

Still, it must have seemed to the English that God had his own plans for the succession. Edward himself, in the *Vita Aedwardi*, is said

---

*Other medieval sources claim this Agatha may have been a niece, or even the sister, of Emperor Henry, though which Henry, III or IV, is not specified.

to have had another of his visions, this time a visitation by St. Peter, who told him, "The kingdom of England belongs to God, and after you he will bring forth a king according to his own will."

And God wasn't finished. He kept on clearing the Godwins' opponents off the board. Around the end of August, Earl Leofric of Mercia died. He had been the heaviest counterweight to the ambitions of the Godwins, a stabilizing factor in the back-and-forth swirl of court politics. "For his entire life," admitted Worcester, "this earl's wisdom was of the greatest use to the kings and the whole kingdom of England."

His son Aelfgar, on the other hand, had proven himself to be an unpredictable troublemaker in the tradition of Earl Godwin's late son, Sweyn. King Edward apparently recognized this tendency in earls' eldest sons. He conceded to Aelfgar taking over Mercia, but Aelfgar's earldom of East Anglia was not awarded to his own eldest son, Burgheard. Little is known of this Burgheard ("Brave Fortress"), but evidently neither king nor *witan* wished to give Aelfgar the kind of two-earldom power his father and he had wielded. Instead East Anglia went to the king's cousin, Ralf the Timid.

Aelfgar, as might be expected, did not react well to this.

Having lost Ambrières and Mayenne to Normandy, Geoffrey of Anjou knew better than to think Duke William would stop there. Desperate for an ally, the Hammer turned again to France.

Since his last invasion of Normandy, King Henry had been chafing over his decision to concede victory to Duke William without a fight. "The king could not love Normans," insisted Wace. "He preferred to go back on his word rather than let them claim victory at Mortemer. As advised by Geoffrey Martel, around August, when the grain was new, he summoned all his barons and assembled the horsemen, everyone who held fiefs from him and owed him service."

Together again, France and Anjou were determined to finish what they had started. Poitiers wrote, "Martel the Angevin who, in spite of many setbacks was not yet defeated, far from giving up, brought the largest army he could collect by any method. It would hardly have satisfied this man's raging hatred if all Normandy had been totally crushed and laid waste."

That appeared to be the goal when the French and Angevins entered Normandy from the south, headed north by forced march toward Bayeux and Caen, with the goal of cutting Normandy in half.

Even William had to think twice about engaging these combined armies. As he had before Mortemer, he played a waiting game, withdrawing to Falaise while the French and Angevins marched past, then emerging to shadow them as they marched almost to the sea. When they reached the ford over the Dives River (Celtic *Dēuā*, god, divine) at Varaville, just two and a half miles from the coast, he saw his chance. "The king had crossed the Dives, the river which runs through that part of the country," wrote Wace. "The bulk of the army did its best to keep up, but it trailed a long way behind them."

At Varaville the Dives splits and widens into its estuary, a marshy bog of almost 25,000 acres. In the summer the water levels are extremely low, but like so much of the Normandy coast, the Dives is tidal, and the water level of tidal rivers doesn't simply rise, gradually and predictably. The incoming tide is held up by the river until, with enough pressure behind it, the sea finally overcomes the flow, and the water runs upstream as a tidal bore, a deep-water surge. The French and Angevins were halfway across the shallow-water ford when suddenly the Dives became impassable. "The king did indeed get across," recorded Jumièges, "but half his army was halted by the tide, and the river having swelled, could not reach the far side."

"The sea came up and the waves grew high," agreed Wace. "You would have seen a great deal of equipment floating off, men swept into the river and sinking to the bottom. No one but a skilled swimmer could live through that." Those already across could only look back in horror as those in mid-crossing were overwhelmed by the inrushing water. Those who had not yet reached the crossing looked back in terror as well. For now was the moment that Duke William and the Norman army appeared behind them.

William did not need to defeat the French army. He had only to defeat half of it. As Wace put it, "The duke saw he had the advantage over those who were cut off."

Jumièges wrote, "The duke launched a vigorous surprise attack on those who had remained behind, and wrought great carnage on them."

"Those caught on that side of the river were nearly all slaughtered under the eyes of the king," gloated Poitiers, "except for those who, stricken by panic, preferred to take their chances in the torrent."

The French rear guard were completely outnumbered. The baggage train was easy prey for the Norman horsemen. The only escape was a rickety bridge across the ford. As Wace heard it, "When they came to the bridge, there was a great mob, with everyone struggling to cross at once. The bridge was old and the weight was too much for it. The planks gave way."

The survivors fared little better. "Those not put to the sword were taken prisoner," reported Jumièges, "and sent into hard captivity in various parts of Normandy."

"Never in Normandy, it is said, was so much loot won with such little loss of life," agreed Wace. "William thanked God. The river and the sea washed away many. The king, who saw it all, was despondent."

Once again King Henry had lost half his army without having ever engaged with the enemy himself, and once again he lost the will to go on. Poitiers wrote, "Sorrowing for the dead and fearing the destruction of the rest of his army, the king, with the tyrant of Anjou, departed Normandy as quickly as he could."

Yet William must have watched his enemies with grim realization. As long as Martel and Henry lived, they would remain threats to his dukedom. It was not enough to defeat them in Normandy. He would have to take the battle to them.

XXIX

SUPREMACY

1058–1060

[King Henry] even sought the duke's friendship, in consideration of its value, and returned to him the castle of Tillieres, which he had taken away from him a long time ago.

Jumièges

Duke William was celebrating Eastertide of 1058 in his ancestral home at Fécamp when a delegation of French bishops came to visit. Their mission was not so much religious – William had his half-brother Bishop Odo of Bayeux to handle the necessary services – as diplomatic. They had come as emissaries of King Henry in Paris, to sue for peace. Poitiers, who may have witnessed the event, recorded, "Though valiant and renowned in war, he [Henry] realized with dismay that it would be madness to ever attack Normandy again."

Henry surely realized more than that. Normandy was a bear that France had perhaps poked one too many times. In three battles – three invasions – William had gone out of his way not to personally engage Henry in conflict, which would have constituted a breach of his feudal obligations. And yet every victory gave him more confidence to do so. If the king made no accommodations to the duke, in a short time he would have bloody-handed Normans on the very doorsteps of Paris.

No evidence exists that it happened on this specific occasion – but it certainly happened *by* this occasion – that Henry ceded back to William the fortress of Tillières that he had confiscated, razed and rebuilt some twenty years before. It was a noble gesture, one that righted an old wrong, but it was about twenty years too late. Duke William accepted the offer, but no Norman warlord would have seen it as anything but a gesture of appeasement – and of weakness.

William called up Gilbert Crispin, the knight from whom he and Henry had taken the original castle of Tillières all those years before, and gave him charge of the new castle Henry had built in its place. Then he marched his army past Tillières, sixteen-odd miles further down the road to Thimert-Gâtelles, over the border in France. The castle there commanded a strategic crossroad from which the Normans could advance further south to Chartres, southwest to Le Mans, or even east toward Paris. The garrison evidently did not expect the Duke of Normandy to arrive at their gates in anger. They submitted without a fight.

And Thimert wasn't the only place where Duke William saw fit to expand his borders. In a kind of flanking maneuver he installed Gilbert's brother William at Nielfam, modern Neaufles-Saint-Martin, about forty miles northwest of Paris, for almost 150 years the border between France and Normandy. That this loss came at the expense of Count Walter of the Vexin, elder brother of Earl Ralf the Timid, nephew of King Edward and conceivable heir to the English crown in opposition to Duke William, was merely icing on the cake.

———

Ralf the Timid died on the 12th of the calends of January 1058 – December 21, 1057 on the modern calendar. He had held the earldom of East Anglia for only a few months. Gaimar shrugged, "He was a good enough man, the short while he lived."

His son Harold being not yet of age, another earl had to be found. It can be assumed the *witenagemot* held over that Christmastide was a contentious one. The former earl, Aelfgar, had three sons, Burgheard, Edwin and Morcar. The two eldest at least were probably eligible for the post. Old Earl Godwin's son Wulfnoth was still a guest of Duke William in Normandy, but the rest were already earls, even if, like Gyrth and Leofwine, of smallish earldoms. (The dates are approximate, but by this time Gyrth was probably Earl of

Cambridgeshire and Oxfordshire, and Leofwine of Essex, Middlesex, Hertford, Surrey and possibly Buckinghamshire.) Small earldoms, though, still gave each a voice in the *witan*. Aelfgar was outnumbered. His sons were passed over.

East Anglia reverted to Earl Gyrth. Leofwine, if he wasn't already, was named Earl of Kent. Together with Harold's Wessex, the family territory now ran from the Channel in the east to the Cornish coast in the west, and that wasn't counting Tostig's Northumbria. All alone in Mercia, Aelfgar found himself outnumbered and outmaneuvered. He still had his old ally Gruffydd of Wales at his back, though, and it seems that early in 1058 he sought to renew their alliance, presumably with the goal of again making trouble for England. Gruffydd, still bound by his oath of friendship with Edward, may have been hesitant to break it, so Aelfgar threw a sweetener into the deal: his daughter, Ealdgyth.

For one whose career would be so illustrious, and so tragic, there are surprisingly few details recorded of this Edith of Mercia. Jumièges described her as *pulchram*, beautiful, and Walter Map, himself Welsh, agreed Gruffydd had "a most beautiful wife," usually taken to mean Edith. She was, after all, a granddaughter of the famous beauty Lady Godiva. Her age is not known, but evidently she was not too young for marriage. At this point Gruffydd was probably about fifty, and whether still wed or a widower to his unnamed first wife, or even a third, is unknown, and immaterial. Welsh kings, like Vikings, took as many wives as they liked.

Despite the fact that Edward and Gruffydd had struck a similar bargain not that long before, the threat of a renewed alliance between Aelfgar and Gruffydd was not one the English court took lightly. Aelfgar was once again outlawed on a charge of treason.

This was certainly an overreaction on Edward's part, if it was his decision. If it was the *witan*'s, it may have been a play to have the last non-Godwin earldom of England made vacant for a son of Godwin to occupy. Either way, it had the effect of stirring a rebellion that might not otherwise have arisen. If he had not intended to before, Aelfgar now had every reason to rebel.

On their arrival at the Welsh king's court at Rhuddlan ("Red Riverbank") on a rise above the River Clwyd in the far north of Wales, Edith and her father would have learned she was not the only youth involved in the enterprise. Whether by prior plan or coincidence, as in 1055, the Welsh and Mercians were to have Viking allies.

The fleet arriving in from the Irish Sea that year was nominally commanded by Prince Magnus Haraldsson, son of King Harald of Norway, though in reality by the king's more veteran warriors. Magnus could have been little more than a figurehead, and like Edith little more than a child. His father Harald was still busy warring against Denmark, but had sent his eldest son off on an easy first expedition through the Orkneys, Western Isles of Scotland and the Isle of Man to learn the ropes and perhaps get his first taste of blood. He was evidently a quick study, or had able lieutenants. Even the Welsh account of events, the *Brut y Tywysogion*, gives him most of the credit, casting Gruffydd as backup and Aelfgar not at all.

English rebels, Welsh, and Vikings; England had been down this road before, but contrary to the *Brut* there does not seem to have been ravaging in 1058 on the scale of that in 1055. English accounts give it little notice. In fact, the only version of the *Chronicle* to so much as mention it in 1058 is the Worcester edition, and its writer sounds almost bored with the topic, or perhaps is glossing over a mistake: "It is tedious to tell how it all happened." It may be that the chronicler erred with the dates, and that the two episodes are one and the same, the only difference being the specific mention of Magnus.

But that mention is important. Because both young Magnus and young Edith would grow to rule their respective thirds of old King Cnut's North Sea Empire.

Briefly...

———

With events in the west at least temporarily settled again, events in the north now took precedence. By this time Macbeth was dead. Malcolm was left as the apparent heir to the throne. Gaelic tradition demanded he reward his supporters with a *crech ríg*, a "royal plundering" or "royal preying" on his neighbors. The Scots probably raided into Strathclyde and the Viking fiefs in the Orkneys, but minor warfare in those regions was so endemic and of little note, and local documentation so spotty, that it can't be confirmed. Part of Malcolm's purpose, though, was undoubtedly to prove to his chieftains that he was no mere English puppet. It was Earl Siward who had put him on his rightful throne, not Earl Tostig, and the Scots considered their debt to England void. Geoffrey Gaimar noted that "they often harried Northumberland."

"When Earl Tostig ruled," concurs the *Vita Aedwardi*, "the Scots, since they had not yet tested him and so thought less of him, often harassed him with raids instead of war."

Having proven his worth to his chieftains, Malcolm convinced them it was better to show loyalty to Earl Tostig, as the *Vita* proclaims: "And so they and their king thought it better to serve him and King Edward than to carry on fighting, and, what is more, to confirm the peace by offering hostages."

Part of this 1059 treaty is thought to have been the betrothal of Malcolm to Margaret, daughter of the late Edward Aetheling. She was probably in her early teens, and not present at the meeting, so an actual wedding would have to take place later. (As shall be seen, events would intervene, putting off the nuptials until 1070.) The truce with Scotland sounds strikingly like that made with Wales, in which Edith of Mercia was bargained away to King Gruffydd in exchange for a ceasefire. In both cases it merely gave each side time to rest and re-arm before resuming battle. As Gaimar described the peace, "It lasted but short while."

For that matter, the same could be said for the peace between Normandy and France.

In the midsummer of 1059 King Henry laid siege to the Norman garrison William had installed in his newly captured castle at Thimert. The struggle was to drag on and on with neither commander paying much attention to it. Both were busy fortifying the entire Epte River valley, with seven castles eventually built or rebuilt on the Norman bank and eight on the French. William rewarded his lieutenants, among them William fitzOsbern and possibly Roger de Beaumont, with charge of these redoubts, and, mindful of his back, around this same time he also named his younger half-brother Robert as Count of Mortaine in far western Normandy. Malmesbury described Robert as "thick and dull-witted," but he would prove to be another of William's most steadfast men.

And about this time there were other edifices that William and Matilda undertook to build. In January there had been a new Pope elected, Nicholas II. (Actually there had been several popes since Leo IX's death in 1054 – Victor II and Stephen IX, not to mention an usurping antipope, Benedict X – but Nicholas, a Burgundian, took a pragmatic view of William's marriage to his very distant cousin Matilda.) By this time the ducal marriage had already been blessed with six children: Robert (born circa 1051), Richard (1054), Adeliza (1055), Cecilia (1056), William (1056) and Constance (1057). And they weren't done yet. Malmesbury wrote of the duke, "He had many children by Matilda, whose submission to her husband and fecundity stirred in him the tenderest love for her, although there were some who grumbled about him renouncing his former chastity."

The duke had been doing in good faith what he could to expiate his supposed sin, establishing a hundred pretends – paid clerics – to care for the poor and downtrodden in various cities across Normandy. In this spirit, Nicholas absolved him and Matilda of sin, at a price: the construction of two abbeys in Caen, one for men and one for women. The Abbey of Saint-Étienne and Abbey of Sainte-Trinité, better known as the *Abbaye aux Hommes*, "Men's Abbey," and the *Abbaye aux Dames*, "Ladies' Abbey," still stand in Caen today.

In France King Henry, too, had similar reasons to look to the future instead of the past. In May of 1059 he had crowned his eight-year-old son as co-king, Philip I. Perhaps he and William, being symbolic father and son as well, felt it was time to settle their differences for their children's sake. The siege of Thimert had been going on unabated all this time, but August of 1060 found William at Courdemanche, just across the Eure from Henry at Dreux, and it's thought they came together to undertake peace negotiations.

Unfortunately God had a different peace in mind for Henry. Jumièges wrote:

The most skillful of doctors prescribed him a potion to heal his body. But this potion having given him a burning thirst, he disdained the orders of his first doctor, and during his absence had himself given to drink by his *valet de chambre*, and drank before he had been purged. He became much sicker, and died the same day, after having received the Holy Eucharist.

At fifty-two, Henry had lived longer than most men of that time, and as has been amply shown, sudden death was not unusual even among nobles. Judging by the description, this doctor's potion, whatever it was – and who knows what ill-considered medieval ingredients were in it – sounds less medicinal than toxic. Even Malmesbury declared that "Henry, king of France, a good and energetic warrior, died of poison."

Then, a few months later, in November 1060, another of William's opponents dropped dead.

"Geoffrey Martel also died, as wished by many, either those whom he had oppressed, or those who feared him," reported Poitiers with his usual lack of objectivity. "Thus nature puts an inevitable end to earthly power and human pride."

Coincidence? Possibly. What matters is, with Henry and Martel dead, perhaps no one in Western Europe sat so secure in power as Duke William of Normandy...other than the earls Harold, Tostig and their brothers, the sons of Earl Godwin, in England.

XXX

FRAGILE PEACE

1061

And so, the kingdom being strengthened by these princes on every side, the most kind King Edward led his life in security and quiet, and spent most of his time hunting in the forests and glades.

Vita Aedwardi Regis

When King Henry and Count Geoffrey died, in their early fifties, King Edward was already nearing sixty. Surely everyone at court, not least the king himself, realized he was in the sunset of his reign. This is the period of his life by which he is best known to history, in which his legacy as Edward the Confessor was made.* His *Vita* declares, "He showed much mercy to the poor and weak, and supported many such not only every day in his royal court, indeed, through most of the places of his kingdom, at his own expense."

Edward would become famous for the King's Touch, the ability to remedy disease by a laying-on of hands or anointing with the royal washwater. By this he is said to have cured several of his subjects of blindness, and a woman of both scrofula (a tuberculous infection of the lymph nodes) and barrenness, after which she bore twins.

---

*The title of "Confessor of the Faith" once referred to any saint who confessed Christianity publicly and suffered persecution for it, though not fatally (which would make him or her a martyr instead). By medieval times, when Christians were no longer persecuted, it referred to any worthy soul who lived religiously and died peacefully.

Work on his abbey at Westminster was ongoing. The *Vita* declares, "There was no concern for the costs, spent or to come, as long as it proved appropriate to, and justifiable by, God and St. Peter."

As with the Normans, building, restoring and decorating churches was a common pastime among Anglo-Saxon nobles. Earl Tostig and his Countess Judith were great patrons of Durham Cathedral in Northumbria and its shrine of St. Cuthbert, despite the fact that the countess herself, as a woman, was not allowed entry. "When he gave alms," Edith's *Vita* says of Tostig, "he gave lavishly, and more often this was done at the religious urging of his spouse in the honor of Christ, than for any frail support of men."

For his part Earl Harold poured his devotions into Waltham Abbey. Tovi the Proud having died in the 1040s, and his son being caught up in Osgod Clapa's rebellion, King Edward had given the abbey, along with the Black Rood, to Harold. According to the *Vita Haroldi*, he had it rebuilt in stone. Instead of a monastery (and perhaps befitting one raised to be a man of letters), Harold endowed Waltham as a collegiate church, with clerks, secular priests, a dean, and his old benefactor Adelard of Liege as chancellor. He gifted it with estates and valuables, said to include seven shrines (three gold, four gilded silver), four bibles bound with gold, silver and gems, four gold and silver censers, six candelabras (two gold, the rest silver), four crosses worked in gold, silver and jewels, priestly vestments decorated with gold and gems and much more. No doubt in reverence for the Black Rood, the church was dedicated on May 3, 1060: Roodmas, the feast day of the Finding of the Holy Cross, the day when Saint Helena discovered the True Cross in Jerusalem in AD 326. The service was attended by no less than King Edward, Queen Edith, and the leading churchmen of the kingdom, presided over by Archbishop Cynesige of York.* The ceremonies and celebrations went on for a week, in the course of which the king confirmed Harold's gifts with a charter he signed in gold lettering.

---

*Archbishop Stigand had refused to give up his sees of both Canterbury and Winchester, and held the abbeys of Gloucester and of Ely, and probably others too. It was for this pluralism that he was excommunicated by five consecutive popes, and though neither Stigand nor Edward seem too bothered by this – as has been seen, excommunications were not uncommon and easily rescinded – Earl Harold evidently preferred a canonical minister to consecrate his church.

In his personal religious pursuits, however, King Edward is said to have gone in the other, more austere, ascetic direction, taking seriously his role of patriarch, and gradually assuming a biblical look, as his *Vita* describes: "His person was very decent, of distinct height, with hair and beard marked with milky gray hair, a full face and rosy skin, thin and snow-white hands, and also with long shining fingers, the rest of the body a perfect and regal man."

Part of the look was the king's disregard for ostentation, which Queen Edith took pains to overcome. "Even the pompous royal finery in which she dressed him as her queenly duty, he wore only on occasion, making it plain that he took no pleasure in it, and would not care a whit if he was not adorned at so much expense."

Of course, according to Queen Edith's account, Edward was said to appreciate the fact that she saw to it he was properly dressed. To judge by certain parts of the *Vita Aedwardi Regis*, it might more properly be titled the *Encomium Edithae Reginae*, because the queen's writer is not remiss in singing her praises. Not to be outdone by her husband's and brothers' church work, she turned her favors on her *alma mater*, Wilton Abbey. The nuns there had raised her to be a worthy queen, but they were not educated in construction and they were too poor to hire workmen. Like her brother and husband, Edith adopted their church as her own, undertaking to have the wooden nunnery rebuilt in stone. Edward's *Vita* admits, "In this way the king and queen competed, which was pleasing to God and agreeable to both. But the frugal queen's building, because it was better planned, was finished more quickly."

Despite their friendly rivalry, the queen was ever careful to defer to her husband. "Though by custom and right a throne was kept for her at the king's side, she preferred to sit at his feet at the front of the church and at the royal table, unless he might hold out his hand to her, or by a gesture invite her to sit beside him, or command her to."

Reading between the lines, it might be pointed out that Edith was in this way placing herself between the king and any subjects who might approach him. And Edward's reputation is equally suspect, made for him by later writers after his death. In life he was perhaps not quite as saintly as described. Riding to the hunt with hawks and hounds is not exactly a holy pursuit, and even his *Vita* admits he had a temper "as terrible as a lion," though he was circumspect in showing it. That is most likely because he had no real power over those most likely to anger him – namely, the Godwins. And Edward had time for all that hunting and prayer because he entrusted the hard work of governing to others, as the *Vita* also admits: "Imposing the cause of God upon his bishops and men of law, he admonished them to act accordingly, ordering the princes of the judiciary and the lawyers of his palace to judge justly."

Edward's casual – not to say slovenly – dress, his disregard of duty, his concealed anger toward underlings, might also mark a man who felt keenly the loss of all his power to a domineering wife and her brothers, and along with it his self-respect, which is why he took every opportunity to get away into the woods with his hounds and hawks.

Who can say what kind of king Edward the Confessor would have been, given all his royal power and the will to use it? It mattered little to his subjects whether their king was a figurehead, particularly those old enough to remember the bad old days of his father's reign. The various editions of the *Chronicle*, in these entries for the early 1060s, report little more tumult in England than the pilgrimages, deaths and replacements of bishops and archbishops. They are a summary of uninteresting, peaceful times, which is the important thing to any people and which, as the *Vita* records, they attributed to King Edward: "In his wisdom abolishing unjust laws and establishing just ones, he made all Britain happy, over which, by the grace of God and by hereditary right, the pious king presides."

Archbishop Cynesige of York, who had helped secure the peace between Edward of England and Malcolm of Scotland in 1059 and consecrated Harold's abbey at Waltham that May, died three days before Christmas of 1060. On Christmas Day, Bishop Ealdred of Worcester – the unsuccessful military commander and mediocre royal diplomat, but social-climbing church officer – was raised to the archbishopric. (This was probably King Edward and the *witan* hoping that a southern bishop would help the southern earl, Tostig, keep a lid on the rambunctious northerners.) Like Stigand, however, Ealdred did not give up his bishopric of Worcester. That was not unprecedented. York was a step up from Worcester in status, but not income, and Ealdred probably thought it his just due to hold both.

The recent rapid turnover in popes had sent waves of trouble rippling through the church. Archbishop Stigand of Canterbury and Winchester, appointed by the king in 1052, had received his pallium, his mantle of office, from Pope Benedict X in 1058. But Benedict, being just one of the claimants to the title of pontiff at the time, had been chased out of Rome and declared an usurping antipope by Nicholas, which put Stigand's legitimacy in question. Meanwhile, for his own legitimacy, Ealdred needed a pallium for himself. When Edward furthermore wished to raise two of his clerics to bishoprics, neither Stigand nor Ealdred could ordain them. In light of Ealdred's travels (he had visited Rome in 1050, and in 1058 had been the first English bishop to journey to Jerusalem), in the spring of 1061 King Edward decided to send him and the bishops to straighten things out with Nicholas. As a negotiating tool, they took along the previous year's *Romescot*, the Rome Tax reinstituted in the days of King Cnut.

All this figures into our story because the deputation was to be escorted by Earl Tostig.

He had succeeded in pacifying his earldom of Northumbria, proving himself just as violent as the most murderous of his vassals. Edward's *Vita* attests, "This son of God and great lover of peace had so weakened the evildoers at that time, purging the country by torture or by killing them, and sparing no one of any nobility who was caught in a crime, that people could travel alone with whatever goods they liked, without fear of attack."

With Northumbria quieted, Tostig felt free to visit Rome, accompanied by his wife Countess Judith and his brother Earl Gyrth of East Anglia. They were joined by Burgheard, eldest son of Earl Aelfgar of Mercia, but whether as a guest or a hostage against misbehavior by his father while two Godwinson earls were out of the country is anybody's guess.

In addition to the Rome Tax, Cnut had negotiated for the safety of English pilgrims on the road to Rome, and though the signees to that agreement were all dead it seems the deal still held in Tostig's day. "He crossed over [the Channel], through Saxony and the upper Rhine, and reached the borders of Rome," recounts the *Vita Aedwardi*. "And what language or what words could properly explain with how much devotion and generosity he venerated each shrine along the way...?"

As it turned out, the trip over the Alps and through Lombardy was more pleasant than the embassy's welcome in the Eternal City. Tostig was received with due respect by Pope Nicholas, who even seated the earl beside him at the Easter synod. However, Ealdred's diplomatic skills – not for the first time, putting it nicely – let him down. Pope Nicholas was a reformer, not inclined to look favorably on his predecessors' wheeling and dealing in church matters, and furthermore he was willing to make an example of faraway England, which to Rome was something of a hinterland. What Ealdred saw, and freely admitted to, as his legitimate rise to the duties of the archbishopric, Nicholas saw as simony (the trade in religious offices), pluralism (holding the two sees, York and Worcester, at once) and translation (transferring between sees without papal permission). The *Vita* admits, "When the apostolic and pontifical decrees were examined his request was rejected by the whole synod. Not only did he not obtain the use of the pallium, indeed he had to step down from the episcopate and retreat in confusion."

Ealdred was to leave Rome no longer an archbishop, or bishop, or so much as a parish deacon. He was all but excommunicated. William of Malmesbury, in addition to writing his *Gesta Regum Anglorum*, "Deeds of the Kings of the English," also wrote the *Vita Wulfstani*, a biography of Bishop Wulfstan of Worcester, who replaced Ealdred in that see. In it he recorded Ealdred's disgrace, and Tostig's reaction: "Earl Tostig, who had come with him, threatened greatly that after this the money which England had contributed to the Roman pope for so many years, would no longer be paid."[*]

Suffice to say the royal delegation had failed miserably. Adding insult to injury, the *Chronicle* reveals, "The bishop and the earl met with great difficulty as they returned home."

The *Vita Aedwardi* goes into more detail: "when they were returning together from Rome, they met with robbers on the same day [they left], and were despoiled and plundered, some of them even to nakedness." (Luckily Earl Tostig had sent Countess Judith ahead earlier. She and her ladies made it home with their money and virtue intact.)

---

[*]This was not just a hotheaded reaction from Tostig, but a tactic popes and English kings would use repeatedly in their dealings with each other, right up to Elizabethan times.

This was no mere robber band, however, but friends of the antipope, Benedict X, who were either extremely lucky in their choice of victims, or had accomplices inside Nicholas's court. They appear to have had advance knowledge of when and by which route the English delegation was headed home (the inland Via Cassia, as opposed to the coastal Via Aurelia), that its purse was still full of *Romescot*, and furthermore that even if ex-Archbishop Ealdred was now worthless, Earl Tostig would make a fine hostage for ransom.

There was a struggle. Burgheard, it's thought, was wounded before Tostig (somewhat to his disgrace) and the rest of the party escaped back to Rome.

Pope Nicholas was so humiliated by this demonstration of his lack of real power anywhere more than a few miles outside the Eternal City – and in light of it, doubtless advised by his synod that offending all of England, and losing that future income, was not a good idea – that he agreed to reinstate Ealdred on the condition that he give up one of his sees (hence his replacement the next year by Wulfstan as Bishop of Worcester). Then he loaded the English with gifts and sent them on on their way.

But they didn't all make it. They had to pause their journey in northern France, at Reims, to conduct a funeral.

Apparently from wounds sustained in the struggle outside Rome, Burgheard, son of Aelfgar and presumed heir to the earldom of Mercia, had died.

This was just the beginning of Tostig's problems.

In 1059, or even earlier, Tostig and Malcolm of Scotland had sworn an oath of brotherhood, but in 1061, with the English brother away in Rome, the Scottish one took the opportunity to steal behind his back. The Holy Island of Lindisfarne is a tidal islet off the extreme north coast of Northumbria. The monastery there was famous as the first bastion of Christianity in the north, the home of its patron saint, Cuthbert, but also, in AD 793, the site of the first Viking raid in England, today taken as the beginning of the Viking Age. Remote monasteries, both helpless and wealthy, were always inviting targets for raiders, and with Harald of Norway and Svein of Denmark still preoccupied in warring on each other – and the Earl of Northumbria gone south – there was opportunity for lesser men to take advantage.

The Scots, a people of the highlands and glens, were never as renowned as the Scandinavians or Irish as seagoing pirates. But Lindisfarne is a tidal island – at low tide, not an island at all, but a peninsula connected by an ithsmus to the mainland – and only a little over eleven miles from the Scottish border. For the Scots it would have been a mere day trip down to the pilgrims' path across the sand beach and mud flats, to enjoy six hours of Viking-esque pillage before the tide rose again, but they could not have tarried long at their work. Lindisfarne was only about five miles across the water (though about twice that far along the coast) from Bamburgh, formerly *Bebbanburh*, the one-time capital of Celtic *Bernicia* before the coming of the Anglo-Saxons. It had been razed by returning Vikings in 993, but the Bamburghers might have expected God to protect them from fellow Christians. The Scots were apparently not the same creed of Christian. Gaimar wrote, "Holy Island was then harried, which before had been always spared."

For pagan Vikings to have ransacked the monastery was bad enough. They had at least gone home across the North Sea afterward. These Scots still lurked just over the border, threatening to raid again at any time. Earl Tostig did not need this kind of trouble, not after the fatal wounding of Earl Aelfgar's son Burgheard in Italy while Tostig had made good his escape, or his near-break with Pope Nicholas (who, it must be said, had died that July and was replaced by Alexander II, probably even before Tostig's party arrived home). Bamburgh was so far north that it had only been part of Northumbria for ten years, after Siward, on King Harthacnut's orders, had treacherously slain Earl Eadwulf. Earl Tostig may not have even been sure his subjects would fight for him, against either Malcolm or Aelfgar. It was necessary to throw cold water on the whole situation. Gaimar said simply, "Peace was made with Malcolm."

This did little to calm the northerners, to whom it must have looked as though this southern liege of theirs had left them to be preyed upon by the Scottish king, and done nothing to exact retribution. This simmering unrest would soon spread across all Northumbria. Gaimar wrote, "The people of York, on his return, hated Tostig so that he could not enter the city."

XXXI

CONQUERORS
1062–1063

After having gloriously triumphed over the armies of the Franks, the great Duke William, remembering the insults that Count Geoffroy had made him, directed his arms for some years against the city of Le Mans.

Jumièges

Count Herbert II of Maine, who to escape the grip of Geoffrey Martel had thrown himself on Duke William's mercy back in 1056, died in March 1062. He being only about fifteen, his pledge to marry one of the duke's daughters went unfulfilled. More importantly, his pledge that, if he died childless, his countcy of Maine was to go to Duke William still stood – at least, in William's mind. (This claim, made by Poitiers and no one else, sounds suspiciously like the only slightly more corroborated claim that Edward the Confessor had willed England to Normandy.)

As usual, the rulers of France and Anjou might have objected to Normandy annexing Maine. For a change, neither was powerful enough to do anything about it. Young King Philip of France was guided by his co-regents, his mother Anne of Kiev and Duke William's father-in-law Count Baldwin V of Flanders, who naturally enough refrained from advising his ward to go against the interests of his daughter, Duchess Matilda. On the other side, Count Geoffrey the Bearded of Anjou was an ineffectual commander who would eventually be usurped by his younger brother Fulk, and was not in a position to do anything about Duke William.

312

One person of a mind to interfere in William's plans was Walter, Count of the Vexin. The duke's recent encroachment on his lands in the Epte River valley, Mantes and Chaumont, had him on the lookout for new territory, and being married to the late Count Herbert's aunt, he felt he had something of a hereditary right to make himself the next Count of Maine. As King Edward's nephew he had never followed up his claim to the English crown, but he wasn't going to let Duke William take Maine without a fight. As well, in this dispute he had the backing, from the other side of Maine, of Geoffrey of Mayenne.

Having been let down by Geoffrey the Hammer those few years before, Geoffrey of Mayenne had been building up his forces to take on William himself. "Whenever he needed he could easily have mustered a thousand knights without much effort," admitted Wace. "He was a man of extensive property and very great power."

Geoffrey had sworn fealty to William, but by force. He was married to the late Count Herbert's sister and doubtless entertained aspirations of his own in Maine. "In his impudent audacity he forgot how previously, in defeat, he had pleaded for mercy," wrote Poitiers. "In his shameless villainy he was not afraid to break his sworn oath."

About thirty miles south of Alençon the city of Le Mans, today best known for its grueling twenty-four-hour motorcar race, was then the capital of Maine. It dated from the pre-Roman days of Gaul, though the Romans had taken it in 47 BC and named it *Vindunum*, "White Citadel." With the advent of Christianity Le Mans became home to one of the largest bishoprics in France, and a center for craftsmen – wheelwrights, carpenters and saddlers. It was a bigger city than any in Anjou, Mayenne or the Vexin, and a ripe plum for the man who could rule it.

Geoffrey might wish to be that man, even as a vassal of Walter of the Vexin, but he had no intention of letting Duke William trap him inside. "He entered Le Mans once, but did not stay long and quickly abandoned it," wrote Wace. "He did not dare await the duke and would not have been able to defend himself."

"Indignant at this rebellion," continued Poitiers, "William, who had more than enough right to succeed Herbert, took up arms to recover what had been taken from him." Summoning the fighting men of Normandy, and allies from Brittany and Flanders, he marched on Maine, burning towns and villages along the way.

The campaign dragged on into 1063. William had proven himself adept at besieging castles, but besieging a walled city was something else. Poitiers, ever supportive of his lord, put things in a favorable light: "To immediately burn or level the whole city, and to slaughter those who dared iniquity, with his abundant skill and strength he could easily have done. But rather than shed blood, even from the guilty, he preferred moderation, and left that most powerful city intact, as capital and strength of the land which he held in his hand."

Jumièges was less flattering: "Who could say by how many invasions of his horsemen, by how many expeditions of his legions, he maltreated this city?"

The Normans could not break into Le Mans, and the citizens would not come out. "They frequently called on Geoffrey whom their governor, Walter, had named as their lord and defender," Poitiers jeered. "They sometimes threatened to give battle, but never dared."

So Duke William undertook a campaign of scorched earth around the city and across the countcy. Terror raids, fields burned, lesser fortresses taken and garrisoned with Normans, and general havoc soon convinced the people of Maine that Walter and Geoffrey could not protect them, and let the people of Le Mans know their freedom came at the price of a devastated countryside.

Poitiers claimed Walter of the Vexin was willing to give up what he had never really ruled, to avoid goading the Normans into taking Mantes and Chaumont, much closer to him. According to Orderic Vitalis, negotiations took a sinister turn while Walter and his wife were the guests of the Normans in Falaise: "While the gallant duke was launching attack after attack against the rebels, now winning, now losing, as war goes, Count Walter and his wife Biota both died at the same time, poisoned – according to rumor – by the evil schemes of their enemies."

Bereft of everything including a leader, the defenders lost heart. Jumièges concluded, "Finally, and after he had subdued every fortress in the land, the people of Le Mans, defeated, reached out their hands to the duke, and pledged their fealty to him with the most solemn oaths."

William did not sack Le Mans. Poitiers recorded, "The champion thought they had been punished enough, being subdued and brought under his control, and that the citadel of the town should henceforth host a Norman garrison."

"He had stone and lime brought there and built a tower," concluded Wace. "He took their oaths and homage and accepted hostages from the barons so that they would keep their word, maintain the peace and serve him loyally."

That did for Maine.

Now for Mayenne.

In England, as on the Continent, the death of a lord often led to war. In 1062 it was Earl Aelfgar of Mercia. The date is uncertain. His signature on a royal charter dated December 31 is of doubtful authenticity. His last certain appearance in the records is as a witness to the appointment of Wulfstan to replace Ealdred as Bishop of Worcester on September 8. Sometime between then and the end of the year, he passed away.

This was an event of great import, to the Godwins and to England. Aelfgar had been the last man standing between them and total domination of the court of King Edward. His eldest surviving son, Edwin, birthdate unknown but at least fourteen, was, like Harold, a second son, not raised to rule, but thrust into the job. He would be easily influenced, easily guided, and he was no threat to the Godwins. (He received not the slightest mention in the *Chronicle* until 1065, and may not have been immediately confirmed as earl.) Harold and his brothers likely even preferred a Mercian to continue to rule over Mercia, to maintain at least the appearance of a balance of power.

But the balance of power that Aelfgar's death upset was the one spanning the River Dee, with Wales.

With his father-in-law's death, and despite being married to Edwin's sister Edith, King Gruffydd apparently felt his partnership with Mercia to be at an end. The *Vita Aedwardi* testifies that he immediately resumed raiding onto English soil: "He launched unjust war across the Severn, and England endured his hostile attacks until worthy and famous King Edward compelled him to regret it."

News of the attacks would quickly have reached the king, who that Christmas was holding court at Gloucester, not far from the Welsh border. There it was decided that Earl Harold should put an end to Gruffydd's depredations once and for all. The task was to be accomplished by a surprise midwinter raid on his castle at Rhuddlan.

By tradition Welsh kings let their war bands go home for Christmas. Gruffydd would be caught defenseless. According to Worcester, Harold "put himself in charge of a small body of horse, and proceeded by rapid ride from Gloucester, where the king then was, to Rhuddlan."

From Gloucester to Rhuddlan, as the crow flies, is a little over a hundred miles. In midwinter the riders probably did not take that route through the barren Welsh hill country, but stayed east of Offa's Dyke, in English territory, perhaps loosely following the modern *Llwybr Clawdd Offa*, Offa's Dyke Path. An average hiker can cover that route, about 175 miles past the Black Mountains, through forest and moor country, in about twelve days, and given the need to rest and graze their horses, a medieval cavalry troop probably did little better. At its northernmost extremity near the Irish Sea coast, the path comes within four miles of Rhuddlan.

Lookouts on the barren Welsh hilltops, however, could easily have spotted horsemen from miles away. Word of Harold's coming arrived ahead of him. Worcester reported, "Gruffydd, being alerted to the earl's approach, fled with his household, and with extreme difficulty escaped by ship. Harold, finding him gone, burned his palace, set fire to his ships and rigging, and began marching homeward the same day."

That was a disappointment, but Harold wasn't done yet. Gruffydd might think he could always escape by water, but that needn't be so. Come spring the earl gathered a fleet at Bristol and had it sail around the Welsh coast, launching raids inland and positioning itself to cut Rhuddlan off from the sea. Meanwhile Earl Tostig came down from Northumbria with his own troop of horsemen, riding right across Mercia (which Earl Aelfgar might have taken as an act of war, but to which his son Earl Edwin made no recorded objection). Now the Welsh got a taste of the ransacking they had so often inflicted on the English. Unable to match the brother earls in battle, Gruffydd withdrew into the wild mountains of Snowdonia, from which to draw the English into a war of attrition. The *Brut y Tywysogion* confirms: "The once invincible man was now left to the desolate glens after claiming immeasurable spoils, winning countless battles, and possessing uncounted gold, silver, jewels, and purple raiments."

Gruffydd wanted attrition. Attrition he got. The 12th/13th-century Welsh cleric and historian Gerald of Wales would claim that Harold "scarcely left a man there alive."

All summer the English pressed the Welsh so hard that they grew to desire peace more than they loved their king. Gruffydd had attained his throne through the assassination of his precedessor, Iago ab Idwal ap Meurig. Now Iago's son, Cynan ab Iago, claimed vengeance. The *Chronicle* reports, "King Gruffydd was slain on the nones of August [the 5th] by his own men, as a result of the war he waged with Earl Harold. He was king over all Wales. His head was brought to Earl Harold, who sent it to the king [Edward], with his ship's prow, and the rigging with it."

Harold laid down the law on the vanquished foe. Any Welshman caught with a spear on the wrong side of Offa's Dyke was to have his right hand struck off. Wales was to be divided again, between Gruffydd's brothers, who gave King Edward hostages, swore their fealty and paid him tribute. Gruffydd's widow Edith, sister of Edwin and Morcar of Mercia, survived her husband, either becoming Edward's prisoner or going home to her brothers. As her husband's conqueror, Earl Harold might rightfully have claimed her as a war bride – he had so decimated the male population of Wales that King Edward gave special permission for Welsh women to marry Englishmen – but then Harold was already married, even if unofficially, to his own Edith, Edith Swanneshals. He and Tostig went home, having ended a threat that had tormented England for a generation.

Furthermore, Harold's conduct as a military commander – his quick-march raid, his combined land-sea operation in coordination with his brother, uniting the warriors of Wessex and Northumbria – was proof that he was more than a diplomat, more than the king's ambassador. So the Welsh would not forget this, Gerald of Wales recalled, he dotted their countryside with standing stones inscribed HIC VICTOR FUIT HAROLDUS: *Here Harold Was Victorious.*

They marked him out as what his father Godwin had been: the true power behind the English throne, in all but title, king.

"The wily Geoffrey of Mayenne," recorded Poitiers, "learned just how far out of Duke William's favor he was, when the city of Le Mans surrendered." With Maine lost to him, and his liege lord Walter of the Vexin dead, Baron Geoffrey fled home to his castle on the outcrop above the Mayenne River. "Repeatedly called upon by messenger to submit, he persevered in his stubborn course. Flight, cunning, and strong fortifications served him well."

Geoffrey was right to feel secure. His keep was actually one of the most well sited and advanced in the region. To guard against Breton attacks, the original wooden fortress had been rebuilt in stone sometime after AD 900, with two floors, a staircase turret and square tower. Poitiers wrote, "The far side of this citadel is washed by a rocky, rapid river, for it is situated on a steep mountainous rock above the bank of the Mayenne, cannot be attempted by any man, by any trick, or by human skill. On the other side, it is defended by stone ramparts and equally difficult approaches." The Normans, he reported, were skeptical and downtrodden at the prospect of attempting to storm such a castle. "Indeed, with swords, lances, and missiles, nothing is to be done, nothing is expected to be done, neither with a battering ram, nor with a ballista, nor with any other instruments of war. The place is completely unsuited for siege machinery."

Only William maintained his optimism. His men duly settled in, as at Arques, to starve the defenders out, but the duke had other ideas. Poitiers had the attackers launching fireballs over the walls onto the buildings inside, but according to Jumièges, "The duke led his army there, besieged it for some time, and seized it, having set it on fire by means of two children who had entered the place secretly, to play with other children."

"The guards and defenders," wrote Poitiers, "stunned by the sudden defeat, abandoned the gates and walls and ran in panic to first help their burning buildings and property."

With the walls undefended, the Normans were able to attack the castle gate directly. They burst inside, driving the defenders into the central tower. Deprived of their provisions, with no one coming to their rescue, Mayenne and his men had little hope of holding out. The Normans were already dividing the outer spoils when, Poitiers wrote, "The defenders, who had taken refuge in the citadel, surrendered the next day, not trusting any defense against William's skill and courage."

Geoffrey was taken alive and made to swear fealty to Duke William (again), who repaired the castle and stocked it with his own fighting men as yet another outpost of Normandy. Geoffrey, having finally learned his lesson, was lucky to experience the benign side of his duke's retribution.

For the Duke of Normandy, aged about thirty-five, the fall of Mayenne closed a chapter of his life that had begun with the death of his father Robert, almost thirty years before. His neighbors in Anjou, in Poitou and Boulogne, and Brittany and Flanders and France, looked on him with trepidation, for any new territorial aspirations he dreamed would come at their expense.

Unless he looked across the sea, to England.

The addition of the Island Kingdom to Normandy would create a new maritime empire even greater than old King Cnut's, and William would not have to fight the rest of the empire to take it. Up in Scandinavia, the kings Harald of Normandy and Svein of Denmark had spent sixteen years fighting to a bloody draw that had brought the age of the Vikings to near conclusion. Both countries lay prostrate and exhausted. Svein was happy just to keep what he had. And to satisfy his own ravenous need for conquest, Harald, ever the aggressor, was not looking south but east, to Sweden. Scandinavia had become a backwater of Vikings busier killing each other than outsiders.

The conquests of 1063, of Maine and Mayenne, and that of Wales, established Duke William and Earl Harold as the two preeminent military commanders of Western Europe. Each man stood unopposed in his own domain. Both England and Normandy were finally at peace, and left to their own devices might have remained so for years. Yet, even in modern times, economic growth is necessary to feed population growth, and in that violent age economic growth came mostly through military expansion. In retrospect a clash between England and Normandy would seem almost inevitable, but at the time it was almost out of the question. The English Channel presented an insurmountable obstacle to the Normans, who – as William's father Robert had proven – were not sea raiders like their Viking forefathers.

It was equally unlikely that the English crown itself would cross the Channel to Normandy. The rumor that King Edward had promised William his throne was still no more than rumor. Earl Harold, the *de facto* King of England, had not yet had his say in the matter. He and Duke William had never even met, at war or in peace.

That was about to change. And with it, the future of the Island Kingdom.

XXXII

UBI HAROLD DUX ANGLORUM ET SUI MILITES
EQUITANT AD BOSHAM
HIC HAROLD MARE NAVIGAVIT
ET VELIS VENTO PLENIS VENIT IN TERRAM
VVIDONIS COMITIS

Where Harold, an earl of the English, and his soldiers ride to Bosham.
Here Harold sailed the sea
And, the wind full in his sails, he came to the country of Count Guy.

Bayeux Tapestry

The Bayeux Tapestry, like an 11th-century comic strip, reads left to right. The far-left end, the beginning, is carefully planned, with a border trimmed and embroidered at the chosen starting point. Whether, as various historians opine, commissioned by Duke William's brother Bishop Odo of Bayeux, or his queen Matilda, or even King Edward's Queen Edith, the Tapestry is indisputably pro-Norman in its storytelling. And for the Normans the story starts with Earl Harold's trip to the Continent in 1064. Anything that came before doesn't matter, not even the supposed pledge of the kingdom to Duke William by King Edward. By the time the Tapestry was woven, that pledge was moot.

And the Norman version of this event is, for the most part, the only one extant. The *Anglo-Saxon Chronicle* makes no mention of Earl

Harold's trip. In fact, its only mention of the year 1064 is mistaken, recounting events that actually took place in 1065. (Though we might note that no mention was made in the chronicles of Harold's trip to Flanders in 1056 either.) It's almost as though the English, or Harold himself, had his 1064 trip stricken from the official record – for which, as it turned out, he might have had good reason.

Why Harold would cross the Channel in the first place is even more mysterious. Wace took the English view that Harold wished to retrieve his brother Wulfnoth and nephew Hakon, Sweyn's son – both sent by Edward to Duke William as hostages during the unpleasantness of 1051–1052 and never returned – but his ship lost its way: "I cannot say what mistake was made, either the helmsman or the navigation, but I know he went astray."

Orderic, Poitiers and Jumièges took the Norman view that Harold went on Edward's orders to personally confirm Duke William as rightful heir to the English throne. Malmesbury wasn't so sure. "Some agree that the king sent Harold to Normandy on this mission," he admitted. "Others, who knew Harold's more secret intentions, claim he was driven there against his will by a violent wind, and made up this story as an excuse." He believed that Harold, with Wales pacified and the English earldoms finally under his firm control, went to the family estate at Bosham merely to relax on a fishing trip, and was simply caught in a storm.

The views are not mutually exclusive. The English Benedictine monk and historian Eadmer of Canterbury, born right around this time and later to become Bishop of Selsey, probably heard about the trip from the earl's kinsman Aethelric, the monk who had been passed over by King Edward for Archbishop of Canterbury in 1050 in favor of Robert of Jumièges. Around the end of the century Eadmer included what he heard in his *Historia Novorum in Anglia*, "History of Recent Events in England." According to him, Harold crossed the Channel with the king's permission to secure the release of his brother and nephew, but was blown off course: "The turbulent sea terrifies the sailors, and the ship is violently driven by the rising waves. Finally, with all that she was carrying, she was blown to Ponthieu."

For what it's worth, the Bayeux Tapestry depicts Harold's ship with a dragon prow and gunwales lined with shields, making it a very militaristic fishing boat. The Anglo-Saxons wade ashore with their leggings removed and their tunics tucked up between their legs, to be immediately met by the locals.

The last we heard of Ponthieu, Normandy's northern neighbor, was ten years prior, after Count Enguerrand II was killed outside Arques, and his brother Count Guy was defeated and taken prisoner at Mortemer. Duke William had held Guy prisoner for two years until he pledged fealty. (During this time Ponthieu was ruled as a regency by Guy's uncle, another Guy, Bishop Guy of Amiens, whose account will shortly become one of our sources.) Having been a prisoner himself, Count Guy was not reluctant to make prisoners of others. HIC APREHENDIT VVIDO HAROLDUM, reads the Tapestry: *Here Guy arrests Harold.*

"He and his men were seized and taken captive," wrote Poitiers. "Such a proud man would gladly have rather been shipwrecked."

Captivity was only to be expected. Ponthieu, like Normandy and most other medieval coastal lands going back to Roman times, maintained its right of salvage: the claiming of flotsam, jetsam and derelict goods of ships washed up on its shores. Poitiers admitted that some made a business of using lights to lure ships onto the rocks, confiscating everything they could and selling survivors for ransom or even into slavery.

The wealthiest, most powerful earl in England, brother-in-law of the king, was worth a very high price indeed. Guy's problem was collecting it. The taking of such a high-profile prisoner could not remain secret for long. As soon as he heard about it, Duke William realized that here was a prize worth much more than mere money. He sent word to his vassal, offering him the choice of surrendering his prisoner or his *comté.* Guy had spent too much time in his duke's prison cell to disobey him now. He delivered Harold little the worse for wear to William, for which he was well rewarded.

The duke escorted the earl and his retinue to Rouen, wined and dined them, and made them comfortable as his honored guests. This was the first meeting between two of the most powerful men in Western Europe, but only one of them held the power at the moment, and William was quick to exploit his advantage. Poitiers admitted, "Of course he was very pleased with his guest, the ambassador of his dearest kinsman and friend [Edward], whom he hoped would be the most faithful intermediary between himself and the English, among whom he was second only to the king."

By all accounts the earl was well treated. Malmesbury recorded, "The duke entertained him with great respect, both in food and clothing, according to the custom of his land."

Poitiers, however, claimed that that was a sham, that William "treated his guest and envoy as his man-at-arms, an honor making him more faithful and obligated to him."

According to Eadmer, Harold knew full well his life was in the duke's hands: "Harold was in danger on all sides, nor could he see any way to escape, unless William agreed to let him go."

The duke, Malmesbury claimed, had other plans: "To better learn his temperament, and at the same time to test his courage, he took him along an expedition he led against Brittany."

The duke's troubles with the Bretons had been ongoing. His young kinsman Duke Conan II had finally gained control of Brittany, capturing and imprisoning his uncle Odo, and now aspired to make himself a threat to Normandy. William had encouraged one of his barons, Rivallon I of Dol in eastern Brittany, to rebel, for which Conan besieged him in his own city. It was time for William to intervene.

To support Rivallon, the Normans rode across the foot of the Cotentin to the estuary of the River Couesnon, the border with Brittany, where it lets out into the bay of Mont Saint-Michel. At this time the now-famous abbey which stands atop the tidal island a half-mile offshore was brand new, having been raised at the orders of William's uncle, Duke Richard II. The surrounding mud flats, washed in by the tide and stirred up by the river, were just as treacherous then as now. Some of the Normans were trapped by the rising water or got bogged down in what amounted to quicksand. The Norman chroniclers make no mention of it, but the Tapestry famously shows Earl Harold performing a feat of valor, taking one man on his shoulders and dragging out another behind him: HIC HAROLD DVX TRAHEBAT EOS DE ARENA, *Here Duke Harold pulled them out of the sand.* William was evidently impressed. Malmesbury wrote, "There Harold, proving both his ability and courage, won the Norman's heart."

On his kinsman's approach, Duke Conan abandoned his siege of Dol and withdrew about thirty miles south to Rennes, then another thirty northwest to Dinan, where he holed up in a hill fort, the type William had great experience at taking down. The whole matter being a mere family spat, rather than lose everything including his position, Conan is pictured as leaning out over the wall to offer William the literal keys to the dukedom on the point of his lance. Probably both knew the peace between them would be merely temporary. Their differences simply had not yet risen to a level requiring one of them to die.

By now Duke William saw in his captive Anglo-Saxon earl a man of quality, perhaps even a man worthy of being made Norman himself. As the (somewhat biased) Waltham chronicler described him, "Harold was a fine soldier, tall in stature, very strong, the handsomest of all the great men in the land, and the king's right-hand man. He was gifted with wisdom, skilled in all the military arts which became a warrior, and in every way showed himself to be a man of excellence."

The Tapestry shows Duke William bestowing *arma*, arms, on Earl Harold, with one hand outstretched to his face, in either a lordly embrace or – and this is a critical point – in *adoubement*, the cheek-slap as in the dubbing of a knight, to make sure the recipient never forgot that he was now a vassal of his overlord.

The duke and the earl would have of course discussed the future. Specifically, the future of England. In his account Eadmer of Canterbury noted, "He said that King Edward, back when he was a young man living in Normandy, had promised by the faith between them, that if he were king of England he would pass the rule of the kingdom to him by right of inheritance after his death." He gave the duke voice:

If you, too, promise to support me in this endeavor, and also dig a well for the castle of Dover, I will give your sister to one of my barons as a wife at the proper time. You have not yet promised

---

*The keep at Dover, nowhere yet near the imposing stone citadel built during the reign of Henry II (r. 1154–1189), was to be known as the "Key to England." That William wished to have a well dug for it, down 290 feet through the chalk cliff to groundwater, might indicate that he was thinking ahead strategically, wanting a base made ready for his long-term occupation and defense in case his return to England went badly.

to take my daughter as your wife. Then, and only then, will you have your nephew, and when I come to reign in England, you will receive your brother safe. If I am confirmed by you in that kingdom, I guarantee you will obtain everything that you reasonably ask me to grant you.

It's thought Harold had two little sisters even younger than his brother Wulfnoth: Aedgiva (or Aelfgiva or Aelfgifu) and Gunhilde. In a scene which has long puzzled and fascinated historians, around this point in the Tapestry a woman makes a cryptic appearance under the legend AELFGYVA, as yet unexplained though not lacking for explanations. (Over the years no less than a dozen different women, including the late Queen Emma and her nemesis Aelfgifu of Northampton, have been nominated for the position.) She is accompanied by an unnamed, tonsured cleric, with his hand to her face in the same manner as William to Harold a few scenes later – perhaps as though, just as a knight's *adoubement* came with a slap in the face to make it official, so did a woman's betrothal. As for William's daughters, he had at least three, possibly five: Agatha, Adeliza, Adela (who may have been the same person), Constance and Cecilia. Of Agatha, Orderic wrote, "She had seen and loved the Englishman," as well she might. "This Englishman was distinguished by his greatness and elegance, and by his strength of body, and boldness of mind, and fluency of language, and much admirable wit and valor."

Of course, Harold already had a wife, Edith the Gentle Swan. But as William doubtless well knew, that was a Danish marriage, held valid by the English and Scandinavians, but not so much on the Continent and not at all by the Church of Rome. As far as the duke was concerned, it could be disregarded as though it had never happened. Nor did the age difference matter. Harold was in his forties, and Agatha/Adeliza/Adela probably only in her teens, but the important thing was that a child of theirs would unite the two most powerful families of Normandy and England. With William, still only in his mid-thirties, as father-in-law, of course.

The party returned to Normandy. Sources differ on exactly where. Jumièges specified no location. Orderic claimed Rouen; Poitiers Bonnavilla, modern Bonneville-sur-Touques near the Eure estuary. The Tapestry, naturally enough, depicts *Bagias*, Bayeux. The crypt in its modern chapel is of Norman origin, and may already have housed the bones of a saint. (Bayeux had already been home to several – St. Exuperius, St. Loup, St. Patricius – though just whose bones resided in the crypt at this time, if any of theirs, is unclear.) As long as they were sanctified, they suited William's purpose: Harold's debt to him had to be made ironclad, set in stone, for he well knew the Godwins' reputation. Malmesbury wrote of Harold, "This man, though possessing many good qualities, was said to have cared little for avoiding deceit, so that he could contrive a way to get out of any agreement."

According to Wace, William had the bones collected and put in a chest, and covered that with a silk cloth on which sat a fereter, a portable reliquary or container for relics, the finest available, but presumably of less commanding status than holy bones. Harold could have no inkling of those within the chest on which he was to swear.

Poiters set down what happened next.

And, as the most honest and exemplary men who witnessed it have related, at the critical point in the oath he clearly and of his own free will swore that as long as he lived he would be the representative of Duke William in the court of his lord King Edward, with his utmost counsel and wealth ensure that the English crown should be pledged to him after Edward's death, that meanwhile he would see to the fortification of Dover Castle at his own expense for William's men, and that he would fortify, provision and garrison various other castles as the duke directed. Before he had sworn the duke had already accepted his vassal's hand, and confirmed his lands and powers. For Edward, who was sick, was not expected to live long.

"The congregation said: 'May God grant him this!'" wrote Wace. "After Harold had kissed the reliquary and arisen, the duke stood him beside the chest. He took off the brocade which had hidden everything and showed Harold the relics inside, on which he had sworn. On seeing the relics Harold felt great fear."

He was right to fear. This was not just any oath. Bad enough for a man to tarnish his honor by breaking his word. An oath sworn over holy bones, the way William had made his barons swear on relics to uphold the Truce of God back in 1047, put a man's soul on the line. This was just as William intended. After all, there was a kingdom at stake.

Malmesbury and Jumièges attested to Harold's oath, though only Wace mentioned William's trick, and Eadmer claimed the pledge was made under duress instead of deception. Either way, if Harold's oath was compelled, he could comfort himself that he could renounce it and make amends with God later. In truth, what else could he do? He was totally in William's power. The duke had held his brother and nephew, both of whom were politically more or less worthless, hostages for over a decade. William could simply have done the same to Harold, or murdered him outright, as he had supposedly just done to Edward's nephew Walter of the Vexin and his wife, to remove him as an impediment to his own power, and where would England be then? That William was allowing Harold to swear fealty was, in that respect, a sign of his good intentions.

William, for his part, held up his end of the bargain, allowing Harold's nephew Hakon to return with him to England. But he kept the earl's brother Wulfnoth hostage, to be delivered only when Harold handed over the kingdom.

"Then when everything was readied for his journey home, he took his leave," concluded Wace, "and William charged him with being true to his word, and kissed him in the name of good trust and amity. And Harold went home a free man, arriving safely in England."

Yet Orderic, after lauding all those qualities of Harold's that made him so attractive to the duke's daughter, lamented, "But what mattered so many gifts to him without honor, which is the source of everything good?"

If, as the Normans asserted, Earl Harold was now a vassal of Duke William, it was not made widely known in England. On his return Harold certainly would have reported to King Edward, as shown on the Bayeux Tapestry. An oath to a foreign lord, freely made, amounted to treason, but not if compelled by duress or deceit. As events would soon show, if any oath had been sworn, both king and earl regarded it as invalid. But, as though God knew the earl's heart, his fortunes soon took a turn for the worse. Mostly due to his brother Tostig.

Though he had ruled Northumbria for ten years, Tostig and his subjects had never warmed to each other. He had cracked down on their constant feuding and murdering. His Wessex blood alienated them. His amity with the troublesome Scots angered them. His treasury had been depleted by the Welsh war, and since Northumbria enjoyed a lower tax rate than the southern earldoms (and an earl customarily claimed a third of all tax revenue before remitting the rest to the king), Tostig hiked the taxes. When this was naturally resented by his subjects, he wielded a heavy hand in meting out justice.

Worcester accused him of inviting two of the opposition leaders to his own chambers at Earlsborough, where he had them murdered. Shades of Eadric Streona, you might say, and of Tostig's predecessor Earl Siward as well, who in 1041 murdered Eadwulf of Bamburgh on King Harthacnut's orders. At Christmas 1064 another leader of the resistance, the Northumbrian *thegn* Gospatric, son of Uhtred the Bold, appeared at the court of King Edward, where he was assassinated, supposedly on Queen Edith's orders on her brother's behalf. As Huntingdon recorded, Tostig's depredations stained the entire family: "Such was the avarice of these brothers that on seeing a well-run farm, they had the owner killed in the night with his entire family and confiscated the dead man's property. And these men were the justiciaries of the realm."

While Tostig was giving the family a bad name, Harold – especially considering his recent affair in Normandy – was doing his best to stay on King Edward's good side. In the summer of 1065 he had a hunting lodge built for the royal pleasure at Portskewet in the Severn estuary. That, however, evidently stirred up old hatreds, on both sides of the river. On August 24, the feast day of St. Bartholomew, a force of Welsh raiders descended on the site, killed most of the workers, and made off with everything they could carry. A cryptic comment in the *Chronicle* – "We do not know who planned this wicked deed" – might seem to imply that one of Harold's enemies at the English court was behind the raid.

As for Duke William, both king and earl might well have crossed him off the list of possible heirs to the throne. In 1065 it was not a given that he would outlive Edward. For in Normandy the duke had come down with, as a contemporary record puts it, a "sickness in which he was worried of losing his life."

The details, unfortunately, are even more unclear than usual. None of William's biographers, Wace, Poitiers or Jumièges, make direct mention of his illness – not because it never happened, but very probably because it was not to be publicized. A duke of the Normans on his deathbed would likely have lit off another struggle for supremacy among the barons, much as had the death of William's father Robert.

Our only inkling comes from the *Archives départementales de la Manche*, the "Channel Archives," established in 1790 to curate, among other records, the charters and grants by the nobility to the local churches going all the way back to AD 911. The originals are lost, but 17th- and 19th-century copies survive, though like the various editions of the *Chronicle* the texts sometimes differ in wording and detail. From them can we glean that, somewhere in the period 1063–1066, most likely in 1065 when he was uncharacteristically quiet, Duke William – for almost all his life in good health – was "cast down to the ground as if he were about to die."

The number of personages in Normandy in those days who suddenly dropped dead is surely more than coincidence. William's uncle Duke Richard III and his father Duke Robert I, Duke Alan III of Brittany, Count Walter of the Vexin and his wife Biota, and that's not counting William's external enemies like King Henry I and Geoffrey the Hammer. Hygiene, diet and medicine being what they were, perhaps these deaths could be put down to the continental version of *aelfscot*, but certainly people had their suspicions at the time. At this point Duke William really only had one enemy left standing: his kinsman Duke Conan II of Brittany. Their struggle was ongoing, and as Conan probably believed his father Alan had died of Norman poison, he might have wished to strike first.

Poitiers does perhaps make oblique reference to the episode. Around this time he reported William contemplating the afterlife, "For he knew not only that the flourishing dominions in the world should eventually end, but the world itself would pass away, crushing tyrants too devoted to earthly pleasure. The diadems and palaces of the unfaithful cannot outshine the splendor of God's servants, and mean nothing in that most glorious city, the land of the true and the highest good."

William pledged to dedicate a church in Cesarisburg (modern Cherbourg) and gift it with relics from his personal collection, and Duchess Matilda made offerings in order for God and St. Mary to restore the duke's health. All of Normandy, according to Poitiers, feared for his life: "The land, therefore, rightly sheds tears and prays, for his sake, whatever illness lays him low, with such prayers as to enable him to come back from the dead, praying that he would not soon die, fearing his premature death would again stir the storms which had previously tormented them."

All those prayers and offerings must have worked, for the accounts have William soon back on his feet, "as if he had been resurrected."

This brush with mortality must have affected the duke's mindset, though, like having his boyhood guardian murdered in front of him, or narrowly escaping assassination plots by rebellious barons. For him to have lived this long was surely due to more than mere luck or coincidence; to have come back from death's door when so many others had passed through was, to a medieval mind, a sign of God's blessing.

William could now rest assured that, whatever came, he had the Lord behind him.

Events in England came to a head at the beginning of October. Tostig had gone south to court on official business and lingered to go hunting with the king. Some Northumbrian *thegns* saw their chance and rose up to march on York. As Queen Edith's *Vita* puts it, "That region which had rested for so long in the tranquility of peace under the rigor and justice of a most illustrious earl, was all overthrown by the malice of a few nobles seeking the extermination of his family."

Tostig's housecarls were the first to be put to death, caught trying to escape and executed outside the city walls. The following day the rebels seized all of the treasure and weaponry in Earlsborough, then went on a killing spree. Every family feud from generations past was sorted out by the most final, violent method. Whoever had once been a member of Tostig's court, some 200 in total, was put to death without trial.

The rebels being led by an assortment of low-level *thegns* – the only ones to have survived Tostig's persecutions – they cast about for a leader to give their uprising an appearance of legitimacy. They passed over young Waltheof, son of the previous earl, Siward. Instead they settled on Morcar, brother of Earl Edwin of Mercia. "He went south with all the people," records the *Chronicle*, "and with Nottinghamshire and Derbyshire and Lincolnshire, until he came to Northampton, where his brother Edwin met him with the men of his earldom. Many Britons also joined them."

The sons of Aelfgar had nursed the family grudge against the Godwins long enough. With Mercia allied to Northumbria, they held the sword hand over the neck of Wessex and the south. The uprising threatened to become a civil war.

News of all this came as a shock to Earl Tostig and King Edward. The royal party retreated south, with the king calling an emergency meeting of the *witan*. Some of the assembled lords accused Tostig of having provoked the rebellion through his own misrule and greed. According to the *Vita* – sympathetic to the queen's favorite brother – others, including Tostig himself, accused Earl Harold of fomenting the crisis in order to remove his brother from power.

"I dare not, nor would I, believe a prince capable of such detestable wickedness to his brother," penned the queen's writer on her behalf. Harold cleared himself by means of compurgation, swearing to his innocence and having a sufficient number of peers attest to it. With him absolved of wrong, the king sent him to negotiate with the rebels.

This was the greatest test of Harold's diplomatic skills to date. The fate of the entire kingdom, not to mention his own family, hung in the balance. His brother would have to lose his earldom, or civil war would ravage the land. There was no in-between.

He met Edwin and Morcar at Northampton to hear out their demands. These were simple: Tostig to be banished, and Morcar to be accepted as the new Earl of Northumbria. While he hurried back to the king with this list, the rebels kept up the pressure. "The Northern men did much damage about Northampton while he went on this errand," attests the *Chronicle*, "slaying men, burning houses and grain, or taking all the cattle they came across, which amounted to many thousands. Hundreds of people they took north as well, so that not only that shire, but others around it were the worse for many winters."

Edward was of a mind to stamp out the rebellion by military force. Some of his lords objected. It was by now the end of October.

Winter was coming on. It would not be easy to assemble the army, they claimed, much less mount an offensive. Even the *Vita Aedwardi* admits they simply dreaded the prospect of civil war: "They did not so much deflect the king from determination on war as wrongfully, and against his will, abandon him."

It should be pointed out that the most powerful members of the *witan* who were not from Mercia or Northumbria were Harold and his brother earls Gyrth and Leofwine, or their supporters. Around this time even young Waltheof finally gained his own earldom, of Northamptonshire and Huntingdonshire in the Midlands, probably as reward for backing Harold. Tostig, who was already effectively powerless in this dispute, saw his own brothers turn on him. If the consensus was that avoiding war was simply a matter of replacing one Earl of Northumbria with another, then let it be done. The *Vita* records, "The king, beloved of God, when he could not protect his earl, bestowed upon him plentiful gifts and, distressed at his own impotence, let him go."

Queen Edith was said to have wept at the decision. It was to cost Harold's family in more ways than he could know. To seal the bargain, Edwin and Morcar evidently demanded that the Earl of Wessex marry their sister, Edith, widow of King Gruffydd. (The accounts do not state this implicitly, but the fact is that soon after the negotiations the two were married, making this the most likely time for it to have been agreed.) A union of the families meant all three great earldoms, Mercia, Northumbria and Wessex, would at last be as one. The assumption had to be that there would be a child of that union as well, who might even be raised to take his father's place as *dux Anglorum*, as *subregulus*, vice-king.

What the earls' sister Edith thought of the match was left unsaid, and didn't matter. She had already been pawned off to one husband, Gruffydd, to make the peace, and lived with him six years. She may have been grieved by his death, but for all we can know she had been relieved by it, and may have even expected to be taken as a war bride. To become a countess was a step down for a woman once queen, but it was a step up from being a widow.

Also unmentioned in the chronicles is the reaction of Harold's wife, Edith the Gentle Swan.

She must have known it might eventually come to this. When they had married, her husband had been a minor earl, with an elder brother ahead of him in line even for the earldom of Wessex. Now he was in effect a head of state, and in those days matters of state were often resolved through marriage. She might well have expected, though, that such a time would never come. The Island Kingdom had long been at peace, with no marriage alliance required to maintain it. (There was supposedly that vow of Harold's to marry Duke William's daughter, but that was of little consequence. She was a child, and across the Channel as well. Harold would have disregarded that vow even more easily than his oath of fealty to the duke.)

But now war was here, in England, against the north, and Edith and her husband were duty-bound to do their utmost to resolve it.

Besides, a second marriage for Harold did not mean he must renounce the first. After all, for most of his life King Cnut had been married to two wives, Emma and Aelfgifu. They had hated each other, but there did not need to be hate between the two Ediths. A love match need not be threatened by political marriage. There could only be one Countess of Wessex, of course, but the first Edith would still have her own household and her own sons. The eldest, Godwin, was now in his late teens or even his early twenties, old enough for his father to groom him for office, perhaps an earldom of his own. If a woman could not be the wife of an earl, being one's mother was almost as good.

The reaction of Earl Tostig – ex-Earl Tostig – to his brother's bargain is better known. The *Chronicle* passes over the story, but six decades after the fact it was still remembered well enough for Henry of Huntingdon to write it down. "That same year, in the king's palace at Winchester, Tostig seized his brother Harold by the hair in front of the king, while he was serving the king wine, for it had been a cause of envy and hatred that the king had higher regard for Harold."

Nine decades after Huntingdon, Roger of Wendover was still telling the story. "Provoked to action, Harold seized his brother with both arms, lifted him and threw him to the ground. At this the soldiers rushed forward from around them, ended the fight between the famous brothers and separated them. The king then predicted that the brothers' destruction was at hand, and that God's vengeance would not be long in coming."

Tostig left in a rage, going to Hereford, where his brother had collected a large store of provisions to stage a feast for the king. "There," wrote Huntingdon, "he butchered all his brother's servants."

"He cut the limbs off all the servants," added Wendover, "and sank an arm, or some other member, in each of the containers of wine, mead, ale, or pickling. Then he sent a message to the king, that on visiting his lodge, he would find the food seasoned to his taste, and that he should feel free to take some of the delicacies with him."

"For this horrible crime," Huntingdon concluded, "the king ordered him banished and outlawed."

"And not long afterward," wrote Wace, "Tostig said farewell to his sorrowing mother and many of his friends, and with his wife and infant children and a good number of his *thegns* crossed the Channel and came to that old friend of the English people, Count Baldwin."

Baldwin V, Countess Judith's elder half-brother, would seem to have been a friend only to those Anglo-Saxons who were on the outs with King Edward. Flanders had been the refuge of expelled English aristocrats going back to the days of Queen Emma and Earl Sweyn, and a source of fighting men when, like Earl Godwin back in 1052, they wished to stage a return. Baldwin, now in his early fifties, was already looking after young King Philip, the late King Henry's son, as his regent. Conceivably, through the count's influence, the military might of France might be put at Tostig's disposal. Baldwin was also William of Normandy's father-in-law, and might convince the duke to put his formidable power behind Tostig as well. Then again, Tostig could have gone to Normandy directly to ask for William's aid. His brother's treatment there the previous year doubtless put him off. Norman help came at a high price. Tostig did not wish to be the second Godwin swearing to support a Norman claim to England.

So Tostig accepted Baldwin's hospitality at St. Omer. "He gave him both a house and an estate there, and put the town revenues at his disposal," records the *Vita* (the anonymous author of which is thought to have been a monk in St. Omer at the time), "and he ordered all the troops stationed there to serve Tostig as his deputy commander." "And," the *Chronicle* records, "they stayed there all the winter."

The shock of these events hit old King Edward hard, and in a sense he never did recover. "Afterward King Edward suffered a lingering illness," confided Worcester, "but he held his Christmas court at London as well as he could."

Christmas courts were usually held at Gloucester, but the king's pet project, the abbey of Saint Peter at Westminster, was finally complete, and was to be consecrated on Sunday, Christmas Day. (Queen Edith's abbey at Wilton had been dedicated the previous October.) In this the hand of God might be seen, because the abbey had always been intended to serve as Edward's mausoleum, and was ready just in time. As Osbert of Clare, the 12th-century prior and abbot of the church, recorded, "He had become aware the end of his mortal life was approaching, and was driven to complete his purpose before he reached his end."

Earls, *thegns* and knights converged on the city for the event. Archbishops, bishops, abbots and monks made ready to perform the service. Sulcard, a Benedictine monk at the abbey, recorded, "Everything necessary for the great building's dedication was prepared at the royal expense, as was just, and from the whole of Britain men assembled there."

Alas, the happy event soon took on a funereal tone. On Christmas Eve the king fell ill. He was able to soldier on, making a glad face for the attendees, but he abstained from attending the feasting and celebrations. The consecration was postponed until December 28, by which time Edward had taken to his bed and advised Archbishop Stigand and the other priests to proceed without him. Queen Edith took charge, seeing to it the church was properly sanctified in time for its first holy service. Her *Vita* records, "When King Edward, full of faith, felt the disease overcoming him, he commended himself to the funeral rites with the praise and prayers of God's most faithful."

For several days he drifted in and out of consciousness, sometimes comatose, sometimes mumbling deliriously. The Bayeux Tapestry depicts the scene – HIC EADVVARDVS REX IN LECTO ALLOQVIT FIDELES,

Here King Edward in bed speaks to his faithful followers – with the king surrounded by his innermost councillors: his kinsman (and Duke William's), the *staller* Robert fitzWimarc; Queen Edith in her accustomed place, warming his feet in her lap; Stigand the Archbishop of Canterbury (though at this time still regarded by the papacy to be uncanonically elected and possibly excommunicated); and Harold, Earl of Wessex.

At some point, according to the *Vita*, Edward awakened long enough to relate a dream in which he met two monks he had known as a young man in Normandy, both long dead, who imparted a message to him:

> Since those who have reached the heights of greatness in this English kingdom, the dukes, bishops, and abbots, and all who have obtained the holy orders are not what they appear to be, but on the contrary ministers of the devil, in one year and one day after your death God will deliver this entire kingdom, cursed by him, into the hands of the enemy, and the devils will invade this entire land with fire, sword, and hostile destruction.

Edward replied that he would have the people repent and beg God's mercy, which surely would be given. The monks insisted that neither repentance nor mercy would be forthcoming. At Edward's pleading, they prophesied that punishment would only end when a green tree in full bloom, cut in two and the top carried three furlongs away, would of its own accord become one, grow and bloom and bear fruit again – in short, never.

Now, since the *Vita* was penned afterward, this scene is another of those rather obviously concocted in hindsight. It is thought to be a rebuke by its sponsor, Queen Edith, putting blame for ensuing events on Stigand, who invoked God's wrath (and the Pope's) by holding the bishopric of Canterbury in plurality with Winchester – the two halves of the tree – and receiving his pallium from the antipope Benedict X. Her *Vita* makes a point that Stigand, "who should either have been first to fear or speak comfort," whispered in Earl Harold's ear, and Malmesbury recorded, "Though others were worried about this prediction's truth, Archbishop Stigand laughed it off, saying the old man was delirious with disease."

A curious sentiment, for the king's next words concerned all the kingdom, and if made in delirium would not – should not – have been preserved. Asking his men not to grieve and to pray for his soul, and for God's grace toward his wife who had served him like a daughter, Edward stretched out a hand to Earl Harold: "I commend to you the protection of all the kingdom. As to your queen and sister, it is for you to be a faithful servant, so that as long as she lives, she will not be deprived of the honor she received from me."

It certainly sounds, even in Edith's account, as though there was animosity between her and Harold, which the king with his dying wish desired to end. He further requested that Harold take his French housecarls and servants into his own service, or otherwise see them sent safely home, as though to prevent a postmortem purge of the foreign elements at court. (Robert fitzWimarc doubtless wanted that part set down in writing.) Then he comforted Queen Edith that he would yet regain his strength and live, and in this he spoke the truth. Edward the Confessor died on January 5, 1066, but as the *Vita* sees it, "he has not died, but has passed from death to life with Christ."

Wendover intoned, "With him died the line of English kings which began with Cerdic, the first English king of Wessex, and continued unbroken for five hundred and seventy-one years, except for a few Danish overlords, who because of the sins of the English nation reigned a short while."

The next day's funeral service was the first at Westminster Abbey, and was immediately followed, in the same location, by its first coronation, that of Edward's successor, Harold of Wessex, henceforth to be known (Harefoot being Harold I) as King Harold II.

To modern eyes that might seem a rather abrupt transition of power. Not a few of the later chroniclers agreed. Huntingdon wrote, "Some of the English wished to name Edgar Aetheling king, but Harold, backed by his power and his noble birth, seized the crown."

In Malmesbury's opinion, Harold "seized the crown and forced the nobles' consent, though the English say it was granted him by the king. I however find it hard to believe, knowing Harold, that Edward would in sound judgement transfer his kingdom to a man of whose power he had ever been jealous."

They were writing years later, however, when it was unwise, even dangerous, to claim Harold might be England's rightful king. At the time, it came down to a matter of 11th-century *realpolitik*. Harold was, after all, King Edward's choice, and before witnesses, as the *Chronicle* attests: "The wise monarch left the realm to the nobility and to Harold, the highborn earl, who always obediently heard and obeyed his master in word and deed, nor ever left to anyone what the king wanted."

The *aetheling* Edgar, grandson of King Edmund Ironside, still resided at court, but was barely a teenager, and might not yet have even spoken English. William of Normandy was just as much a foreigner. With Harold, no real change was required. No new royal court had to be brought in and trained to their tasks. He was already regarded as *subregulus*, vice-king. Now he would reign as *regulus* in fact. Who better than this man who, a mere eight weeks or so earlier, and at no small personal cost to himself, had finally united all the great earldoms in England as one family? The *witan*, all the most powerful men of which were already in Harold's camp, would hardly have given the matter a second thought. As the *Waltham Chronicle* argues, "Earl Harold was unanimously elected king, for there was no one in England more shrewd, better at war, more educated in the laws or more capable in every way. Those who had been his prime enemies to this point could not oppose him, for England had not raised a man that distinguished to decline the task."

Harold's chief enemies, however, were not in England. They were across the Channel. In Flanders, Tostig was plotting revenge. And as far as the Normans were concerned, Duke William was the rightful heir to the English throne, and Harold had sworn fealty to him. If he reneged, William was not one to let him get away with it. As the *Chronicle* records, in hindsight, "He enjoyed little peace while he ruled the kingdom."

PART THREE

THE NORMANS
AD 1066

Always, unfailingly, one of three things will threaten men in their fated hour: illness, or old age, or the sword's hate will tear the life out of those doomed to die. And so it is for each man. The praise of the living, of those who speak afterwards, is the best epitaph. He should work before he must go, show bravery in the world against the devil's enmity, perform daring deeds against the fiend, so that the sons of men will praise him afterwards, and his fame will live on with the angels for ever and ever, the glory of eternal life and happiness with the heavenly host.

From "The Seafarer"
Anglo-Saxon, late 9th/early 10th century

XXXIII

Challenge Accepted

Spring 1066

We have few words for you, Harold. What were you thinking, after everything that happened, to dare take away William's inheritance, to war on he to whom you submitted yourself and your nation with a sacrosanct oath, by your words and your hand?

Poitiers

Duke William, having recovered from his near-fatal illness, had achieved the peak of power. Poitiers wrote of the nobility of Europe visiting Normandy to gain his favor, and being amazed that the roads were so safe that people went about unarmed: "This peace, this dignity, the virtue of William bestowed on his country."

Yes, William was still a duke, and of a small nation, but in terms of power and wealth he was a duke to be envied by kings, and could comfort himself that he would soon be a king to be envied by emperors. Over the last months of 1065 would have come word of the tumult in England, of the uprising in Northumbria, the banishing of its earl Tostig, and the declining health of King Edward. The most powerful man in England was Earl Harold of Wessex, and he had sworn his allegiance to William. It was only a matter of time until the duke became a king.

Early in the new year, William, accompanied by his entourage of lords, knights and attendants, took part in a hunt at Quevilly, today Petit-Quevilly in the suburbs of Rouen. In 1066 this was a hunting park originally cleared by the Viking Rollo, both habits in which his descendant William indulged; Malmesbury attested the duke was "so enamored with the thrill of the hunt, that he evicted the inhabitants and let an area of many square miles grow wild so that, when free of other obligations, he might take his pleasures there."

Wace has William stringing his bow when a messenger arrives to whisper in his ear. The duke promptly abandons the hunt and, without saying a word, stalks back to his hall in a rage. Only his seneschal, William fitzOsbern, dares say what everyone in town already knows – that Edward has died and Harold Godwinson has reneged on his oath to William – and he urges the duke to act: "Summon all the men you can muster, cross the sea, and take the kingdom from him. A bold man should begin nothing he will not finish."

Build a fleet, man it with troops, and cross the Channel? His father Robert's ill-fated attempt must have given William pause. As he had with so many rebellious liegemen in the past, he first gave the transgressor a chance to do the right thing. Jumièges attested, "The duke immediately sent deputies to invite Harold to renounce this senseless usurpation, and with proper fealty keep the faith he had sworn by oath."

In England, King Harold got off to a good start with his new crown and throne. He showed himself to be a just lord, rescinding bad laws and enacting good ones, urging his earls and *thegns* and shire reeves to enforce them. He was a friend of the church; within a few weeks of his coronation he had appointed his first abbot, to replace one who had died at Abingdon Abbey. As was the perogative of a king, he swiftly saw to the creation of coinage. Almost every *burh* in England worthy of the name had its own mint, some fifty in total, but the dies were only available in London. (Counterfeiters were punished by the loss of a hand.) The coins put Harold's name, likeness and title, *Rex Anglorum*, in every man's pocket and mind. Even Malmesbury admitted, "Harold would have ruled the kingdom with wisdom and courage, as was his character, if only he had done it lawfully."

The arrival of Duke William's embassy would not have been unexpected, nor their message. As Wace put it, "Duke William was very angered that Harold was so disrespectful to him and had not bothered to consult him before being crowned. He had stolen what Edward had given William and what Harold had sworn to him, completely denying and breaking his oath."

"Harold not only did not want to hear this view," wrote Jumièges, "but even more faithlessly he turned the entire English nation against the duke."

The messengers returned to Duke William with the king's reply. As Wendover wrote it:

> King Harold of England says it is true that, under duress, he swore to confer the kingdom on you, and to marry your daughter in Normandy, but he asserts that a forced oath is not binding. For as a maiden's vow or oath made in her father's house without her parents' knowledge should be regarded as invalid, so much more should an oath made by a king's vassal, without informing him, have no effect. He also says that it would have been the height of effrontery for him, without consulting the *witan*, to designate a stranger to inherit the realm, and that it is unfair to ask him to hand over a kingdom, when by general assent the nobles chose him to rule.

Back and forth went the messengers, each time with more threatening words. "William repeatedly told Harold that he should uphold his vow," reported Wace, "and Harold replied back shamefully that he would neither take his daughter nor confer the kingdom on him. William challenged him. Harold always replied that he had no longer had any fear of him."

At this point, William had little choice. A duke of Normandy could brook no defiance from a vassal, which is what he, and his other vassals, considered Harold. Poitiers wrote, "Duke William, after consulting with his men, determined to avenge this insult with arms, and claim his inheritance by force."

And Wace concluded, "If he could attack and punish him without crossing the ocean, he would gladly do so, but he would rather cross the sea than not avenge himself and secure his rights. So he determined to cross the sea, and get his revenge."

William was not the only man on that side of the Channel plotting vengeance. Tostig Godwinson was seeking backers. From Flanders he rode north, through Frisia to the realm of his cousin, King Svein of Denmark. He and King Harald of Norway, having spent years fighting each other to bloody exhaustion, had recently declared peace between them. There was nothing stopping Denmark from invading England again. Snorri wrote, "The earl requested King Svein's aid and manpower. King Svein invited him to stay, promising that he would have a domain in Denmark large enough to make him a *jarl*."

Tostig did not wish to be a Danish *jarl*: "My wish is to go back to my lands in England." If Svein would assist him with men and ships, Tostig promised to pay him back in kind when England was conquered, "as Cnut, your mother's brother, did."

Svein, for his part, did not wish to be an emperor of the north. He admitted, "I am a lesser man than Cnut the Great. I can barely defend my own land against the Norwegians. King Cnut inherited Denmark, nearly lost his life conquering England, and took Norway without a fight. I prefer to know my limits rather than try to imitate King Cnut's lucky victories."

Tostig replied, "I had hoped for more from a gallant king for a kinsman in need. I may just go seek help elsewhere, from a chieftain who is less afraid of a great undertaking."

"Then," wrote Snorri, "the king and the earl parted, not the best of friends."

An area of greater concern for King Harold was the north, where the earls Edwin and Morcar looked on his crowning with trepidation. Their bargain, and standing, had been made with King Edward. Harold had evidently reneged on one oath, to Duke William; would he now set aside their agreement and bring back his banished brother Tostig to rule over Northumbria? If so, they were prepared to rise up again.

To put the brothers at ease, Harold journeyed north in person, accompanied by Bishop Wulfstan of Worcester. More than the uncanonical Stigand or grasping Ealdred, Wulfstan was renowned for his simplicity, humility and religious conviction, as a social reformer and foe of slavery. (In 1203 he would be canonized as a saint.) No one would accuse him of being anything but honest with the northern earls. "Harold set out to resolve the rebellion by gentle mediation," wrote Malmesbury in his *Vita Wulfstani*. "Since he did not intend to break the sword, he brought the holy man along."

Earninga Stræt, "Ermine Street," the old Roman road from London to York by way of Lincoln, ran some 195 miles. A trip of a week or more might seem longer when ridden with Wulfstan, since, as Malmesbury confided, "Wherever he traveled by horseback, he would run through the psalms again and again, repeating over and over any prayer verses that came to mind, until his fellow travelers grew impatient."

But Harold let Wulfstan do the talking when the *thegns* of the north convened at York. The bishop had no sympathy for them. "Of course he was a good clergyman, meek and mild," wrote Malmesbury. "He did not, however, flatter the wicked, but argued and threatened against their methods. If they were to proceed, he said openly, he foretold they would be punished with much suffering."

If Wulfstan was the stick, Harold was the carrot. If he had not already married the earls' sister Edith, he probably did so now.* A royal wedding, one that united north and south, would have gone a long way to keeping the peace in the kingdom, if not in King Harold's household.

On the ride back south Bishop Wulfstan, perhaps taken aback by the copious drink and boisterous partying at a northern, Viking-style wedding, mused to the king about England's future. According to Malmesbury, "He openly expressed to Harold what great loss it would be, both to him and to England, if such iniquitous behavior went uncorrected. For in those days almost everyone in England was living in such dissolute manner, and instead of piety the worship of luxury was habitual."

This from a man who so objected to long Viking-style hair on men that he was known to wield a small knife, normally for cleaning his fingernails or scraping ink blots off manuscripts, to slice a lock off any long-haired man who came in reach. "He would openly charge anyone who objected with effeminacy, and threaten to punish them.

---

*Remarkably little is recorded of this marriage, and equally little mention is made of Edith as queen, which goes some way to demonstrating her pairing with Harold was not a love match, but a political expedient.

Men who blushed to have been born male, and let their hair flow like women, would be of no more use than women in defending England against foreigners."

In Normandy, Duke William had likewise to get balky vassals in line. He brought his barons together at Lillebonne, old Roman Juliobona, where the ruins of the Roman baths and 3,000-seat theater served as reminders of fallen empires. Among the assembled lords were the duke's half-brothers, Count Robert of Mortain and Bishop Odo of Bayeux, their kinsman Roger "the Bearded" de Beaumont, Roger de Montgomery, Walter Giffard, William de Varenne and Raoul de Tosny and many more, plus neighbors from Brittany, Le Mans and Anjou, Ponthieu and Boulogne and Flanders and Maine. William laid out the situation for them: Harold's betrayal, the loss of William's rightful kingdom, his plan to invade England by sea within the year. For that, he needed their help. He demanded that each lord contribute men and ships to the effort.

The barons were not enthusiastic. As Poitiers recalled, "Who would not fear that, by this new campaign, the most beautiful state of the land would be reduced to poverty? Who would not think that the wealth of a Roman emperor would be insufficient for victory?"

Here Poitiers gives Duke William one of the longest speeches attributed to him, which he may have heard in person:

We know Harold's wisdom. It instills fear, but increases hope. For he expends his own wealth uselessly, dispensing gold but not buying honor. He has not the spirit to dare promise even the least of what is mine. But both what is mine, and what he claims as his, will be promised and given according to my will. He who is able to give away the enemy's possessions as easily as his own shall undoubtedly be called victorious. We shall not be hindered by a lack of ships, for we will soon have a sufficient number. Moreover, he fights to keep what he has stolen. We require what we have received as a gift and earned with favors. Our basic confidence, overcoming all danger, will give us the greatest triumph, the highest honor, the most illustrious name.

The barons requested time to talk it over among themselves, which the duke – rather generously, considering he was their overlord – gave. "They discussed among themselves what they should say, what reply they should make, and what help they would afford.... Some said they would bring ships and cross the sea with the duke. Others said they would not, for they were poor and in debt. Some would, others would not, and there was great dissension amongst them."

At this point the seneschal William fitzOsbern stepped in:

Why do you haggle with your natural lord, who seeks greater honor? You are owed nothing. You owe him service for your lands, and what you owe him you ought to give with all your might. Do not wait for him to ask you. Make no excuse, but step up at once, and offer him even more than you can perform. Give him no cause to complain, nor give up this undertaking on your account. He has a quick temper. If he fails, he will undoubtedly soon blame you. Take care that he has no cause to say that his expedition failed because of you.

The barons protested. They did not object to serving their duke, only to serving him across the water. They were not sailors. Their feudal obligations for land did not include service over the waters. "They said that Harold had more than enough wealth with which to bribe dukes and powerful kings to his side," wrote Poitiers. "He had a large fleet and skilled sailors, hardened in many dangers and sea-battles, and both in riches and manpower his kingdom was much stronger than Normandy."

They did, however, agree to let fitzOsbern speak for them to the duke. And did he ever:

Sire, sire, look around. There are no people under Heaven that love their lord as much, or will do so much to honor him, as your people; and equally you should love and protect them. For you they say they would swim the ocean, or throw themselves into raging flames. You may depend on them, for they have long served you and followed you at great cost, and they will gladly serve you again. If they have so far done well, after this they will do even better. They will cross the ocean with you, and double their contribution.

He who owes twenty fighting men, will cheerfully bring forty. He who should contribute thirty, will now send sixty, and he who should bring a hundred will gladly bring two hundred. As for me, I will in good love offer my lord, in his hour of need, sixty ships, well equipped and manned with fighting men.

The chamber burst into an uproar, with barons objecting that fitzOsbern was making promises he – and they – could not keep. As Poitiers wrote, "Who could believe that within the projected time of one year a fleet could be built, or that sailors could be found to man it?"

The chaos was such that William finally took each of his vassals aside in turn, to personally assure them their help in this crisis would not be forgotten, and nor would their refusal. Put on the spot, every one of them agreed to support his lord. Roger de Montgomery vowed to match fitzOsbern's sixty ships. William's brother Count Robert of Mortain, his brother-in-law Richard le Goz, and Roger de Beaumont each did as well. Walter Giffard promised thirty, Bishop Odo one hundred and twenty, Bishop Arnald of Le Mans one hundred. Even Duchess Matilda promised to outfit a ship for her husband. On and on, each contribution was set down in writing, along with William's promise of payment, gifts and – should he conquer – land in England.

Other allies required more delicate handling. The German king Henry IV promised aid if William required it, but he had only attained his majority in 1065, was recovering from a near-fatal illness and had his hands full with his own unruly barons and bishops. William also dispatched a priest to Rome, to secure the blessing of Pope Alexander II for what he described as something of a holy crusade. (This was several decades before the First Crusade to the Holy Land.) His reasoning was that, besides being a usurper, Harold had been unlawfully crowned by Stigand, the uncanonical Archbishop of Canterbury. (This was false. Harold, not wishing to get his reign off to a bad start, had himself crowned by Archbishop Ealdred of York, but Stigand's mere existence gave the Normans an excuse.) More to the point, the church in England, so far from Rome, tended to do things its own way, in deviation from church doctrine. England had declined to continue paying Peter's Pence to Rome. The practice of simony continued to spread among the priesthood. The Island Kingdom,

348

both church and state, had practically descended into barbarity and sin, from which only a God-fearing king could deliver it. Of course, William promised to bring the English clergy under Rome's control. Not to mention resume annual payment of Peter's Pence.

While awaiting the papal reply, William rode to France to seek approval for his expedition from his suzerain, the boy king Philip I. William was, after all, the king's vassal, and if he conquered England with France's help, he promised to remain his vassal, to hold all the land in fief to France.

Philip's councillors advised the king to refuse. They had long looked on the powerful duke's rise with apprehension, and knew as King of England he would not long be in thrall to a king of France. "Because of what the French said, and they would have said worse if they could, the king refused the duke aid," recounted Wace. "In fact he hindered him as best he could."

Spurned but undaunted, William next went to his father-in-law, Count Baldwin of Flanders. As King Philip's co-regent, he might have been expected to sway the boy over to William's way of thinking, but by all accounts Baldwin did not meddle in French politics. According to Wace the count would not even agree to help William himself without first knowing how much of England he would receive for doing so. William said he would discuss the matter with his barons. On his return to Normandy he sent the count a sealed letter promising he would have everything as written. When opened, the letter was blank. The count would get nothing.

It may have been, though, that some help was forthcoming from Flanders after all. By some accounts William did receive a visitor that spring, one who was, if possible, even more intent than he on the destruction of King Harold: his brother, Tostig Godwinson.

XXXIV

Opening Moves

Summer 1066

Then all across England such a sign was seen as no man ever saw before. Some said it was the comet-star, which others call the long-haired star.

Anglo-Saxon Chronicle

At the end of April, into the beginning of May, the "long-haired star" now known as Halley's Comet passed within a million miles of Earth, appearing brighter than Venus and comparable to the moon. It was so notable, so widely observed on both sides of the Channel, that it was thought worthy of inclusion not only in the *Chronicle* but on the Bayeux Tapestry, which depicts a crowd pointing upward at it with the caption ISTI MIRANT STELLA, *These wonder [at the] star*. One man, his face turned to the others and cast down, might be foretelling disaster. Jumièges did, when he called it "a comet bearing three long rays, which illumined the greater part of the South for fifteen consecutive nights, announcing, as many thought, a great change in some kingdom."

England's new king was determined to shield his realm from any ill-starred fate. Poitiers recorded, "Harold, ready to fight on land or at sea, arrayed the coastline with a huge army, and dispatched cleverly disguised spies."

It was critical for the English to know the Norman timetable for invasion. Harold's *hird*, the highly trained and well-equipped elite *thegns* and housecarls, rotated on duty one month out of every three. They could be assembled quickly, ready to march against any threat, but even all together they were relatively few in number. To call up the *fyrd*, the vast mass of manpower from the countryside, required shire reeves to fan out across the road network, notifying the chieftain of each village and hamlet along their routes that his contribution of fighting men was to answer the king's call. That took time. Anglo-Saxon *fyrds* signed up for two months of duty, and it's thought that Harold only summoned half his available manpower at first, ready to call up the other half at the end of two months or upon the Norman landing, whichever came first. "The earl, however, was in all ways ready for war during that entire year," Malmesbury wrote, "retaining his personal soldiers with increased pay, and enlisting those of others."

And across the Channel, Duke William was equally busy recruiting. Mercenaries from across Europe converged on Normandy to join the invasion, willing to fight for pay or, when victorious, for grants of English land. Not all, however, were sympathetic to William's cause. According to Poitiers, they caught an English spy. The man doubtless expected a brutal punishment, but Duke William cared not in the least if King Harold knew of his preparations – in fact, he was happy for him to know all about it. He told the spy that Harold could expect to see the Norman army for himself within the year, or if not, need not worry he would ever see it at all.

The spy's report surely came as cold comfort to Harold. Shortly after the comet faded from view, he was in London when word came that invaders had landed on the Isle of Wight.

Nobody could have imagined the Normans could have built and manned a fleet so quickly, much less become trained sailors. There was, of course, another possibility: that with the war over between Denmark and Norway, either King Harald or King Svein had decided to take the other third of Cnut's North Sea Empire. Yet from Scandinavia Vikings would have taken the traditional, direct route and attacked Northumbria, not come all the way down through the Strait of Dover (and two opposing fleets) to attack the Isle of Wight. A landing there would only require them to put to sea again to attack the mainland.

It soon turned out that the invaders were not Vikings at all, or Normans either. By reports, they were not intent on pillage, more on simply squeezing money and supplies out of the islanders. And their leader was none other than the king's brother, Tostig.

———

Though some of his men were undoubtedly Norman, and Flemish, and for that matter English, Tostig was not accompanied by Duke William. (Or his wife Judith, presumably left at home in Flanders, though he did bring along his teenaged son Skuli.) When Tostig had approached William about a partnership in invading England, the duke's response had been noncommittal. He had no intention of taking on English allies. If Tostig, with his little band of outcasts and Flemish mercenaries, wished to sail home and make trouble for his brother, the duke would not stop him, but neither would he join him. He had already been betrayed by one son of Godwin. It would not do to depend on this one, only to have the renegade earl desert him at a critical moment. William would, however, take great interest in this test of King Harold's preparations and response. Jumièges wrote simply, "the duke sent Earl Tostig to England."

Tostig's landing on the Isle of Wight, and the bullying of the inhabitants into giving up payment and supplies, was no less than what Earl Godwin had done, preparatory to his return from exile in 1052. Tostig may even have recruited men from the Godwin family estates along the south coast, but he did not receive the same warm reception his father had. Before Harold could prepare his own reception, Tostig raised anchor. His little pirate fleet harried its way east across Sussex. Selsey, Shoreham, Brighton, Rottingdean and more felt the exiled earl's vengeance. Around the prominence of Kent he went, records the *Chronicle*, "and ravaged the coast wherever he landed, until he came to Sandwich."

Sandwich was now one of the navy towns that had furnished King Edward with ships and men against the Viking threat. Ships and men were still there, and fell into Tostig's hands with little trouble. In 1052 this had been the turning point for his father and brothers, when they took their fleet inland and sailed up the Thames to face down King Edward. Tostig's fleet now numbered some sixty ships, about the same number old King Harthacnut had brought to declare himself king. He might have sailed upriver like his father and demanded Harold's submission. He did not. Harold, in London, had the people of England behind him the way Edward, at least in the old days, had not. As soon as he learned of his brother's incursion, he whistled up a troop of horsemen and ordered the fleet to rendezvous with him at Sandwich.

On the approach of the king with his army, Tostig raised anchor again and made off, up the coast to the Humber estuary, the way Forkbeard had in his conquest of the north. It wasn't King Harold and England that Tostig was after, not yet. It was Northumbria and its new earl, Morcar Siwardsson.

Morcar, however, was ready for him. While Tostig had been dawdling his way up the coast, burning and pillaging, the Northumbrian had been gathering his army, and in Mercia his brother Edwin the same. When Tostig attempted to land, they met him together and drove him back into the sea. Of the sixty ships in his fleet, he escaped with only a dozen, with many men killed and many others abandoning his cause. "The Flemings, when they saw this, deserted, and left Tostig," wrote Gaimar. "They went back home laden with loot from the miserable English."

Having run out of friends in Denmark, Normandy, Flanders and now England, Tostig and his remaining men continued north, up the coast to Scotland, to seek shelter from his old brother in arms, King Malcolm.

"Then King Harold went to Sandwich, where he awaited his fleet," records the *Chronicle*, "for it was some time before it could be collected, but when it was assembled, he took it to the Isle of Wight, and waited there all summer and autumn."

The Isle of Wight, lying directly between Normandy and the English mainland, was not the best place to begin an invasion, but it was the best place from which to intercept one. Even with his massive army Harold could not hope to defend the entire southeastern coast of England, but an English fleet at Wight would be well positioned to cut off Duke William from ever reaching shore. In the event the navy failed to head him off, the land forces, scattered though they were, would immediately send word of any Norman landing, and might even fight a forlorn delaying action long enough for the king to converge the rest of the army on the spot.

Harold's more immediate problem was keeping all those farmers on standby all summer. By this time the *fyrd*'s first tour of duty was up; the second half had been called up to replace them. The Isle of Wight and southeastern England would have been fairly stripped of edibles to feed what amounted to a huge army of occupation. And the harvest season was coming up. If all these men weren't home to take in their crops, the nation would face starvation over the winter.

By now Duke William had the approval of the Holy Roman Emperor and Pope Alexander, who had sent him a papal flag – a blue-bordered white square with a gold cross – to carry into battle and a ring, said to contain beneath the gemstone a relic of Saint Peter, perhaps a tooth or hair. Wace wrote, "The duke rejoiced greatly at receiving the banner, and the sanction which the pope gave him."

With the promise of absolution from God, and of vast riches from what would amount to the greatest invasion of England since the days of Forkbeard and Cnut or even the Great Heathen Army under the sons of Ragnar Lodbrok in the year 865, more than enough men had answered William's call to arms. "Many foreign troops came to help him," wrote Poitiers, "attracted in part by the duke's well-known generosity, but all fully trusting in the justice of his cause."

Wace concurred. "There was no fighting man in the land, no good warrior, archer, nor peasant of brave heart and old enough for battle, that the duke did not call upon to go with him to England, promising payment to the vassals and honors to the barons."

Poitiers put their number at 50,000, and other old chroniclers at anywhere up to three times that, though modern historians estimate less than a tenth of it, and only a third of those with horses. In medieval times, though, that was a respectable army. Forkbeard and Cnut had conquered the Island Kingdom with less. William's more immediate problem was keeping them from taking over Normandy.

Poitiers would have it that all those fighting men acted as perfect guests, stealing nothing from the locals, leaving their herds and crops safe. An army needs to eat, however, and somebody must provide the food. If no herds were poached, crops confiscated or locals molested it was because those alternatives could always be inflicted on any who refused to contribute. Nobody could gather a mixed army of Normans and medieval mercenaries together in anticipation of war, then have them get along for an entire summer without some brigandage, thievery and mayhem. Nobody, perhaps, except Duke William, who appears to have understood that the first principle of keeping soldiery out of trouble is to keep them busy. Wace wrote, "He assembled carpenters, smiths and other workmen, so that great commotion was seen in every Norman port, wood and materials being collected, planks being cut, ships and boats framed, sails stretched and masts raised, with great effort and at great expense. They spent all summer and autumn in fitting out the fleet and gathering the forces."

The size of this navy, according to various sources, ranges from almost 700 to over 3,000 ships – dragon ships, longships, cargo cogs – capable of carrying 10,000 men and all their gear. Such was the duke's application of man-hours to the task that it's thought the Norman fleet, which many had believed impossible to assemble within the promised year, was ready by the end of June. The *drakkar* gifted to William by Duchess Matilda was christened the *Mora*. (The name refers to the Morini, the original Belgic inhabitants of Matilda's Flanders homeland.) It was the biggest ship in the fleet, capable of carrying ten or twelve knights – the Companions – along with their entourage, some forty or fifty men in addition to the crew. Its prow bore a heavenly cherub, pointing the way forward.

Heaven, however, did not immediately cooperate. Poitiers and Bishop Guy of Amiens (whose *Carmen Widonis*, "Poem by Guy," takes up the story here) both allude to contrary winds out of the north, blowing in the Normans' faces. Old hands, veterans of Duke Robert's aborted invasion of 1034, might well have advised against sailing into it.

By late August or early September, though, Duke William evidently ran out of patience. Poitiers recorded, "Now the whole fleet, furnished with great care, from the mouth of the Dives and neighboring ports, where they had awaited a south wind for their passage, was blown by the breath of the Zephyr [west wind] to the harbor of Saint-Valery [modern Saint-Valery-sur-Somme, in the Somme estuary]." He spoke of terrible shipwrecks and men deserting the cause, so he may be glossing over a first Norman attempt at a Channel crossing, rebuffed by a summer storm. William, Poitiers wrote, made the best of things: "Indeed, meeting adversity with good spirit, he hid the loss of the drowned as much as he could by burying them in secret. By daily increasing rations he relieved want, and with sundry encouragements he soothed the terrified and gave heart to the fearful."

For whatever reason, the Norman fleet had put in up the coast at Saint-Valery, in Ponthieu. We can assume that Count Guy, who had played such a critical role in the first meeting of William with Harold, willingly assisted in his second; though the count could not leave his domain, according to the *Carmen*, his brother Hugh joined William's crusade. And, if not as good a harbor as at the Dives, Saint-Valery had the advantage of being nearer to English soil.

It had a disadvantage, however, in being at the opposite end of Normandy from Brittany, and Duke Conan II.

Two years prior, Duke William's cousin had handed over to him on his spearpoint the keys to his castle at Dinan. Since then he had been simmering in his hatred for the Normans. He was fighting yet another border war with yet another neighbor, Anjou's Count Geoffrey III the Bearded, when he received notice from William (as the duke sent to all surrounding rulers) of his intent to cross the Channel, advisement of his papal blessing, and a warning not to meddle in Normandy while the Normans were in England. Conan replied that William should first look to the home front. Jumièges quoted him thus:

> I hear, that you now wish to go beyond the sea and conquer for yourself the kingdom of England. Now Robert, Duke of the Normans, whom you pretend to regard as your father, at the moment of leaving for Jerusalem, handed over his entire inheritance to Alan, my father and his cousin; but you and your accomplices killed my father with poison at Vimeux in Normandy. Then you invaded its territory, because I was still too young to be able to defend it, and against all justice, since you are a bastard, you have retained it to this day. Now then, either give me back this Normandy that you owe me, or I will make war on you with all my might.

Duke William could hardly abandon his duchy while Duke Conan was on the loose, but to give up his invasion plans meant breaking his vow of English land and loot to all his men. To invade Brittany instead might have appeased them, but it would not gain William his kingdom nor his crown. Conan would have to be dealt with otherwise. Messages were sent to Brittany, but not in answer to its duke.

Conan, having taken Pouance on the Anjou border, pushed fourteen miles into Angevin territory to take Segres. In the following months he would turn north to capture Castrum Gunterii, modern Château-Gontier in Mayenne, from which he might invade southern Normandy while the Normans were away.

He never got there. Jumièges recorded, "One of the great Breton lords, who had sworn loyalty to the two counts and carried the messages to each other, rubbed poison on Conan's saddle pommel, his horse's reins and the inside of his gloves, for he was valet of Conan's chambers."

When Conan mounted his horse to accept the castle's surrender, he handled the reins, saddle or gloves, probably all three. "He died shortly afterwards," wrote Jumièges, "to the great regret of all his family, for he was a clever man, brave and partisan of justice. It is asserted that if he had lived longer, he would have done much good, and would have rendered himself very useful in the administration of his country."

That may be so, but we will never know, because for all that Conan made one great mistake, in crossing his kinsman William. The duke was widely suspected in his assassination, but nothing was ever proven. The only witness, the valet, immediately deserted the army of Brittany and went into the service of Normandy.

———

"By the time of the Nativity of St. Mary [September 8]," records the *Chronicle*, "the men's provisions were gone, and no one could keep them there any longer. Then the men were permitted to go home, and the king rode home, and the ships were dispatched to London."

All England breathed a collective sigh of relief. The Norman invasion that everyone feared had not come to fruition. All believed, as Malmesbury claimed even Duke William's own men did, "that he must be mad, wishing to subjugate a foreign land, that God opposed him by withholding the wind, that his father had made a similar attempt, and was similarly frustrated, that it was ever the way of that family to desire that which was out of their reach, and to find God against them."

Come winter the storms in the Channel would grow even more wicked, the waves even higher. Duke William and his would-be sailors would not dare another attempt until spring, by which time his vast mercenary army would have eaten Normandy down to the ground, driven the locals near to rebellion, and perhaps even mutinied themselves over loot promised and not delivered. Meanwhile the English soldiery, disbanded, scattered back to their farms. The harvest moon was still several weeks off. There was plenty of time for everyone to bring in their crops and rest assured they would be fed through the winter.

It was probably the second week of the month that messengers arrived in London and Harold received awful news. An invasion had come after all, and where least expected: not in the south, but in the north. A fleet had come ravaging down the coast of Northumbria and turned inland, up the Humber, right into the heart of the kingdom. From there they might move south, as Forkbeard and Cnut had, to Gainsborough, or north to cut off York from aid.

Worst of all was hearing who led them.

Tostig, his own brother.

With Harald Sigurdsson, the King of Norway.

And 300 dragon ships.

The Vikings had returned to England.

XXXV

Return of the Vikings

September 1066

*When King Harold, in the south after he had returned from the fleet,
was told that Harald, King of Norway, and Earl Tostig had landed
near York, he went northward day and night, as soon as he had
collected his army.*

Anglo-Saxon Chronicle

Tostig's quest for an ally had taken him to Scotland and the court of
his old friend King Malcolm, but he had fared no better there than
in Flanders, Denmark or Normandy. Malcolm was willing to grant
him asylum, but if Tostig insisted on invading England he would offer
nothing more than moral support. Malcolm was still betrothed to
Margaret, old King Edward's great-niece, and though the marriage
had not yet come to fruition, Malcolm desired continued good
relations with his powerful neighbor to the south. Scotland was, after
all, surrounded to the east, north and west by Vikings, minions of
Norwegian king Harald III.

Having run out of friends and options, Tostig had little choice but to
sound out King Harald himself for aid. In 1066 Harald was fifty-one
– old for a man of that time and place – the most widely traveled and
combat-experienced Viking of the age. He had fought Pecheneg nomads
on the Russian steppes, desert bandits in the Holy Land, Saracen armies
in Sicily, and Norman mercenaries in Italy. That in a decade and a half
he had failed to conquer Denmark was something of a blemish on his

resumé, for which he had lately consoled himself by tyrannizing his own subjects, earning the sobriquet *Hardrada*, Hard Ruler.

"If you wish to conquer England," Tostig told him, "I can talk most of the lords there into becoming your comrades and allies. The only difference between me and my brother Harold is the title of king. You are well known as the greatest champion in the North, and I am surprised that you have spent fifteen years attempting to conquer Denmark, yet hesitate to invade England, which is ripe for the taking."

"King Harald carefully weighed the earl's words," his own saga relates, "and saw at once there was truth in much of them." Some of his courtiers believed a conquest of England would be the pinnacle of his career, making him an equal in history of Forkbeard and Cnut. Others reminded him the Island Kingdom was much larger and much better defended than Denmark. It was common knowledge that any English housecarl was equal to any two Vikings. In the end, however, Hardrada could not resist. His saga concludes, "He, too, longed to conquer new realms."

"Tostig swore an oath of loyalty to King Harald," relates the *Morkinskinna*, "promising the king his aid and assistance in their invasion of England. King Harald swore in return that Tostig would rule that land, and that he would have power in accordance with territory they won there."

It's likely that neither party bargained in good faith. The sons of Godwin were not renowned for their honesty. "People say," Harald grumbled, "the English are not to be trusted."

Yet the Norwegian king was also notorious for going back on his word whenever it suited him. As soon as England was conquered, neither man would have much use for the other.

———

Tostig and his new Norwegian friends crossed the North Sea to pick up more fighting men in the Orkneys, Shetlands and Scotland. That brought their total invasion force to about 300 ships, but perhaps as many as 500, with at least 9,000 men, maybe 12,000, and by some analyses as many as 18,000 – half again the number with which Cnut was said to have conquered the Island Kingdom, fifty-one years earlier.

They went ravaging down the coast of Northumbria. The far northern towns, Clifflond (modern Cleveland) and Mydilsburgh (Middlesbrough) and the villages around them were more Viking than English, and submitted without a fight. Forty miles down the coast, in Skardaborg, Skardi's Fort, modern Scarborough, the villagers were manifestly English. They stood off the invaders from within a palisaded ditch around their town, at least until the Vikings lofted firebrands over the wall to light up their thatched roofs. From Skardaborg a road led directly inland to York, but even after all these years Vikings still hated to march when they could sail. Tostig and Harald may also have intended to draw the Northumbrian army toward the coast while they circled around, seventy miles south to the mouth of the Humber. Getting an assist from its tidal bore to coast up its northern feed river, the Ouse, on Wednesday, September 20 they landed at Riccall, within ten miles of York. They had only marched about seven miles when they came to a choke point at Fulford, "foul water ford," between the banks of the Ouse and an impassable riverside swamp.

There they found their way blocked by a wall of shields a quarter-mile across. Above it flew the banners of Morcar, Earl of Northumbria, his brother Earl Edwin of Mercia, and even Earl Waltheof of Northamptonshire and Huntingdonshire. The north had united against the invaders.

And probably that same day, far to the south, King Harold received word of the Viking invasion.

From the king's perspective, the one bright spot in these events was that the invasion had not come a few weeks or even days earlier. Then, half the *fyrds* of Mercia and Northumbria had been in the south, with him, on the lookout for a Norman invasion. As it was, the northern *fyrds* had had the better part of two weeks to march home and rest. Edwin and Morcar had their full troop strength at their disposal.

Judging by the reported size of the Viking fleet, however, even that might not be enough. News out of the north, even by high-speed riders, would have been days out of date. As far as Harold knew, the Vikings were still harrying the Northumbrian coast, but in such strength that this was no minor raid. Whether an attack on York or, like Forkbeard and Cnut, via the Humber from which to strike inland north or south, their goal could be nothing less than conquest. It was imperative for the king to come to the earls' rescue as soon as possible.

That, however, might well require a miracle. With the *fyrd* disbanded and dispersed, Harold himself had only his housecarls and those of his brothers, the earls Gyrth of East Anglia and Leofwine of Kent. They were the best fighting men in Western Europe, but he commanded at most 3,000 of them. Tostig and the Vikings might have three or four times as many men, in which case even the housecarls' famous two-for-one advantage would not be enough. Harold would have to recall the *fyrd* and take it north. At a reasonable pace, say twelve hours per day, a march from London to York might require a week, and that was after a day, or more likely days, for the *fyrd* to assemble. By that time the fate of the north would almost certainly have already been decided.

No matter. It was a king's duty to go to the aid of his vassals. If King Harold could not save his earls and their people, he would avenge them.

He ordered his housecarls to make ready for the march. He sent riders north to fan out on both sides of Ermine Street and call up the *fyrd* again. Those to the south would have to catch up. All of it this time, no halfway measures. The militias were to rendezvous with the king along the way. He departed London with a barebones force, but with luck would arrive in York with an army.

If only he arrived in time.

At Fulford, time had already run out for Edwin, and Morcar, and Waltheof.

Historians have questioned whether it was wise for the earls to come out from York and risk battle with Tostig and King Harald. After all, the city had once been Roman, and was still ringed with Roman walls. The northerners might have stood off a Viking siege long enough for King Harold to come to their rescue.

But they could not assume he was coming at all. That old animosity between Wessex and the north may have been in everybody's minds, leading pessimists inside the walls to think Harold might leave them to the Vikings' mercy in order for his rivals to destroy each other.

Even disregarding that, by any reasonable estimate, it would be weeks before the king could arrive. The earls could not wait.

September in medieval days was a time of some privation, with the previous year's stock of food running low and the current crop yet to be harvested. Rather than tending their fields, half the farmers in the north had spent the summer in the south with King Harold. Now they were all back, but with the Vikings afoot they were not out in their fields working their crops. They were all in York, eating up whatever food was left.

So the earls had to gamble all on one battle. They had defeated Tostig once already, on the banks of the Humber that summer. Even with his new Viking allies backing him, they could have some hope of defeating him again. With the River Ouse to their right and that impassable swamp to their left, the enemy could not flank them to either side. A ditch ran between swamp and river; they arrayed their shield wall with their best men, their armored housecarls, to the front along its lip, Edwin's Mercians nearest the river and Morcar's Northumbrians nearest the swamp, forming one invincible line along the trench, with ranks of fyrdmen backing it. From there they dared Tostig and Harald to come at them. The Vikings would have to wade across the trench and scramble up the far side, straight into the spears and Dane axes stabbing and chopping from behind the shield wall.

And so they did. The *Heimskringla* records, "When King Harald saw the English army had lined the ditch against him, he ordered the charge sounded, and urged on his men."

To the wail of horns, the beat of drums, and the bellow of maddened warriors, the invaders surged forward toward the English. Man-to-man on level ground, Vikings might have had some chance of breaking the shield wall, as long as they kept their formation. Clambering through the waterlogged trench and slip-sliding up the other side, however, was impossible to do in unison. Some men reached the shield wall ahead of the others, and paid the price for their aggression. All alone, facing two or three spears, and swords and axes striking from behind shields was futile, and fatal. The men behind them found themselves tripping over their dead and wounded fellows sliding back down into the ditch, sinking in the turbid water.

It went on like that for what must have seemed a long time, but it could not go on forever, not against English housecarls. Behind the safety of their shield wall, Edwin and Morcar were content to let the enemy learn the lesson. That summer, along the Humber, those of Tostig's pirates and marauders who hadn't been killed had promptly deserted. The earls knew that, if pressed hard enough, Tostig's hired swords would fold again.

But very likely, King Harald knew that too.

"The king's banner [a black raven on white silk, called Land-Waster] was next to the river," records the *Heimskringla*, "where the line was thickest." While Tostig and his renegades faced Morcar, toward the swamp, Harald faced Edwin's Mercians. His Vikings were veterans of the long war with Denmark, and many had fought with him prior to that, in the Holy Land, Sicily and Italy. It would not be they who broke.

Sure enough, at some point, Tostig's pirates and marauders decided they'd had enough. Rather than charge yet again, they turned their backs and ran.

"The wing of the Northmen's line nearest the ditch gave way," recorded Snorri, "and the English followed, thinking the Norse would fly."

On seeing the enemy retreat, the urge to chase and kill, to seize victory – or at least be done with all the death – was overpowering. Morcar's housecarls felt triumph in their grasp. If they chased off Tostig, they would turn King Harald's flank – attack him from the side while Edwin's Mercians engaged from the front. They plunged down into the ditch and up the other bank, after the fleeing invaders. The fyrdmen behind them, with no better grasp of tactics than following the housecarls, charged.

But retreat – feigned retreat – was a time-honored medieval tactic. If a shield wall could not be broken by frontal attack, or outflanked around the ends, the only way to defeat it was to lure the defenders into deserting it themselves.

The moment the Northumbrians abandoned their position, the battle at Fulford became two battles. Toward the river, the Mercians and Vikings still opposed each other along the gully, but toward the swamp, the Northumbrians' pursuit of Tostig's men had moved the fight out beyond it. Half the English line was overextended, leaving a gap in the shield wall.

Whether or not Tostig's retreat had been feigned, Harald saw the opening. Snorri wrote, "He ordered the banner which was called the

Land-Waster to be carried before him, and made so severe an assault that all had to give way before it."

Vikings poured across the ditch, up the bank, and into the gap between the English armies. Suddenly it was the Northumbrians who were surrounded, with their backs to the swamp, and the Mercians who were outflanked. Droves of fyrdmen armed with pitchforks and wood hatchets were exposed to the swords and axes of the Vikings. "Mercilessly the king bloodied weapons on the English near the Ouse River," records the *Morkinskinna*. "A greater slaughter will never be inflicted on a brave army."

Those English who could escape, did, the Mercians along the riverbank, and the Northumbrians into the swamp. Most did not escape at all, though Edwin and Morcar both survived. Waltheof was captured, but King Harald let him go with a promise to never fight him again. After all, the Vikings wanted allies in England. "As King Harald had won such a decisive victory against such great chieftains and so large a host," wrote Snorri of York, "the people were fearful, and doubted they could stand against him. The city elders therefore decided, in a council, to tell King Harald they would hand over the city to him."

Leaving 150 of their men in York as a garrison, the Vikings took an equal number of citizens as hostages and arranged to take more from the surrounding hamlets and villages. The two sides were to meet the following Monday, September 25, a few miles east of the city at a bridge over the River Derwent, then called *stan ford*, "stone ford," or *Samfordesbrigge*, "the bridge at the sandy ford," today Stamford Bridge.

With the army of Northumbria destroyed and that of Mercia scattered, come Monday Harald deemed two-thirds of his force sufficient for a simple hostage exchange. The other third he ordered to stay behind at Riccall to protect the fleet. The weather was clear and hot. "So the men laid aside their armor," wrote Snorri, "and went ashore with just their shields, helmets and spears, wearing their swords, and many had also arrows and bows. All were very merry."

They arrived on the high ground south of the bridge about midday. Harald and Tostig led a few men across the slender footbridge to reconnoiter the far bank. They soon spotted a cloud of dust in the distance, above the road from York. Harald asked Tostig, "What is that yonder, a whirlwind or the dust of horsemen?"

Tostig guessed it was the delegation from York, but when the procession topped a rise about a mile and a half away, the sun glittered on the spearpoints and armor of an army. It's thought they numbered 10,000 infantry and 2,500 cavalry – at least a third again as many northmen at the bridge. Above them fluttered a banner bearing a fighting man woven in gold, the personal standard of King Harold II of England.

———

While the Vikings and Northumbrians were haggling over hostages, King Harold had pulled off one of the greatest military feats of the Middle Ages: assembling an army while on the move, and force-marching it 200 miles in a less than a week. Even recalling the *fyrd* just days after he had released it from service was an achievement in itself. To gather and lead thousands of men, most of them on foot, many in full armor, twenty miles or more a day, required remarkable kingship. Norman writers would ever denigrate Harold as a shameless oath-breaker, but only a respected, even beloved leader could have achieved so much.

Somewhere along the way he would have learned of the English defeat at Fulford, and that he would have to prevail over the Vikings without the help of his brothers-in-law, the northern earls. Locals must have reported the whereabouts of the Viking fleet too, which Harold might have attacked directly. Burning the ships, however, would have denied the Norwegians any escape, and compelled them to fight all the harder. Instead, the Anglo-Saxons skirted around Riccall to approach York from the west, coming to within ten miles of the city by Sunday night. On Monday morning, the day of the hostage exchange – presumably having killed or imprisoned the token Viking garrison in York – the Anglo-Saxon army marched through the city toward Stamford Bridge.

As soon as they got over the shock of the English army's arrival, Tostig and King Harald made plans. They could have simply retreated, but that was not in Hardrada's nature. The Vikings held the footbridge and the high ground beyond. If there was to be a fight, let it be here. Harald sent riders hastening back to the fleet to summon every man to the battle and went back over the bridge to order his army, leaving it to Tostig to say what he would to his countrymen.

The English army pulled up a few hundred yards short of the bridge. King Harold and a few trusted lieutenants rode forward to where Tostig and his retainers awaited, to see if there was still a way to resolve matters without bloodshed. It's notable that Harold went incognito, his face probably hidden beneath an ornate, Saxon-style full-face helmet, not trusting the Vikings in Tostig's party to honor the truce. Yet he still trusted his brother, who surely recognized him, not to give him away.

The conversation between the English king and his disgraced brother is one of the most famous in English history. Different versions exist in different chronicles, but they vary only in detail, and putting them together, it is possible to hear two sons of Godwin decide the future of the Island Kingdom.

Harold called out, "Is Earl Tostig with this army?"

Tostig said, "There is no point in denying it."

"Your brother, King Harold, sends God's greetings," said Harold, "and offers to atone for past deeds."

Tostig asked, "What does he offer now that he did not before?"

"He regrets that offer now," conceded the king, "after all that's been done."

"We won't set that right with money," said Tostig. "What is his offer?"

"A fifth of England, no more. But you have laid waste the land, and for that must make amends."

Tostig said, "I do not accept."

Harold raised his offer. "You shall have all of Northumbria, and rather than fight you for it, he will award you a third of the kingdom to rule beside him."

"That is preferable to the contempt and treachery he offered last winter," said Tostig, "and if he had made such an offer then it would have saved many lives, and been better for England." Across the span of a thousand years, Tostig's anger and resentment can still be heard. "But it is too late for such bargaining. I have often heard the Norwegians say that if an acceptable offer were made I would quickly leave them to fight their own battles, but I will not."

"Then hear the king's final offer," Harold said. "He would rather you have half of England, than you both fight over it, with the survivor taking all."

Tostig said, "But if I accept, what will he give King Harald Sigurdsson for his trouble?"

The king replied, "He has also spoken of this. He will give King Harald seven feet of English ground, or as much more as he is taller than other men, but no more."

"Then tell King Harold to make ready for battle," Tostig said, "and never let it be said that Earl Tostig betrayed King Harald Sigurdsson to his enemy, when he came west to fight for England. We would all rather die with honor, than lose the kingdom."

The brothers had come too far for anything else. One of them would have to die.

"Then," Harold told him, "the king declares the blame for this business to be on your head." He wheeled and with his silent companions rode back to the English lines.

With a word, Tostig could have loosed his Viking dogs on his brother and seen him killed then and there. Yet he did not. And when, on his return, Viking king Harald demanded why, Tostig replied, "I knew he would offer me peace, lands and title, and that I, on the other hand, would be his murderer if I gave him away. I would not break faith with him when he came trusting my honor, and if one of us must die I prefer that he killed me rather than I killed him."

———

On the far side of the river, the Viking army had withdrawn up the slope beyond arrow range, but left a detachment on the English side to defend the bridge. Or, at least hold it long enough for the other third of the invaders to arrive.

Harold of England would have known he was not facing the entire Viking army. He had to defeat this contingent before their reinforcements could arrive to tip the balance. To do that, he had to take the bridge.

The Vikings there knew they would die that day. Their defeat was a foregone conclusion, hardly worth mention in the annals. Yet they made their deaths worthwhile, with least one among them passing anonymously into legend. His story appears in but a single version of the *Anglo-Saxon Chronicle*, the one from Abingdon Abbey – actually, as its last entry, which is mysteriously cut off in mid-paragraph – and there only as an addendum inserted by an equally unknown 12th-century annalist: "The Norwegians fled before the enemy, but one stood firm, preventing them from crossing the bridge or clinching victory."

As Malmesbury heard it, "However hard it is to believe, for some time a single Norwegian halted the advance of so many great men. Standing on the entrance of the bridge, which is called Standford Brigge [*sic*], killing several of our warriors, he prevented the rest from crossing over."

Stamford Bridge was narrow enough to be covered by the swing of a Dane axe as tall as a man. Huntingdon recorded, "A single Norwegian, whose name should have been remembered, posted himself on a bridge and, chopping down more than forty English with a battle-axe, his country's weapon, halted the advance of the whole English army."

Whether this anonymous Viking actually killed forty English himself, or was simply credited with every foe who died trying to take the bridge, hardly matters. At some point even the English housecarls, themselves expert axemen, felt it better to offer him quarter.

"Given the chance to surrender, and being assured that a man of such bravery could expect the greatest mercy from the English," wrote Malmesbury, "he ridiculed those who tried to bargain with him, and instead, with grim expression, scorned the cowards who were unable to overcome one man."

By now no one on the English side wished to face this Viking axman, and yet even he could not stand forever against such odds. One might think he was a prime target for an arrow, and Malmesbury claimed he was hit by a javelin, but Huntingdon assigned him a less glorious end: "Finally someone went under the bridge in a boat and stuck a spear up into him through a gap in the planks." And the anonymous scribe in the Abingdon *Chronicle* agreed that someone "went under the bridge and stabbed him under his coat of mail."

At any rate, when he and the rest of the dead Vikings had been dragged from the bridge or rolled off into the water, the way to the enemy was clear. Tostig and King Harald had used the delay to form their shield wall at the top of the opposite slope where the English, exhausted by their long march from London, would have to march uphill to attack. King Harald expected King Harold to fight him the way Vikings and Anglo-Saxons had fought each other for the better part of three centuries: on foot, man-to-man.

But, though not as traveled as King Harald, King Harold was an experienced, worldly war-leader in his own right. He had been to the Continent, had fought the Bretons in Normandy, and recalled how the Normans fought: from the saddle. He sent his housecarls clattering across the bridge and up the slope on horseback. If the cavalry could get around the ends of the shield wall, they would be able to assault the Vikings from the rear, even as the English *fyrd* engaged it from the front. The Vikings would be surrounded.

"Then the Englishmen gave out their war cry," recorded the scribes. (For the Anglo-Saxons that was either "God Almighty!" or "Holy Cross!")

To their credit, Tostig and King Harald adapted their tactics on the fly. Before the horsemen could ride around the shield wall, they bent its ends back and around to form a complete, unflankable circle, with the king and the earl in the center.

"Our archers will be inside with us," Harald ordered. "Those in the front rank should set the butts of their spears in the ground, aiming the points at the riders' chests if they charge us, and those in the second rank should aim theirs at the chests of the horses."

Horses, even goaded and spurred, will refuse to throw themselves on a hedge of spears. Those which stopped too suddenly hurled their armor-weighted riders overhead and down before the shield wall, where they were helpless prey for Viking spears and axes. The rest circled around the hilltop, seeking a weak point and finding none. "The English rode at the Norwegians," recounts the *Morkinskinna*, "only to meet that impenetrable defense. The way the spears were set, the horses could not get past them."

The cavalry thundered around the circular, spear-bristling Viking shield wall but could neither find a break in it, nor inflict one. Spears stuck in shields could be battered loose. Spears tossed over the shield wall might hurt someone inside, but not help to break the wall itself. "Both sides fought with the greatest ferocity, and at first suffered few casualties," admitted Snorri.

King Harold's experiment with cavalry had failed. Or, more precisely, he learned that a Norman-style cavalry assault was ineffective against a Scandinavian-style shield wall. "The fighting was sporadic while the Norwegians maintained the proper formation," claims the *Heimskringla*, "with Englishmen charging hard and withdrawing as soon as they saw they had achieved nothing."

Yet as Harald of Norway had demonstrated at Fulford, there was more than one way to defeat a shield wall, even one that could not be outflanked. Harold of England sent his footsoldiers up the hill. "There was such a large difference in numbers," recounts the *Morkinskinna*, "that the English, engaging the Norwegians, surrounded them, and attacked from all sides. As might be expected, men began to fall."

A spear or axe or sword can only kill one man at a time. With more than their own number facing them, the Norwegian spear-hedge was gradually trimmed back. Still, the shield wall might have lasted until reinforcements arrived from the fleet, had not the Anglo-Saxons, perhaps on signal, given up the fight and fled down the hill.

The Vikings could taste blood. Some of them broke out of the safety of the shield wall to pursue their foes, and if their king and Tostig tried to recall them it was no use. As soon as they had lured the Vikings far enough down the hill, the English horsemen wheeled and circled back up behind them, while the Anglo-Saxon housecarls turned and began hewing away with their axes. The Norwegians on the slope, cut off and surrounded, were annihilated. Worse, those at the top could not close the gap in the shield wall before the English cavalry poured in through it. "The circle broke and fell back," laments the *Morkinskinna*, "and many of King Harald's men were killed."

For the Vikings, not all was yet lost. Taking it upon himself to personally win the battle, King Harald broke out beyond the shield wall, swinging his sword two-handed. "Neither helmets nor mail coats could protect against him," the scribes proclaimed, "and everyone in his way fell back before him. To all it seemed the English were going to be routed."

It was not King Harald's destiny, however, to be another Forkbeard or another Cnut, and conquer England. It was his destiny to personify the end of the Viking Age. For at that moment an arrow or javelin – as some Scandinavian accounts would have it, launched by King Harold himself – struck him in the throat. Dying, he called Tostig to his side and advised, "You should come to terms with your brother, and tell him I accept that portion of the kingdom that he offered me."

With the Norwegian king dead, the English king promised his men quarter. Tostig, now in command, declined both King Harald's advice and King Harold's offer, determined to fight to the death. And so he did. The English cavalry broke up the shield wall, and the outnumbered defenders were cut down piecemeal. Like Hardrada, Tostig was killed by an arrow, in his case to the eye. Nearly all the Vikings died with him, including the reinforcements who arrived too late from Riccall. The few still alive fled for their ships and asked for mercy.

King Harold granted it. He could afford to. According to the *Chronicle*, of the 300 ships of the original invasion fleet, the survivors only needed twenty-four for the return journey. Seventy-odd years later Orderic wrote, "Visitors can easily discern the battlefield, for a great mountain of dead men's bones still lies there, bearing witness to the terrible slaughter on both sides."

Stamford Bridge was the greatest battle, if greatness is reckoned by the number of dead, in English history to that time. Greater than Maldon, greater than Sherston, greater than Assandun. As the victor, King Harold II – king for less than a year – could already count himself among the great monarchs of England. If he did nothing more in his reign, he would be remembered for that.

In York the celebrations went on for a week. There was of course some mourning among Harold and his brothers Gyrth and Leofwine for their lost brother, but death had been Tostig's own choice, and if he had not lived honorably he had at least died so. Edwin of Mercia and Morcar of Northumbria reclaimed their earldoms, thanks to their brother-in-law the king. The hostages were restored to their families. With the Vikings repelled and the Normans outlasted, the future of the Island Kingdom was secure. Drink flowed and music played in the Earlsborough…at least, until a rider arrived along Ermine Street with terrible news.

In the south, the wind direction had changed.

A few days earlier, even as the king was celebrating in York, the Norman fleet had landed at Pevensey, in the far south of England.

Duke William had arrived after all. With twice as many ships as the Viking fleet.

XXXVI

Hastings

October 1066

Not the countless denizens of the land, nor a treacherous sea, nor a shore marked with punishing rocks, nor even the threatening onset of winter deterred you from seeking the kingdom left to you by your kinsman. Justice and rightful law supported you before posterity; therefore, for you there was no fear.

Amiens

Having waited all summer for a favorable wind, and with his seamen and warriors chafing to either raise sail or go home, Duke William had taken it upon himself to remind God of his papal blessing. As the fleet lay at Saint-Valery-sur-Somme, he called upon no less than St. Valery himself, a monk-turned-hermit dead some 450 years, to deliver his message. Poitiers recorded, "He raised holy prayers to the extent that he had the body of Valery, a confessor most pleasing to God, borne out of the basilica to calm the contrary wind and bring a favourable one."

Valery – Walaric in the original Frankish – was said to deliver miraculous cures from beyond the grave, and sure enough the gilt-brass windvane on the duke's *drakkar* soon swung round to point north. Orderic recorded, "When finally in answer to so many prayers and by the grace of God the favourable wind arrived, the duke impatiently summoned all his men to the ships at once and commanded them to bravely set sail."

William had the papal banner fixed to the masthead of his flagship *Mora*, and a lantern as well. Amiens and Poitiers, both of whom may have taken part in the crossing, claimed the fleet, apparently anxious to take advantage of the wind while it lasted, departed at dusk, only to lie at anchor overnight around the duke's beacon.* Come daylight the fleet raised sail northwest. Saint-Valery does not lie on the Channel's narrowest point; from there to Pevensey is almost seventy miles of open water, and for a good bit of it both coasts are below the horizon. The fearless Norman warriors, most of whom had never been out of sight of land in their lives, might have been more eager to face Anglo-Saxon swords than all that open sea, and looked forward to that first sighting of the English coast regardless of whether or not it was full of English housecarls awaiting them.

Today the Sussex coast at Pevensey is a gentle curve of clay miles wide, long ago eroded and silted full. In 1066 it extended further out to sea as a peninsula and tidal islands, offering safe harbor and plenty of convoluted shoreline on which a thousand ships could land all at once. First ashore, according to Wace, were the Norman archers, ready to lay down covering fire. Behind them came the horsemen, armed and armored, splashing through the waves and riding up across the beach into the woods beyond to clear any resistance. All must have been surprised, and perhaps disappointed, to find none. Only when the all-clear was sounded did Duke William himself come ashore. As he waded through the surf, however, breaking waves knocked him to his knees.

A murmur of dismay went up among the troops. It was a bad omen for a commander to appear clumsy in front of his men. (It's said that Harald of Norway's horse stumbled and threw him prior to his disaster at Stamford Bridge.) But William arose with his fists full of English soil. "See, my lords, by the grace of God I have seized England with both hands!"

He set his men to work. Earthworks were dug and reinforced to protect the landing site. The ruins of a nearby Roman fort, leftover from the days when Pevensey was *Anderitum*, "Great Ford," part of

---

*It's very believable that even William's most experienced seamen would hesitate to make a Channel crossing at night. Medieval navigation was rudimentary at best, and few other than Vikings dared voyages beyond sight of land.

the fortifications raised 600 years past against the first Saxon raiders (who called it *Andrades ceaster*), were occupied and strengthened as a base of operations. Resistance was expected. Normans who had landed up the coast at Romney had been set upon by locals and taken heavy casualties. Cavalry patrols ranged out into the countryside in search of the English usurper, terrorizing and taking captive anyone who denied the rightful king was William of Normandy.

"One of the English," wrote Amiens, "lying hidden behind sea-rocks, saw the countless ranks spread far and wide and the fields glittering with arms. He saw the citizenry, their homes burned for their disloyalty, put to the raging sword, and the children's tears shed for their fathers' slaughter. He ran to mount a horse and rushed to tell the king."

Wace has King Harold, in York, sorry on hearing the news. Not that the Normans had come, but that he and the army had not been on hand to drive them back into the sea: "So it has pleased the heavenly king, however, and I could not be everywhere at once."

His problem now was to assemble yet another army. His had not come through the battle at Stamford Bridge unscathed. Those of Edwin of Mercia and Morcar of Northumbria had been virtually wiped out at Fulford. The fyrdmen Harold had collected on the way north would have hurried homeward in anticipation of the harvest; the *Waltham Chronicle* concedes that "almost all his men had dispersed to different regions." Certainly the survivors would not be eager to join another forced march with a battle at the end of it.

Of course, there was another alternative: to cede southern England to William and try to take it from him later. According to Amiens (who could not possibly have witnessed the scene, but recreated it), Harold called together his commanders to put the question to them.

You are my fortress, my help, and defense. You have heard that a predatory Norman has set foot in our kingdom, robbing and despoiling. William does this to make you his subjects. He has a great name, but his heart is small. He is vain, covetous and pompous. He knows neither peace nor faith. If he can do it easily, he desires to take what is ours. Almighty God will not be patient with this. How great will be the grief, how great the pain and shame, how ruinous for the kingdom, how dark the day, if he gains what he wants, if he holds the royal scepter!

He put an ultimatum to his men. "Let all those who wish to, depart from us."

To their credit (according to Amiens), they considered this only briefly. "We would have war rather than bow our necks to the yoke of another king. We would rather die!"

"He ordered his men to ready themselves as quickly as they could," recorded one of Wace's sources, "that he might surprise the Normans and their leader William, before they could flee England."

Another 200 miles in a week or so. Probably Harold set out from York at the beginning of October with only the hard core of his army: his and his brothers' housecarls, said by some sources to now number no more than 500 men. Most would have been mounted, though, so the trip south may have been swifter than the one north. Again messengers rode out ahead, this time toward Wessex, Essex and Sussex, with orders for the *fyrd* to assemble yet again and rendezvous with the king at London. "All who could bear arms, and had heard about the duke's invasion, rose to defend the land," wrote Wace, "but none came from beyond the Humber. They had other business at hand, the Danes and Tostig having greatly slaughtered and weakened them."

Harold was not in so much haste that he could not make a side trip to his abbey at Waltham. Over the years he had bestowed even greater treasures upon it, including relics collected on his forays to the Continent, which he had wisely not housed in gold or silver reliquaries attractive to thieves and raiders, but preserved in clay vessels secretly buried on the site. Still, the abbey's greatest treasure was, of course, the Black Rood. The anonymous author of the *Waltham Chronicle* tells the story:

> He entered the church of the Holy Cross early that morning, and in his chapel placed relics which he brought with him upon the altar. He vowed that if the Lord granted him victory in the war he would endow the church with many estates as well as many clerics to serve God, and he swore to serve God like a bought slave for all time.

Accompanied by the priests, and with a procession going ahead, he entered the apse where, facing the Rood, the king in his devotion prostrated himself on the ground in the form of a cross and prayed.

The king almost certainly knew well "The Dream of the Rood," an Old English poem then already some 300 years old, so old that lines from it are to be found carved in runes on an eighteen-foot, 8th-century stone cross in Ruthwell, on the Scottish border. The poem, in part, tells the story of the Crucifixion from the point of view of the Holy Cross: how it began life as a tree, "felled at the forest's edge, torn up from my roots," only to be made a spectacle to which men nailed their criminals, until at last came the Christ to make his final sacrifice.

"I trembled when he embraced me," admits the Rood, "but I dared not bow to the ground.... I had to stand fast." Stand fast, as the nails driven through the man were driven into it as well. Stand fast, through the mockery and the blood. Stand fast, under the weight of the world, a weight that no thing, no man should bear – even a king – except to absolve sin.

The *Waltham Chronicle* attests:

Then occurred something touching to tell and miraculous from an earthly point of view. When the king prostrated himself the image of the crucified one, which to this point had been looking directly ahead over him, bowed its head as if in grief, a portent of events to come. Turkill, the sacristan, testified to having seen this while he was collecting and arranging the gifts the king had set on the altar. He told many people about it. I heard this from him myself, confirmed by many onlookers who saw the figure's head upright, though only Turkill witnessed its bow.

Alarmed at the sight, the elders appointed two of their monks, Osgod Cnoppe and Aeltheric Childmaister, to accompany the king to battle, to look after his spiritual health.

Or, if things went badly, to retrieve his body.

At the end of the week, probably Friday, October 6, Harold and his footsore troops arrived in London. He was doubtless relieved to find that William, who after all was only fifty miles away, had not used the time to reach and occupy the capital before him. In fact both sides, after the hustle-bustle of the previous days, paused for something of a breather. Harold needed time to rest the troops who had come south with him and to gather more. William was using the time to consolidate his new territory.

The tidal flats at Pevensey would leave the fleet stranded if the English attacked at low tide, so the ships had moved about ten miles up the coast to Hastings (Old English *Hæstingas*, after the tribe of a 7th-century Anglo-Saxon chieftain, Hæsta). Today just another section of the gentle miles-long Sussex beach, in those days Hastings was a little peninsula extending out between two estuaries that have since then largely dried up, forming an isthmus that would be easily defensible if need be. *Hæstingaport* itself was at *Winchelse*, Old Winchelsea, which was long ago lost to coastal erosion, but back then the docks and such were at *Icoleshamme*, modern Icklesham. On the summit above the town was another ex-Roman fortification, *Hæstingaceastre,* made into something of a *burh* in the days of King Alfred against the Vikings. Here the Normans set about doing what they did best: building castles, or at least fortresses. For the time being, at Hastings, a simple motte-and-bailey would have to do. Wace recorded, "The sailors were ordered to beach the ships, hole them and break them up so that cowards could not return and use them to escape."

Masts and oars, deck planks and hull boarding went into the new fortress and surrounding palisade. Meanwhile Norman riders laid waste the surrounding villages. The locals abandoned their homes, fleeing ahead of the invaders, driving their livestock before them. Word went even further of the Normans' depredations, all the way to King Harold's ear, as Duke William knew it would. He was goading the king to come meet him.

Harold's family tried to turn him from his course. His mother Gytha, already mourning the death of Tostig, dreaded losing him, and Gyrth and Leofwine as well. For his part, Gyrth begged Harold to rest and let him and Leofwine do the fighting: "We, who are not obligated, should be the ones to defend our land. It can be seen that if you fight, you may face flight or death, but if we fight, our cause will live on in any case, for you will survive to both rally fugitives and avenge the dead."

"At this Harold flew into a mad rage," reported Orderic. "He rejected his friends' wise advice, rebuffed his brother who was only voicing the best for him, and when his mother clung to him to restrain him, insolently pushed her off with his foot."

The common wisdom is that Harold rushed to engage with the Normans before his forces were ready. As the *Waltham Chronicle* puts it, "He was stubborn and put too much faith in his own bravery. He thought he could strike the Normans when they were weak and unprepared, before reinforcements from home could bolster their forces."

Worcester agreed: "Although he knew that many of England's bravest men had died in the two battles [Fulford and Stamford Bridge], and that half of his troops were not yet assembled, he hurried to meet the enemy in Sussex."

In Orderic's opinion, "His plan was to catch them by surprise and overwhelm them by a sudden or night attack."

This does not sound like the crafty, calculating Harold we have come to know. Any good *hnefatafl* player knew the idea was to surround the enemy, prevent his escape, and force his capitulation.

Harold knew the Hastings terrain well. His father Godwin had owned local property, as did the king himself. About six miles northwest of town, the London road ran up the side of a 1,600-foot stretch of crossridge, eroded to the north and south into inclines impassable to cavalry. At the foot of the hill lay a marshy valley which (alone among the old sources) Orderic named "Senlac."

(Considering that over a thousand years the Battle of Hastings has spawned a minor industry of historians and writers, the dispute over this name might at least fill a few books. In Old English *lacu* means pond or stream, but *sen* is not a word. Orderic being the son of a French priest by an English mother, *Senlac* was long thought to be a corruption of the Old English *Sandlacu*, "sandy pond" or "sandy stream," possibly of his own invention, or that of Norman chroniclers approximating Old English sounds. An alternative origin might be *isenlacu*, "iron stream," after the brook which drains it and is said to run red after a rainstorm, supposedly from blood washed out of the ground but actually from local iron-rich sandstone deposits that had fueled a Roman-era iron industry. Afterward the Normans were said to have corrupted the name to *Sanguelac*, "Blood Lake," but English writers simply called the site, in Latin, *Bellum*, "Battle.")

The unflankable ridge presented a roadblock to any Norman advance from the peninsula. The swampy valley floor would be an impediment to their cavalry. While the English army held the invaders at bay, the English fleet would be able to come out and cut off, or at least hinder, their retreat or resupply. Even Orderic admitted, "To prevent their escape he [Harold] put seventy heavily armed ships to sea."

With the Normans contained, winter would eventually decide victory, as they both froze and starved. Harold was not in a hurry to defeat William in battle. He was in a hurry to imprison him on his peninsula.

On Wednesday, October 11 the English army, such as it was, marched out of London. After yet another grueling march – sixty miles in three days – on Friday evening it camped on Caldbec ("Cold Brook") Hill, about a mile from Senlac. Harald sent a messenger to the Norman camp to deliver a final ultimatum – hardly the move of a man hoping to take the enemy by surprise.

When the royal envoy arrived, William gave him due courtesy. He is shown on the Tapestry holding the papal flag as the messenger rattles off the king's terms or, according to Poitiers, his demands:

> King Harold commands you thus. You have entered his land, with what confidence, with what recklessness, he does not know. He indeed remembers that King Edward long ago decreed that you would be the heir of the English kingdom, and that he himself in Normandy assured you of the succession. However, ever since blessed St. Augustine came into this country, it has been a common custom of our people that a gift which a man bestows on his deathbed [as Edward did] is regarded as valid. Therefore he demands that you return to your land, taking your men with you. Otherwise, he will dissolve the friendship and all agreements he made with you in Normandy. It is entirely up to you.

The duke was furthermore informed that Harold had just defeated the Viking army and killed both its king and his own brother, and was at the head of a huge army of (Amiens said) "twelve hundred thousand men." If William would hand over his captives and looted property, war might yet be avoided, but the king could barely control his troops.

Duke William was unimpressed, a little insulted, and only too pleased the English had offered battle so soon. He told the messenger to remind Harold of his sworn fealty and that he still held his little brother Wulfnoth hostage. From this position of strength, William (Poitiers claimed) was willing to leave the decision of who should rule to the courts, either Norman or Anglo-Saxon, and abide by it. Failing that, and since neither the Norman nor English soldiers were at fault in their dispute, he was also willing to face Harold in single combat, winner take all. Otherwise, Poitiers recorded, "I will not hide behind a rampart or palisade, but will instead fight Harold. I trust that he and his men will be crushed by the strength of mine, as God wills, even if I had only ten thousand men such as the sixty thousand I brought."

Both men, or their writers, were clearly bluffing with numbers. For his part William had nowhere near 60,000 men, let alone the 150,000 he is sometimes credited. Modern estimates give him 14,000 at most, more likely eight to ten thousand. And no medieval army ever numbered the 1.2 million men Amiens gave Harold. It was to flatter their Norman sponsors that Norman writers inflated English numbers; English writers, in view of the outcome, downplayed English strength. Between the three of them, Harold, Gyrth and Leofwine probably mustered no more than 13,000, more likely half that, and possibly as few as 5,000. "Many said afterward that Harold had fewer men," wrote Wace. "But many others say, and I agree, that he matched the duke man for man. The duke did not have more men, but he had certainly more nobles, and his men were better. He had plenty of good horsemen and archers."

The messengers returned to the English camp to report that, judging by their clean-shaven faces, the Norman army was full of priests.* "The king smiled at their simplicity," wrote Malmesbury, "revealing, with a gentle laugh, that they were not priests, but soldiers, well equipped, and eager to fight."

The duke's challenge was a more serious matter.

---

*Going all the way back to the Britons of Julius Caesar's day, English men took pride in their moustaches. For their part the Normans shaved the backs of their heads, probably to keep the hair from catching in a chain mail aventail. Both styles are depicted on the Bayeux Tapestry.

To judge by their later appearances, the king's mother Gytha and his first wife, Edith the Gentle Swan, had joined him in the royal camp. Their eldest son, Godwin, and perhaps the younger ones Edmund and Magnus, were likely old enough for battle, but as princes of the realm may have stayed behind with their young sisters Gunhilde and Gytha for safekeeping. The whereabouts of Harold's second wife, Queen Edith, are unknown. There's a likelihood, this being several months after their marriage, that she was pregnant, and so remained behind at court. The family must have had a heartfelt discussion in the royal tent, as to whether Harold should accept William's offer. The king perhaps recalled how his predecessors Cnut and Edmund Ironside were said to have settled their differences by personal combat, on the island of Alney in the Severn. He could not be confident that William, like Cnut, would offer to split the Island Kingdom between them. Nor was he confident the duke would accept a decision by English courts. The *witan* had already made that decision, and William had not accepted it.

The king would leave the matter in the hands of God.

"So the brave leaders prepared for battle, each according to the way of his people," wrote Malmesbury. Norman writers would have us believe the English, exhausted as they were, sat up through the night drinking and singing, while the pious Normans spent the night in prayer and received the sacrament in the morning. William, according to Poitiers, "attended the mystery of the Mass with the greatest devotion, and fortified his body and soul by receiving in communion the body and blood of the Lord. He hung around his humble neck the relics, the protection of which Harold had lost by violating the oath that he had sworn on them."

Early on Saturday, October 14, the Normans set out on the London road, with the archers and infantry leading the way and the cavalry bringing up the rear. About mid-morning they crested Telham Hill and looked out over the Senlac valley. (The etymology of Telham is even more obscure than Senlac, possibly from Old English *tæl*, blame, blasphemy or disgrace, and *ham*, home.)

Across the valley, behind a wall of overlapping shields, bristling with spears and stretching the length of the Senlac ridge, awaited the Anglo-Saxons.

Like the origins of the name Senlac, arguments over the positioning of the opposing armies at Hastings could fill several books in itself. Was the English shield wall a straight line, or curved back on itself, like the Vikings' at Stamford Bridge? Was the battle fought face-on toward Hastings, or oblique toward one angle or another? Was the battle line a few hundred yards wide, or a mile? Few of the early writers were alive at the time; even fewer, with the possible exception of Poitiers, attended the battle, and even he admitted, "The most articulate writer who had seen that battle with his own eyes could scarcely have followed every detail."

Since then, seemingly every historian with an interest in the subject has his own theory and his own map of the battle, few of which exactly match the existing terrain. As has been shown, the entire coastline of Sussex, which back then was pocked with bays and tidal islands, has since silted up into a single length of beach; it's not too much a stretch to think that since 1066 the field at Senlac has changed as well. Cases have been made, with varying degrees of believability, that the struggle did not even take place on the currently celebrated site.

It seems King Harold's order of battle, at least, was not complex, possibly because it consisted mostly of fyrdmen who knew little more of tactics and maneuver other than to stand facing the enemy and do their best to kill them, which was all that would be required of them this day. Harold's best men, the housecarls, stood to the front behind the shield wall. Those from Kent, according to Wace, went where the Normans were most likely to attack (the center?), for theirs was traditionally the honor to strike the first blow. It was Londoners' duty, on the other hand, to defend their king to the last, so they gathered round Harold and his brothers under the wyvern standard of Wessex and King Harold's personal flag, the Fighting Man. Malmesbury, the half-Norman Englishman, recorded, "The king himself stood on foot with his brother near the standard, so that all shared equal danger, and none would consider retreat."

Wace, all Norman, depicted Harold a little less bravely, having him upon first sighting the enemy turning to his brother Gyrth. "With so great an army opposing us, I dare not do anything but fall back to London. I will return there and assemble a larger army."

"You have given up your pride too soon," Gyrth tells him. "Quickly indeed has this sight diminished your courage. If you turn back now, everyone would say you ran away. If you are seen to flee, who will hold your people together? And once they scatter, they will never be united again."

From what we have seen of Harold's nature, he was not given to fear on the battlefield. Second-guessing oneself prior to the fight, on the other hand, would only be natural. But Gyrth was right. All would be well as long as the shield wall held. Wace wrote, "He [Harold] commanded his men, and advised his leaders, to stay together and fight as one, for if they became separated, they would have a hard time achieving victory."

Having witnessed the failure of his own cavalry against the Viking shield wall at Stamford Bridge – and like the Vikings there, holding the high ground here – Harold put his faith in traditional Anglo-Saxon tactics. Poitiers wrote of the English, "Dismounting from their horses, the footsoldiers formed a dense formation," and Orderic concurred: "All the men dismounted and sent their horses to the rear, making their stand on foot."

Whether by coincidence or according to some divine inspiration, William arranged his army rather like a map of his duchy. He commanded the center, his Normans, along with his half-brothers Bishop Odo and Robert of Mortain. To his right, Normandy's east, were the men of Flanders, Picardy, Boulogne and France, under Count Eustace, Roger de Montgomery and William's seneschal William fitzOsbern. To his left, west, were the warriors of Anjou, Poitou, Maine and even some Bretons under Alan Rufus, Alan the Red, a kinsman of both William and his antagonist Duke Conan. These Bretons, marching in the lead, formed the vanguard as the army turned left off the Hastings road and formed up in front of the English. "The duke of Normandy arranged bowmen and crossbowmen in the front rank," recorded Orderic, "armored footsoldiers in the second, and finally squadrons of horsemen. He himself, surrounded by his best fighting men, took his place in the center, so that all could see and hear him as he led the battle."

Duke William was no less nervous than King Harold. He was a master of warfare, particularly the siege, but his experience of battle command was actually limited. At Val-ès-Dunes in 1047 he had served as one of King Henry's cavalry commanders; he had taken no direct part in the victories at Saint-Aubin in 1053 or Mortemer in 1054, and at Varaville in 1057 he had seen to the slaughter of a baggage train only while the French army was trapped across the river. Now he was said to have at first donned his mail coat backwards, another ill omen. "A lesser man would have been mortified, putting his hauberk on back to front," declared Poitiers, "but William laughed at this reversal as a mischance and did not worry it was a bad sign."

As Malmesbury told it, the duke simply shrugged off the mail, turned it around and put it back on, saying, "My dukedom shall be turned into a kingdom."

He then declared to one and all, "I vow to found a monastery on this battlefield for the salvation of all, and especially for the fallen, in honor of God and his saints, where servants of God may find favor, a fitting monastery with a worthy endowment. Let it be an atonement, a haven for all, as free as the reparation I make for myself."

He had his war horse brought to him, and the papal banner as well, though he had difficulty finding a man to bear it. Raoul de Tosny, son of Roger the Moor Eater, and Walter Giffard both declined, preferring to lead their men in combat rather than mind a flag; Giffard was now old enough to have a son of the same name in the fight. Finally the duke settled the banner on Turstin fitzRolf, "le Blanc," whose descendants enjoyed freedom from service ever after. (Though the Bayeux Tapestry shows it carried by Count Eustace of Boulogne, more of whom later.)

"Meantime, while everyone awaited battle in nervous anticipation, with the terrible threat of death hanging over them," recounted Amiens, "a minstrel, to the glory of his most valiant soul, rode out before the duke's vast army."

"He was named Taillefer," confided Gaimar, "a minstrel, but a bold one. He was armed and rode a good horse, a daring and worthy warrior."

Amiens, Gaimar, Huntingdon, Malmesbury and Wace all tell the story of Taillefer (most often translated from Old French as "cleaver of iron"), though they differ in the details. In the original Latin he was a *histrio*, actor, and in the Norman a *joglere*, minstrel, and perhaps something of a jester. As Wace told it, he had a favor to ask of Duke William. "A boon, sire! I have served you a long time, and you owe me for it. Today, if it please, you may pay that debt. I ask as my recompense, and ask it resolutely, that you allow me to strike the first blow in the battle."

This William granted. Taillefer rode out between the lines. "He inspired the French and frightened the English," wrote Amiens, "tossing his sword high and cavorting with it."

He is said to have gone out singing lines from *La Chanson de Roland*, which was after all a tribute to a previous French conqueror in a foreign land: "*Charles the king, our great emperor, seven full years has been in Spain; as far as the sea he conquered the land, there is no castle that resists him nor town left to conquer....*"

That the Song ends in disaster, with the useless but valiant death of Roland at the Battle of Roncevaux Pass, was surely not lost on Taillefer. Then as now, no one lives forever, except in legend. Like Roland – like that nameless Viking at Stamford – Taillefer, the singer of songs, would make certain that, of all those men in this valley of death, his death at least would be remembered.

"He handled his lance by the butt as if it had been a baton," continued Gaimar. "Up high he threw it, and caught it by the head. Three times he threw his lance thus."

The sight of one man, riding out alone from amid thousands to tempt death, got the better of some unknown Anglo-Saxon warrior, who left the safety of the shield wall and came downslope to meet this mad minstrel. Single combat – champion warfare – was not just the private domain of the nobility, but a martial tradition going all the way back past Cnut and Ironside to Achilles and Hector, or even David and Goliath. And if King Harold and Duke William would not risk themselves, it was left to these two warriors to decide which would become famous.

"Taillefer," wrote Amiens, "as soon as he came within reach, spurred his horse, pierced the Englishman through his shield with his sharp spear and with his sword hewed the head from the fallen body." Here was Achilles, here was David, here was a champion for all time. "Turning to his comrades, he displayed his grisly trophy, showing that fortune favored them. All rejoiced and called on the Lord, exulting that the first blow was theirs. Both a shiver and a thrill ran through every heart."

"Then he drew his sword, and struck again," declared Wace, "crying out 'Come on! Come on! Why do you wait, sirs? Lay on! Lay on!' After the second blow, the English rushed forward to envelop him."

"He struck an Englishman with his sword," declared Gaimar, "making his hand fly right off. Another he struck, as well as he could [but] he received an ill reward that day, for from all sides the English hurled javelins and spears at him. They killed both him and his steed."

It was the morning of Saturday, October 14, 1066. "The raucous bray of trumpets," recorded Poitiers, "signaled both sides to battle."

As with the terrain and formations, the tactics at Hastings are also open to question. Only a few things seem certain. The Anglo-Saxons dominated the crest of a ridge, forcing the Normans to attack them head-on. The vaunted Norman cavalry could not simply ride around the English flanks to attack from the rear. We know this because if they could have they would have, and they did not. Perhaps the ground was too soft, or too steep, or – a millennium ago – too thickly wooded. And that's the most important thing, the one thing that all sources agree on, and all historians concede: Although the Normans employed cavalry at Hastings, the English did not.

Duke William's strategy this day was not as clever as at Varaville, nor as sly as at Mortemer, but though unimaginative, did not stray far from basic battlefield tactics that have lasted to this day.

Soften up an entrenched enemy with artillery.

Send in the infantry to break the line.

Turn the cavalry loose to run down the scattered survivors.

It didn't work out that way.

"The first rank, of archers, attacked from a distance, transfixing bodies with their shafts," wrote Amiens, "and the crossbowmen pierced shields like a hail-storm, shattering them with countless blows."

It's estimated William employed as many as a thousand bowmen. They were cheaper than knights to equip, wearing little in the way of armor, and in contrast to the expensive sword, the bow was a poor man's weapon. Orderic and Amiens both mention crossbows, but that technology having been basically lost to medieval Europe from the departure of the Romans until the 10th century, at this time would have been a relatively new battlefield innovation. They had a much slower rate of fire, but a much greater draw weight, and were capable of putting a quarrel right through a wooden shield into the man behind it. As Orderic noted, "Against crossbow bolts shields are of no use," but there were probably few crossbowmen at Hastings. (Indeed, none are shown on the Tapestry.) The vast majority of arrows simply feathered the shield wall.

Yet the English could not answer back in kind. As the Welsh had learned, they had not yet developed their tradition of archery, or the throngs of longbowmen who would dominate the battlefields of France in centuries hence. Yes, the bow was a poor man's weapon, but in late Anglo-Saxon England, recreational hunting was a privilege of rich and powerful men like King Edward and the Godwinsons. (At Stamford Bridge both Earl Tostig and King Harald were felled with arrows, but those old accounts which name the archers, name them as noblemen.) Royal hunting parks proscribed to the common man have generally been thought to have been introduced to England by the Normans, but of late that view is being reassessed, and King Edward, with his Normanesque love of the hunt, may have instituted aristocrat-only hunting parks during his reign. In sum, the English in 1066 numbered few archers. Some idea of the ratio of English to Norman bowmen is that only one of the former is depicted on the Tapestry, and he is very diminutive compared to his mailed and helmeted fellows, and no fewer than twenty-three of his Norman counterparts.

"Then the Norman foot-soldiers closed to assault the English, killing and crippling many with their missiles," wrote Poiters. Tossing javelins into and over the shield wall, the Normans reached for their swords, but before they could come to grips with the English it was their turn to be showered. "Each Englishman resisted bravely however he could," wrote Poitiers. "They threw javelins and spears of various types, lethal axes and even stones tied to sticks."

But the Norman footmen had shields too. Like a rising wave their line came relentlessly up the slope. Then, with each side calling on God's help and cursing in a language the other did not understand, the two lines smashed together.

"Loud and far sounded the note of the horns," recorded Wace, "and the impact of the spears, the weighty stroke of clubs, and the rapid clatter of swords."

All along the ridge crest, housecarls set grimly to their work. Spears stabbed, swords hewed and axes hacked. Blood spurted and spattered the grass, and the crash of weapons echoing across the valley was soon mixed with the cries of the wounded and the cheering and jeering of the fyrdmen in the rear, urging their heroes on. "The Normans press the attack, and the English defend their position well," admitted Wace. "They pierce hauberks, cleave shields and give and take killing blows."

Amiens was equal in his admiration for the housecarls. "They gave missile for missile, sword-stroke for sword-stroke. Bodies could not fall down, nor did the dead give way to the living, for each lifeless corpse stood as though living and held its post."

In this contest of foot soldiers, the Anglo-Saxons proved superior. The Norman infantry reeled back, leaving the ridge crest littered with dead and dying. Before the attack collapsed, however, William ordered his third wave, the cavalry, to their aid. In a thundering mass they spurred up the slope, pitched their javelins ahead of them, and rushed the English line. Poitiers wrote, "The horsemen come up, and those who had been behind become the first. Ashamed to fight at a distance, they dare to carry the battle with swords. The loud cries, on one side Norman, on the other barbarian, are overwhelmed by the sound of weapons and the groans of the dying."

The Anglo-Saxons might be unused to fighting cavalry, but the Norman horsemen were unprepared for the Dane axe. With the shield wall's spear-hedge holding off the horsemen, the housecarls could step out and set to swinging those murderous blades. To the cries of wounded men were added the screams of crippled, dismembered horses.

This carnage went on all morning, with neither reprieve nor advantage for either side.

It was the Normans – or rather, the men of Brittany on the Norman left – who faltered first. Poitiers admitted, "Terrified by this savagery, the footsoldiers, Breton cavalry and other mercenaries on the left turned tail."

Reining their animals around, those horsemen galloped back down the hill through their own infantry and archers, who joined the flight. The Bretons had come up the slope in good order, but fled back down it in complete disarray, which was almost the undoing of the entire Norman army.

"In the valley was a fosse, now behind the Normans, who had passed it in the advance with little notice," wrote Wace, *fosse* being an Old French word for a ditch or trench, probably meaning the little creek-gully running along the marshy valley bottom. "The English charged and drove the Normans ahead of them, causing them to fall back into this fosse, overturning steeds and men into it."

The Tapestry vividly depicts horses tumbling end over end at the bottom of the hill: HIC CECIDERVNT SIMVL ANGLI ET FRANCI IN PRELIO, *Here at the same time English and French fell in battle.* It must have been a horrific scene as the fight went hand-to-hand, men struggling amid downed and kicking horses to stab, strangle and drown each other in the mud. "Many fell in there, one rolling over the other, with their faces in the mire, unable to stand," wrote Wace. "Many English, whom the Normans pulled in along with them, died there as well. At no time during the day's battle did so many Normans perish, as did in that fosse."

The Norman left wing had failed. The English on that side saw their chance. Amiens admitted, "They saw the enemy's left wing had broken, and the way was wide open to destroy the rest."

If, while the rest of the Norman army was engaged with the English at the top of the hill, the English right flank swept down and around to envelop them from the side, the result would be slaughter. Everyone could see that, and seeing it, the Normans in the center panicked and fell back, and then the French on the right, all fearing disaster. Orderic wrote, "They turned to run, and almost the duke's entire battle line fell back, for a rumor spread that he had been slain."

From his position in the center of his army, William and his brothers saw defeat looming. They rode into the thick of the fighting. Wace has Bishop Odo, recognized by his white horse and priestly garb under his mail hauberk, riding to the left, the ditch. He carried a baculus, a wooden rod symbolic of royal or ecclesiastical authority, but in battle, as shown on the Tapestry (which Odo is often thought to have commissioned), more as a club, which might not pierce mail armor, but instead beat the wearer to death inside it. "Stand fast! Stand fast!" he tells his men. "Keep calm and hold your position! Fear not, for if God please, we shall yet conquer."

Meanwhile William, according to Poitiers, spurred his horse into the midst of his fleeing men, striking and threatening them. The Tapestry shows him bearing a baculus as well, standing in his stirrups to tip back his helmet and show his face. "Look at me! I live, and with God's help I will conquer. What madness causes you to run? Which way is escape? You can slay the men who pursue and slaughter you like cattle. You are handing away victory and everlasting glory, to hurry to doom and perpetual infamy. Not one of you will escape death by fleeing."

On the Tapestry, Count Eustace, now bearing the papal banner, points out the duke. Under their curses and threats, the Norman center and right regained their courage, for unlike the left wing they had not been pursued. Most of the Anglo-Saxons still held the crest of the ridge; only those on their right, the Norman left, had disobeyed their king's orders and deserted the shield wall.

Maybe that had been a mistake, or maybe the mistake was that the entire English army had not also come rushing down the hill as well, to upend horses, spill riders to the ground and see them finished off by knife-wielding fyrdmen. Either King Harold did not realize his opportunity, or perhaps, as he fought on foot in the middle of that huge army rather than mounted like William, his order was lost.

Instead of the Norman left, it was now the English right that was exposed. Unlike Harold – but like Harald Hardrada at Fulford – William did not miss his chance. He sent his horsemen charging up across the slope and into the gap to cut off the men who had come downhill. Instead of their own fyrdmen, the housecarls in the ditch found enemy riders behind them. Amiens would have it that the king's brother Earl Gyrth was among them – perhaps as the leader of the imprudent English right wing – hurling a spear that killed Duke William's horse under him: "But as a foot-soldier, he fought even better, rushing on the young earl like a roaring lion. Cutting him limb from limb, he shouted, 'Take the crown you have earned from us! My horse is dead, thus I slay you as a common soldier!'"

HIC CECIDERVNT LEVVINE ET GYRD FRATRES HAROLDI REGIS depicts the Tapestry, *Here were killed Leofwine and Gyrth, the brothers of King Harold*, one with a Dane axe and the other with a sword and round Viking-style shield. (It has them slain early in the battle, and other accounts later, but in none of them do the brothers survive. Their mother Lady Gytha's worst fears were coming true.)

The duke remounted by dint of tearing a passing horseman of Maine out of the saddle and taking his horse, but that one was felled too. Count Eustace gave the duke his mount, and himself claimed that of another rider. Together, count and duke led the counterattack. "With their swords the two cleared the field of English," trumpeted Amiens, "and some deserted, staggering, exhausted. As a thinned wood falls to the axe stroke, so the forest of Englishmen was reduced to nothing."

Poitiers gloated, "The eager Normans surrounded some thousands of their pursuers and slaughtered them together, so that not one survived."

Wace admitted, "From tierce (the third hour of the day, 9am), when the combat began, until nonce (ninth hour, 3pm), the battle was up and down, this way and that. No one knew who would win."

No army could keep that up for six hours. At some time, probably multiple times, the battle paused as both sides regrouped, treated wounds, counted friends lost and those still alive, wiped gore from notched weapons, and perhaps washed down a bit of food while there was the chance. For none reckoned the battle was over yet. Dead Normans littered the top of the ridge, and dead English the slope, and both clogged the fosse in the valley bottom, all for naught. Nothing had changed. Duke William had nothing to lose by continued assault.

It began again with archery, but by now the Norman bowmen were running low on ammunition – too few English archers shooting back. The Normans could not reload with enemy arrows pulled from the ground, nor from their own dead or wounded. Needing to make every draw count, they could not afford to waste points, firing into the English shield wall. "The Normans decided to shoot their arrows up in the air," recorded Wace, "so that they might fall on their enemies' heads and faces."

Now, for the first time, the great mass of fyrdmen behind the shield wall felt the full sting of the arrow storm. There was no cover. Only a few wore armor or carried shields. Even fewer had helmets to protect them from the descending clouds of shafts. "The falling arrows struck them in the head and face, putting out many of their eyes," allowed Wace, "and all feared to look up, or leave their faces unguarded."

Yet the shield wall held firm...at least, until someone among the Normans recalled that the English could be enticed to abandon it. Poitiers wrote, "When the Normans and their allies saw they could not easily overcome the enemy's defenses, they retreated, deliberately feigning flight. The barbarians, with the hope of victory, rose up with great joy."

Feigned retreat was the same tactic the Vikings had used to defeat the northern earls at Fulford, and the English to defeat the Vikings in turn at Stamford Bridge, and this time it was the English left wing that could not resist chasing the Normans. Poitiers sneered, "As before, thousands of them dared to descend, almost as if they had wings, in pursuit of those they thought fleeing."

Wace wrote of an English housecarl cleaving Normans left and right with his axe, attempting to behead a mounted knight with a blow that instead glanced off his helmet and decapitated the horse. "Roger de Montgomery galloped up with his spear ready, unheeding of the long-handled axe which the Englishman brandished, struck him down and left him stretched out on the ground. Then Roger cried, 'Frenchmen strike! The day is ours!'"

"The Normans," wrote Poitiers, "suddenly wheeling their horses around, halted and encircled them, and slew them to the last man."

"The English fell back to higher ground," continued Wace, "but the Normans followed them across the valley, attacking on foot and horseback." Wading through high grass now trampled, blood-soaked and tangled with guts and limbs, dead and dying horses and men, the Norman footsoldiers came to grips with the Anglo-Saxons while the cavalry swept around and behind them. Without a shield wall at his back, no housecarl could wield his axe to full advantage. "The English did not know how to fight from the saddle, or even bear arms on horseback, but fought with hatchets and axes," chided Wace. "A man wanting to strike an axe-blow had to hold it with both hands, and could not at the same time, it seems to me, both defend himself and strike with it."

"The English, growing weaker, endured their punishment as though atoning their sins through defeat," wrote Poitiers. "So fortune changed for William, quickening his victory."

Wace and Orderic in particular extoll the feats of Norman heroes, the Companions of Duke William and many more. Roger de

Montgomery, William fitzOsbern. Walter Giffard (elder and younger), William Warenne. Roger de Beaumont and Ralf of Tosny. Normans of Evreux and Calvados, the Bessin and Cotentin, of Rouen and Caen and Falaise and Fécamp, and their neighbors of Anjou and Poitou and Pontheiu and Boulogne, "and many others of military renown and great fame," added Orderic, "whose names deserve to be recorded in the annals of history amongst the very greatest warriors. But Duke William surpassed them all in courage and wisdom."

Wace agreed. "Duke William fought gallantly, hurling himself wherever the fighting was heaviest and beating down many who found no respite, so that all might easily see that the business at hand was his."

By this time the very borders of the Tapestry are cluttered with dead, many hewn to pieces, severed limbs and heads serving as decoration. Afterward an English monk agonized over the crash of weapons, the wails of the dying, and that the matter of succession could only be resolved by such violent means: "It is truly astonishing that the miserable human condition is typified by the lamentation of sadness."

Both wings of the Anglo-Saxon line had been decimated. For the survivors to spread out and cover the flanks meant opening breaches in the shield wall that could not properly be filled by unarmored fyrdmen, but not doing so meant leaving their flanks exposed. For the first time, Norman cavalry could get around behind the shields. As at Fulford, the English line bent back on itself, round the banners of royalty and the king.

"Duke William pressed the English hard with his spear," wrote Wace, "striving to reach their flag at the head of his men and eagerly seeking for Harold, upon whom the whole war was blamed."

Malmesbury at least credited the last Anglo-Saxon king as a fighting commander this day: "Harold, not merely content to lead, diligently fought as a soldier should, often at close quarters. None could approach him unscathed, for he immediately levelled both horse and rider with one blow."

Few English writers of the time, and none of the Normans, cared to imagine what King Harold was thinking as the Norman tide crested the Senlac ridge and closed around him. In the eye of the storm, amid the circling riders, under the banners of Wessex and of the Fighting Man, he may have realized he was a king on a *hnefatafl* board: surrounded, awaiting only the final moves. Amid mounting adrenaline, anger and expectation of death, he might be excused for being too preoccupied to feel the winds of history swirling about him, from those that first brought Saxon raiders to the Kentish coast in the early 400s, then Vikings to Northumbria in the late 700s, and finally the changeling breeze that had borne the Normans to Sussex. No one in those days could have expected that, after almost 275 years of struggle between Vikings and Anglo-Saxons, a bastard from Normandy would sweep in to claim the Island Kingdom. Yet the Bastard was here, and it was Harold's fate to be the man from whom the kingdom was taken. It would be only natural that a God-fearing man would have – and certainly later chroniclers, in seeking divine retribution for Harold's sins, noted this – lifted his face heavenward.

At which point, Huntingdon wrote, "A shower of arrows came down around King Harold, and he himself was hit in the eye."

And here is yet another bit of confusion about the Battle of Hastings: whether King Harold Godwinson was indeed felled by an arrow to the eye.

The story originates with the Normans. The contemporary writers Poitiers and Jumiéges did not specify how the king was slain. An account from a Norman monk in Italy, circa 1080, wrote of Harold that they "burst his eye with an arrow," but that is from a 14th-century translation of the lost original, perhaps untrustworthy. Malmesbury, around 1120, recorded that Harold "fell with his brain pierced by an arrow." It was Huntingdon, ten years after that, who first connected arrow to eye. By 1170 or so, a hundred-odd years after the battle, Wace had embellished the tale:

It was then that an arrow, shot upwards, struck Harold above his right eye and put it out. In agony he pulled the arrow, broke it in both hands and threw it away, but the pain in his head was so great that he leaned upon his shield. This the English were like to say, and still tell the French, that the arrow was well shot which went up against their king, and the archer won them great glory, who put out Harold's eye.

Of course, it's the Bayeux Tapestry that made the story famous. HIC HAROLD REX INTERFECTVS EST, *Here King Harold has been killed*, it says of an armored man standing by the wyvern standard of Wessex, gripping a golden shaft protruding from his eye, in the next scene chopped down by a sword-swinging rider.

The problem is, the Tapestry as it exists today is not the Tapestry as originally created.

We can thank D. Bernard de Montfaucon and his artist Antoine Benoît, who first sketched the Tapestry after its rediscovery in the 1720s. In their rendition, the armored man does not grasp an arrow protruding from his eye, but a stylized spear, *sans* fletching, raised for throwing or thrusting. (Though he does appear to have a second spear standing or slung behind him.) The upraised spear was replaced with an arrow by a later embroiderer during a 19th-century restoration, as can be verified by its more modern dyes and machine-spun threading. The style of the new arrow's fletching, with the "feathers" more tightly spaced, does not match that of the arrows in the spearman's shield, or of any others in the Tapestry. The arrow's shaft is even slightly bent, in order to connect with its target.

It behooved both sides to peddle the story of the arrow. The Normans could depict Harold – slain almost accidentally by a humble, anonymous archer – as laid low by fate, or the will of God. The Anglo-Saxons could equally claim their hero had not been defeated in combat but, as Malmesbury put it, "received the deadly arrow from a distance and yielded to death." Random chance, literally *aelfscot*.

The probable truth is more mundane.

Bishop Guy of Amiens wrote his account within months of the event, for presentation to William and Matilda at Eastertide, 1067. It being meant to flatter his benefactors, not mock them, it is unlikely Guy would have fabricated what everyone, on hearing it, would know to be a lie. He has Duke William spotting Harold atop the hill, hewing down the Normans closing around him. William calls Count Eustace to his side. Hugh of Ponthieu (brother of Count Guy) and Walter Giffard (not the Companion of William, but his son) answer the call as well. Together the four ride through the maelstrom of battle to set upon the king. Amiens declared, "If anyone doubts this, the truth of the action proves it." He continued:

> The first, splitting his shield and his breast with his sword, drenched the earth with a spurting rush of blood. The second struck off his head beneath the helmet and the third pierced his innards with his spear. The fourth hacked off his thigh and carried off the severed limb. The body, thus destroyed, was left where it lay.

"The banner [of Wessex] was beaten down, the golden gonfanon [of the Fighting Man] was captured, and Harold and his best men were slain," wrote Wace. William would have Harold's banner delivered to Pope Alexander as a trophy.

With its leaders dead, the Anglo-Saxon defense collapsed. The Norman cavalry overrode the last of the king's housecarls. The rest of the English realized the day was lost. "Their ranks broke and they ran, fast as they could, to meet sundry fates," wrote Orderic. "Some tried to catch and mount horses, others fled afoot along the roads or through the unmarked woods."

The sun was setting, on the day and on Anglo-Saxon England. As twilight descended, the Norman horsemen pursued the survivors into the woods behind the ridge. They were overconfident with victory, however, and unfamiliar with the terrain.

For Jumiéges this was almost the only part of the battle worth mention. "For the growing weeds hid from them an old ditch, towards which the Normans rushed hastily, and they fell there with their horses and their arms, killing one another, as they fell into it, one upon another."

"It may have been a natural gully in the earth or maybe it had been washed out by storms," wrote an English monk. "But in those woods it was full of thorns and thistles, and could hardly be seen in time. It engulfed great numbers, especially of Normans chasing the English."

"At this the fleeing English regained their courage," wrote Orderic. "Seeing as they could be protected by the broken slope and maze of gullies they reformed their ranks and made a surprise stand, inflicting heavy casualties on the Normans."

Poitiers recorded, "But when the duke, leading the conquering forces, saw that the enemy had unexpectedly regrouped, even though believing them a freshly arrived relief force, he neither turned aside nor paused." He called again on Eustace of Boulogne, but even with fifty riders at his back the count preferred to let the English go rather than fight them in the dark. As he advised William to do the same, however, he was struck between the shoulders by an unknown weapon – arrow, spear, or stone – and his men had to help him off the field, blood streaming from his mouth and nose. He would survive, but William carried out the counterattack himself. Poitiers declared, "The duke, utterly scorning fear and dishonor, charged and laid his enemies low. In that fight died some of the noblest Normans, for their valor was no advantage on such unfavourable terrain."

"This deep pit has been named for this incident," wrote the English monk, "and today it is called *Malfosse* [Evil Ditch]."*

"Having thus achieved victory, and returned to the battlefield," wrote Poitiers, "William beheld the slaughter with some amount of pity, although it had been wrought upon the wicked. To slay a tyrant is just and glories a man's name, worthy of praise. The flower of English nobility and youth lay covered in blood." Though advised to sleep elsewhere, and under guard against any retribution by the defeated, the duke ordered his tent to be raised on the battlefield, and passed the night among the dead.

"This was a fatal day for England," lamented Malmesbury, "a sad tragedy for our dear land, through its change of masters."

"After the glorious sun rose to cleanse the world of dark gloom," wrote Amiens, "the duke considered the field, and ordering the bodies of his fallen collected, had them interred in the breast of the earth. The English dead, strewn across the area, he left to be consumed by worms and wolves, birds and dogs."

---

*Whether this *fosse* was the same as the one in mid-battlefield – the scenes are similar, with various chroniclers placing them during or after the main combat – is the last of the mysteries of the Battle of Hastings. The very location of this ditch is one of the unknowns that keep historians up at night, for no such ditch is readily apparent on the modern battlefield, and over the years practically every gully for miles around has been designated as the likely site. It's even been suggested that the *Malfosse* story is actually cover for a mass grave, for after the battle there was a multitude of bodies both human and equine needing disposal. Alas, no archaeological dig has succeeded in finding it.

As shown on the Tapestry, looting of the dead had begun even as the living still fought. Overnight the poorer soldiers and even locals would have converged on the field, as advised by their elders who had done the same at Maldon, Sherston, Assandun, and every other English – and indeed, every other medieval – battlefield since time immemorial, for such remains were a rare and precious trove. By daylight most of the English dead would have been stripped of weapons, armor, jewelry and even shoes and clothing, lying naked in the sun.

The priests of Waltham, Osgod and Aethelric, as was their mission, searched the blood-scabbed grass for their late king, without success. "They hurried among the dead, turning them over one side and the other, but were unable to recognize that of the king," testifies their abbey's chronicle. "This is because a man's body, when dead and emptied of blood, does not usually look the same as when alive." With one leg severed, the top of his head taken off, and his helmet and royal trappings delivered (as was customary) to Duke William as proof of death, King Harold was said to be unrecognizable...except to some.. And that leads to one of the most sorrowful scenes of the entire story of the Island Kingdom. "They decided there was only one thing to do. Osgod returned to camp and brought back the woman whom the king had loved before he became king: Edith, called 'Swanneshals,' which means 'Swan-neck.' She had once been the king's mistress, and as his lover knew the secret marks on his body better than anyone."

Poor, grieving Edith the Gentle Swan had to walk the battlefield, picking her way through the naked tangled bodies, searching among the dead faces for that one she had known so well, only to find that face smashed beyond recognition, that body she had so long lain beside butchered, and the memory of that man, whom she had so loved, forever tainted by the memory of that last sight of him.

"She pointed out the king's body amid the heaps of dead, according to several identifying marks," continues the *Waltham Chronicle*. "The brothers placed it upon a bier, to which many of the Normans paid their respects."

Not so much Duke William. According to Amiens, "Harold's mother, overwhelmed with grief, sent word to the duke himself, pleading with him to restore to her, a sorrowing woman, a widow bereft of three sons, the body of one if not the three. Or, if he wished, she would give him the body's weight in pure gold."

English tradition claims the king was interred at Waltham Abbey, where a stone is said to still mark the spot. (The *Vita Haroldi*, the 13th-century biography of Harold sponsored by the abbey, would have it that their patron did not die at Hastings, but escaped, badly wounded, to Winchester and then to Saxony and Scandinavia to raise an army, only to return to England and live out his life disguised as a hermit.) Poitiers, however, recorded that William declined to release the body to the family. "For he felt it unseemly to accept gold for such business. He thought it unworthy for Harold to be buried as his mother wished, when so many men lay unburied because of his overbearing greed."

"Fickle fortune often brings a hard and bitter end to mortal men on earth," intoned Orderic. "Some climb from nothing to the heights of power. Others fall from greatness to sorrow in the pit of despair."

"We do not revile you, Harold," wrote Poitiers, "but like the pious conqueror weeping over your fall, we pity and mourn you. You have won what you deserved, and your efforts gained you nothing but blood. You will lie in a grave on the coast, and be an abomination to future generations, both English and Norman."

And though any evidence has been lost, Amiens agreed the Normans buried Harold on a seaside cliff top with a stone to mark the spot, carved with an epitaph allowing the last Anglo-Saxon ruler of England to perform in death the duty he had done as king:

> By the duke's command, here rests King Harold,
> Ever guarding the coast and the sea.

AFTERWORD

Domesday

1066–1154

There can be no doubt that a good part of this strip of tapestry has been lost in the passage of time. What remains of it only goes as far as Harold's defeat and death, and William's victory. The work had to go at least up to his crowning, which is not there. The last part of this monument is so spoiled, that we should not be surprised if what follows is entirely lost.

Montfaucon

When, in 1729, Dom Bernard de Montfaucon received his artist's copies of the mysterious tapestry in the cathedral of Bayeux, he was both astounded and disappointed. Astounded, because the initial drawings by the late Monsieur Foucault of Normandy represented only one-seventh of the embroidery's actual total length: just short of 225 feet. Disappointed, because the far-right end of the work came to an abrupt, ragged stop, and with it the story. (It's thought that at least a scene or two from that end, perhaps as much as seven yards, has been lost over time.) He lamented, "The end of the tapestry is so spoiled that we know almost nothing further. The writing is absolutely erased. We see only in a few less spoiled places Frenchmen who, pursuing their victory, kill the Englishmen whom they meet."

The drawings arrived too late for inclusion in Volume I of Montfaucon's *Les Monumens De La Monarchie Françoise*, "The Masterpieces of the French Monarchy." Instead he published engravings of the Foucault

401

originals, done in a florid 18th-century style. For his second volume, in 1730, he treated his readers to the new, cruder but more accurate medieval-style rendition from Bayeux as illustrations for his version of the tale. As a proud Frenchman writing for a French audience, Montfaucon was not exactly impartial, and as his five volumes were intended to serve as a history of France, not England, he concerned himself with the Norman Conquest up to the point where the Island Kingdom received a continental king. "The tapestry as it is at present only comes so far," he told his readers. "There can be no doubt that it went at least as far as the coronation of King William. But though all that end is gone, I must admire that what remains has been preserved for six hundred and fifty years. In order not to spoil this imperfect story, I am going to pursue it up to the coronation of William."

Duke William may have thought – hoped – killing the King of England would be enough to make him its ruler. It would not be quite that easy.

England had plenty of would-be leaders, from Archbishop Stigand of Canterbury and Archbishop Ealdred of York to the earls Edwin and Morcar, who had belatedly marched down to London to either support or take over from any new king. What they needed was a figurehead, someone to fight for. The *witenagemot* elected Edgar Aetheling, grandson of Edmund Ironside and great-nephew of Edward the Confessor, as king. A year earlier he had been thought too young to rule. Now he was the only ruler on whom, for the time being at least, they could all agree.

Meanwhile, from Hastings William moved northeast to secure Dover, guardian of the Channel, along the way brutally punishing Romney for its initial resistance. In view of that treatment, Dover submitted, then Canterbury. When the Normans reached Southwark and laid waste to it, however, the citizens of London mounted a defense of the London Bridge that convinced William the city was too big to take by direct assault.

Instead he moved west, accepting the submission of Winchester and along with it Harold's sister, Edward's widow Edith. She, having lost most of her family and two kings in the span of a year, had lost the will to fight as well, and being the widow of the king who had supposedly bequeathed the kingdom to William, was well treated for her trouble. As for the other Ediths, Edith the Gentle Swan, having performed her last service in identifying her husband's body, but having no official status to protect her, wisely vanished from history, while Harold's widowed queen Edith of Mercia took refuge with her brothers Edwin and Morcar. Many historians believe she gave birth to twin sons, Harold and Ulf, before fleeing to sanctuary in Ireland. Grown to manhood, Harold would journey to Norway and fight for Harald Hardada's grandson, Magnus III Olafsson, called Barefoot, in that king's raids around the Irish Sea in 1098. Ulf, captured, would be raised in captivity in Normandy and ultimately train and fight as a Norman knight. The rest of the family was resolute in their resistance to the Normans. Harold and Edith's mother Countess Gytha retreated to Exeter, while Harold's elder sons Godwin, Edmund and Magnus, as their father had once done, voyaged to Ireland to raise an army to bring to her assistance.

Resistance at home, however, soon crumbled, beginning with Archbishop Stigand. When the Normans crossed the Thames upriver at Wallingford, plainly intending to encircle London from the northwest, he submitted. By the time they reached Berkhamstead, still two dozen miles from the city, the capitulation of the Anglo-Saxon leadership was complete. Archbishop Ealdred, the earls Edwin and Morcar, and even Edgar Aetheling (elected king but never crowned) recognized William as lord, and soon afterward leaderless London did as well. "It was very ill-advised that they had not done so already," records the *Anglo-Saxon Chronicle*, "seeing that God, because of our sins, would not improve matters."

In Edward the Confessor's Westminster Abbey on Christmas Day, 1066, Duke William was crowned as King William I of England. It was a portent of future events that, hearing the clamor acclaiming the new monarch, his mercenaries thought him under attack and in retribution set fire to some of the neighboring houses.

The year 1066 would be remembered forever as the Year of the Three Battles, the end of almost 275 years of Viking strife, and of six centuries of Anglo-Saxon rule. For Hastings was not just a battle for part of the Island Kingdom, as the Saxons and Vikings had so often fought, but for all of it.

William I, called the Conqueror, reigned for just short of twenty-one years, hardly any of it peacefully. Rebellions soon broke out in Exeter and York and had to be put down. The English aristocracy, which William had initially left largely in place, by their duplicity brought about their own downfall. After leading rebellions Harold's mother Gytha was forced into exile, Edwin of Mercia betrayed and murdered, Morcar of Northumbria imprisoned for life, and their sister Queen Edith lost to history. Then it was foreign threats, with Harold's sons Godwin and Edmund and Magnus, Eustace of Boulogne and Svein of Denmark launching separate invasions, unsuccessfully. In the course of the latter, Svein's ally, Edgar Aetheling, married his sister Margaret to King Malcolm of Scotland, with whom he continued to make mischief. Out of patience, King William subdued Scotland, ran Edgar off the island and resorted to the Harrying of the North: a campaign of scorched earth, brutality and genocide that even Orderic condemned:

> Never before was William so cruel. Here he gave in to villainy, made no attempt to control his rage, and slew the innocent along with the guilty. In his fury he ordered all food, crops and cattle to be burned together, so that all the provisions throughout the land north of the Humber were totally destroyed. As a result, soon afterward a great famine afflicted England, and the hapless commonfolk suffered such starvation that more than a hundred thousand Christians, of both sexes and all ages, died. In many respects our story has gladly commended William, but I do not dare to praise him for using famine as a weapon against both the just and the wicked. For when I see innocent infants and young men and gray-haired old men dying of hunger, I feel more compassion for the distress and anxiety of the miserable people, than I wish to vainly encourage such guilty deeds by frivolous flattery.

Malmesbury took a more lenient view. "Their fate drove the king to tears," he wrote of the northern lords, "for he would have long before granted them marriages with his kinswomen, and the honor of his favor, had they but agreed to terms of peace." To his mind, his mother's people got no more than they deserved for their Saxonish treachery. "For this reason perhaps the king's conduct might reasonably be excused, if he was sometimes rather hard on the English, for he hardly ever found them faithful."

He took greater issue with William's ever-increasing greed: "He would say and do some things, and in fact, practically anything, unbecoming such great majesty, when the prospect of income lured him. This he sought always to accrue, he cared not how. I offer no defense whatsoever, unless it is that, as someone once said, 'Of necessity, he must fear many, whom many fear.'"

That cupidity, however, and the Norman aptitude for figures and records, is something for which modern historians can thank William the Conqueror. To determine exactly what was owed him in taxes, about twenty years after Hastings he ordered a survey of the entire Island Kingdom, including the property of every archbishop, bishop, abbot, earl and *thegn*, by name, right down to the last hide of land in the last shire, the last ox, cow and pig. Men were dispatched across the realm to gather this information and bring it all back to the royal treasury at Winchester, where it was compiled into what became known in Old English as the *Domes Dæg Boc*, and by the 12th century, from the Middle English, as the Domesday Book, because the records set down therein were as final as those of the Last Judgment on Doomsday. As currently preserved in the National Archives of the United Kingdom, the Book is the oldest such document in English history, and very likely all of Europe. Nothing of such magnitude was even attempted in England for another 800 years. Historians, geographers, topologists and even genealogists owe King William a debt of gratitude.

If only he had managed his personal life as adroitly.

By every account William remained loyal all his days to Queen Matilda, but when she died in 1083, he was left with no moderating influence. Yes, these were the same years he saw to the completion of the Domesday Book, but physically all the decades of constant warfare had caught up to him. "He was tall, unusually fat, fierce-faced, partially bald," recorded Malmesbury. "Sitting or standing he was majestic, although his rotund belly marred his royal dignity."

In 1087, in the course of attempting to conquer the Vexin from Philip of France, William was besieging Mantes when he fell ill. Orderic put it down to heat exhaustion. Malmesbury claimed his horse bolted from some flames, throwing the heavyset king forward onto his saddle pommel and rupturing something inside him.

William withdrew to Rouen, where doctors found blood in his urine and pronounced the injury fatal. According to Malmesbury, the king lamented his life's unfinished business, but saw to possibly its greatest mistake: the division of his empire among his sons. "Reluctantly, and under compulsion, he bestowed Normandy on Robert [called *Curthose*, 'Short Stocking']. To William [*Rufus*, 'the Red'] he gave England, while Henry [*Beauclerc*, 'Handsome Clerk'] received his mother's properties."

William died on the eighth of the ides of September – September 6 – 1087, at the age of fifty-nine. The principle of "might makes right," engrained in him from his childhood as a bastard on the run, set a horrible precedent for the future of European politics, for there was no such thing as a peaceful transition of power in the Norman dynasty. As with his father Robert, William's death set off a power struggle, this time consuming England as well as Normandy.

His eldest son, Robert, now Duke Robert II of Normandy, resented that his younger brother William was now King William II of England, and even younger Henry resented that he was nothing more than Count of the Cotentin. (The second-eldest son, Richard, had died of a riding accident in 1070.) All three brothers fought a dynastic war for control of William's empire – in which Harold Godwinson's son Ulf fought for Curthose – but which saw Henry come out on top. Normandy was henceforth held as a fiefdom of England instead of France, which had the effect of setting those two kingdoms at odds for hundreds of years. A generation later King Stephen, son of the Conqueror's daughter Adela, fought another fifteen-year civil war with his cousin Matilda, Henry's daughter, a period of such violence and lawlessness that it's been called "The Anarchy." At the end of it, Matilda's son Henry, son of Count Geoffrey V of Anjou, finally attained the throne, marking the end of the Norman dynasty.

As a result of all these rebellions and wars, the Normans studded the English countryside with their castles, and developed them from the wooden motte-and-bailey style to sophisticated stone keeps like London's White Tower, a form which would mark the Middle Ages until the advent of gunpowder. And as they had done in Normandy, to expiate their sins the Normans built a profusion of abbeys and cathedrals as well, which had the unexpected effect of strengthening the church until, in Stephen's reign, it challenged royal authority.

Secular wars resulted as well, as William's nobles took advantage of the existing, egalitarian Anglo-Saxon form of government. Norman barons found they held more power as English earls. Over the centuries their assertion of that power, in the form of the Magna Carta and the creation of Parliament, led slowly, and not always peaceably, to the democratization of England.

And as the years went on, the Normans' dominance of the native Anglo-Saxons became gradually less heavy-handed. Through intermarriage and mutual opposition to almost everybody else in Europe, the two peoples gradually became one. In court circles the official language was Old Norman – English kings would speak French until the reign of Henry IV beginning in AD 1399 – but commoners continued using Old English. The trickling down of French words and the trickling up of English grammar eventually melded the two into Middle English, antecedent of the modern tongue spoken today, if only as a second language, by the majority of the planet.

The last version of the *Chronicle*, the one from Peterborough Abbey, was lost when the church accidentally burned in 1116. Two years later its rebuilding was undertaken in the Norman style, and in 1122, beginning from a copy of Winchester Cathedral's *Chronicle*, the monks resumed their work. There is a noticeable jump in the language from the Old English of the Winchester chronicle – noun genders and such – as the later scribes worked in a tongue different from that of their predecessors 200 years gone. When a final annalist took over the job in 1132, he wrote in a single voice, one lonely man chronicling the onset of The Anarchy, a time of torment, terror, chaos and famine, the burning down of the Norman dynasty. Toward the end his edition bundles multiple years into one entry – 1135, '37, '38, '40. "Then England was much divided. Some supported the king [Stephen] and some the empress [Matilda]" – and finally all the way to the last, in 1154. By now, thirty years after work resumed (and the better part of 200 years since it was first undertaken) the writing is all in Middle English:

In this year died King Stephen. He was buried where his wife and his son were buried, at Faversham, in the monastery they founded. When the king died, then the earl [Henry Curtmantle, Henry fitzEmpress, Henry Plantagenet; the future King Henry II] was beyond the sea, but no man dared do anything but good for great fear of him. When he came to England, he was received with great acclaim, and blessed to become king in London on the Sunday before midwinter day.

Henry II, son of a Norman mother but an Angevin father, the first of the Plantagenet dynasty, was crowned on December 19, 1154, eighty-eight years almost to the day after his great-grandfather William the Conqueror, almost eighty-nine years after Harold Godwinson, England's last Anglo-Saxon king, and 114 years after Harthacnut, its last Danish king. The Peterborough *Chronicle*'s description of Henry's royal procession trails off in mid-sentence, as though the annalist was taken away from his work in mid-stroke, as though the Plantagenet court saw no point in further recording the doings of Normans, Vikings and Anglo-Saxons. They considered the battle for the Island Kingdom to be over. Won. And perhaps it was. Factions would quarrel, dynasties would end and be replaced, foreign kings would be invited to rule, but the bloodline of William the Conqueror never died. The Plantagenets and all English dynasties since then – the Tudors, Stuarts, Hanoverians and Windsors – claim descent from William I.

And every English-speaking person today owes something to those men and women who fought and died on that island, particularly in the six and a half decades leading up to the year 1066. In those years things could have gone in any direction and, as a result, our world would be very different. The thousand years since are all owed to those who fought and died for the Island Kingdom, and those who made sure they are remembered.

To record the deeds, the words, and mannerisms of our forefathers, to tell of the felonies of felons and the baronage of barons, men should read aloud at feasts the gests and histories of prior times. Therefore they did well and should be highly regarded and rewarded, those who first wrote books and set down the noble deeds and worthy orations which barons and lords did and spoke in olden days. Long ago such things would have been forgotten, were it not that such tales have been retold, and their story duly recorded and remembered.

So wrote Wace. He undertook his *Roman de Rou*, his "History of the Norman People," around 1160 at the behest of Henry II, to record the glories of the king's ancestors, and he may have taken fifteen years to complete it. That's a substantial part of anyone's lifework. Wace and his fellow historians – Orderic, Poitiers, Malmesbury, Huntington, the anonymous Anglo-Saxon chroniclers and the rest – all wrote laboriously, by hand and by candlelight, but for all that they wrote in ink.

It's the generations of whom they wrote – six hundred years of them, Vikings, Anglo-Saxons, Normans, all – who wrote this story in blood.

SOURCES

ADAM of Bremen, German chronicler and historian, wrote his *Gesta Hammaburgensis Ecclesiae Pontificum*, "Deeds of Bishops of the Hamburg Church," in the second half of the 11th century. Documenting the Archdiocese of Hamburg-Bremen near the Danish border, it includes the history and the geography of northern Germany, Denmark and the other Scandinavian countries, at the time including England. Adam spent time in the court of Danish King Svein II.

AELFRIC of Eynsham was educated at Winchester's Old Minster, a teacher in the Benedictine New Minster, and an abbot at the abbey of Cerne Abbas in Dorset. He was not so much an historian as a biblical commentator and recorder of hagiographies and homilies. He picked up Bede's use of *Engla-lond* and popularized the term in his writing of the late 990s, indicating the Anglo-Saxons finally had a sense of national identity.

Bishop Guy of AMIENS served as regent of Ponthieu after the Battle of Mortemer, when his nephews Count Enguerrand II of Ponthieu and Waleran were killed and Count Guy I imprisoned. He later served as chaplain to Duchess Matilda of Normandy. He wrote the *Carmen de Hastingae Proelio*, "Song of the Battle of Hastings" (see below), to flatter her husband Duke William after he became King William I, since Guy had been relieved of his bishopric by Pope Alexander II.

BEDE the Venerable, a monk in the Northumbrian monasteries of St. Peter and St. Paul during the 5th and 6th centuries. The five books of his *Historia Ecclesiastica Gentis Anglorum*, "The Ecclesiastical History of the English People," cover the ecclesiastical and political history of England from the period of Julius Caesar up to AD 731. It includes what may be the first written use of the term "*Engla-lond*."

BENOÎT de Sainte-Maure was a 12th-century French poet, and probably the author of the *Chronique des ducs de Normandie*, thought to be the oldest surviving Old French text on the Continent.

Hector BOYCE was a 15th-century Scottish historian and principal of King's College in Aberdeen. In 1527 he wrote the *Historia Gentis Scotorum*, "History of the Scottish People," which proved popular and won him royal acclaim, but contains numerous errors and must be compared with other accounts.

John BROMPTON was a 15th-century English abbot of the Cistercian monastery at Jervaulx in Yorkshire. He either wrote, or commissioned someone to write, a *Chronicon* which compiled material from previous histories, some now lost. It accepts many stories as fact and is of dubious historical value, but useful for flavor.

The *BRUT CHRONICLE* is a 13th-century collection of medieval chronicles of English history, thought to have been composed by the clerks of the Royal Chancery in Westminster, which produced all royal charters and writs.

The *CARMEN WIDONIS*, "Poem by Guy," in modern times retitled the *Carmen de Hastingae Proelio*, the "Song of the Battle of Hastings," is the earliest history of the Norman Conquest. It is thought to have been written in 1067 by Bishop Guy of Amiens (see above), who was a contemporary of and even related to some of the figures in the story.

Richard of DEVIZES was a late 12th-century English chronicler at Winchester Abbey. He was best known for his *Chronicon de rebus gestis Ricardi Primi*, "Chronicle of the Deeds of Richard the First," but is also credited with the *Annales de Wintonia*, the "Annals of Winchester," which document events in England from AD 519 to 1277.

DUDO of Saint-Quentin, a dean of the monastery there, wrote his *De moribus et actis primorum Normannorum ducum*, "On the manners and acts of the first Norman dukes," or in short the *Gesta Normannorum*, "Deeds of the Normans," at the bidding of Richard II, Duke of Normandy. Compiled from oral traditions rather than written sources, it is very pro-Norman in outlook and served as the basis for the works by William of Jumièges and other later writers. Dudo had died by 1043.

EADMER of Canterbury was born in England circa 1060, personally knew kinsmen of the Godwins, and in the early 1100s wrote the *Historia Novorum in Anglia*, "History of Recent Events in England" from 1066 to 1122.

The *ENCOMIUM EMMAE REGINAE*, "Elegy of Queen Emma," is a paean to the English queen Emma of Normandy, although it actually makes little mention of her. It is more a telling of her version of Cnut's story, and in the Middle Ages was actually titled the *Gesta Cnutonis Regis*, "Deeds of King Cnut." Often of dubious veracity, it was written in the early 1040s at Emma's behest by the anonymous ENCOMIAST, probably a Flemish monk of St. Bertin's or St. Omer's Abbey, who lived at the time of the events depicted and saw Cnut personally when the king visited the abbey during his trip to Rome.

FOLCARD of St. Bertin, a Flemish monk who lived in England during the reign of Edward the Confessor and served at the monastery of Christ Church, Canterbury. Thought by some historians to be the author of the *Vita Aedwardi Regis*, see below.

Geoffrey GAIMAR was an Anglo-Norman chronicler who in the AD 1130s translated Old English accounts to Anglo-Norman. His *L'Estoire des Engleis*, "History of the English People," is the oldest known history written in French. It begins with the reign of King Arthur and ends with the death of William II in 1100, biased toward the Normans as the true heirs to the English throne.

Eleventh-century Benedictine monk Rodulfus, or Raoul, GLABER, "the Bald," wrote the *Historiarum libri quinque ab anno incarnationis DCCCC usque ad annum MXLIV*, "History in five books from 900 AD to 1044 AD." He was born in Burgundy, lived in Italy, and returned to France in 1031. He died around 1050, making his a contemporary account.

Another 11th-century Benedictine monk, GOSCELIN OF SAINT-BERTIN, was born in Flanders around 1040 but moved to England around 1058. He was a compiler of hagiographies of English saints.

Henry of HUNTINGDON was a 12th-century English priest and historian who wrote his *Historia Anglorum*, "History of the English," in the mid-1100s.

The *JOMSVIKINGA SAGA*, "Saga of the Jomsvikings," was written by Icelandic skalds in Iceland during the 13th century, concurrently with the *Knytlinga Saga* (see below).

William, a monk of the abbey of JUMIÈGES, was born around the year 1000, died around 1070, and was a contemporary, if not a witness, to many of the events on the Norman side of the Channel. He wrote his *Gesta Normannorum Ducum*, "Deeds of the Dukes of the Normans," in the 1050s, building on and extending the pro-Norman work of Dudo of Saint-Quentin (see above). It was later extended by ORDERIC VITALIS and finally completed in the reign of Henry I (r. 1106–1135).

The *KNYTLINGA SAGA*, "The Saga of Cnut's Descendants," is thought to have been written in Iceland in the 1250s by Olaf Thordarson (d. 1259), called *hvitaskald*, "the White Poet." It details the kings of Denmark from the early 10th century.

The *LIBER ELIENSIS*, "Book of Ely," was composed by the monks of Ely Abbey, on the island of Ely in eastern Cambridgeshire. Its three-book account begins with the abbey's founding in AD 673 and ends in the mid-12th century.

William of MALMESBURY, half Norman and half English, in the 12th century was his country's greatest historian. He patterned his *Gesta Regum Anglorum* ("Deeds of the English Kings"), completed in 1127, on the work of Bede.

Walter MAP, a Welsh official in the 12th-century court of Henry II, wrote *De nugis curialium*, "Of the trifles of courtiers," a collection of tales and rumors of varying truth on historical and contemporary events.

The *MORKINSKINNA*, "Moldy Parchment," was an Icelandic saga of Norse kings circa 1025–1157, written anonymously in Iceland around 1220.

English chronicler and Benedictine monk ORDERIC VITALIS, 1075–c.1142, wrote the *Historia Ecclesiastica*, a great English social history of the Middle Ages. He used both Jumièges and Poitiers as sources, but his English mother instilled in him the native, not-so-sanguine view of the Conquest, and his take on events is fair to both sides. He wrote a long speech attributed to Duke William on his deathbed.

Ottar *svarti*, "OTTAR THE BLACK," so named either for a swarthy complexion or dark demeanor, was an Icelandic skald who served in the courts of Svein Forkbeard, Olaf Haraldsson and Cnut the Great.

Matthew of PARIS, despite his name, was a Benedictine monk, chronicler and artist of Herefordshire in the first half of the 13th century. He wrote and illustrated the Anglo-Norman *La Estoire de Seint Aedward le Rei*, "The History of Saint Edward the King," probably based on the *Vita Beati Edvardi Regis et Confessoris* by Aelred of Rievaulx, see below.

William of POITIERS is thought to have trained as a Norman knight before joining the priesthood, gaining an education in Poitiers. He ultimately became chaplain to Duke William of Normandy, as well as his earliest biographer, as set down in his *Gesta Guillelmi ducis Normannorum et regis Anglorum*, "The Deeds of William, Duke of the Normans and King of the English."

Abbot Aelred of RIEVAULX was a 12th-century English monk and writer, held by Anglicans and Catholics to be a saint. His *Vita Beati Edvardi Regis et Confessoris*, "The Life of Saint Edward, King and Confessor," was written to commemorate the 1161 canonization of Edward as propaganda to justify the accession of his descendant Henry II, the first king of the House of Plantagenet, in 1154. About a century later it was used as the basis for Matthew Paris's illustrated *History of Saint Edward the King*.

SAXO GRAMMATICUS, a 13th-century Danish theologian, historian and author, wrote the *Gesta Danorum*, "Deeds of the Danes," a history of Denmark. His telling of the legend of Danish prince Amleth would inspire Shakespeare to write *Hamlet*.

SNORRI STURLUSON, a 13th-century Icelandic historian, poet and politician, wrote the *HEIMSKRINGLA*, a history of the Norwegian kings from prehistory into the Middle Ages.

Around AD 1129 Benedictine monk and chronicler SYMEON OF DURHAM composed his *Historia Regum Anglorum et Dacorum*, "History of the English and Dacian Kings" (not the kingdom of the Dacians in southeast Europe, but Dacia, a combination of the toponyms Dania and Suecia – in medieval Latin, Denmark and Sweden). In contrast to the writers of the *Anglo-Saxon Chronicle*, his work concentrated on events in the north of England.

The two books of the *VITA AEDWARDI REGIS*, "Life of King Edward," were written shortly after the Conquest. It is thought to have been sponsored by Edward the Confessor's widow Queen Edith to promote her view of events, meaning that although it's a biography of King Edward, it is very pro-Godwin in outlook. British historian Tom License recently made a convincing case that its author was Folcard of St. Bertin, see above.

The *VITA HAROLDI REGIS*, "Life of King Harold," was composed at Waltham Abbey, which Harold patronized, in the late 12th century from a shorter, primary source, supposedly derived first-hand from the king's confessor. It has been called little more than a historical romance – most of the story consists of Harold's adventures after he "survived" Hastings – but is also thought to contain some truths.

WACE, sometimes called Robert Wace, was a medieval Norman poet born on the island of Jersey and raised in Normandy. Wrote the *Roman de Rou*, the "History of the Norman People."

The WALTHAM CHRONICLE, more properly *De Inventione Sanctæ Crucis Nostræ*, "The Discovery of our Holy Cross," is a 12th-century account of the Black Rood. It is flattering throughout to Waltham Abbey's patron, Earl Harold Godwinson, though it attributes his defeat to his headstrong courage and pride.

Roger of WENDOVER was a 12th–13th-century monk of St. Albans Abbey. His *Flores Historiarum*, "Flowers of History," was a compilation of earlier chroniclers' work, notable not so much for its content as Roger's style.

John and Florence of WORCESTER, monks and chroniclers of Worcester Priory. Florence was long thought to be the author of the *Chronicon ex chronicis*, "Chronicle of Chronicles," a world history beginning with the Creation and ending in 1140. Due to the similarity of writing style before and after Florence's death in 1118, John is now thought to be the probable author of the work up to the year 1141. It was continued from 1152 to 1265 at the Benedictine abbey of Bury St. Edmunds by the 13th-century English Benedictine chronicler John de Taxster and then to 1295 by John of Eversden.

BIBLIOGRAPHY

Adams, D.C.O. *The Saints and Missionaries of the Anglo-Saxon Era*. A.R. Mowbray & Co., 1901.

Adam of Bremen. *Gesta Hammaburgensis ecclesiae pontificum*. Impensis Bibliopolii Hahniani, 1876.

Aelred of Rievaulx. *The Life of Saint Edward, King and Confessor*. Translated by Jerome Bertram. St. Edward's Press, 1990.

Ahrholdt, Judith. "Nordic Names." 2004. https://www.nordicnames.de/. Accessed June 17, 2022.

Andersson, Theodore Murdock and Kari Ellen Gade. *Morkinskinna: The Earliest Icelandic Chronicle of the Norwegian Kings (1030–1157)*. Cornell University Press, 2012.

Anonymous. *Jomsviking Saga and Knytlinga Saga*. Translated by Carl Christian Rafn. *Old Norse Sagas*, Vol. 11. Copenhagen, 1839.

Bailey, Paula and Ann Smith. "Daughters, Wives, and Widows: A Study of Anglo-Saxon and Anglo-Norman Noble Women." Henderson State University, 2001.

Barlow, Frank. *Edward the Confessor*. Eyre Methuen, 1979.

Barlow, Frank. *The Godwins: Rise and Fall of a Noble Dynasty*. Routledge, 2013.

Barlow, Frank. *The Life of King Edward Who Rests at Westminster: Attributed to a Monk of Saint-Bertin*. Oxford University Press, 2008.

Barlow, Frank. "Two Notes: Cnut's Second Pilgrimage and Queen Emma's Disgrace in 1043." *The English Historical Review*, Vol. LXXIII, Issue 289 (October 1958), pp. 649–656.

Barthram, Phil. "Old English Translator," 2014. https://www.oldenglisht ranslator.co.uk/.

Bates, David. "The Character and Career of Odo, Bishop of Bayeux (1049/50–1097)." *Speculum* 50, No. 1 (1975), pp. 1–20.

Bates, David. *William the Conqueror*. G. Philip, 1989.

Bates, David. *William the Conqueror*. Yale University Press, 2018.

Battle Abbey. *The Chronicle of Battle Abbey*. Clarendon Press, 1980.

Baxter, Stephen. "Edward the Confessor and the Succession Question." *Edward the Confessor: The Man and the Legend*. Edited by Richard Mortimer, pp. 77–118. Boydell & Brewer, 2009.

Beech, George T. "How England got its name (1014–1030)." *Nouvelle revue d'onomastique*, No. 51 (2009), pp. 17–52.

Bender, Brandon Michael. "The Anglo-Saxon Invasion of Normandy: When, If at All, Did It Take Place?" March 15, 2020.

Benoît, de Sainte-More. *Chronique Des Ducs de Normandie*. Translated by Francisque Michel. Imprimerie Royale, 1836.

Birch, Walter de Gray and Harvard University. *Vita Haroldi. The Romance of the Life of Harold, King of England. From the Unique Manuscript in the British Museum*. E. Stock, 1885.

Bolton, Timothy. "Ælfgifu of Northampton: Cnut the Great's 'Other Woman.'" *Nottingham Medieval Studies*, Vol. 51 (2007), pp. 247–268.

Borman, Tracy Joanne. *Queen of the Conqueror*. Bantam, 2012.

Bouquet, Martin. *Recueil des historiens des Gaules et de la France*. Victor Palmé, 1876.

Boyle, J.R. "Who Was Eddeva?" East Riding Antiquarian Society. *Transactions* Vol. IV (1896), pp. 11–22.

Brayley, Edward Wedlake. *The History of Surrey*. R.B. Ede, 1841.

Brie, Friedrich. *The Brut; Or, the Chronicles of England*. Early English Text Society, 1906.

Brooks, Nicholas. "'Anglo-Saxon Chronicle(s)' or 'Old English Royal Annals'?" *Gender and Historiography: Studies in the Earlier Middle Ages in Honour of Pauline Stafford*. Edited by Janet L. Nelson, Susan Reynolds and Susan M. Johns. University of London Press, Institute of Historical Research, 2012, pp. 35–48.

Bumke, Joachim. *Courtly Culture: Literature and Society in the High Middle Ages*. University of California Press, 1995.

Butler, Denis. *1066, The Story of a Year*. G.P. Putnam & Sons, 1955.

Butler, Malcolm. "Regia Anglorum." https://regia.org/. Accessed June 28, 2022.

Cambridge Digital Library. "Christian Works: Life of St Edward the Confessor." Cambridge University, 2015.

Campbell, Alistair, ed. *Encomium Emmae Reginae*. Internet Archive. Camden Third Series. Vol. LXXII (1949). Offices of the Royal Historical Society.

Caradoc of Llancarvan, John Williams and University of Toronto. *Brut Y Tywysogion: Or, the Chronicle of the Princes*. Internet Archive. Longman, Green, Longman, and Roberts, 1860.

Chaillu, Paul Belloni Du. *The Viking Age: The Early History, Manners, and Customs of the Ancestors of the English-Speaking Nations*. AMS Press, 1889.

Chilcott, Tim. *Six Old English Poems*. The Chilcott Literary Translations, 2012.

Crouch, David. *The Normans: The History of a Dynasty*. Continuum, 2007.

Croxton-Smith, Patricia. "The Site of the Battle of Assandun, 1016." *Saffron Walden Historical Journal*, No. 3 (Spring 2002).

Davies, Michael, and Sean Davies. *The Last King of Wales: Gruffudd Ap Llywelyn, c. 1013–1063*. The History Press, 2012.

Davis, R.H.C. and Marjorie Chibnall, trans. *The Gesta Guillelmi of William of Poitiers*. Clarendon Press, 1998.

DeVries, Kelly and Robert Douglas Smith. *Medieval Military Technology*. University of Toronto Press, 2012.

DeVries, Kelly. *The Norwegian Invasion of England in 1066*. Boydell, 2003.

Dewhurst, Sir John. "A Historical Obstetric Enigma: How Tall Was Matilda?" *Journal of Obstetrics and Gynaecology* 1(4) (1981), pp. 271–272.

Douglas, David C. *William the Conqueror: The Norman Impact upon England*. University of California Press, 1964.

Dudo of St. Quentin. *Dudo of St. Quentin's Gesta Normannorum: An English Translation*. Edited by Felice Lifshitz and Kathryn Talarico. ORB: Online Reference Book for Medieval Studies. College of Staten Island, City University of New York, 2004.

Dugdale, William. *Monasticon Anglicanum: A History of the Abbies and Other Monasteries, Hospitals, Frieries, and Cathedral and Collegiate Churches, with Their Dependencies, in England and Wales; Also of All Such Scotch, Irish and French Monasteries, as Were in Manner Connected with Religious Houses in England*. J. Bohn, 1846.

"Early English Laws." University of London. https://eel.cch.kcl.ac.uk/. Accessed August 7, 2022.

The Exeter Book. Published for the Early English Text Society. Oxford University Press, 1958.

Fairweather, Janet, trans. *Liber Eliensis: A History of the Isle of Ely from the Seventh century to the Twelfth*. Boydell, 2005.

Faroux, Marie, ed. *Recueil des Actes des Ducs de Normandie (911–1066)*. Mémoires de la Société des Antiquaires de Normandie. Vol. XXXVI. Caen, 1961.

Flight, Tim. "Aristocratic Deer Hunting in Late Anglo-Saxon England: A Reconsideration, Based upon the Vita S. Dvnstani." *Anglo-Saxon England* 45 (2017), pp. 311–331.

Flint, B.W. "Edith the Fair: Visionary of Walsingham." Gracewing, 2015.

Florence of Worcester. *The Chronicle of Florence of Worcester with the Two Continuations*. Translated by Thomas Forester. H.G. Bohn, 1854.

Freeman, Edward Augustus. *The History of the Norman Conquest of England, Its Causes and Its Results*, Vol. II: *The Reign of Edward the Confessor*. Clarendon Press, 1867.

Freeman, Edward Augustus. *The History of the Norman Conquest of England: Its Causes and Its Results*, Vol. III: *The Reign of Harold and the Interregnum*. Clarendon Press, 1869.

Gaimar, Geoffrey. *Lestorie Des Engles Solum La Translacion Maistre Geffrei Gaimar*. Printed for H.M. Stationery office. Eyre and Spottiswoode, 1889.

Gameson, Richard. *The Study of the Bayeux Tapestry*. Boydell Press, 1997.

Garmonsway, George Norman. *Canute and His Empire*. H.K. Lewis, 1964.

Garmonsway, George Norman, trans. *The Anglo-Saxon Chronicle*. Everyman's Library, Vol. 624. Dent, 1967.

Giles, John Allen. *Old English Chronicles: Including Ethelwerd's Chronicle, Asser's Life of Alfred, Geoffrey of Monmouth's British History, Gildas, Nennius, Together with the Spurious Chronicle of Richard of Cirencester*. G. Bell, 1906.

Goodman, Ryan T. "'In a Father's Place': Anglo-Saxon Kingship and Masculinity in the Long Tenth century." Student thesis, University of Manchester, 2019. https://research.manchester.ac.uk/en/studentTheses/in -a-fathers-place-anglo-saxon-kingship-and-masculinity-in-the-lo.

Grammaticus, Saxo. *Danmarks Krønike*. Translated by Fr. Winkel Horn. A. Christiansen, 1898.

Gravett, Christopher and Christa Hook. *Norman Knight 950–1204 AD*. Osprey, 1993.

Grierson, Philip. "A Visit of Earl Harold to Flanders in 1056." *The English Historical Review* 51, No. 201 (1936), pp. 90–97.

Hagland, Jan Ragnar and Bruce Watson. "Fact or folklore: The Viking attack on London Bridge." *London Archaeologist*. No. 12 (Spring 2005), pp. 328–333.

Hemingus. *Hemingi Chartularium Ecclesiæ Wigorniensis*, ed. T. Hearnius, 1723.

Henry of Huntingdon, 1084?–1155, Thomas Forester ed. and trans. *The Chronicle of Henry of Huntingdon. Comprising the History of England, from the Invasion of Julius Cæsar to the Accession of Henry II. Also, the Acts of Stephen, King of England and Duke of Normandy.* H.G. Bohn, 1853.

Herschend, Frands. "Semiramis: An Early 11th C. Norman Text with Anglo-Danish Connotations Reviewed as a Dramatic Script." www .academia.edu. Accessed November 1, 2022.

HighFive. "Explore the Bayeux Tapestry Online." Bayeux Museums. www .bayeuxmuseum.com/en/the-bayeux-tapestry/discover-the-bayeux -tapestry/explore-online/. Accessed December 27, 2022.

Ingulf. *Ingulph's Chronicle of the Abbey of Croyland: With the Continuations by Peter of Blois and Anonymous Writers.* H.G. Bohn, 1854.

Lethaby, William Richard. *London before the Conquest.* Macmillan, 1902.

Lettenhove, Kervyn de and Joseph Marie Bruno. *Istore et Chroniques de Flandres, d'Aprés Les Textes de Divers Manuscrits.* F. Hayez, 1880.

Licence, Tom. *Edward the Confessor.* Yale University Press, 2020.

Licence, Tom. "A New Source for the Vita Ædwardi Regis." *The Journal of Medieval Latin* 29 (2019), pp. 1–19.

Liuzza, R.M., trans. "The Dream of the Rood." *The Broadview Anthology of British Literature,* Vol. 1: *The Medieval Period,* edited by Joseph Black et al. Broadview Press, 2006, pp. 23–25.

Lowther, A.W.G. "The Saxon Cemetery at Guildown, Guildford, Surrey." *Surrey Archaeological Collections,* Vol. 39 (1931), pp. 1–50.

Luard, Henry Richards, ed. *Lives of Edward the Confessor: I. La Estoire de Seint Aedward le Rei. II. Vita Beati Edvardi Regis et Confessoris. III. Vita Æduuardi Regis qui Apud Westmonasterium Requiescit., Rerum Britannicarum Medii Aevi scriptores.* Longman, Brown, Green, Longmans, and Roberts, 1858.

MacKinney, Loren C. "The People and Public Opinion in the Eleventh-century Peace Movement." *Speculum* 5, No. 2 (April 1930), pp. 181–206.

Map, Walter. *De Nugis Curialium.* Translated by Frederick Tupper. Chatto & Windus, 1924.

Mason, J.F.A. "Roger de Montgomery and His Sons (1067–1102)." *Transactions of the Royal Historical Society,* Vol. 13 (1963), pp. 1–28.

McGuigan, Neil. *Máel Coluim III, "Canmore."* John Donald, 2021.

Medievalists.net. "The Arrow in King Harold's Eye: The Legend That Just Won't Die." 2022. https://www.medievalists.net/2022/10/arrow-king-harold-eye/

Moberg, Ove. "Slaget Vid Helgeå Och Dess Földjer." *Scandia* Vol. 53, No. 1, 1987, pp. 175–185.

Montfaucon, Bernard de. *Les Monumens de La Monarchie Françoise Qui Comprennent l'Histoire de France Avec Les Figures de Chaque Règne Que l'Injure Des Tems a Epargnées. Tome Premier.* Julien-Michel Gandouin & Pierre-François Giffart, 1729.

Montfaucon, Bernard de. *Les Monumens de La Monarchie Françoise Qui Comprennent l'Histoire de France Avec Les Figures de Chaque Règne Que l'Injure Des Tems a Epargnées. Tome Second.* Julien-Michel Gandouin & Pierre-François Giffart, 1730.

Napier, Arthur Sampson and William Henry Stevenson. *The Crawford Collection of Early Charters and Documents Now in the Bodleian Library.* Clarendon Press, 1895.

O'Brien, Harriet. *Queen Emma and the Vikings: Power, Love, and Greed in Eleventh-century England.* Bloomsbury, 2006.

Orderic Vitalis. *The Ecclesiastical History of Orderic Vitalis.* Clarendon Press, 1969.

Pastan, Elizabeth Carson. "Montfaucon as Reader of the Bayeux Tapestry." *Medieval Art and Architecture after the Middle Ages,* ed. Janet T. Marquardt and Alyce Jordan. Scholar's Press (2009), pp. 89–110.

Pratt, David. "The Making of the Second English Coronation Ordo." *Anglo-Saxon England* 46 (December 2017), pp. 147–258.

"Prosopography of Anglo-Saxon England." Department of History and the Centre for Computing in the Humanities, at King's College, London, and in the Department of Anglo-Saxon, Norse, and Celtic, at the University of Cambridge, 2010. https://pase.ac.uk.

Richard of Devizes. *Annales de Wintonia,* in *Annales Monastici.* Translated by Henry Luard. Longman, Green, Longman, Roberts, and Green, 1864.

Rivers, Theodore John. "Adultery in Early Anglo-Saxon Society: Æthelberht 31 in Comparison with Continental Germanic Law." *Anglo-Saxon England* 20 (1991), pp. 19–25.

Robertson, A.J., ed. *Anglo-Saxon Charters.* Cambridge University Press, 1956.

Rodulfus Glaber, *Raoul Glaber: Les Cinq Livres de Ses Histoires (900–1044).* Translated by Maurice Prou and Harvard University. 1886.

Roffe, David. "The Historia Croylandensis: A Plea for Reassessment." *The English Historical Review* 110, No. 435 (1995), pp. 93–108.

Roger of Wendover. *Flowers of History.* H.G. Bohn, 1849.

Savill, Benjamin. "Remembering St Brictius: Conspiracy, Violence and Liturgical Time in the Danish Massacre of 1002." *The Journal of Ecclesiastical History* (2021), pp. 1–25.

Sawyer, Birgit I.L. "Marriage, Inheritance and Property in Early Medieval Scandinavia." www.academia.edu. Accessed June 5, 2022.

Schulz, Jonathan F. "The churches' bans on consanguineous marriages, kin-networks and democracy," CeDEx Discussion Paper Series, No. 2016-16, The University of Nottingham Centre for Decision Research and Experimental Economics (CeDEx), 2016.

Shack, William A. "Collective Oath: Compurgation in Anglo-Saxon England and African States." *European Journal of Sociology / Archives Européennes de Sociologie / Europäisches Archiv Für Soziologie* 20, No. 1 (1979), pp. 1–18.

Shoesmith, R. "Hereford City Excavations Volume 1: Excavations at Castle Green 1980 the Council for British Archaeology."

Sondheimer, J.H. "Encomium Emmae Reginae. Edited by Alistair Campbell." *Revue Belge de Philologie et D'Histoire* 29, No. 4 (1951), pp. 1275–1277.

Sparks, Nicholas. "The 'Parker Chronicle': Chronology Gone Awry." *The Medieval Chronicle VII* (May 2011), p. 63.

Stafford, Pauline. *Queen Emma and Queen Edith: Queenship and Women's Power in Eleventh-century England.* Blackwell, 1997.

Steckel, Richard H. "New Light on the 'Dark Ages': The Remarkably Tall Stature of Northern European Men during the Medieval Era." *Social Science History* 28 (2) 2004, pp. 211–29.

Stenton, Frank Merry. *William the Conqueror and the Rule of the Normans.* G.P. Putnam's Sons, 1908.

Steven, Leslie and Sidney Lee, eds. *Dictionary of National Biography, 1885–1900.* Vol. 24. 1890. London: Elder Smith & Co.

Stevenson, W.H. "Senlac and the Malfossé." *The English Historical Review* 28, No. 110 (1913), pp. 292–303.

Strickland, Agnes. *Lives of the Queens of England from the Norman Conquest.* Lea & Blanchard, 1841.

Sturluson, Snorri. *The Heimskringla.* https://en.wikisource.org/wiki/Heimskringla.

Sutton, Dana F. "Hector Boethius, Scotorum Historia (1575 Version)." The University of California, Irvine, February 26, 2010.

Tichy, Martin Rocek, Ondrej. "Bosworth-Toller's Anglo-Saxon Dictionary Online." https://bosworthtoller.com/.

Tsurtsumia, Mamuka. "Couched Lance and Mounted Shock Combat in the East: The Georgian Experience." *Journal of Medieval Military History* XII (January 1, 2014), pp. 81–98.

Turner, Ralf V. "The Children of Anglo-Norman Royalty and Their Upbringing." *Medieval Prosopography* 11, No. 2 (1990), pp. 17–52.

Van Houts, Elisabeth M.C. "The Origins of Herleva, Mother of William the Conqueror." *The English Historical Review* 101, No. 399 (1986), pp. 399–404.

Wace. *The History of the Norman People: Wace's Roman de Rou.* Translated by Glyn S. Burgess. Boydell Press, 2004.

Wace. *Master Wace: His Chronicle of the Norman Conquest, from the Roman de Rou.* Translated by Edgar Taylor. William Pickering, 1837.

Walker, Ian W. *Harold, the Last Anglo-Saxon King.* The History Press, 2010.

Warner, David A. *Ottonian Germany: The Chronicon of Thietmar of Merseburg.* Manchester University Press, 2008.

Watkiss, Leslie and Marjorie Chibnall, trans. *The Waltham Chronicle: An Account of the Discovery of Our Holy Cross at Montacute and Its Conveyance to Waltham.* Oxford University Press, 1994.

Weston, L.M.C. "Women's Medicine, Women's Magic: The Old English Metrical Childbirth Charms." *Modern Philology* 92, No. 3 (1995), pp. 279–293.

White, Geoffrey H. "The First House of Bellême." *Transactions of the Royal Historical Society* 22 (1940), pp. 67–99.

Wido, Bishop of Amiens. *The Carmen de Hastingae Proelio of Guy, Bishop of Amiens.* Clarendon Press, 1972.

Wilcuma – Anglo-Saxon – Englisc Heritage. https://www.wilcuma.org.uk/ Accessed April 18, 2022.

William of Malmesbury, translated by John Allen Giles. *William of Malmesbury's Chronicle of the Kings of England. From the Earliest Period to the Reign of King Stephen.* H.G. Bohn, 1847.

Williams, Mary Wilhelmine. *Social Scandinavia in the Viking Age.* Macmillan, 1920.

ACKNOWLEDGMENTS

I'd like to thank Kate Moore, Osprey Publisher, for her help in cutting down my initial epic take on this subject to a more palatable size. When too close to the work to see which scenes are crucial to the story instead of simply interesting, it's great to have someone who's gentle in pointing out the difference.

At the micro vs. macro scale, I'm also grateful to Gemma Gardner, Osprey's Senior Desk Editor, for her patience, diligence, and attention to detail in implementing the various and all-too-numerous little tweaks necessary to polish my drafts to perfection.

As always, thanks go to my agent, Scott Mendel, Managing Partner of Mendel Media Group LLC, for taking care of business so I can concentrate on the writing. I'm a little pony in his large stable, but he treats me like his best war horse, ready for battle.

And lastly, thanks to Jesse Lovell and Robert and Constance Lovell for their assistance with their ancestor Tom Lovell's classic painting of the Battle of Hastings, herein. That image was the centerpiece for my first professional magazine article in 1994. For it to serve as the climactic illustration in this book on the same subject brings me full circle.

INDEX

ABOUT THE AUTHOR

Don Hollway is an historian, illustrator, historical reenactor and classical rapier fencer. For over twenty-five years his writing on history, aviation and reenacting has appeared in magazines ranging from *Aviation History, Excellence, History Magazine, Military Heritage, Military History, Wild West* and *World War II* to *Muzzleloader, Porsche Panorama, Renaissance Magazine* and *Scientific American.* Many of his articles are available free on his website, donhollway. com, where a number of them rank in the top two or three in global search results. His first nonfiction book, *The Last Viking*, a gripping history of Norse king Harald Hardrada, is an Amazon best seller in the US and UK, acclaimed by *The Times* of London and Michael Dirda, Pulitzer Prize-winning critic for *The Washington Post*. His first professional publication, in August 1992, was a magazine article about the Battle of Hastings.